AF767415

MANAGERIAL ACCOUNTING

MANAGERIAL ACCOUNTING

PRINCIPLES, ANALYTICS, AND ARTIFICIAL INTELLIGENCE

Joseph Ugrin
Amy Igou

WILEY

This edition first published 2025

Registered Offices
John Wiley & Sons, Inc., 111 River Street, Hoboken, NJ 07030, USA
John Wiley & Sons Ltd, New Era House, 8 Oldlands Way, Bognor Regis, West Sussex, PO22 9NQ, UK
For details of our global editorial offices, customer services, and more information about Wiley products visit us at www.wiley.com.

The manufacturer's authorized representative according to the EU General Product Safety Regulation is Wiley-VCH GmbH, Boschstr. 12, 69469 Weinheim, Germany, e-mail: Product_Safety@wiley.com.

Wiley also publishes its books in a variety of electronic formats and by print-on-demand. Some content that appears in standard print versions of this book may not be available in other formats.

Library of Congress Cataloging-in-Publication Data Applied for:

Print ISBN: 9781394265831
ePDF ISBN: 9781394265855
epub ISBN: 9781394265848

Cover image: © Iurii Motov/Shutterstock
Cover design: Wiley

10/12 Janson Text LT Std by Lumina Datamatics

We dedicate this book to our families, whose support and encouragement have made this journey possible; to our mentors and colleagues who have inspired us throughout our academic journey, and innovators and critical thinkers who will shape the evolving landscape of managerial accounting.

CONTENTS

PREFACE

Future businesspeople must not only be proficient in well-established technology tools like spreadsheets but also be familiar with emerging technologies like artificial intelligence, machine learning, and robotic process automation, and how such technologies impact business disciplines. In our role as accounting educators, we see the value of integrating technologies into various business courses but have also seen the challenges students and instructors face when traditional textbooks fail to keep pace with current and emerging business tools.

This textbook was conceived to bridge that gap by integrating managerial accounting with technology and data-driven decision-making frameworks. Managerial accounting is the foundational course for learning how business leaders use data and information and the ideal context for learning how technology can improve business decision-making. Drawing on our experience in academia and industry, we have crafted a resource that not only covers fundamental managerial accounting principles and their application in a modern business environment but also familiarizes students with the analytical skills and technologies necessary to advance in their business and accounting curriculum and thrive in today's workplaces.

We were inspired to create this book after years of engaging with students, professionals, industry leaders, and educators who consistently emphasized the need for a more practical and future-focused approach to managerial accounting. We also concluded that it is imperative to introduce students to the foundational technological and analytical tools within context, but a comprehensive, instructor-friendly resource did not exist.

Throughout the writing process, we have carefully crafted real-world examples, case studies, and insights into technology to make the material engaging and relevant. Each chapter aims to simplify complex topics and bring them to life in our "Accounting in Life" and "Accounting in Business" vignettes. Additionally, our "Technology, Application, and Artificial Intelligence" segments at the end of each chapter highlight cutting-edge advancements that are redefining accounting and business and integrate hands-on activities and video demonstrations that make it easy for educators to embed technology into their courses without additional burden.

We hope this book provides readers with an understanding of the critical managerial accounting concepts and inspires them to embrace current and emerging technologies used in the field. We encourage readers to approach accounting with curiosity, adaptability, and a readiness to apply modern tools to traditional financial challenges.

We thank our colleagues, students, and industry professionals who contributed their insights, feedback, and support throughout the development of this book. We are excited to share this journey with you and look forward to seeing how the next generation of business students leverage managerial accounting in the era of artificial intelligence.

Joseph Ugrin & Amy Igou

ACKNOWLEDGMENTS

This book is the result of many years of learning, working, teaching, and collaborating. We owe a great deal of gratitude to those who have supported us and sacrificed with us along the way.

First, we recognize the contributions of researchers and industry professionals who have laid the foundation for the intersection of managerial accounting and technology and developed the tools integrated throughout this book. Their efforts have paved the way for the next generation of accountants and business professionals to embrace innovation in their careers.

We are grateful to our colleagues in the academic community who provided valuable insights that contributed to the development of this book by impacting our decisions about content, structure, and associated resources.

Thank you to the many thousands of students whom we have been privileged to teach and who continue to inspire us with their curiosity, enthusiasm, and drive to apply accounting concepts in real-world scenarios. Their engagement and feedback have shaped this book's practical and technology-driven approach.

Most importantly, we thank our families for their patience, support, and understanding. The long hours and late nights would not have been possible without their patience, encouragement, and love.

ABOUT THE AUTHORS

Joseph C. Ugrin, PhD, CPA, is the RSM Chair of Accounting and head of the Department of Accounting at the University of Northern Iowa (UNI). Dr. Ugrin has taught managerial accounting and accounting information systems courses for nearly two decades, among other classes. He is an advocate for integrating technology and accounting. Under his leadership, the Accounting programs at UNI became STEM-designated, and the accounting department was awarded the 2024 KPMG Innovation Award in Accounting Education. He has a undergraduate degree in accounting from Dickinson State University, an MBA from the University of North Dakota, and a PhD in business with an emphasis in accounting and a secondary focus in information systems from Southern Illinois University Carbondale. He also holds a graduate certificate in artificial intelligence for business from Rennes University in France.

Dr. Ugrin researches accounting and information systems. He has published more than 30 peer-reviewed articles, and his research has been supported by the National Association of State Boards of Accounting (NASBA), the Institute of Managerial Accountants (IMA), the Pontikes Center for Information Systems Research, Koch Industries, John Deere, and more. He has received numerous research awards from the American Accounting Association, and his research has been featured in numerous business publications, such as *Forbes* and *Accounting Today*. He serves as associate editor for *Advances in Accounting* and served on the editorial boards of the *Journal of Information Systems* and the *Accounting Educator's Journal*.

Dr. Ugrin has professional experience in public accounting, corporate financial management, and manufacturing operations. Prior to his academic career, Dr. Ugrin spent 10 years in public accounting and industry, including 5 years as the head of accounting and finance at a diversified manufacturer. He also served as a consultant in designing the managerial accounting curriculum for the AICPA. He maintains an active CPA license, has been a member of the American Accounting Association, the AICPA, and IMA, and served as the chair of the AICPA's Pre-Certification Education Executive Committee and other committees and task forces at state and local levels.

Amy Igou, PhD, CMA, is the Halverson Associate Professor of Accounting at the University of Northern Iowa. She primarily teaches accounting information systems and accounting analytics at the graduate and undergraduate levels and received the UNIBusiness award for Innovation in Teaching in 2016. Dr. Igou received her undergraduate degree in accounting and computer science from Luther College, her MBA from St. Ambrose University, and her PhD in business with an emphasis in management information systems from Southern Illinois University Carbondale. She also holds a graduate certificate in artificial intelligence from Rennes University in Rennes, France. Amy is a certified management accountant and is an active member of the Institute of Management Accountants.

Amy researches accounting standards' effect on IT operations, IT use in nonprofit organizations, data analytics in the classroom, and artificial intelligence ethics. Amy has been published in the *Journal of Accounting Education*, *Issues in Accounting Education*, and *Journal of Emerging Technologies in Accounting*, among several other academic and practitioner journals. She recently published a book, *Emerging Technologies for Business Professionals: A Nontechnical Guide to the Governance and Management of Disruptive Technologies*.

Prior to joining UNI, Amy Igou worked for 19 years at Deere and Company in a variety of accounting systems positions, including information systems audits and the implementation of SAP projects. Many of the experiences from leading and participating in the system development project are used as a foundation for her teaching and research.

CHAPTER 1

Introduction to Managerial Accounting

Learning Objectives

1.1 Define managerial accounting and describe the managerial accountant's role in business operations.
1.2 Compare and contrast managerial and financial accounting.
1.3 Explain how to use the accounting information to implement business strategy and exercise business control.
1.4 Identify trends in managerial accounting.

Accounting in Life

Kampus Production / Pexels / Public Domain

Many decisions in your life are similar to those faced by businesspeople. Learning to think like a managerial accountant will improve your personal decision-making. For example, a managerial accountant evaluating the decision to attend college would ask the following questions:

- Is college worth the cost based on your future income with additional training?
- What is the *real* cost of college, considering you would have to give up four years of income that you would have made if you were working?

Businesspeople are confronted with similar questions daily, and managerial accountants help them assemble the appropriate information to make sound decisions. Throughout the remainder of this book, we will cover many different types of decisions that businesses face and some of the equivalent situations you might encounter in your personal life.

What Is Managerial Accounting, and How Does Managerial Accounting Help Businesses?

Learning Objective 1.1
Define managerial accounting and describe the managerial accountant's role in business operations.

The use of accounting information to assist in making operational decisions is a managerial accounting function. **Managerial accounting** is a facet of accounting that focuses on internal operations and assists the company's owners, managers, and employees in making operating, investing, and financing decisions. **Managerial accountants** are internal business partners who use data to support management's formulation of strategies and decisions regarding how a business operates, invests its resources, and solicits financing. For example, a managerial accountant might aggregate and communicate information useful in answering questions like the following:

- How much do the business's products cost?
- Should the business outsource operations overseas?
- How can the business manage scarce resources most profitably?
- How much employee labor will need to be budgeted to meet expected production demands?
- What is the cause for costs overrunning expectations?

Managerial accountants play an important role in helping organizations formulate strategies, plan for operations, implement initiatives, guide activities, and evaluate results to assess performance and control future operations. They work closely with other business leaders and are often part of cross-functional teams that operate a business through planning, facilitating, and controlling.

Planning

Managerial accountants assist businesses in developing strategies, goals, objectives, and profit plans at a high level. Managerial accountants assist in **planning** for operations through the development of operating budgets and financial forecasts. Managerial accountants must be familiar with all areas of business and work closely with people throughout the organization when formulating budgets and forecasts; thus, communication skills are essential.

Facilitating

Facilitating involves creating mechanisms that promote business strategies and initiatives that bring them to fruition. Consider these examples of initiatives:

- Development of structures that align employees' interests with the interests of owners, such as paying employee bonuses in shares of stock rather than cash
- Mechanisms that facilitate continuous improvement, such as basing employee bonuses on obtaining a performance target
- Production systems that minimize the amount of costly inventory the business keeps on hand, such as a just-in-time inventory system

Controlling

Operational control is accomplished through monitoring, evaluation, and feedback. **Controlling** keeps business plans on track by performing the following tasks:

- Identifying and developing focused performance measures
- Monitoring the measures by comparing them with targets
- Reporting the results and offering recommendations

Controlling is the last phase of a continuous loop of planning, implementing, evaluating, and making adjustments.

Managerial accountants play a vital role in evaluating performance and communicating the performance results to a diverse group of stakeholders. An effective managerial accountant can articulate results, explain why the results happened, outline the decisions the managers made that influenced the results, and present the strategies the business is employing that influenced the decisions. This analysis adds value to information.

ACCOUNTING IN BUSINESS

Stanley Morales / Pexels / Public Domain

Effective teamwork is critical for business success. Professors from the University of Amsterdam and the University of Michigan published an article chronicling two essential roles managerial accountants played: a *watchdog* role and a *team member* role.[1] The watchdog role emphasizes accountants' responsibility to outside stakeholders, such as stockholders and creditors, to ensure that the economic position of the company is presented fairly in financial reports. The team member role is concerned with making strategic and operational decisions to run the organization. The professors found that managing these two conflicting roles—operating as a team member while simultaneously serving as the watchdog of the team—is a particularly challenging part of managerial accountants' jobs.

[1] Maas, V. and Matejka, M. (2009). Balancing the dual responsibilities of business unit controllers: Field and survey evidence. *Accounting Review*, 88(4), pp. 1233–1253.

LEARNING ACTIVITY 1.1

Identify if the following are planning, facilitating, or controlling functions.

1. Preparing a balance sheet.
2. Establishing organizational objectives.
3. Comparing budgets with actual results.
4. Implementing a computer system to track inventory.
5. Designing an incentive structure for traveling sales staff.
6. Preparing an operating budget.
7. Assessing if purchasing a new piece of equipment will improve profits.
8. Employing a system to automate routine accounting tasks.
9. Presenting quarterly business results to the board of directors.
10. Evaluating the costs and benefits of outsourcing production to China.

What Is the Difference Between Financial and Managerial Accounting?

Learning Objective 1.2
Compare and contrast managerial and financial accounting.

Financial and managerial accounting are similar in that they deal with data and they aggregate and communicate that data in a manner that is useful for decision-makers. They typically differ in key ways:

- Serve different groups
- Aggregate and communicate different types of data and information
- Prepare different types of reports
- Deliver reports at different intervals

We explore each of these areas in the discussion that follows.

Focus of Financial Accounting

Financial accounting provides information for external decision-makers, such as outside investors, lenders, customers, and the federal government. It generally records and aggregates accounting events needed to prepare typical financial statements such as income statements, balance sheets, and statements of cash flows. Businesses prepare financial statements on a consistent basis, usually monthly, quarterly, or annually.

Focus of Managerial Accounting

Managerial accounting, on the other hand, focuses on information for internal decision-makers, such as the company's owners, managers, and employees. It aggregates and communicates a broad range of data and information in the form of managerial reports that focus on the data needed for the decision. Managerial reports vary by the impending decision and are prepared when needed, often on an ad hoc basis. Managerial reports commonly contain both financial and nonfinancial data. Finally, verification of the accuracy, consistency, and legitimacy of managerial reports is the sole job of the managerial accountant. Financial statements, in contrast, are often audited by Certified Public Accountants (CPAs) to ensure they offer a faithful representation of the business. Table 1.1 illustrates some of the differences between financial and managerial accounting.

Table 1.1 Differences Between Managerial and Financial Accounting

Financial Accounting	Managerial Accounting
Provides information for external decision makers.	Provides information for internal decision-makers.
Aggregates and communicates financial information related to "accounting" events.	Aggregates and communicates detailed financial, nonfinancial, operational and "other" information.
Prepares regular financial reports, including the income statement, balance sheet, and statement of cash flows.	Prepares unstructured reports related to operational, investing, financing, and other ad hoc decisions.
Relies on auditors to verify reports for faithful representation.	Does not verify reports with outside parties.

LEARNING ACTIVITY 1.2

Identify if the following are functions of financial or managerial accounting.

1. Preparing a monthly balance sheet.
2. Working with the marketing department to develop a pricing structure for a new product.
3. Helping auditors with inventory test counts.
4. Working with the marketing department to set the price of a new product.
5. Ensuring that financial information is prepared in accordance with generally accepted accounting principles.

How Do Managers Know if They Are Implementing Plans Effectively?

Learning Objective 1.3
Explain how to use the balanced scorecard approach to implement business strategy and exercise business control.

Today's businesses use data to manage operational activities more than ever. They capture internal operational data like defect rates, production time, or internal costs. They record customer data like buying patterns or customer satisfaction and track broad business and economic data like industry trends or interest rates. Businesses use the data to make predictions, analyze results, and drive future business activity.

For example, consider the case of **Vinted**, a Europe-based online marketplace that allows users to buy, sell, and exchange secondhand clothing and accessories, focusing on a community-driven shopping experience. In 2008, while packing for a move, Milda Mitkute realized she had too many clothes she no longer needed and wanted a way to give them a second life. She shared the idea with Justas Janauskas, a programmer who helped build an initial website to sell the secondhand clothes, and Vinted was born. Vinted grew rapidly but encountered challenges faced by all businesses, especially startups and those that grow quickly. Cofounder Janauskas recalled in a *Wall Street Journal* interview, "At first, the biggest challenge for us was scraping together the €600 we needed to run our servers each month." Vinted struggled financially for nearly a decade but made a turnaround after hiring a Dutch consultant, Thomas Plantenga, who now serves as CEO. Plantenga recommended the organization revise its fee structure, reduce staff, overhaul the app, and centralize operations. To monitor

Sarah O'Shea / Pexels / Public Domain

progress, Vinted implemented key metrics like user engagement, transaction volumes, and customer satisfaction. This data-driven approach fueled Vinted's transformation into a leading secondhand fashion marketplace in Europe, with a valuation of $5.26 billion and its first annual profit of €18 million in 2023.[2]

Large businesses are not the only ones that make use of data. Galen Hafla, owner and manager of a **Hokulia Shave Ice** franchise in Parker, Colorado, uses a number of nonfinancial metrics to evaluate essential aspects of his business. "My franchise provides a great product, but I still have to sell it. I operate as a merchant tenant at Walmart. The keys for my business to be successful are to capture Walmart's foot traffic, provide pleasing customer service, and upselling. I look closely at measures like customers per hour, percent of Walmart customers that convert to sales in my store, sales mix including the percent of sales contributed by add-ins, and average ticket price. I also monitor customer reviews on social media closely. If the numbers show that I am capturing a big percentage of Walmart's foot traffic, selling my more profitable items and add-ins, and have positive social media reviews, financial results follow."[3]

Balanced Scorecard

The **balanced scorecard** is a performance management tool that links key nonfinancial performance indicators to financial results. When implementing the balanced scorecard approach, managers select **key performance indicators (KPIs)**, which are important measures of success within one of four business perspectives: *learning and growth*, *internal business*, *customer value*, and *financial performance*. Measures within the **learning and growth, internal business**, and **customer value perspectives** represent factors that indicate the successful implementation of a business's strategy that should eventually lead to desired financial results. KPIs in the learning and growth, internal business, and customer value perspectives are commonly nonfinancial.

- **Learning and growth:** Indicators of the development of intellectual capital and technologies through training and investment
- **Internal business:** Indicators of the development and improvement of internal business processes
- **Customer value:** Indicators of the firm's satisfaction of customer desires
- **Financial performance:** Traditional performance indicators used by external stakeholders

The perspectives are interrelated. That is, investments in learning and growth should lead to improvement in a firm's internal operations by applying what has been learned through training or the implementation of new technologies. For example, investment and training in inventory management systems and techniques will likely lead to advancements in operational

[2] Moss, T. (2024, December 8). How an app selling secondhand clothes went from near collapse to worth $5 billion. *Wall Street Journal*. Available from: https://www.wsj.com/business/retail/vinted-vintage-clothes-app-65e6c2ed
[3] Source: Author interview with Galen Hafla, owner and manager of a Hokulia Shave Ice franchise in Parker, Colorado.

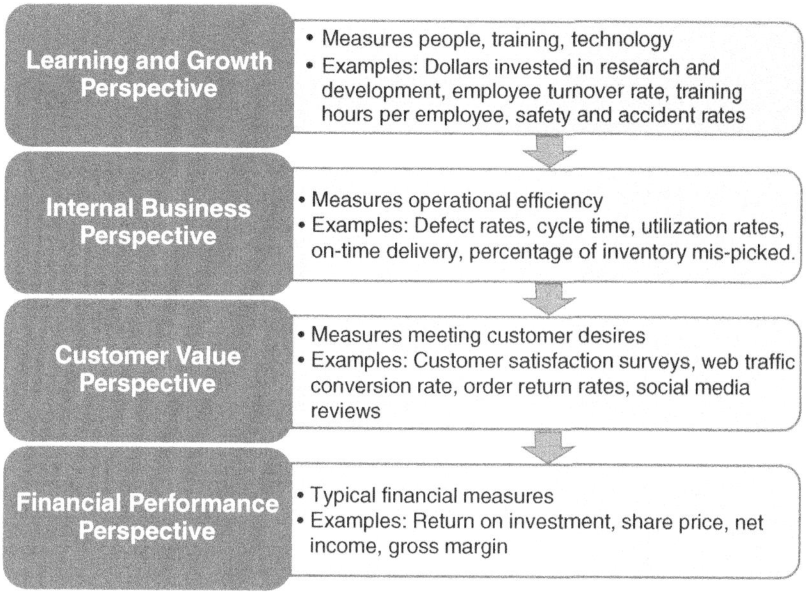

Figure 1.1 Four perspectives of the balanced scorecard.

performance, like more on-time delivery. Operational improvements should then lead to an ability to meet customer desires. For example, more accurate and timely deliveries should lead to a lower amount of returned merchandise and increased customer satisfaction. Increased customer satisfaction should lead to more orders in the future, a willingness by customers to pay higher rates for quality service, and eventually, greater financial results for stakeholders. See Figure 1.1 for the four perspectives of the balanced scorecard.

Question: How do businesses use data when putting strategy into action?
Answer: Many businesses use the balanced scorecard approach to implementing business strategy. The balanced scorecard approach focuses on reporting nonfinancial metrics related to business operations, recognizing that financial results are byproducts.

Strategy Maps

Firms can use the balanced scorecard approach and strategy maps to operationalize business strategy. **Strategy maps** outline strategic objectives across the four perspectives. Businesses select KPIs to measure progress on the objectives and set benchmarks for each KPI by researching industry norms or using professional judgment. Businesses then put initiatives in place to try to meet or exceed the benchmarks.

Denmon Electronics Strategy Map			
Strategic Objectives	**KPIs / Measures**	**Targets**	**Initiatives**
Financial Performance Increase Revenue and ROE	Market Share	30%	Reduce stock ownership with a stock buyback program
	Revenue Growth Rate	20%	
	ROE	25%	
Customer Value Customer Satisfaction	Customer Satisfaction	90%	Implement customer satisfaction survey
	Web Conversion Rate	5%	
Internal Business Advertising Optimization Product Speed to Customer Inventory turnover	Inventory Turnover	60 Days	Implement an inventory storage area redesign
	Time from Order Receipt to Shipment	7 Hours	Website redesign
	Web Hits Per Hour	5000	
Learning and Growth Investment in Analytics Support Warehouse Automation Expansion	SG&A as % of Sales	15%	Purchase data analytics software and train marketing staff
	Investment in warehouse as % of total capital expenditures	40%	Review and select warehouse automation vendor and obtain equipment

Figure 1.2 Denmon strategy map.

An example strategy map for Denmon Electronics, a fictitious internet-based electronics retailer, is illustrated in Figure 1.2. Denmon's ultimate objectives are to increase revenue and return on owner's equity (ROE). Denmon's keys to success as an internet-based retailer are convenience, large selection, and fast delivery. Denmon's strategy map illustrates how financial performance objectives are a function of investments in learning and growth, which lead to improvements in internal business that should help Denmon become more valuable to customers and ultimately more profitable. Denmon's learning- and growth-related objectives are to invest in data analytics software and training to evaluate website traffic and to invest in warehouse automation equipment to make the handling of inventory more efficient.

Denmon has two key performance indicators that gauge their progress on the objectives: (1) selling, general, and administrative expenses as a percentage of company sales and (2) the amount invested in warehouse automation as a percentage of total capital expenditures. Targets for the measures are 15% of sales and 40% of capital expenditures, respectively. To obtain those targets, Denmon is undertaking active initiatives to select data analytics and warehouse automation vendors and obtain analytics software and warehouse automation equipment.

Denmon expects to use analytics software to analyze the effects of various online advertising methods and optimize ad placement to increase website traffic. Denmon is acquiring the warehouse automation equipment to make inventory selection and warehouse operations more efficient. Denmon gauges its internal business objectives with three KPIs: inventory turnover, time from receipt of an order to getting a shipment out to the customer, and number of website visits per hour. Targets are 60 days' worth of inventory on hand, orders shipped within 7 hours, and 5,000 daily website visits, respectively. Denmon is initiating redesigns of the inventory storage area and its website to achieve these targets.

Optimized advertising and fast inventory handling and delivery should result in happy customers, consistent with Denmon's objective of high customer satisfaction. Key measures of success at satisfying customer demand are their customer satisfaction ratings and the percentage of website visits that convert to sales (conversion rate). Targets are 90% and 5% for the two metrics, respectively. Denmon has initiated an online customer satisfaction survey that it sends to customers a week after an order has been placed online. They hope that information gleaned from the survey will help them identify how well they are satisfying the customer and potentially improve the customer experience.

Happy customers should eventually lead to increases in sales revenue and more profits for the owners (return on owner's equity or ROE). Key measures of success are market share, revenue growth rate, and percentage return on owner's equity. Targets are 30%, 20%, and 25%, respectively. One way in which return on owner's equity can increase is to reduce the dollar amount of investment by the owners, so Denmon has implemented a plan to purchase stock back from shareholders. If overall profits remain stable, dividing the same amount of profits by a smaller amount of stock ownership will increase the profits available to be paid out to remaining owners or stockholders, increasing return on equity.

Remember, sequential objectives are set along the four balanced scorecard perspectives. Investments in learning and growth lead to internal business improvements, which help companies satisfy customer demands, which should lead to greater financial performance. Once objectives are set, KPIs are selected, targets are established, and operational initiatives are put into action to achieve the targets.

LEARNING ACTIVITY 1.3

Match each key performance measures with the balanced scorecard perspective to which it belongs:

Performance Measures	Balanced Scorecard Perspective
1. Net income 2. Number of shipments per hour 3. Social media rating 4. Number of safety violations 5. Research and development costs as a percentage of sales 6. Stock price 7. Gross profit margin 8. Website visit-to-sales conversion rate 9. Manufacturing defect rates 10. Percentage of employee ownership	Learning and Growth Perspective Internal Business Perspective Customer Value Perspective Financial Performance Perspective

What Will Managerial Accounting Look Like in the Future?

Learning Objective 1.4
Identify trends in managerial accounting.

Historically, managerial accountants were concerned with compiling and reporting cost data in financial reports and using the resultant information to evaluate product costs. Both functions remain vital today and are a focus of a subsequent chapter in this text. The modern managerial accountant's role, however, has expanded to encompass the managerial support functions we have discussed and future roles that we will now describe.

In the past, businesses evaluated operational performance by preparing financial reports and making simple return on investment calculations. Those straightforward measures were adequate for businesses that produced a limited amount of products and competed in limited markets with limited geographic dispersion; they are not adequate for today's multinational, e-commerce-powered businesses, nor will they be adequate in the future.

ACCOUNTING IN BUSINESS

Jim Deichert, Business Unit Manager at **Steffes, LLC**, a diversified manufacturer of products for the energy industry, relies on accurate and timely accounting information to make operational decisions that ensure the company is making progress on strategic initiatives. A customer-focused company, Steffes is committed to providing innovative solutions at competitive prices. Comparing the cost of building component parts in-house versus outsourcing to suppliers is just one example of how Deichert and his supply chain team manage the cost of products. Per Deichert, "It is essential for us to have a good understanding of the cost of the components we produce when we compare them with the cost of outside suppliers that have the capabilities of producing them for us. We have to be careful to incorporate the right data into our evaluations; it can be tricky." Deichert and his team work closely with managerial accountants to capture and analyze cost information. "Cost information is available in our accounting system, but sometimes, decisions require information that exceeds system limitations. We work closely with the accounting staff to capture relevant data and formulate projections in those situations; it takes a lot of teamwork."[4]

The supply chain team at **Steffes, LLC** is concerned with more than just supplier prices. "Quality and delivery from our outsource suppliers weighs as heavy, or even heavier, than cost from them," says Deichert. Thus, Jim and his team analyze supplier performance data that includes defect ratios and on-time delivery rates.

Introduction to Modern Tools

Today's businesses operate internationally with ease, using internet sales. They are as likely to have a virtual storefront as they are to have a brick-and-mortar building. They are often large and complex, employ people with all ranges of business expertise, produce and sell a wide range of products with more options and customization than ever before through the use of sophisticated manufacturing principles, automation, and robotics. They use technology to capture large quantities of data and incorporate **data analytics**, the use of statistical techniques to analyze, evaluate, and turn data into information useful for decisions. Today's managerial accountant's role is equal parts technical accountant, communicator, and data analyst.

Managerial accounting jobs are expected to grow at a double-digit rate over the next decade,[5] but tomorrow's managerial accountants will see their role as data analyst and communicator grow in importance. Accountants' function as technical accounting experts will decline as businesses expand their use of *artificial intelligence*, *machine learning*, and *automation* of routine managerial and accounting tasks. **Automation** is the performance of tasks by a machine that were previously done by a human. Many corporations already automate accounting and managerial tasks such as recording and compiling data for reports, but in the near future, companies will be using automation to query data, analyze reports, and make comparisons.[6]

[4]Source: Author interview with Jim Deichert, business unit manager at Steffes, LLC.
[5]Source: Bureau of Labor and Statistics, Occupational Outlook Handbook, https://www.bls.gov/ooh/business-and-financial/accountants-and-auditors.htm
[6]Source: Vasarhelyi, M. and Rozario, A. (2018). How robotic process automation is transforming accounting and auditing, *CPA Journal*, July.

Historically, automation has been done by IT departments by writing programs or coding. Now software called **Robotic Process Automation** or RPA allows users to automate simple processes through a point-and-click interface. Now managerial accountants can automate processes, such as complex data analyses, without programming skills. RPA works similar to an Excel macro, except that it can use multiple applications rather than being limited to just one.

Question: How do new technologies affect managerial accounting?
Answer: New technologies will automate many routine tasks and leave more time for managerial accountants to analyze and interpret information.

Managerial accountants are also using newer tools to allow for more in-depth data analysis. One of these tools is **artificial intelligence (AI),** which is when a machine emulates the cognitive functions of a human through complex reasoning. AI systems will likely add human-like abilities to organizational information systems in the future. **Generative artificial intelligence (GenAI)** is a subset of AI that can produce new content in response to conversational prompts. Output can be computational, text, graphics, or video. GenAI programs utilize large volumes of data and information to learn relationships and then uses that knowledge to respond to prompts. Output from GenAI systems is constantly changing as the system learns from more data.

Another form of AI is machine learning. **Machine learning** uses large volumes of data and analyzes it for existing patterns. Based on the existing data, machine learning builds a model to help predict future outcomes. For example, **IBM Watson** is a supercomputer that uses machine learning by incorporating new data with old to constantly adjust predictive models and make them more accurate. Machine learning is an important aspect of AI systems.

There are two primary types of machine learning: supervised and unsupervised. **Supervised machine learning** involves algorithms that use labeled data and known inputs and outputs to develop a best-fit model. The model can be improved as subsequent data are labeled or subsequent results are obtained from new inputs. For example, a supervised machine learning model is built from credit card transaction data. Each transaction is labeled as fraudulent or not fraudulent. Machine learning uses this data to build a model to analyze incoming credit card transactions. As new transactions are made, the model will flag those it predicts are fraudulent. The new data will be incorporated into the model. **Unsupervised machine learning** is the process where the machine uses unlabeled data from large data sets to find patterns without the supervision of a human. For example, to develop an unsupervised model, the program could use the detailed purchase information by customer for a large supermarket. The machine learning program will analyze the data to look for patterns among customers and build a model to group the most similar customers together. This can be used for targeted marketing and other personalization features.

LEARNING ACTIVITY 1.4

Match the following examples of business activities with the appropriate key word.

Activities	Key Word
1. Using internet search data to sense a change in an existing customer's preferences. 2. Completion of repetitive accounting transactions by a machine. 3. Tracking driving patterns to develop a driver risk profile in the insurance industry. 4. Readjusting formulas after obtaining new information. 5. Using a voice-activated computer that assists in answering general questions.	**Automation**
	Machine Learning
	Artificial Intelligence

Technology, Analytics, and AI

AI is rapidly changing the way we live and work. According to a 2023 study by OpenAI, a leader in AI and producer of the GenAI platform ChatGPT, "... approximately 80% of the US workforce could have at least 10% of their work tasks affected by the introduction of GPTs, while around 19% of workers may see at least 50% of their tasks impacted."[7] Some popular AI tools include ChatGPT, a chatbot that takes instructions from you and provides a detailed response; DALL-E, creates realistic images and art from a text description; Looka, an AI-powered platform to design a logo; Eightify, summarizes YouTube videos; and Decktopus AI, creates presentations in a flash.[8]

Workers will learn to incorporate AI technologies to enhance their productivity, much like they incorporated calculators, personal computers, and spreadsheets. Consider the following data table and the use of ChatGPT to analyze it quickly and accurately:

[7] Source: OpenAI.com. (2023). *GPTs are GPTs: An early look at the labor market impact potential of large language models* [online]. Available from https://openai.com/index/gpts-are-gpts/.

[8] Source: Kahn, S. (2023). *The ultimate 100 AI tools* [online]. Available at: https://www.joinsuperhuman.ai/p/100-ultimate-ai-tools.

Transaction Number	Transaction Date	Company Name	Dollar Amount
1001	7/4/2024	Ashworth Industries	$ 240.50
1002	7/6/2024	SamsonCo	$ 333.99
1003	7/6/2024	Feralite	$ 175.75
1004	7/7/2024	Ashworth Industries	$ 39.00
1005	7/7/2024	Ashworth Industries	$ 19.99
1006	7/7/2024	HBC Incorporated	$ 924.00
1007	7/8/2024	Feralite	$ 116.00
1008	7/8/2024	Ashworth Industries	$ 119.87
1009	7/10/2024	Joneboro Controls	$ 230.00
1010	7/10/2024	SamsonCo	$ 600.00
1011	7/10/2024	Ashworth Industries	$ 289.99
1012	7/11/2024	JeneBuilt	$ 320.00
1013	7/12/2024	Ashworth Industries	$ 44.99
1014	7/12/2024	Feralite	$ 69.00
1015	7/13/2024	Joneboro Controls	$ 50.00
1016	7/13/2024	HBC Incorporated	$ 704.44
1017	7/15/2024	Feralite	$ 32.77
1018	7/16/2024	Ashworth Industries	$ 75.00
1019	7/18/2024	Edinbaugh Technologies	$ 99.99

ANALYSIS USING CHATGPT

Professor

Organize the following table by company.

ChatGPT

Sure! Here's the table organized by company name:

Company Name Transaction Number Transaction Date Dollar Amount

Ashworth Industries 1001 7/4/2024 $240.50 Ashworth Industries 1004 7/7/2024 $39.00 Ashworth Industries 1005 7/7/2024 $19.99 Ashworth Industries 1008 7/8/2024 $119.87 Ashworth Industries 1011 7/10/2024 $289.99 Ashworth Industries 1013 7/12/2024 $44.99 Ashworth Industries 1018 7/16/2024 $75.00

Edinbaugh Technologies 1019 7/18/2024 $99.99

Feralite 1003 7/6/2024 $175.75 Feralite 1007 7/8/2024 $116.00 Feralite 1014 7/12/2024 $69.00 Feralite 1017 7/15/2024 $32.77

HBC Incorporated 1006 7/7/2024 $924.00 HBC Incorporated 1016 7/13/2024 $704.44

JeneBuilt 1012 7/11/2024 $320.00

Joneboro Controls 1009 7/10/2024 $230.00 Joneboro Controls 1015 7/13/2024 $50.00

SamsonCo 1002 7/6/2024 $333.99 SamsonCo 1010 7/10/2024 $600.00

Please note that this is a basic organization by company name, and the table only includes the provided columns. Let me know if you need any further assistance!

Professor

Which company had the most transactions?

ChatGPT

To determine which company had the most transactions, we can count the number of transactions associated with each company in the table. Here's the breakdown:

- Ashworth Industries: 7 transactions
- Feralite: 4 transactions
- HBC Incorporated: 2 transactions
- JeneBuilt: 1 transaction
- Joneboro Controls: 2 transactions
- SamsonCo: 2 transactions
- Edinbaugh Technologies: 1 transaction

From the given data, Ashworth Industries had the most transactions with a total of 7 transactions.

Professor

Which company had the highest dollar amount of transactions?

ChatGPT

To determine which company had the highest dollar amount of transactions, we can calculate the sum of the dollar amounts for each company. Here's the breakdown:

- Ashworth Industries: \$240.50 + \$39.00 + \$19.99 + \$119.87 + \$289.99 + \$44.99 + \$75.00 = \$829.34
- Feralite: \$175.75 + \$116.00 + \$69.00 + \$32.77 = \$393.52
- HBC Incorporated: \$924.00 + \$704.44 = \$1,628.44
- JeneBuilt: \$320.00
- Joneboro Controls: \$230.00 + \$50.00 = \$280.00
- SamsonCo: \$333.99 + \$600.00 = \$933.99
- Edinbaugh Technologies: \$99.99

From the given data, HBC Incorporated had the highest dollar amount of transactions with a total of \$1,628.44.

The illustration demonstrates the potential for workers to save time and maximize their efficiency by using AI to their advantage. As man and machine work together, humans will need to understand the concepts well enough to interact with AI, read the output, monitor results, and take corrective action when AI goes awry.

Key Terms

artificial intelligence (AI) When a machine emulates the cognitive functions of a human.
automation Performance of tasks by a machine that were previously done by a human.
balanced scorecard A reporting approach that integrates key financial and nonfinancial measures to connect business results and business strategy.
controlling The process of monitoring, evaluating, and providing feedback to keep business plans on track.
customer value perspective Indicators of the firm's satisfaction of customer desires.
data analytics The use of statistical techniques to analyze, evaluate, and turn data into useful information for decision-making.
facilitating The creation of mechanisms that promote the implementation of business strategies.
financial performance Traditional performance indicators used by external stakeholders.
generative AI (GenAI) A subset of AI that can produce new content in response to conversational prompts.
internal business perspective Indicators of the development and improvement of internal business processes.

key performance indicators (KPIs) Important measures of success within one of four business perspectives.
learning and growth perspective Indicators of the development of intellectual capital and technologies through training and investment.
machine learning When a machine recognizes patterns and improves accuracy with each subsequent decision.
managerial accountant An accountant who serves as an internal business partner and assists the business in the use of data to formulate strategies and make decisions regarding how a firm operates, invests its resources, and solicits financing.
managerial accounting Focuses on information for internal decision-makers, such as the company's owners, managers, and employees.
planning The process of developing strategies, goals, objectives, budgets, and forecasts.
Robotic Process Automation Software that allows end users to automate processes using a point-and-click interface.
strategy map A diagram that depicts organizational goals across the four balanced scorecard perspectives on one page.
supervised machine learning Involves algorithms that use labeled data and known input and outputs to develop a best fit model in advance.
unsupervised machine learning The process where the machine uses unlabeled data from large datasets to find patterns without the supervision of a human.

LEARNING ACTIVITY SOLUTIONS

Learning Activity 1.1

1. *Controlling—Financial statements are prepared to evaluate and control financial performance and assess financial position.*
2. *Planning—Businesses set organizational objectives to support the business's mission. Activities and initiatives are then put into place to achieve the objectives in the future.*
3. *Controlling—Comparing actual results with budgeted plans helps businesses evaluate performance and formulate corrective actions.*
4. *Facilitating—Installing a computer system facilitates the performance of business operations.*
5. *Facilitating—This is an example of designing and implementing a managerial strategy to facilitate efficient operations.*
6. *Planning—Budgeting is a quintessential part of the planning process. Forward-looking budgets set operational and financial goals that businesses aim to achieve.*
7. *Assessing if purchasing a new piece of equipment will improve profits. Planning—Assessing the viability of purchasing and implementing new equipment is part of a business leader's forward-looking planning duties.*
8. *Facilitating—Employing a system to automate routine accounting tasks would help facilitate efficient operations.*

9. *Controlling—Evaluating and presenting financial results helps business leaders understand the business's financial performance and financial position and formulate plans for corrective action.*
10. *Planning—Evaluating a potential outsourcing opportunity is a forward-looking, planning function.*

Learning Activity 1.2

1. *Financial—A balance sheet is used to assess a company's financial position, a financial accounting function.*
2. *Managerial—Developing a pricing structure is an example of a way managerial accountants help facilitate business operations.*
3. *Financial—Auditors are primarily concerned with the accuracy of external financial statements.*
4. *Managerial—Setting pricing is a business operating decision that utilizes managerial accounting information.*
5. *Financial—External financial statements are prepared in accordance with generally accepted accounting principles. Auditors are concerned with ensuring the principles are applied correctly.*

Learning Activity 1.3

Performance Measures	*Balanced Scorecard Perspective*
1. *Net income* 2. *Number of shipments per hour* 3. *Social media rating* 4. *Number of safety violations*	*Learning and Growth Perspective* *Research and development costs as a percentage of sales* *Percentage of employee ownership*
5. *Research and development costs as a percentage of sales* 6. *Stock price* 7. *Gross profit margin* 8. *Website visit-to-sales conversion rate*	*Internal Business Perspective* *Number of shipments per hour* *Number of safety violations* *Manufacturing defect rates*
9. *Manufacturing defect rates* 10. *Percentage of employee ownership*	*Customer Value Perspective* *Social media rating* *Website visit-to-sales conversion rate*
	Financial Performance Perspective *Net income* *Stock price* *Gross profit margin*

Learning Activity 1.4

Activities	*Key Word*
1. Using internet search data to sense a change in an existing customer's preferences. *2. Completion of repetitive accounting transactions by a machine.* *3. Tracking driving patterns to develop a driver risk profile in the insurance industry.* *4. Readjusting formulas after obtaining new information.* *5. Using a voice-activated computer that assists in answering general questions.*	***Automation*** • *Completion of repetitive accounting transactions by a machine.*
	Machine Learning • *Tracking driving patterns to develop a driver risk profile in the insurance industry.* • *Readjusting formulas after obtaining new information.*
	Artificial Intelligence • *Using internet search data to sense a change in an existing customer's preferences.* • *Using a voice-activated computer that assists in answering general questions.*

Review Questions

1. Managerial accounting is primarily concerned with preparing data for external stakeholders. **(Learning Objective 1)**
   a. True
   b. False
2. Developing a forecast is an example of a planning function. **(Learning Objective 1)**
   a. True
   b. False
3. Implementing a program to incentivize employees is an example of a facilitating function. **(Learning Objective 1)**
   a. True
   b. False
4. Which is the best example of a controlling function? **(Learning Objective 1)**
   a. Preparing a budget
   b. Comparing results with budgets
5. Which of the following describes a managerial accountant's job? **(Learning Objective 1)**
   a. An internal business partner
   b. A trusted advisor to clients
6. Managerial accounting reports are usually audited. **(Learning Objective 2)**
   a. True
   b. False

7. Which type of accounting typically focuses on aggregating accounting events into financial statements? **(Learning Objective 2)**
   a. Financial
   b. Managerial
8. Which type of accounting is more likely to report on operational data? **(Learning Objective 2)**
   a. Financial
   b. Managerial
9. What mechanism is used to link business strategy and financial results? **(Learning Objective 3)**
   a. The operating budget
   b. The balance scorecard
10. Which balanced scorecard perspective focuses on improvement in business processes? **(Learning Objective 3)**
    a. The learning and growth perspective
    b. The internal business perspective
    c. The customer value perspective
    d. The financial performance perspective
11. A __________ is a tool that integrates all four balanced scorecard perspectives. **(Learning Objective 3)**
    a. strategy map
    b. key performance indicator
12. Data analytics can best be defined as **(Learning Objective 4)**
    a. the use of statistical techniques to turn data into useful information.
    b. the use of tools to make managerial accounting more efficient.
13. ________ involves recognizing patterns in data and using the patterns to improve the accuracy of future decisions. **(Learning Objective 4)**
    a. AI
    b. Machine learning
14. Which tasks are most likely to be automated? **(Learning Objective 4)**
    a. Recording and compiling data for reports
    b. Interpreting data from reports
15. New technologies will give managerial accountants more time and tools for analyzing and interpreting data and information. **(Learning Objective 4)**
    a. True
    b. False

Short Exercises

S:1-1 (Learning Objective 1)

Which of the following is *not* a traditional managerial accounting function?

a. Planning for operations
b. Instigating operations through negotiating prices

c. Facilitating operations through developing structures and strategies
d. Controlling operations through preparing performance reports
e. All of these are traditional managerial accounting functions.

S:1-2 (Learning Objective 1)

Emerson James is the corporate controller for True-Built Trailor Company in Miles City, Montana. Which of the following parts of Emerson's job would *not* be considered a planning activity?

a. Performing a cost-benefit analysis before purchasing a new tube bending machine
b. Analyzing labor costs from a production job in the factory
c. Budgeting for material purchases
d. Developing profit targets to meet stockholder objectives
e. All of these are planning activities.

S:1-3 (Learning Objective 1)

Which of the following communications skills are necessary to be an effective managerial accountant?

a. An ability to articulate results
b. An ability to explain why results happened
c. An ability to outline the decisions that led to the results
d. An ability to link the strategies that influenced the decisions
e. All of these are important communication skills.

S:1-4 (Learning Objective 2)

Which of the following is a primary difference between financial and managerial accounting?

a. Financial accounting reports are primarily prepared for external users.
b. Management accounting reports are not usually evaluated by auditors.
c. Financial accounting reports are generally prepared at specific intervals.
d. All of these are primary differences.

S:1-5 (Learning Objective 2)

Aram Stevens owns a boutique clothing store. Which of the following metrics would help Aram operate the store effectively?

a. Monthly gross profit percentage
b. Annual net profit
c. Average amount of sale per customer
d. All of these are important metrics.

S:1-6 (Learning Objective 2)

Consider Aram Stevens' clothing store. Which of the following metrics would be considered managerial accounting metric rather than a financial accounting metric?

a. Monthly gross profit percentage
b. Annual net profit
c. Average inventory turnover rate
d. All of these are important financial accounting metrics.

S:1-7 (Learning Objective 3)

The balanced scorecard perspective that emphasizes the use of intellectual capital is the

a. learning and growth perspective.
b. internal business perspective.
c. customer value perspective.
d. financial perspective.

S:1-8 (Learning Objective 3)

The balanced scorecard perspective that emphasizes how well businesses meet customer requests is

a. earning and growth perspective.
b. internal business perspective.
c. customer value perspective.
d. financial perspective.

S:1-9 (Learning Objective 3)

The balanced scorecard perspective that emphasizes the process businesses put in place to meet customer requests is

a. learning and growth perspective.
b. internal business perspective.
c. customer value perspective.
d. financial perspective.

S:1-10 (Learning Objective 3)

The balanced scorecard culminates in which perspective?

a. The learning and growth perspective
b. The internal business perspective
c. The customer value perspective
d. The financial perspective

S:1-11 (Learning Objective 4)

Which types of technologies are likely to disrupt the managerial accounting profession in the future?

a. Machine learning
b. AI
c. Automation
d. All of these technologies will likely disrupt the managerial accounting profession.

S:1-12 (Learning Objective 4)

A computer program that incorporates new data to become progressively more accurate would be an example of

a. data analytics.
b. machine learning.
c. AI.
d. automation.

S:1-13 (Learning Objective 4)

Today's managerial accounting job includes which function(s)?

a. Accounting
b. Data analysis
c. Communication
d. All of these are part of a managerial accountant's job.

Exercises

E:1-14 (Learning Objective 1)

Consider the following managerial accounting activities:

a. Preparing a financial statement
b. Comparing budget and actual results
c. Implementing a reward system for production employees
d. Preparing a budget
e. Implementing a new accounting system
f. Evaluating bids from suppliers

Requirement
List the activities under the correct functional category below.

Planning	Facilitating	Controlling

E:1-15 (Learning Objective 2)

Consider the following accounting characteristics:

a. Provides information for external decision-makers.
b. Aggregates and communicates detailed financial, nonfinancial, operational, and other information.
c. Provides information for internal decision-makers.
d. Does not verify reports with outside parties.
e. Relies on auditors to verify reports for faithful representation.
f. Prepares unstructured reports related to operational, investing, and other ad hoc decisions.
g. Aggregates and communicates financial information related to accounting events.
h. Prepares regular financial reports, including the income statement, balance sheet, and statement of cash flows.

Requirement
List the characteristics under the correct column below to indicate if they are financial or managerial accounting characteristics.

Financial	Managerial

E:1-16 (Learning Objective 3)

Consider the following performance indicators:

a. Return on investment
b. Employee turnover rate
c. Customer satisfaction
d. On-time delivery
e. Cycle time
f. Net income
g. Order return rates
h. Employee ownership percentage

Requirement
List the performance indicators under the correct balance scorecard perspective.

Learning and Growth	Internal Business	Customer Value	Financial

E:1-17 (Learning Objective 4)

Consider the following business tasks:

a. Detecting potential nonpaying customers
b. Matching invoices with purchase orders
c. Predicting sales
d. Interacting with customers reporting defective products
e. Selecting samples of data to analyze

Requirement

List the business task with the new technology that will help make that task more efficient.

Machine Learning	Artificial Intelligence	Process Automation

Technology, Applications, and AI

T:1-18 Use GenAI for written response

Managerial accountants can do their jobs more efficiently using the large language models (LLMs), such as ChatGPT, Google Gemini, Anthropic Claude, or Microsoft Copilot. LLMs are a form of GenAI that can generate content based on a prompt. In this exercise, you will learn some basic prompting techniques and see how changing the prompts will provide better information.

Part 1

- Login to ChatGPT or any other LLM of your choice. You may need to create an account to use these tools. For this exercise, the free version of the tool is sufficient.
- Enter the following simple prompt.
  What is the difference between managerial and financial accounting?

Questions to answer

- Based on what you learned in the chapter, is everything correct in the response?
- Was the response overall satisfactory? What would you improve if you were writing the response?

Part 2

Although the simple prompt provided a reasonably complete response, writing better prompts will get the user better information.

Users should consider adding the following to the prompt for a better response:

- **Define the role:** Specify the role or area of expertise you want the LLM to possess. For example, tell ChatGPT to play the role of an accounting expert or a tutor in accounting.
- **Provide context:** Provide any additional background information to ChatGPT.

- **Clearly write the task:** Give specific information on what you want ChatGPT to provide.
- **Set any parameters or restrictions:** If there is specific information to include or exclude, add this to the prompt.
- **Define the format:** Specify any particular format you want the output, such as tabular, paragraph, or bullet points.

Using the listed guidance, write a more complete prompt. Consider what information the first prompt was missing and ask ChatGPT to include it in this prompt. Limit the output to 1,000 words. Give ChatGPT the role of an accounting professor and direct it to write for a beginning accounting student.

Questions to answer

- Did the second prompt improve the answer? What changed?

Part 3 (Optional)

Use an alternate GenAI tool to complete the same exercise. How do the results differ? Which one provided more complete answers? Which response do you prefer?

T:1-19 Use GenAI for data analysis

Accountants can use GenAI tools to analyze data. In this exercise, use the recent free version of ChatGPT and upload the provided file *Office_Supply_Sales_Data_2025.csv.*

Note: if you are using ChatGPT, you must create a free account and sign-in to upload files.

Write prompts in GenAI to answer the following questions:

- Which store sold the most bookshelves?
- Summarize the sales by Product for January 2025.
- Compare January Sales with other months.
- Visualize monthly sales trends for furniture.

CHAPTER 2

Accounting for the Costs of Products and Services

Learning Objectives

2.1 Identify the difference between product and period costs and describe the three types of product costs.

2.2 Explain how product and period costs are accounted for in conformity with the expense recognition principle.

2.3 Explain how production costs flow through an accounting system to determine per unit costs.

Accounting in Life

Mikhail Nilov / Pexels / Public Domain

Keeping track of spending is a crucial aspect of good personal financial management:

- Tracking expenses helps individuals develop and stick to a budget. Developing a personal budget can help people keep their spending below income and give them an opportunity to save money and avoid debt and unnecessary usage of credit and credit cards.
- Tracking expenses helps individuals develop financial awareness as individuals get a picture of how much money is coming in and going out. Tracking expenses over time allows individuals to identify spending patterns and trends.

Similarly, companies need to track various types of expenses to understand its spending trends to make better decisions.

Let's Review

In the previous chapter, you learned that accountants help plan, facilitate, and control business operations. In this chapter, we focus on accounting for the costs of a firm's products or services. Before exploring costs, let's take a moment to review the different types of business activities that fall into the three categories of business operations.

LEARNING ACTIVITY 2.1

For each activity listed, identify if it is a planning, facilitating, or controlling activity.

a. Computing how much to charge for a product
b. Preparing a production schedule to fulfill current customer orders
c. Analyzing the cost to manufacture a product
d. Determining if using a robot will cost less than using manual labor to produce a product
e. Determining why profits for a month were below expected levels

What Costs Do Companies Track?

Learning Objective 2.1
Identify the difference between product and period costs and describe the three types of product costs.

Judgment and decision-making related to planning, facilitating, and controlling require a solid understanding of the cost of a firm's products or services. For example, managers might examine questions like the following:

- How much should the firm charge for a product to make a profit?
- How does the addition of new factory equipment affect the cost of products?
- How much of the cost of a product is labor versus material?

In this section, we look at the two types of costs: *product* and *period* costs.

Types of Costs

Costs are expenses that represent monetary measures of resources consumed, or, given up to acquire another resource in return. For example, a manufacturing company gives an assembly line worker wages and consumes the worker's time in return. Both wages and time are resources exchanged for one another. Businesses incur many types of costs. They might include the costs of making products or performing services, such as the cost of raw material used in manufacturing a product or the wages paid to employees for their time spent assembling component parts on an assembly line, or performing a service for a customer such as an electrician repairing the wiring in a customer's home. Businesses also pay costs for facilities and equipment, training employees, obtaining insurance, marketing, advertising products, and much more.

Businesses often categorize costs in terms of their relationship with a product that is produced and sold to customers. **Product costs** are costs that are either physically part of the product or essential to the production of the product. **Period costs** are costs that pertain to resources exchanged in the selling of products or exchanged during general administering of the business. They are not part of the products or essential to the production of the products.

Question: How does a business that provides services categorize costs?
Answer: In a service business, costs directly associated with providing the service are treated like product costs, categorized together, and expensed when the service is performed. Period costs, such as those related to selling or general business administration, are treated similarly to period costs in a manufacturing firm.

Product Costs

Product costs are categorized as *direct materials*, *direct labor*, or *overhead*. **Direct materials** are raw materials that are eventually converted into finished goods that are available for sale. Direct materials physically become part of the finished product. For example, the steel used to manufacture the fender of an automobile, such as a **Ford** F-150 Pickup, physically becomes part of the vehicle. The steel is direct material. **Direct labor** represents the work that employees exert converting raw materials into finished products. For example, the wages paid to a machine operator who operates a stamping press producing fenders at **Ford's** factory in Dearborn, Michigan, are considered direct labor because the operator is physically participating in the conversion of raw material into a finished product.

Overhead costs represent costs that are essential to the production of products that are not directly part of the product. Overhead costs include raw materials consumed in production that do not physically become part of the finished product (commonly called indirect material), such as shop supplies, small fasteners, or welding wire and gas. It also includes production employee time spent on tasks not directly associated with converting raw material into a finished product, such as cleaning or training (commonly called indirect labor); utilities paid for heating, cooling, or electricity in the manufacturing plant; the salary of the production supervisor who coordinates production operations; the depreciation on the factory and factory equipment; real estate taxes paid on the factory; and more. Overhead costs are *essential* to the production of products or providing services, but they are not physically part of the products, not directly associated with the conversion of material into a finished product, or not directly related to providing services. Table 2.1 identifies the different types of manufacturing costs for an automobile manufacturer.

Table 2.1 Manufacturing Costs

 Rolled Alloys Specialty Metal Supplier / Pexels / Public Domain	**Direct Materials** Manufacturing costs for an automobile manufacturer include direct materials, such as this sheet metal.
 Chevanon Photography / Pexels / Public Domain	**Direct Labor Costs** The wages for this production worker are direct labor costs that are part of the cost of production.
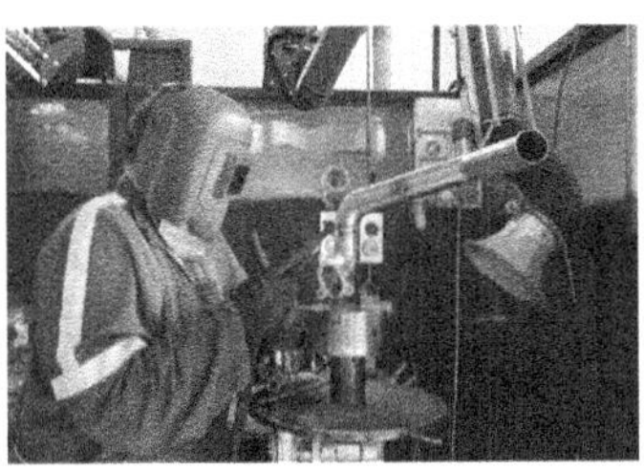 Alex / Pexels / Public Domain	**Overhead Costs** The welding supplies—welding wire and gas—used by this worker are overhead costs because they are raw material consumed in the course of production that do not physically become part of the finished product.

LEARNING ACTIVITY 2.2

Which is an example of a product cost that would be classified as overhead?

a. Real estate taxes covering the home office of a multinational corporation
b. The cost of raw material used to produce a product
c. Payroll taxes associated with the salary of the production supervisor
d. Payroll taxes associated with the wages of assembly line workers

Period Costs

Period costs, on the other hand, are costs that are not directly or indirectly related to the production of products or services. Examples of period costs include travel expenses for the sales staff, wages for accounting and human resources personnel, rent, utilities, and property taxes paid on corporate office space. Businesses expense period costs in the period they are incurred, matching them to the period in which the revenue they help produce is also recorded. The difference between product and period costs at an automotive manufacturer are presented in Table 2.2.

Table 2.2 Period and Product Costs of an Automobile Manufacturer

Costs	Period Costs	Product Costs		
	Selling, General, and Administrative Expenses	Direct Material	Direct Labor	Overhead
Batteries for the automobiles purchased from a supplier		X		
Assembly line worker wages			X	
Factory cleaning supplies				X
Property taxes on the home office	X			
Property taxes on the factory				X
Marketing department traveling expenses	X			
The cost to send the production supervisor to a training seminar				X

(continued)

Table 2.2 (*continued*)

Costs	**Period Costs**	**Product Costs**		
	Selling, General, and Administrative Expenses	**Direct Material**	**Direct Labor**	**Overhead**
Delivery costs for batteries purchased from a supplier		X		
The chief financial officer's annual bonus	X			
Commissions paid to traveling salespeople	X			

Classifying costs is generally contingent on purpose and intent. For example, insurance costs are classified based on *what* they insure. Property insurance covering the home office is a period cost and is part of selling, general, and administrative expenses. Property insurance covering a factory or factory equipment is part of overhead because it ensures an essential element of the production process.

LEARNING ACTIVITY 2.3

Classify each of the following costs as either product or period costs and classify the product costs as either direct materials, direct labor, or overhead.

	Product or Period	Material, Labor, or Overhead
1. Depreciation on factory equipment		
2. Advertising		
3. Property taxes paid on a factory		
4. Component parts purchased from a vendor and used on a product		
5. The CEO's salary		
6. Assembly line workers' wages		
7. Attorney fees		
8. Depreciation on office equipment in the marketing department		
9. Electric utilities in the factory		
10. Product liability insurance		

How Do Companies Account for Product and Period Costs?

Learning Objective 2.2
Explain how product and period costs are accounted for in conformity with the expense recognition principle.

Businesses account for product and period costs in a manner that is consistent with the **expense recognition principle**. The expense recognition principle determines when a company records expenses either by matching revenue, expensing in the period incurred, or expensing over time. In general, it determines that expenses should be recorded in the period that resources are *consumed* or used up.

Recording Period Costs

Businesses typically record *period* costs such as advertising expenses, marketing costs, or other types of general administrative costs as an expense on the company's income statement in the period of the expenditure (that is, the period in which money was paid). The exception is expenditures made in advance of, or after, consumption of the resource the expenditure is associated with. In these particular cases, the value of the period costs is kept in special accounts on the balance sheet (prepaid expenses and unearned revenue) until they are consumed. They are then expensed in the period of consumption.

Recording Product Costs

Expenditures for *product* costs are initially accumulated on the balance sheet as an asset labeled inventory. **Inventory** is made up of goods and materials that businesses intend to sell or intend to convert into a product to sell. Product costs become inventory and are not expensed when money is initially spent because product costs like material have not been utilized or consumed. *Expenditures* for product costs represent changes in the form or nature of resources, but the resources are still in the businesses' possession. For example, money exchanged for raw material is an exchange of one asset, money, for another, raw material.

Table 2.3 illustrates the difference between period and product costs for a company like **Ford**, an automobile manufacturer indicates when the company would record the expense.

Table 2.3 Product or Period Costs Expense Timing

Product Costs—Manufacturing Costs	Period Costs—Nonmanufacturing Costs
Direct Material (e.g., steel, tires, or wiring)	Selling Expenses (e.g., salesperson's salary)
Direct Labor (e.g., factory worker time)	General and Administrative Expenses (e.g., rent, insurance, and property taxes on the home office)
Overhead (e.g., cost of robots and other factory equipment)	
Initially recorded as an asset and then expensed when the asset produced is sold.	Expensed when incurred (usually expensed immediately).

Forms of Inventory

There are three forms of inventory: *raw material*, *work-in-process*, and *finished goods*. **Raw material inventory** is made up of material in its unaltered state. Raw material inventory typically consists of things that the business would purchase from a vendor to convert into a finished good, like the raw steel that is slated to be turned into a fender for the **Ford** F-150 discussed earlier or wood that is to be crafted into a guitar at the **Gibson** acoustic guitar factory in Bozeman, Montana. Raw material inventory can often be returned to a vendor because it is in its original form. **Work-in-process inventory** consists of raw material that has been altered from its original state but is not entirely converted to a form that is ready to sell to a customer. **Finished goods inventory** is inventory in its final form and ready to be sold to a customer, like a J-45 acoustic guitar made in Gibson's Bozeman factory.

Table 2.4 illustrates how an item can be any form of inventory at Byrnes Exhaust Company. Byrnes Exhaust Company makes aftermarket exhaust systems for automobiles and trucks.

Table 2.4 Stainless Steel Tubing—Raw Material, Work-in-Process, or Finished Goods

 Zakhar Vozhdaienko / Pexels / Public Domain	**Raw Material** This tubing from the supplier has not been altered, and thus, it is considered a raw material.
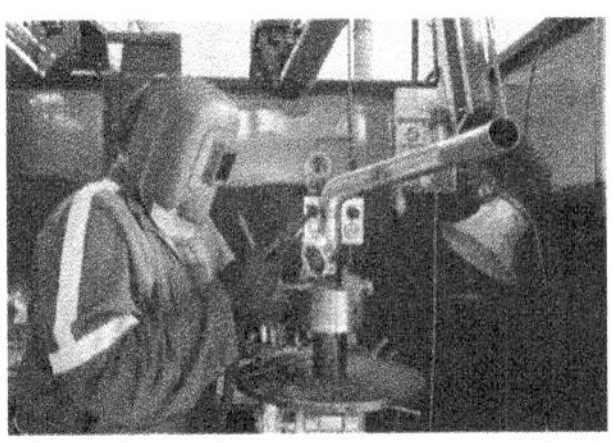 Alex / Pexels / Public Domain	**Work in Process** The welder is modifying the tubing, but it is not yet part of the completed product, thus it is considered a work in process.
 Mathias Redingx / Pexels / Public Domain	**Finished Product** The tubing is altered to become a finished exhaust system, ready to sell to a motorcycle manufacturer.

Byrnes fabricates the exhaust systems from stainless steel tubing. In Byrnes factory, stainless steel tubing can be any of the three types of inventory depending on the stage of production, as illustrated in Table 2.4.

LEARNING ACTIVITY 2.4

Which best describes an inventory item that should be classified as a finished good?

a. Corn that has been harvested
b. Corn that is processed into corn meal that and boxed and sent to grocery stores
c. Corn that is harvested and processed into corn meal in a tortilla factory

Amount of Inventory

In general, businesses like to keep as little inventory as possible because it consumes space, requires money that could otherwise be invested or used to pay off debt, can become obsolete and thus worthless, or can be misappropriated or stolen. Stakeholders who invest or loan money to businesses are also concerned about excess inventory for those reasons and others.

For example, bankers who have loaned money to a business are more worried about the amount of finished goods and work-in-process a company keeps on hand than raw materials. Bankers' primary concern is that the money they loan will get paid back from the business when it is operating or if the business goes bankrupt and is forced to liquidate. From the bank's perspective, raw material is the most valuable form of inventory because it can usually be returned to a vendor at its original purchase price, less a restocking fee. On the other hand, work-in-process inventory has virtually no value because it has been altered and cannot be sent back to a vendor or sold to a customer. Finished goods are also problematic from a banker's point of view. If the finished product were selling, the company would likely not be in bankruptcy!

Question: How much inventory do businesses keep on hand?
Answer: Businesses keep as little inventory on hand as possible because it consumes money that could be used more productively. Companies are particularly cautious about holding large quantities of work-in-process inventory because it is of little external value. Work-in-process inventory cannot be returned to a vendor like unaltered raw materials and is not ready to be sold to a customer like finished goods.

LEARNING ACTIVITY 2.5

Match the key terms with the corresponding definitions.

Raw material inventory	Inventory in its final form and ready to be sold to a customer.
Finished goods inventory	The assertion that expenses should be recorded in the period that resources are consumed.
Expense recognition principle	Raw material that has been altered from its original state but is not converted to a form that is ready to sell to a customer.
Work-in-process inventory	Material in its unaltered state.

How Do Companies Track Manufacturing Costs?

Learning Objective 2.3

Explain how production costs flow through an accounting system to determine per unit costs.

Now that we have described the types of inventory (raw material, work in process, and finished goods), let's examine how the costs of raw material and the costs to convert raw to finished goods are accounted for.

The Flow of Costs Through the Inventory Accounts

Conversion costs are costs incurred to change raw material inventory into a finished product. Direct labor and overhead are conversion costs. Converting raw material to a finished product requires the use of direct labor and the consumption of overhead resources like utilities to power a factory, time spent by a supervisor planning for operations, the cost of robots that perform repetitive functions otherwise performed by people, or cleaning supplies used to keep the production area in good order so conversion can take place. When raw material is removed from storage and work on converting the raw material begins, the business moves the dollar cost of raw material from a raw material inventory account and accumulates it in a work-in-process inventory account. Furthermore, the firm adds the costs of direct labor to work-in-process inventory as they are incurred, along with a percentage of overhead costs. Once the product is fully converted, the firm moves the costs of raw material, direct labor, and overhead that have been accumulated in work-in-process inventory to a finished goods inventory account.

Raw material that is converted to a finished product is merely a conversion of one asset, raw material inventory, to another asset, finished goods inventory. The business is still in possession of the asset, and the asset, regardless of form, remains in an inventory account and is recorded on the balance sheet. The inventory asset finally becomes an expense when the resource is sold to a customer. The finished product (or finished good) is given up in exchange for a customer's

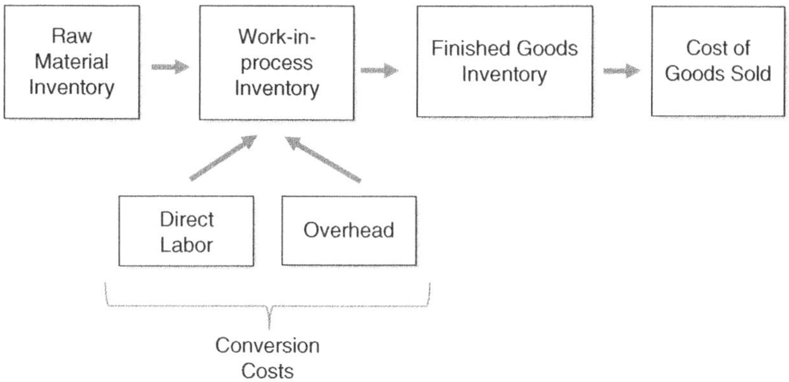

Figure 2.1 Cost flow for a manufacturing company.

resources (money or a promise to pay money later). The finished good is no longer in the possession of the business; it is an expense or cost associated with the item sold, otherwise known as *cost of goods sold*. **Cost of goods sold (COGS)** is defined as the cost of merchandise that has been sold to a customer. Figure 2.1 shows the flow of costs for a manufacturing company.

Calculate Finished Goods Inventory

Businesses track the flow of costs to inform decisions about the cost and profitability of products. Cost flow tracking is based on several key documents and pieces of information:

- Materials requisition forms
- Timecards
- Labor rates
- Shop overhead rate

Let us use Blackhawk Custom Cycles, a fictitious custom motorcycle manufacturing company, to help illustrate the flow of costs through a company. Blackhawk contracted to build three replica **Honda** Superhawk motorcycles made famous by the iconic singer, songwriter, and actor, Elvis Presley, in the movie *Roustabout*. An accounting manager at Blackhawk has been asked to determine the cost per unit of each motorcycle. The first step is to examine information on the materials requisition form to determine the amount of raw material used in the production of the motorcycles. A materials requisition tracks raw material taken from inventory storage or to be purchased from an outside vendor. In our example, the material is directly associated with the production of the three motorcycles Blackhawk contracted to build.

Material Requisition:

$3,500 worth of direct material from Blackhawk's raw material inventor storage consisting of generic components used on all motorcycles Blackhawk builds.

$2,200 worth of direct material purchased from suppliers directly for these particular motorcycles.

$400 worth of indirect material maintained in supplies inventory storage and used to support production of all the motorcycles.

The next step is to examine information on the timecards to determine the labor. Time cards are source documents that accumulate information and data used to track business activity such as employees' time worked, what type of work the employee performed, and what the employee worked on. The shop manager at Blackhawk and a fabricator worked on the custom motorcycles and recorded the following information on their timecards:

Total direct labor hours worked by the shop manager: 50 hours

Total indirect labor hours worked by the shop manager: 6 hours

Total direct labor hours worked by the fabricator: 95 hours

Total indirect labor hours worked by the fabricator: 14 hours

Next, the accounting manager examines additional information related to labor rates and the shop overhead rate and allocation base. An **allocation base** is a factor that links indirect costs to *cost objects*. A **cost object** is an item for which the business tracks costs, in this case the group of three motorcycles. The shop manager's labor rate is $75 per hour, and the fabricator's labor rate is $25. The shop overhead rate is $30 per direct labor hour, the allocation basis. The costs applied to the work-in-process inventory for the group of motorcycles are displayed in Figure 2.2.

Notice that the costs applied to work-in-process inventory only include raw material and labor directly used on the product. The $400 of indirect material and cost associated with the 6 and 14 hours of indirect labor worked by the shop manager and fabricator are not directly applied to work-in-process inventory. Indirect material and labor are overhead costs that are not physically part of the product and are not conveniently traced to the product in process using source documents. They are costs that are necessary for production to take place and are associated with products through allocation.

LEARNING ACTIVITY 2.6

Which of the following is the source document used to track the issuance of raw material into production?

a. The bill of materials

b. The materials requisition

c. The material price list

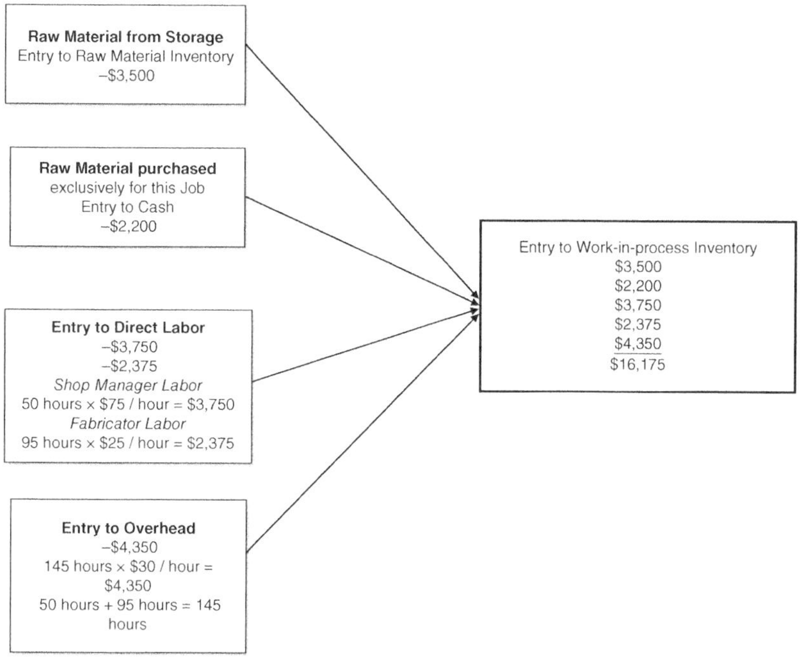

Figure 2.2 Costs applied to work-in-process.

Figure 2.3 Transfer of costs to finished goods.

When Blackhawk completed work on the motorcycles, it moved costs applied to them to finished goods. What dollar amount was moved from work-in-process inventory to finished goods inventory? The answer is $16,175. Blackhawk transferred the total cost that had been applied to work-in-process inventory for the three motorcycles to finished goods when it completed construction of the motorcycles as shown in Figure 2.3.

Calculate Unit Product Cost

Managers can calculate the cost per unit of inventory by dividing the total costs by the number of units produced. In the Blackhawk example, the firm contracted to build three replica motorcycles, and the total cost of the three motorcycles was $16,175. Dividing $16,175 by three results in a cost of $5,391.67 per motorcycle.

Cost per unit:
$16,175 ÷ 3 motorcycles = $5,391.67 per motorcycle

ACCOUNTING IN BUSINESS

In Chapter 1, we introduced Jim Deichert, Business Unit Manager at **Steffes, LLC** in Dickinson, North Dakota, and Galen Hafla, owner of Hokulia Shave Ice in Parker, Colorado. Jim and Galen utilize cost information differently because of the nature of their businesses.

For Jim Deichert at **Steffes, LLC**, understanding the costs of internally produced products is essential to make effective operational decisions around the supply chain. Cost accounting systems help him track costs and associate them with products produced and services provided. "Steffes LLC is a diversified manufacturer, and we tend to specialize in lower-volume products that require a lot of value-added. We are both an original equipment manufacturer, building proprietary products that we market and sell, and a contract manufacturer, bidding on and producing products for other companies," said Deichert. "We track costs as closely as we can to make decisions about things like pricing or outsourcing, along with evaluating our own performance. However, we don't want to spend more money on gathering cost data than we feel we can save through better decision making with the data we collect; it's a delicate balance."[1]

Galen Hafla of **Hokulia Shave Ice** in Parker, Colorado, tracks a more limited amount of cost data. "Trying to drill down on the costs of each shaved ice product or ice cream cone I sell is pointless. The cost of consumables like ice, cups and spoons is marginal. My main costs are labor and facility rent. I generally have one or two people working at the shop depending on traffic volume. If I have two people working, I need sales to make up for that salary because I will be paying it regardless," said Galen Hafla.[2]

Understanding costs and selecting the appropriate method to track costs are vital to both Steffes and Hokulia. Collecting cost information takes time and money, and selecting the appropriate system is an important business decision.

[1] Source: Author interview with Jim Deichert, Business Unit Manager at Steffes, LLC.
[2] Source: Author interview with Galen Hafla, owner of Hokulia Shave Ice of Parker Colorado.

LEARNING ACTIVITY 2.7

Martin and Sons Custom Contract Manufacturing's source documents show the following activities for a contract to build 1,200 trailer hitches for a retailer of aftermarket auto and truck accessories:

Time Cards:
Total direct labor hours worked: 600 hours
Total indirect labor hours worked: 50 hours

Material Requisitions:
$50,000 worth of direct material requested and issued into production
$2,000 worth of indirect material requested and issued into production

Martin and Sons' average labor rate is $25 per hour and its overhead rate is $40 per direct labor hour. Assume Martin and Sons completed all 1,200 units and moved costs applied to the job to finished goods. What dollar amount did Martin and Sons move to finished goods, and what is the cost per unit?

Technology, Analytics, and AI

Companies must capture the data at a detailed level to analyze the cost of their product and overall expenditures. Then, management uses the data for further analysis to help management and accountants better understand the cost of different products. Most companies use an **enterprise resource planning** (ERP) system to capture real-time data as costs are incurred during production. Common ERP systems include Oracle, SAP ERP, and NetSuite, but there are many others as well

ERP systems help integrate many core business processes into a single system. These systems help to centralize data and provide real-time information across departments. In a central system, cost accounting data are collected as a part of the daily operations. By having all the data and processes in the same system, the organization can make better decisions, reduce duplication of effort, and have a real-time view of cost information.

ERP systems are divided into different modules. Some common modules in ERP systems are shown in Figure 2.4.

- **Financial:** This module collects all financial data used for external and internal reporting. Besides the General Ledger, the module contains accounts payable, accounts receivable, budgeting, and financial reporting. The financial module helps track the detailed costs of products and services.

- **Human Resources:** This module tracks employee information, including payroll information, training, and recruitment. This module will provide the financial module with direct labor cost information based on the payroll data.
- **Supply Chain Management:** This module tracks inventory levels, orders materials, and manages the supply chain. The module sends purchasing data to the financial module, determining whether it is a direct material, overhead, or period cost.
- **Customer Relationship Management (CRM):** This module tracks customer information and sales performance to help companies improve customer satisfaction and analyze sales trends.
- **Sales and Marketing:** This module processes sales orders, ships goods to customers, and handles the billing and cash collection. The sales module interfaces with financial to track and record sales and the related costs.
- **Production:** This module plans and manages the production process, from creating the production schedule, maintaining the bill of materials, and tracking the related costs to produce the product. Production sends the information to the financial module to track the inventory movement from raw materials, work in process, and finished goods. These data are used to determine the cost breakdown for each product.

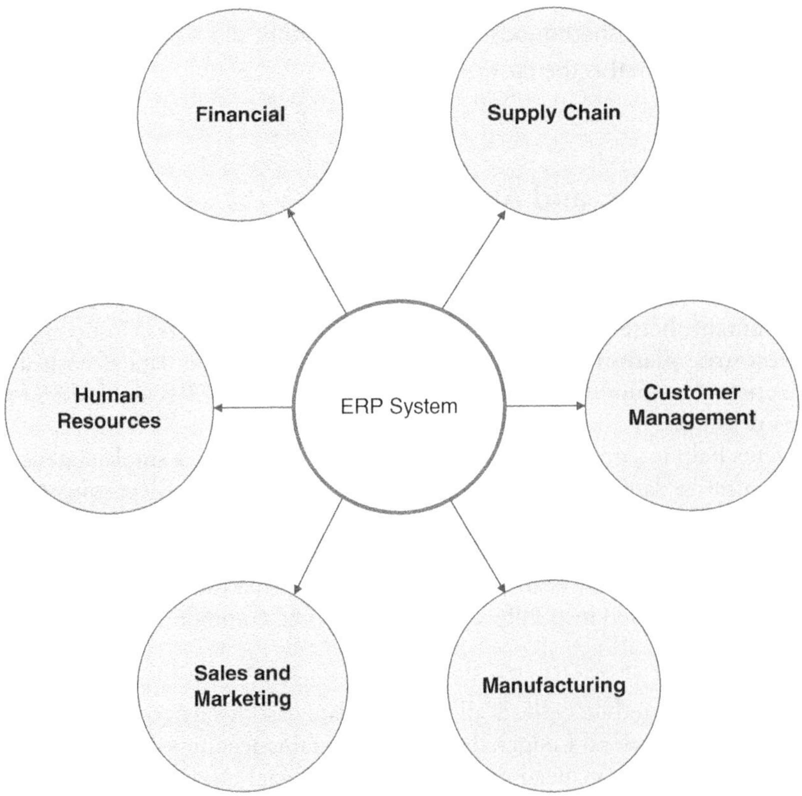

Figure 2.4 ERP system modules.

The modules in the ERP system help to give a single view of business operations and improve accuracy in cost collection. Managerial accounting collects data from each module to help accurately depict costs throughout the company.

Let's examine how the data flows through ERP modules using the example of Blackhawk Custom Cycles.

Supply Chain Management: When Blackhawk buys raw materials, the ERP records the purchase costs, quantity, and supplier information. The system uses the purchase cost as the value of the raw material inventory. The materials will be categorized as assets until sold as finished products.

Production: As Blackhawk manufactures a product, the ERP system tracks each manufacturing step, including the machine hours, labor time, and raw materials. The production module also calculates the overhead costs to add to the final product costs. When the finished goods are completed, the raw materials will be removed from the inventory account and included in the finished goods inventory.

Human Resources: Employees record their time working on various manufacturing activities. The cost for direct labor is calculated using the time information and the wage rates from the payroll system. These costs are included in the finished goods inventory costs.

Sales and Marketing: The ERP system captures the sales price when the goods are sold. The cost of the finished goods is removed from inventory and added to the cost of goods sold.

Financial: The data from the other modules is captured and recorded as journal entries and the general ledger to be used in financial statements and reports used for management decision-making.

The data from the ERP system can be downloaded into a data analytics tool for further analysis. Such tools are Excel PivotTables, Power BI, and Tableau.

LEARNING ACTIVITY 2.8

Blackhawk Custom Cycles is facing challenges with determining the total cost of its finished goods. The company uses an ERP system that includes the Supply Chain Management, Production, and Human Resources modules. Identify how each module impacts cost tracking and explain one specific improvement for each module to ensure more accurate cost reporting.

Use Pivot Tables and Functions in Microsoft Excel

Microsoft Excel is one of the most commonly used tools for analyzing accounting data and can be particularly useful for performing custom analyses of data housed in ERP systems. Other tools like Power BI, Alteryx, and Tableau are also used to summarize data and communicate the information to users. Learning some key features in Excel is essential for an accountant.

In this example, we will use some of these features to analyze period and product costs using the dataset *construction_expense_data_jan_2025*. A sample of the first few lines of data is shown in Figure 2.5.

First, we must classify each cost by type in Column F. We can do this with a lookup table found starting at cell J2 and shown in Figure 2.6, using the function VLOOKUP. This function performs a vertical lookup by looking in the first column of a range and finding a value within the selected range to return. This range is named *Classification* in the spreadsheet.

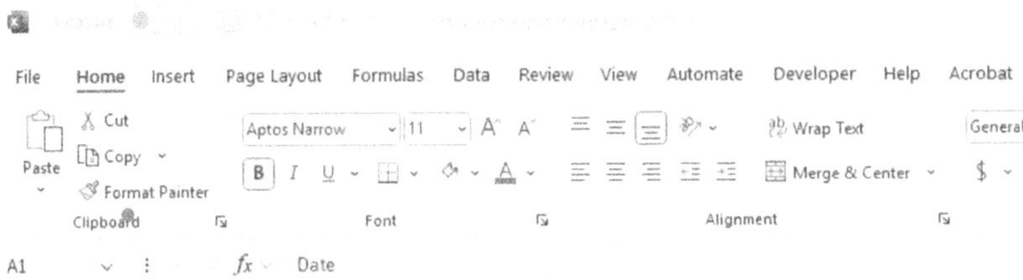

	A	B	C	D	E	F
1	**Date**	**Account Num**	**Account Name**	**Detailed Description**	**Amount**	**Period/Product**
2	1/1/2025	40303	Labor Costs	Electrical work labor charges	918.49	
3	1/1/2025	43404	Marketing	Print media advertisements	3929.06	
4	1/1/2025	40101	Material Purchases	Purchase of nails and fasteners	5058.58	
5	1/1/2025	40505	Site Preparation	Removal of existing structures	458.84	
6	1/1/2025	40505	Site Preparation	Tree removal and land clearing	6817.03	
7	1/1/2025	40505	Site Preparation	Removal of existing structures	751.46	
8	1/2/2025	43303	Utilities	Internet services	837.79	
9	1/3/2025	40101	Material Purchases	Purchase of lumber and wood materials	5067.86	
10	1/3/2025	40101	Material Purchases	Purchase of lumber and wood materials	3349.48	
11	1/3/2025	43101	Office Supplies	Replacement of printer ink	694.5	
12	1/3/2025	40505	Site Preparation	Removal of existing structures	1077.4	
13	1/3/2025	40505	Site Preparation	Tree removal and land clearing	8528.06	
14	1/5/2025	43909	Training	Employee skill development course	1448.53	
15	1/5/2025	43909	Training	Safety training session	2347.49	
16	1/5/2025	40909	Transportation	Fuel costs for construction vehicles	4319.06	
17	1/5/2025	43303	Utilities	Electricity bill payment	2178.9	
18	1/6/2025	40505	Site Preparation	Site grading and leveling	7632.4	
19	1/6/2025	43909	Training	Management workshop	3254.69	
20	1/7/2025	40505	Site Preparation	Site grading and leveling	1070.41	
21	1/7/2025	40505	Site Preparation	Tree removal and land clearing	1679.23	
22	1/8/2025	40101	Material Purchases	Procurement of concrete and cement	4445.34	

Figure 2.5 Excel data for analysis.

I	J	K	L	M
	Cost Type			
	43707	IT Equipment - Office	Period	
	40303	Labor Costs	Direct Labor	
	43404	Marketing	Period	
	40101	Material Purchases	Direct Material	
	43101	Office Supplies	Period	
	43505	Salaries	Period	
	40505	Site Preparation	Overhead	
	43909	Training	Period	
	40909	Transportation	Overhead	
	43303	Utilities	Period	

Figure 2.6 Lookup table for Cost Type.

The parameters of the function are as follows:

=VLOOKUP(Lookup_Value,Table_array,col_Index_num,[Range_lookup])

- Lookup Value—the value you wish to find
- Table Array—the range you are searching for the lookup value
- Column_index—the column to return
- Range_lookup (Optional)—TRUE for an approximate match and FALSE for an exact match. If you are using TRUE, the data in the first column must be sorted.

In our example, place your cursor in cell F2 and enter the following formula:

=VLOOKUP(B2,Classification,3,FALSE)

Note: the formula is using the range name for the cell J3:L12. Since we want the account number to match the values in the lookup table, we will use a FALSE as the last argument.

Now, copy the formula in column F for the length of the data in column E. A quick way is to double-click on the lower right-hand corner of the formula cell. Now, you should have the Cost Type column completed. See Figure 2.7.

Next, we will summarize the data by account by creating a Pivot Table. Put your cursor in any cell in the data. Go to the *Insert* tab, then click *PivotTable* as shown in Figure 2.8.

Then, you will see a dialog box like the one in Figure 2.9.

The Table/Range will automatically select all contiguous data surrounding your cursor. In other words, all cells surrounding the selected cell without a blank column or row will be included in the range. We will place the pivot table in a new worksheet. After reviewing the settings, click OK.

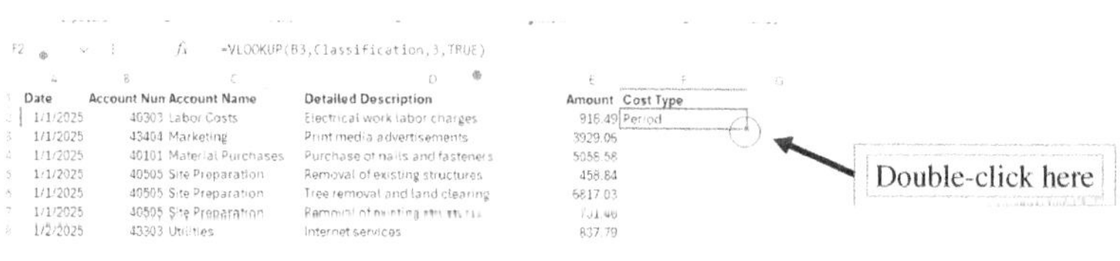

Figure 2.7 Copy formula.

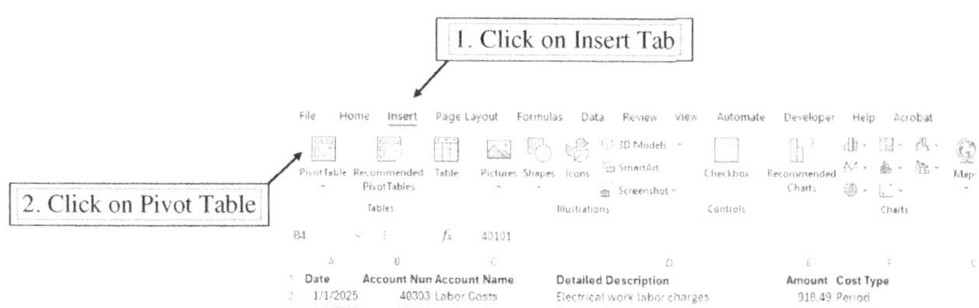

Figure 2.8 Menu path to create pivot table.

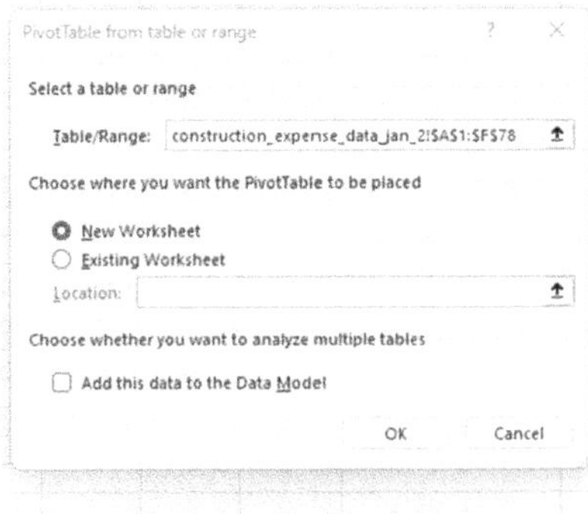

Figure 2.9 Create pivot table dialog box.

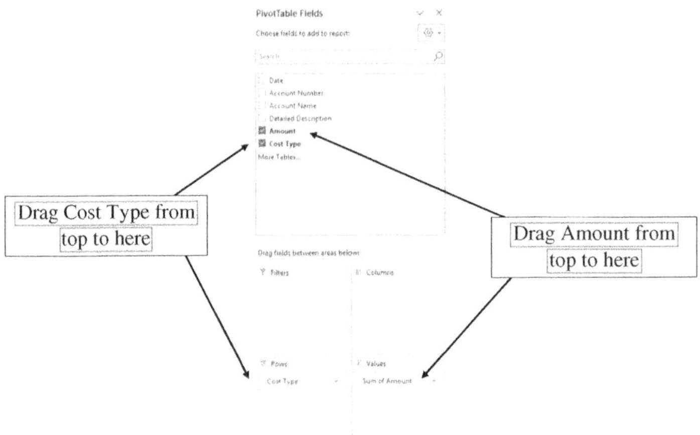

Figure 2.10 Create pivot table.

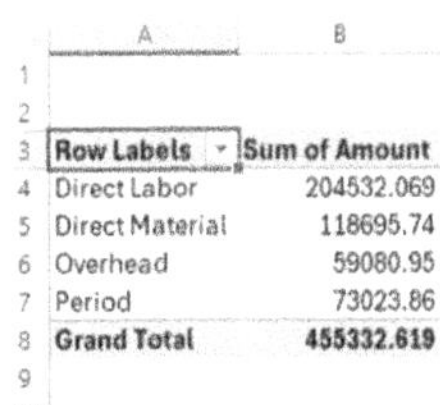

Row Labels	Sum of Amount
Direct Labor	204532.069
Direct Material	118695.74
Overhead	59080.95
Period	73023.86
Grand Total	**455332.619**

Figure 2.11 Completed pivot table.

You will see the PivotTable Fields on the right side of the screen. We will drag and drop the fields to the appropriate areas at the bottom. To summarize by the Cost Type, first drag Cost Type to rows on the bottom of the panel, then Amount to the Values area on the panel as shown in Figure 2.10.

You will then have a simple pivot table similar to Figure 2.11.

Key Terms

allocation base A factor that links indirect costs to cost objects.
conversion costs Costs incurred to change raw material inventory to a finished product.
cost object An item for which the business tracks costs.
cost of goods sold The cost associated with inventory that is sold to a customer.
costs Monetary measures of resources given up acquire another resource in return.
direct labor The work that employees exert when converting raw materials into finished products or performing services.
direct materials Raw materials that are converted into a finished good available for sale.
enterprise resource planning (ERP) An integrated system that integrates most business functions into one system.
expense recognition principle Determines when a company records expenses either by matching revenue, expensing in the period incurred, or expensing over time.
finished goods inventory Inventory in its final form that is ready to be sold to a customer.
inventory Goods and materials that businesses intend to sell or intend to convert into a product to sell.
overhead Costs that are essential to the production of products or performance of services but are not directly part of the product or service.
period costs Costs that pertain to resources exchanged in the selling of products or general administration of the business.
product costs Costs that are either physically part of the product or essential to the production of the product.
raw material inventory Material in its unaltered state.
work-in-process inventory Raw material that has been altered from its original state but is not converted to a form that is ready to sell to a customer.

LEARNING ACTIVITY SOLUTIONS

Learning Activity 2.1

a. Planning
b. Facilitating
c. Controlling
d. Planning
e. Controlling

Learning Activity 2.2

c. Payroll taxes associated with the salary of the production supervisor

Learning Activity 2.3

	Product or Period	Material, Labor, or Overhead
1. Depreciation on factory equipment	Product	Overhead
2. Advertising	Period	
3. Property taxes paid on a factory	Product	Overhead
4. Component parts purchased from a vendor and used on a product	Product	Material
5. The CEO's salary	Period	
6. Assembly line workers' wages	Product	Labor
7. Attorney fees	Period	
8. Depreciation on office equipment in the marketing department	Period	
9. Electric utilities in the factory	Product	Overhead
10. Product liability insurance	Period	

Learning Activity 2.4

b. Corn that is processed into corn meal that and boxed and sent to stores

Learning Activity 2.5

Raw material inventory	*Inventory is in its final form and ready to be sold to a customer.* *Finished goods inventory*
Finished goods inventory	*The assertion that expenses should be recorded in the period that resources are consumed.* *Expense recognition principle*
Expense recognition principle	*Raw material that has been altered from its original state but is not converted to a form that is ready to sell to a customer.* *Work-in-process inventory*
Work-in-process inventory	*Material in its unaltered state.* *Raw material inventory*

Learning Activity 2.6

b. The materials requisition

Learning Activity 2.7

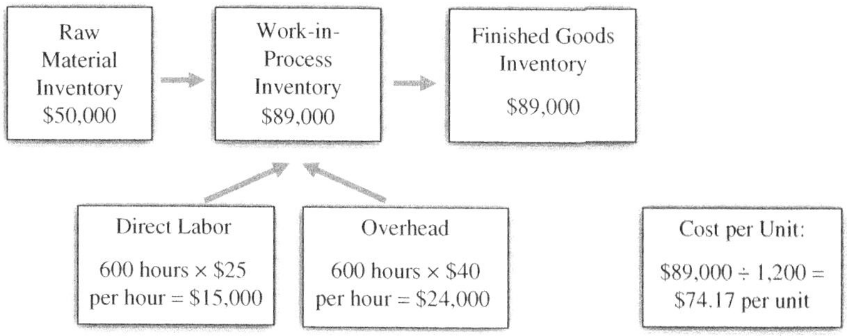

Raw Material		Direct Labor		Overhead		
$50,000	+	$15,000	+	$24,000	=	$89,000

Learning Activity 2.8

Supply Chain Management Module

- *Role: Tracks the cost of raw materials and inventory levels.*
- *Issue: If raw material prices or quantities are incorrect, the inventory value may be inaccurate in the system and financial statements.*
- *Improvement: Can automatically reconcile purchase orders with invoices to ensure material costs are correctly recorded.*

Production Module

- *Role: Monitors machine hours, labor usage, and overhead allocation during manufacturing.*
- *Issue: Overhead costs may be miscalculated if the data on machine usage or production steps is incomplete.*
- *Improvement: Use real-time tracking for material usage and machine hours to allocate costs more accurately.*

Human Resources Module

- *Role: Calculates direct labor costs based on employee time and payroll data.*
- *Issue: Errors in time tracking or delays in payroll processing can lead to payroll problems that impact employees, and inaccurate labor cost allocations impacting financial statements.*
- *Improvement: Electronic time-tracking systems that are integrated with payroll can ensure that direct labor costs are accurately recorded.*

Review Questions

1. Costs are measures of resources consumed. **(Learning Objective 1)**
    a. True
    b. False
2. A cost for things that are essential to the production process represent which type of cost? **(Learning Objective 1)**
    a. Product cost
    b. Period cost
3. Costs that pertain to selling products are which type of cost? **(Learning Objective 1)**
    a. Product cost
    b. Period cost
4. Property insurance paid on a factory is which type of cost? **(Learning Objective 1)**
    a. Product cost
    b. Period cost
5. Payroll cost for the CEO's administrative assistant would be which type of cost? **(Learning Objective 1)**
    a. Product cost
    b. Period cost
6. Shop supplies would be considered what type of cost? **(Learning Objective 1)**
    a. Direct material
    b. Overhead
7. The cost of the time that factory employees spend converting raw material into a finished product is which type of cost? **(Learning Objective 1)**
    a. Direct labor
    b. Overhead
8. The cost of the time that factory employees spend in training learning about a new safety program is which type of cost? **(Learning Objective 1)**
    a. Direct labor
    b. Overhead
9. When should period costs usually be expensed? **(Learning Objective 2)**
    a. In the current reporting period
    b. In a future reporting period
10. Which principle influences the choice of which period a cost is recorded? **(Learning Objective 2)**
    a. The cost principle
    b. The expense recognition principle
11. Which of the following is not an example of a period cost? **(Learning Objective 2)**
    a. Marketing expenses
    b. Insurance costs of the home office
    c. The costs of a safety training seminar for factory employees
    d. All of the above are examples.

12. How would inventory that can be returned to a vendor normally be classified? **(Learning Objective 2)**
    a. Raw material
    b. Work in process
    c. Finished goods
13. Which of the following are part of the cost of holding inventory? **(Learning Objective 2)**
    a. The cost of storage space
    b. The cost of obsolescence
    c. The cost of theft
    d. All of the above are costs of holding inventory.
14. Which type of inventory would probably be most valuable if a company had to liquidate due to bankruptcy? **(Learning Objective 2)**
    a. Raw material
    b. Work in process
    c. Finished goods
15. Which of the following are examples of conversion costs? **(Learning Objective 3)**
    a. Direct material; direct labor
    b. Direct material; overhead
    c. Direct labor; overhead
    d. None of the above are examples.
16. Conversion costs are recorded as which type of cost? **(Learning Objective 3)**
    a. Product cost
    b. Period cost
17. Product costs are initially recorded in ______________ and are expensed as ________________ after they are ______________. **(Learning Objective 3)**
    a. the balance sheet; product costs; incurred
    b. inventory; cost of goods sold; sold
18. A source document used to track raw material usage is a **(Learning Objective 3)**
    a. pick list.
    b. bill of materials.
    c. materials request form.
19. An employee's labor costs can be traced to a particular product using a **(Learning Objective 3)**
    a. Timecard.
    b. standard operating procedure.
20. The item for which an organization is concerned about tracking costs for is called the cost **(Learning Objective 3)**
    a. driver.
    b. object.

Short Exercises

S:2-1 (Learning Objective 1)

Which of the following most accurately describes the difference between product and period costs?

a. Whether the cost pertains to items that are physically part of the product or service
b. Whether the cost pertains to items that are physically part of the product or service or are essential to the production of the product or service
c. Whether the cost is exchanged in the general course of business
d. Whether the cost represents an exchange of resources

S:2-2 (Learning Objective 1)

Which of the following cost is most likely to be considered overhead?

a. The salary of the human resources manager
b. The cost of health insurance for the employees in the assembly department
c. The cost of a software used to analyze financial data
d. Sales commissions paid

S:2-3 (Learning Objective 2)

Logan Anderson operates a sheep ranch. Which of the following would be considered inventory?

a. Sheep held for sheering wool
b. Sheep in a feedlot being prepared for sale
c. Sheep held to be bred
d. None of these would be inventory.
e. All of these would be inventory.

S:2-4 (Learning Objective 3)

Heritage industries builds replica hardwood furniture. Heritage uses direct labor hours to allocate overhead costs. Two Heritage employees worked on a rolltop desk and recorded the following information on their timecards:

Total direct labor hours worked: 60 hours

Total indirect labor hours worked: 6 hours

The employee's labor rate is $25 per hour, and the overhead rate is $30 per direct labor hour, the allocation basis.

Requirement
What labor and overhead costs are applied to the cost of the desk?

S:2-5 (Learning Objective 3)

In a typical cost flow, which of the following would be a reduction to Work-in-Process Inventory?

a. The cost of raw material used in the production process
b. The application of overhead
c. The transfer of the cost of a finished production item
d. None of the above would apply.

Exercises

E:2-6 (Learning Objective 1)

Identify whether each expenditure is a product or period costs, and for product costs, identify if they are part of Raw Material, Direct Labor, or Manufacturing Overhead

Expenditure	Product or Period	Raw Material, Direct Labor, Manufacturing Overhead
Shop supplies		
Wire used to produce circuit boards		
Travel costs for the sales manager		
Lease payments for warehouse used to store raw materials		
Payments to an independent sales representative		
Wages paid to assembly line workers		
Wages paid to the production supervisor		

E:2-7 (Learning Objective 2)

Identify whether the inventory items are Raw Material, Work in Process, or Finished Goods

Expenditure	Inventory (Yes or No)	Raw Material, Work in Process, Finished Goods
Clothing at a department store		
Wire used to produce circuit boards		
A cow used as breeding stock on a cattle ranch		
Headlight assembly for a new car in an automotive factory		
Headlight assembly for sale in an auto parts store		
A cow on a cattle ranch to be sold for processing		
A milk cow		
Fabric at a seamstress shop		
Fabric for sale at a craft store		

E:2-8 (Learning Objective 3)

Suzanne Wong, the controller for Rustin Industries, is evaluating her methods of overhead allocation and is calculating her overhead rate using several different allocation bases, direct labor hours, machine hours, and percent of direct labor costs. Rustin's estimated overhead costs for the upcoming year are $5,000,000. Rustin expects to incur 50,000 direct labor hours with an average wage rate of $25 per hour and 20,000 machine hours.

Requirement
Compute three predetermined overhead rates using the estimated labor hours, estimated machine hours, and estimated labor costs as the allocation base.

Problems

P:2-9 (Learning Objective 3)

Consider the following information related to Spring Creek Outfitter's production of 50 special addition, Driftless model, fly fishing rods.

Material: $1,750 worth of graphite rod blanks, eyelets and other items were pulled from raw material inventory storage.

$500 worth of a special natural cork wrap was purchased from a supplier directly for these specific fishing rods.

$100 worth of indirect material maintained in supplies inventory storage and used to support production of all the rods.

Labor: Total direct labor hours worked producing the rods: 50 hours

Total indirect labor hours worked: 15 hours

Other Information: The labor rate for the skilled rod maker is $35 per hour, and the shop overhead rate is $25 per direct labor hour, the allocation basis.

Requirements

a. Compute the total cost of material, labor, and overhead applied to the fly rods. Assume the rods were started and completed in the current period.
b. How much profit would Driftless make on each rod?

Technology, Applications, and AI

T:2-10 Describe and Discuss ERP

A company implementing an ERP system to track its product costs and overall expenditures notices inefficiencies in the integration between its Supply Chain Management and Production modules. For example, delays in updating raw material usage in the Production module result in inaccurate inventory levels and cost reports.

1. Describe the role of these two modules in ensuring accurate cost tracking.
2. Identify potential reasons for the inefficiencies in integration between these modules.
3. Suggest two strategies the company can implement to improve the synchronization and accuracy of cost reporting across these modules.

T:2-11 Classify and Summarize Period and Product Costs: Excel and GenAI

Managerial accountants are frequently asked to categorize and summarize costs from a list of transactions. You are an accountant for ABC Manufacturing, a small high-end office furniture manufacturer. Your manager asked you to review the individual transactions from January 2025, classify them into Direct Materials, Direct Labor, Overhead, and Period costs, and provide the total costs.

The first few lines of the data are shown here:

Date	Account	Description	Cost ($)
1/2/2025	Internet Service	Internet subscription for offices	11,265.04
1/3/2025	Administrative Salaries	Head office staff salaries	8,376.66
1/3/2025	Product Testing	Product testing expenses	4,585.47
1/3/2025	Safety Equipment	Safety gear for employees	5,560.63
1/4/2025	Lease Payments—Office	Office lease payment	10,184.02
1/5/2025	Factory Wages	Wages for production workers	6,906.61
1/6/2025	Depreciation	Depreciation on factory equipment	4,042.12
1/6/2025	Factory Utilities	Electricity for factory	1,949.73
1/7/2025	Production Supplies	Production-related supplies	9,697.12
1/9/2025	Safety Equipment	Safety gear for employees	1,236.58
1/9/2025	Utilities—Office	Electricity costs for office	14,707.07

Part 1—Excel

1. Open the Excel file *T2-2 Cost Information.xlsx*.
2. Review the transactions in columns A through D.
3. Column J has a list of the accounts used in the transactions. Using the dropdowns in Column K, categorize each account into their respective cost category: Direct Material, Direct Labor, Overhead, and Period Cost. If you need, use the descriptions in Column C for guidance.
4. Using a VLOOKUP function, complete the Cost Type in Column E.
5. Create a Pivot Table to summarize the costs by Direct Material, Direct Labor, Overhead and Period Costs.
6. Summarize the data by Account with a Pivot Table.

Requirements

1. What is the total amount for the following?
   a. Direct materials
   b. Direct labor
   c. Overhead
   d. Period costs
2. What are the total costs for Factory Wages?

Part 2—GenAI (Optional)

Upload the spreadsheet into a GenAI tool. Write a prompt to have GenAI categorize each transaction and then calculate the total Direct Material, Direct Labor, Overhead, and Period Costs. Compare the results to your answer. Are there differences?

T:2-12 Use a Tutor: GenAI

For the following exercise, use the GenAI tool of your choice. The book example uses ChatGPT.

GenAI tools can help students study for exams or understand difficult topics.

Here is a prompt you can use to have a Generative AI tool quiz you on the difference between period and product costs.

> I am a college accounting student and you are a tutor. Please quiz me one question at a time and provide feedback on my answers. I have been learning about the types of costs, such as period and product and how they flow through an accounting system.

Try it! See if it helps your understanding of the topic. Use it in future chapters to help you understand difficult topics.

You can also paste in the chapter learning objectives.

Use this prompt for other classes and as you advance through managerial accounting.

CHAPTER 3

Job Order Costing

Learning Objectives

3.1 Describe the profile of a firm that uses a job order costing system and the main components of the system.
3.2 Explain the role of direct material, direct labor, and overhead in a job order costing system.
3.3 Explain how losses are treated in a job order costing system.
3.4 Outline the elements recorded in a job order cost sheet.
3.5 Illustrate the journal entries associated with job order costing.

Accounting in Life

George Dolgikh / Adobe Systems Incorporated

Have you worked or interned at a job where you had to track time and detail about your daily activities? If so, you likely worked at a business that uses a job order costing system. Professional firms like engineering, accounting, or law firms require employees to record daily time and activities in increments, note the client, and possibly indicate the specific service performed. This level of detail allows the firm to track costs and bill the client accurately for work performed.

Do you use your smartphone to social network, browse the internet, or play games? If so, you might consider tracking your time. Researchers have found that a moderate amount of screen time can improve your performance in school as it can serve as a means of taking a break and clearing your mind.[1] But, as time adds up, performance in school goes down as students miss out on valuable study time, become burned out, stressed, and even depressed. Track your time; you might be surprised by the amount of your life you spend looking at the screen.

Let's Review

In the previous chapter, you learned about the differences between period and product costs and how they flow through the accounting system. This chapter will explain the role of direct material, direct labor, and overhead in a job order costing system. We will examine how the costs are captured and recorded.

LEARNING ACTIVITY 3.1

For each transaction, determine if the costs are product or period costs. If they are product costs, further categorize them into direct materials, direct labor, or overhead.

Transaction	Period or Product	Product Cost Category
Pay factory workers for the week		
Hire a repair person to fix a factory machine		
Pay for raw materials		
Office supplies		

Businesses typically choose one of two systems for allocating product costs to finished goods: a *job order costing system* or a *process costing system.* In this chapter, we examine a *job order costing system;* Chapter 4 examines a *process costing system.* Businesses with heterogeneous products use a *job order costing system* to identify, calculate, and assign costs.

[1] Wu, J., Mei, M., and Ugrin, J. (2018). Student cyberloafing in and out of the classroom in China and the relationship with student performance. *Cyberpsychology, Behavior, and Social Networking*, 21(3).

What Is a Job Order Costing System, and What Kind of Firms Use It?

Learning Objective 3.1
Describe the profile of a firm that uses a job order costing system and the main components of the system.

Pixabay / Pexels / Public Domain

A **job order costing system** is a system of product costing suitable for businesses that identify and calculate specific costs and assign the costs to specific products or services. Generally, companies that use job order costing systems produce heterogeneous products or provide a range of services or are businesses that provide products or services that utilize various internal processes in their production or performance. Examples of such enterprises are custom manufacturers, construction contractors, and law firms, where each item produced or service performed is distinct. Job order costing can help these types of businesses analyze their performance on contracts, compute customer bills, determine appropriate sales prices, or provide data useful for bidding on future business and evaluating performance.

In a job order costing system, a *job* is synonymous with a *batch* or a group of finished goods units produced at one time. A job order costing system calculates the cost of each *job*, not the cost of each specific unit made, unless the job is for a batch of just one unit. To that end, the job is the unique **cost object**, or item for which the business tracks costs. A job can consist of a singular finished good item or service contract or consist of many similar items produced in a batch. A manager computes the cost of the job and divides it by the number of units produced by the job.

In a job order costing system, direct material, direct labor, and overhead costs are captured and then redistributed or applied to each job. Direct material and direct labor costs are typically redistributed by **assignment** to jobs using **source documents**, while **overhead** generally is redistributed through an allocation process using a predetermined formula. Businesses assign costs using a physical mechanism that tracks the amount of cost to redistribute. Source documents such as **timecards** and materials requisition requests serve as physical mechanisms. **Allocation** involves apportioning costs using a formula. Figure 3.1 shows the flow of product costs for a company that uses job order costing.

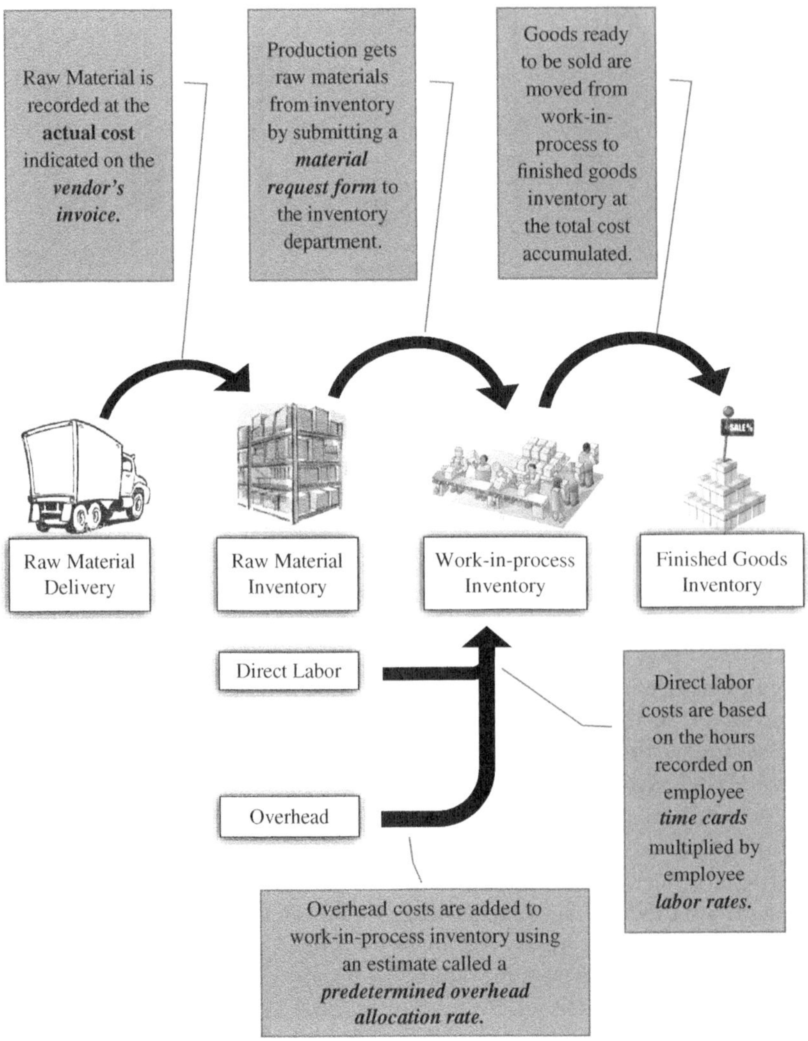

Figure 3.1 Flow of product costs in job order costing.

ACCOUNTING IN BUSINESS

Job order costing data is vital in decision-making and developing estimates for future contracts. In addition to their proprietary products, Steffes, LLC builds a wide variety of products for other companies. Information from its job order costing system helps its contract manufacturing team develop cost estimates for potential new customers. Steffes has decades of contract manufacturing experience and product costing history. Cost estimators can refer to historical job cost data when quoting new business for a potential customer.

Steffes also utilizes job cost data to compute unit costs for cost-plus pricing agreements it has negotiated with some customers. The ultimate selling price in a cost-plus pricing agreement is computed by adding a percentage markup to unit costs, which are calculated using job order costs in Steffes' case. Accurate job costing is essential with cost-plus agreements.

Source: Author interview with Jim Deichert, Business Unit Manager at Steffes, LLC.

LEARNING ACTIVITY 3.2

Select the businesses that would most likely use a job order costing system.

1. Del Dente Food Processing	1. ____________
2. Jessen LLP Attorneys at Law	2. ____________
3. Americo Oil Refining	3. ____________
4. Elwood's Custom Wood Cabinetry	4. ____________
5. Tyron's Chicken Processing Plant	5. ____________

What Are the Main Elements of Job Order Costing Systems?

Learning Objective 3.2

Explain the role of direct material, direct labor, and overhead in a job order costing system.

Let's now take a close look at the main types of information required in a job order costing: direct material, labor, and overhead costs. To illustrate accounting for costs in a job order costing system, we will continue to use Blackhawk Custom Cycle, the custom motorcycle manufacturing company we used to demonstrate cost flow. Blackhawk specializes in custom motorcycles, custom replicas, and classic motorcycle restoration. Blackhawk typically caters to high-end clientele and competes with companies throughout its region and around the country through a bidding process where competing firms present potential clients with detailed mock-ups and pricing. Formulating accurate bids and evaluating financial performance on projects requires precise knowledge of costs. Blackhawk utilizes a job order costing system to capture the required information to account for direct material, labor, and overhead costs.

Accounting for Direct Material

When a business purchases raw material to use in future business processes, it records the price paid to a vendor plus any delivery charges in a raw material inventory account. The raw material inventory account tracks the dollar amount of material the firm has on hand. You can visualize the purchase of raw material from a vendor and the delivery of the material to a warehouse storage area. Blackhawk purchases and stores raw materials such as sheet steel and steel tubing that it customizes into motorcycle frames, fenders, and gas tanks, along with common parts used in most of the motorcycles it produces, such as spoke wheels, cables, brake calipers, and other items. Blackhawk records the quantity and dollar amount of raw material and components delivered after examining shipping documents and *invoices* sent from the vendor and comparing them with a *purchase order* form sent from Blackhawk to the vendor to initiate the transaction. A **purchase order** is a document given to a vendor by a customer that indicates the types, quantities, and prices of goods the customer intends to purchase. An **invoice** is a document provided to a customer by a vendor that displays the charges for goods or services purchased. Figure 3.2 shows the documents needed to record the raw material inventory costs.

When a firm moves raw material that it has accumulated and stored in the raw material inventory warehouse to use in production, it becomes direct material that is assigned to a job and moved from the raw material inventory account to a work-in-process inventory account in the accounting information system. Accounting information systems incorporate several documents to facilitate the process. For example, organizations typically use a *material requisition form* to request that the inventory department provide raw material to production. Figure 3.4 shows an example of a completed material requisition form. A **material requisition form** is a source document that indicates the inventory items and quantities desired by production operations and the job to which the inventory should be assigned. A manager multiplies the number of units on the material request form by the actual unit cost in the inventory records to determine the dollar amount to be assigned to the job.

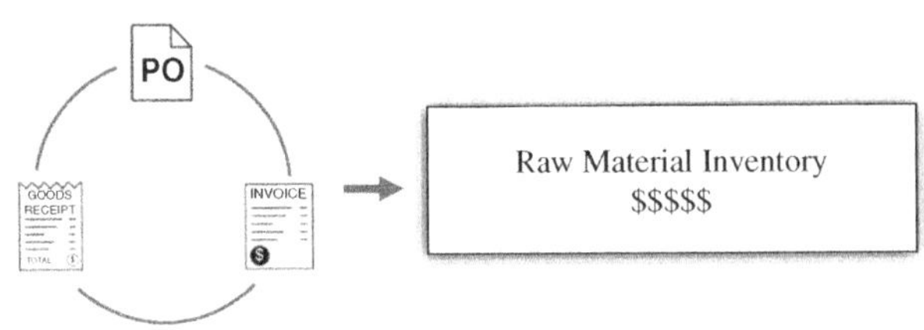

Figure 3.2 Documents used to capture raw materials.

Now, visualize the movement of raw material from the warehouse storage area to the assembly line where conversion into a finished product will take place. Blackhawk Custom Cycle moves sheet steel, steel tubing, and other components from its warehouse for use on a job. The business lists the raw material selected on a materials request form completed by the production operations department. The production operations department presents the materials request form to the inventory department, which then issues the material to production and the raw material becomes work-in-process. Figure 3.3 shows the movement of the costs between accounts. In Figure 3.4, the total cost of the raw material requested on MRQ No. 1 and issued into production is $5,700, which is moved from raw material inventory to work-in-process inventory.

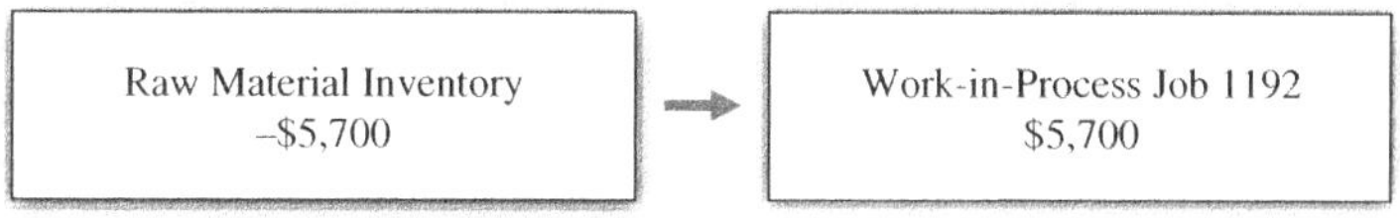

Figure 3.3 Accounting for movement of material to assembly.

Material Requisition Form — **MRQ No. 1**

Date: 6-15-20XX

Job #: 1192

Part No.	Description	Unit of Measure	Quantity Requested	Quantity Issued	Unit Cost	Total Cost
92322-A	1" Tubing	Ln. Ft.	45	45	8.00	360.00
92334	1/2" Tubing	Ln. Ft.	15	15	3.00	45.00
24324	"18 Spoke wheels	Each	3	3	110.00	330.00
24326	"16 Spoke wheels	Each	3	3	80.00	240.00
15324	"16 straight bars	Each	3	3	40.00	120.00
25300	Str8 Stop Brake	Each	6	6	75.00	450.00
15328	Hand grips	Each	6	6	12.00	72.00
38883	3/8 cold rolled steel	Sq. Ft.	90	90	2.00	180.00
47632	Cables	Ln. Ft.	60	60	2.50	150.00
53839	3/4" Clamps	Pkg	3	3	5.00	15.00
10032	Hardware pack	Pkg	3	3	15.00	45.00
55333	350cc OHC engine assy	Each	3	3	985.00	2955.00
50434	Ultraglide transmission	Each	3	3	220.00	660.00
60594	O-ring chain	Each	3	3	26.00	78.00

Completed by the production operations department to request material

Completed by the inventory department after issuing material to production operations

Total Cost of Material Requested on MRQ No. 1 = $5700

Figure 3.4 Material requisition form.

Recording Direct Labor

Businesses accumulate and assign direct labor to jobs much like they do for direct material. At companies that use a job order costing system, employees indicate the amount of time they spend working on particular jobs on their timecards. The timecard provides the information accounting needs to determine direct labor costs and direct labor costs associated with particular jobs. The flow of information from the timecards to work-in-process is as follows:

1. Accounting multiplies the *total* amount of time recorded on the timecards by employees' wage rates and records the amount in a labor expense account that tracks total labor costs.
2. Accounting multiplies the amount of time worked on *particular jobs* by employee wage rates and removes that cost from the labor expense account and applies it to the jobs that constitute work-in-process. The costs remain in work-in-process until the goods are complete.

The work-in-process inventory account now consists of the costs of raw material and the direct labor time spent converting it. Any labor cost not dedicated to a particular job remains in the labor expense account. The business treats the remaining labor cost that is not directly related to a particular job as indirect labor, which becomes part of the overhead costs discussed next.

> Total employee labor recorded from a timecard includes both direct production labor and indirect nonproduction labor. The business *assigns* the *direct* labor to production jobs. Any remaining indirect labor will become part of overhead that is *allocated* to production jobs through the overhead allocation process.

Figure 3.5 shows how an employee's timecard would be used to track work performed on different jobs, including job number 1192 listed on the sample material requisition form in Figure 3.4. Employee number 4 is the shop manager. He tracks his time to jobs for accurate costing and customer billing. The timecard indicates that on June 15, he worked a total of 4.5 hours on job 1192, 1 hour on job 1187, and 1.75 hours on job 1190. Assuming his wage rate is \$75 per hour, \$337.5 of labor (4.5 hours × \$75 per hour) is charged to job 1192, \$75 to job 1187, and \$131.25 (1.75 × \$75) to job 1190. The amounts are posted to work-in-process subaccounts for each job. One half-hour of his time went to job "Train84," a code for a training seminar, and 15 minutes went to "Clean," a code for cleaning. Both training and cleaning are types of indirect labor related to activities that are necessary for production but not officially part of converting inventory to a finished product. Thus, Blackhawk does not allocate \$56.25 (0.75 × \$75) to particular production jobs; instead, it considers it an overhead cost, which is recorded in the manufacturing overhead account.

Recording Overhead to a Job

It is straightforward for a manager to determine the actual cost of raw materials and direct labor for jobs using material request forms and timecards. Companies indirectly associate overhead costs with products or services as they are more difficult to apply to a job because

Employee Timecard			**TC No. 7458**
Employee Number: 4			Date: 6-15-20XX
Job #	Time Started	Time Ended	Time (In Hours)
1192	8:00	10:30	2.5
Train84	10:30	11:00	0.5
1187	11:00	12:00	1
1192	1:00	3:00	2
1190	3:00	4:45	1.75
Clean	4:45	5:00	0.25

Cost to Work-In-Process
Job 1187
1 Hour × $75.00 = $75.00

Cost to Work-In-Process
Job 1190
1.75 Hours × $75.00 = $131.25

Cost to Work-In-Process
Job 1192
4.5 Hours × $75.00 = $337.50

Cost to Manufacturing
Overhead
.75 Hours × $75.00 = $56.25

Figure 3.5 Employee Timecard.

a specific source document is not used to track their consumption. Therefore, businesses use a predetermined overhead allocation rate to estimate the amount of overhead consumed by each job.

The predetermined overhead rate assumes that operating activity drives business costs. A *cost driver* is used to measure operating activity. A **cost driver** is an operating activity that is common to the products or services the business produces and correlates with costs. A measurement of the cost driver typically becomes the basis for allocation or the allocation base (discussed earlier). A manager calculates the predetermined overhead allocation rate by dividing the annual estimated overhead costs, determined during the annual budgeting process, by the expected amount of annual cost driver usage. For example, direct labor is a commonly used cost driver, with direct labor hours being the allocation base. Increases in direct labor typically correlate with increases in operating activity that also result in increases in overhead costs. Thus, one way to represent the predetermined overhead rate is by dividing estimated annual overhead costs by estimated annual cost driver usage (labor hours in this case) at a given level of sales and a production volume that can support that level of sales. The result would be a rate depicted as overhead cost per direct labor hour in Figure 3.6.

Once a business has computed a predetermined overhead rate, it applies overhead to jobs by multiplying the predetermined overhead rate by the *actual* amount of cost driver consumption on the job.

For example, suppose Blackhawk Custom Cycle estimated $600,000 in overhead costs for a year and 20,000 direct labor hours to be performed by its 10 motorcycle fabrication specialists. The predetermined overhead rate would be $30 per direct labor hour, assuming labor hours is the cost driver and allocation base selected. Recall Employee 4, the shop manager, worked 4.5 hours on job number 1192, one hour on job 1187, and 1.75 hours on job 1190. Blackhawk applies $135.00 (4.5 × $30) of overhead to job 1192, $30 (1 × $30) to job 1187, and $52.50 (1.75 × $30) to job 1190 for time worked by employee 4.

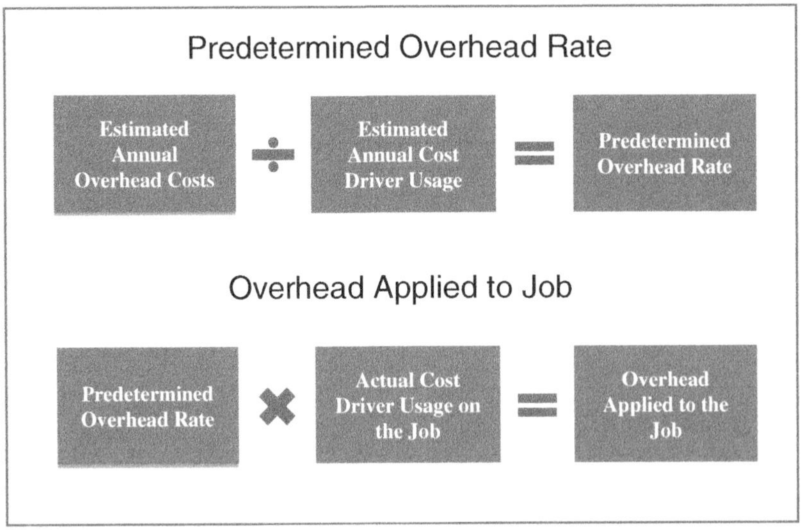

Figure 3.6 Overhead calculations.

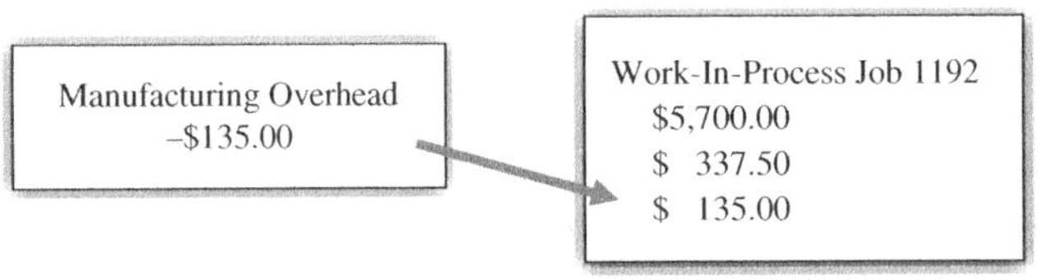

Figure 3.7 Overhead applied.

Predetermined Overhead Rate = Estimated Annual Overhead Costs/Estimated Annual Cost Driver Usage

Predetermined Overhead Rate = $600,000/20,000 DLH = $30/DLH

Overhead Applied to the Job = Predetermined Overhead Rate × Actual Cost

Driver Usage on the Job

Overhead Applied to Job 1192 = $30 / DLH × 4.5 DLH = $135.00
Overhead Applied to Job 1187 = $30 / DLH × 1.0 DLH = $30.00
Overhead Applied to Job 1190 = $30 / DLH × 1.75 DLH = $52.50

You can see in Figure 3.7 that the overhead applied to work-in-process for job 1192 is $135.00.

LEARNING ACTIVITY 3.3

Match each information example with the source document where it can be found.

Information	Source Document
1. Agreed upon purchase price for goods	Invoice
2. Amount of material to be moved from raw material storage to production	Purchase Order
3. Start and stop time worked	Material Requisition Form
4. Vendor charges for goods and services	
5. Quantity of goods purchased from a vendor	Time Card

LEARNING ACTIVITY 3.4

Jay-Dee Company uses a job order costing system and applies manufacturing overhead to its products on the basis of direct labor hours. The business made the following annual estimates:

Direct labor hours	20,000
Manufacturing overhead costs	$200,000

Compute the predetermined overhead (input your answer):

How Are Losses Treated in Job Costing?

Learning Objective 3.3

Explain how losses are treated in a job order costing system.

In job order costing, the occurrence of product and material losses must be accounted for in the overall cost structure. Companies use several terms to describe these losses, such as scrap, leakage, shrinkage, spoilage, or defects. Regardless of the descriptor, they all mean loss of product or material from errors within the production process, whether stemming from human or machine faults, or from losses inherent in the material itself, such as evaporation, or even spoilage that can occur when perishables remain in inventory too long.

In some cases, units can be reworked and eventually sold. Defects that result from errors in the manufacturing process might be rejected during inspection for failing to meet quality standards, but the units might be reworked and eventually available for sale. The effort to rework the units is still an additional cost and is considered a loss. Some units might not be eligible for rework but might be sold for scrap. Other units, such as spoiled perishables, might not be salvageable at all.

The accounting treatment is contingent on whether the loss is normal or abnormal. **Normal losses** are those that fall within an expected tolerance level during production. They are considered inherent to the manufacturing process and are factored into predetermined overhead rates. These expected losses are thus accounted for as part of the cost of the job. **Abnormal losses** are those that exceed the anticipated levels of normal loss. They are treated as period costs and are written off accordingly. Managing and mitigating these various forms of losses is essential for maintaining efficiency and profitability in job order costing systems.

What Do Businesses Record on the Job Order Cost Sheet?

Learning Objective 3.4
Outline the elements recorded in a job order cost sheet.

A business records the dollar amount of raw material, direct labor, and overhead applied to a job on a **job order cost sheet**, a document used in a job order cost system to record all cost associated with a specific job. The business prepares a distinct job cost sheet for each job and uses this information when preparing the balance sheet.

In-process, Incomplete Jobs

The job cost sheet for an in-process, incomplete job would contain all the raw material, direct labor, and overhead applied to date and be part of work-in-process inventory. The total work-in-process inventory balance on the business's balance sheet would consist of the total costs applied to all the incomplete jobs at the balance sheet date. The business moves all the costs that have been recorded on the job order cost sheet to finished goods once a job is completed. Businesses store job order cost sheets in a hard copy or electronic permanent file for later reference.

Figure 3.8 shows Blackhawk's completed job order cost sheet for job 1192. The cost sheet contains entries related to the direct material items used and illustrated in Exhibit 3.4, the labor recorded on the time card for employee 4 and illustrated in Figure 3.5, along with labor for the fabricator who also worked on the job, and the overhead applied based on the usage of labor hours as the cost driver from Figure 3.7 and for the fabricator.

Theoretically, if you were to physically sum the costs applied to job cost sheets at a particular point in time and compare the result with the work-in-process balance on the balance sheet at that date, the figures should match.

Completed Jobs

When jobs are completed, the job is closed, and the products are moved to finished goods. Refer to the job cost sheet in Figure 3.8. The total costs applied to the job are $16,175, consisting of $5,700 of raw material, $6,125 of labor, and $4,350 of overhead.

When the job is completed, the raw material, labor, and overhead costs applied to the job are moved from work-in-process to finished goods as shown in Figure 3.9.

The total cost of the job for a quantity of three CB77 Replica motorcycles is $16,175, resulting in a cost per cycle of $5,391.67 as shown in Figure 3.10.

Job Order Cost Sheet

Job No. 1192

Customer Name: Dave and Julie Peterson, 1405 Cedar Valley Way, Cedar Falls, IA 50613

Start Date: 6-15-20XX

Completion Date: TBD

Item: CB77 Replica

Quantity: 3

Instructions: Replica SuperHawk cycles. Customer will pick up after completion.

$337.50 Labor (See Figure 3.5)

$135.00 Overhead (See Figure 3.7)

Production

Direct Material					Direct Labor					Overhead				
Date	Source	Qty	Rate	Amount	Date	Source	Time	Rate	Amount	Date	Source	Allocation Hours	Rate	Amount
6-15-XX	MRQ #1	45.00	8.00	360.00	6-15-XX	TC 7158	4.50	75.00	337.50	6-15-XX	TC 7458	4.50	30.00	135.00
	MRQ #1	15.00	3.00	45.00	6-15-XX	TC 7464	8.00	25.00	200.00	6-15-XX	TC 7461	8.00	30.00	240.00
	MRQ #1	3.00	110.00	330.00	6-16-XX	TC 7470	7.00	75.00	525.00	6-16-XX	TC 7470	7.00	30.00	210.00
	MRQ #1	3.00	80.00	240.00	6-17-XX	TC 7472	7.50	25.00	187.50	6-17-XX	TC 7472	7.50	30.00	225.00
	MRQ #1	3.00	40.00	120.00	6-17-XX	TC 7480	7.50	75.00	562.50	6-17-XX	TC 7480	7.50	30.00	225.00
	MRQ #1	6.00	75.00	450.00	6-18-XX	TC 7483	8.00	25.00	200.00	6-18-XX	TC 7483	8.00	30.00	240.00
	MRQ #1	6.00	12.00	72.00	6-19-XX	TC 7484	8.00	25.00	200.00	6-19-XX	TC 7484	8.00	30.00	240.00
	MRQ #1	90.00	2.00	180.00	6-20-XX	TC 7491	4.00	75.00	300.00	6-20-XX	TC 7491	4.00	30.00	120.00
	MRQ #1	60.00	2.50	150.00	6-21-XX	TC 7494	8.00	25.00	200.00	6-21-XX	TC 7494	8.00	30.00	240.00
	MRQ #1	3.00	5.00	15.00	6-22-XX	TC 7500	8.00	75.00	600.00	6-22-XX	TC 7500	8.00	30.00	240.00
	MRQ #1	3.00	15.00	45.00	6-22-XX	TC 7501	8.00	25.00	200.00	6-22-XX	TC 7501	8.00	30.00	240.00
	MRQ #1	3.00	985.00	2955.00	6-23-XX	TC 7534	8.00	75.00	600.00	6-23-XX	TC 7534	8.00	30.00	240.00
	MRQ #1	3.00	220.00	660.00	6-23-XX	TC 7535	8.00	25.00	200.00	6-23-XX	TC 7535	8.00	30.00	240.00
	MRQ #1	3.00	26.00	78.00	6-24-XX	TC 7542	3.00	75.00	225.00	6-24-XX	TC 7542	3.00	30.00	90.00
					6-24-XX	TC 7549	8.00	25.00	200.00	6-24-XX	TC 7549	8.00	30.00	240.00
					6-25-XX	TC 7577	8.00	25.00	200.00	6-25-XX	TC 7577	8.00	30.00	240.00
					6-26-XX	TC 7580	8.00	25.00	200.00	6-26-XX	TC 7580	8.00	30.00	240.00
					6-27-XX	TC 7600	8.00	25.00	200.00	6-27-XX	TC 7600	8.00	30.00	240.00
					6-28-XX	TC 7610	8.00	75.00	600.00	6-28-XX	TC 7610	8.00	30.00	240.00
					6-28-XX	TC 7611	7.50	25.00	187.50	6-28-XX	TC 7611	7.50	30.00	225.00

Total Job Costs		
	Material	5700.00
	Labor	6125.00
	Overhead	4350.00

$5,700 Raw Material (See Figure 3.4)

Figure 3.8 Job order cost sheet.

Total Job Costs		
	Material	5700.00
	Labor	6125.00
	Overhead	4350.00

$16,175 in total costs applied per Figure 3.8

Figure 3.9 Total Job Costs.

Work-In-Process Job 1192
–$ 5,700.00
–$ 6,125.00
–$ 4,350.00
–$16,175.00

Finished Goods
$16,175.00

Figure 3.10 Moving the completed job to finished goods.

LEARNING ACTIVITY 3.5

The predetermined overhead rate that you calculated in Learning Activity 3.4 is $10 per direct labor hour. Jay-Dee uses $2,000 of raw material on a production job that requires 200 direct labor hours, and Jay-Dee pays production employees $20 per hour. Assuming Jay-Dee Company uses a job order costing system, compute the cost per unit including material, labor, and overhead assuming direct labor hours is the cost driver for applying overhead and Jay-Dee produced 500 units on the job:

LEARNING ACTIVITY 3.6

CAU Enterprises manufactures a specialty line of women's sandals using a job order costing system. During May, it incurred the following costs in completing Job CAU103: direct materials, $19,600; direct labor, $6,000; administrative, $2,000; and selling, $6,000. CAU applies overhead using a rate of $20 per direct labor hour, and Job CAU103 required 1,000 direct labor hours to complete.

If 6,000 sandals were produced by the jobs, what is the cost per sandal?:

How Are Job Order Costs Recorded in the Financial Accounting System?

Learning Objective 3.5
Illustrate the Journal Entries Associated with Job Order Costing.

When utilizing a job order costing model, the process of making journal entries involves systematically recording the costs associated with each distinct job or project. Here is a step-by-step guide illustrated with a working example for Blackhawk Custom Cycle.

Step 1: Record Direct Materials On 6/15/20XX, Blackhawk Custom Cycle pulled $5,700 worth of raw material from inventory and issued it to the production department for use on job 1192, which involves the production of three replica motorcycles for Dave and Julie Peterson of Cedar Falls, Iowa, who operate a retail marine and cycle shop. The issuance of raw material is recorded on the materials request for, the source document (see Figure 3.4). The journal entry to record the issuance of material into production is as follows:

Work-in-Process	$5,700	
Raw Material Inventory		$5,700

Step 2: Record Direct Labor On 6/15/20XX, employee number 4 worked an 8-hour day, recording 1 hour to job 1187, 1.75 hours to job 1190, and 4.5 hours to job 1192. The remaining time went to cleaning and training (see Figure 3.1). Employee number 4's rate of pay is $75 per hour. The journal entry to record time to job 1192 is as follows:

Work-in-Process	$337.50	
Direct Labor		$337.50

Step 3: Record Manufacturing Overhead Blackhawk Custom Cycle uses a predetermined manufacturing overhead rate of $30 per direct labor hour. The journal entry to apply manufacturing overhead to job 1192 would be calculated by multiplying direct labor hours dedicated to working on job 1192 times the predetermined overhead rate of $30 per hour. The journal entry for employee number 4's time would be 4.5 hours times $30 per hour or $135.

Work-in-Process	$135	
Manufacturing Overhead Control		$135

Step 4: Transfer to Finished Goods Upon project completion and incurring all costs, transfer the total cost to Finished Goods. Notice the summary data at the bottom of the job cost sheet in Figure 3.8. The total material posted to job 1192 amounts to $5,700. Total labor and overhead posted to job 1192 is $6,125 and $4,350 respectively for a total cost of $16,175 to the job, which is moved from work-in-process to finished goods.

Finished Goods	$16,175	
Work-in-Process		$16,175

Step 5: Record Cost of Goods Sold (COGS) at Sale Let us assume that when completed, all three motorcycles in were sold to Dave and Julie Peterson for a price of $8,000 each. When the completed project is sold, corresponding entries are made to record the sale and the expense in the form of cost of goods sold. The expense entry would be as follows:

Cost of Goods Sold	$16,175	
Finished Goods		$16,175

The entry to record the sale, assuming the Peterson's paid in cash, would be as follows:

Cash	$24,000	
Sales		$24,000

These journal entries effectively track the costs for each job, providing companies with a comprehensive understanding of the profitability of individual projects within a job order costing framework. In this case, the gross profit from the job amounted to $7,825, the difference between the sales price of $24,000 and cost of goods sold of $16,175.

Losses

Let us suppose one of the motorcycles did not pass a quality control inspection *before moving it to finished goods* due to a defective engine and poor welding on the frame. Rather than repair the bike, the production supervisor decided to scrap the bike and build a new one from scratch. The defective bike still had usable components that will be sold as used parts for an estimated value of $2,400. The journal entry to record the loss from the scrapped bike would include a credit to work-in-process for the cost of one bike: $5,391.67 ($16,175 ÷ 3). The entry would also include a debit of $2,400 to an asset account called "Scrap Parts" that Blackhawk uses for scrapped parts that still have value. The difference of $2,991.67 would be debited to a loss account because it is unusual and large. In this case, Blackhawk uses an account titled "Losses from Scrap and Rework." If the scrap was normal, it would be accounted for in the predetermined overhead rate calculation.

Scrap Parts	$2,400.00	
Loss from Scrap and Rework	$2,991.67	
Work-in-Process		$5,391.67

LEARNING ACTIVITY 3.7

Homecraft Builders, Inc. is a construction contracting firm that specializes in building residential homes. Homecraft worked on the construction of three homes this month. Each home is considered a job, such as Job #114, Job #115, and Job #116. One home was in progress before the month started, and the other two were started during the month. Job #116 was incomplete at the end of the month. Data for the three jobs is as follows:

	Job #114	Job #115	Job #116
Beginning Work-in-Process	$52,000		
Current Period Activity and Costs			
Raw Material	$78,000	$120,000	$80,000
Direct Labor Hours	1,100	1,375	950
Direct Labor	$44,000	$ 55,000	$38,000

Predetermined Overhead Rate: $75.00 per direct labor hour:

A. Compute the costs applied to job #115 and record the journal entries to apply the raw material, direct labor, and overhead costs to the job.

B. Assume job #115 is completed. Make the journal entry to move the cost of the job to finished goods.

C. Assume the house associated with job #115 is sold for $325,000 on a note receivable with a 20% down payment, paid in cash. Record the journal entries to record the sale and associated cost.
D. How much profit did homecraft make on job #115?
E. Assume Homecraft identified the roof trusses for the home related to job #116 were not the correct pitch. The error was not identified until after the trusses were delivered, and the vendor would not accept a return, since the trusses were custom ordered. The trusses cost $5,000, which was part of the material cost already posted to work-in-process. Although the trusses are not useable on this home, they have a market value of $2,800 if Homecraft sells them to another builder or uses them later. Record the journal entry to remove the trusses from the job and record the loss. Place the trusses back into the Raw Material inventory at their current value and use the account "Loss from Defects" for any expense.

Technology, Analytics, and AI

To allocate and determine the correct costs for each job, managerial accountants need to track large volumes of data. The data need to be sorted and categorized, and then overhead calculations are made before reporting the costs. This can be a very manual process, depending on the systems and tools used by the management accountants.

Accountants have been using various forms of automation throughout the years. Traditionally, this required significant amounts of programming and individuals who knew how to code to achieve the automated process. Accountants would work with programmers to describe the process, the programmers would code, and then the code would be tested to put into production. Then some processes were automated using simple Excel macros, which accountants could record and do tasks within Excel. However, the macros would not interact easily with other desktop applications.

In recent years, a new software category has been developed that puts some automation processes in the hands of the end user. This type of software is called robotic process automation or RPA. This software allows users to design a process and automate it using a graphical interface. RPA works similarly to an Excel macro. A macro runs steps defined by the user and repeats them in Excel. RPA does the same, but it can go across multiple applications, such as enterprise resource planning (ERP) software, email, spreadsheets, and many more. See Figure 3.11 as a sample script using Microsoft's Power Automate.

Calculating the materials, labor, and overhead costs for jobs could be a process fit for RPA. A process is a candidate for automation with RPA if it is relatively simple and does not require human thought, it is easily defined, and it is repetitive. Collecting and calculating job costs would meet these requirements in most companies. A simple test to determine if you can use RPA is if you can flowchart the process; it is likely a candidate for automation.

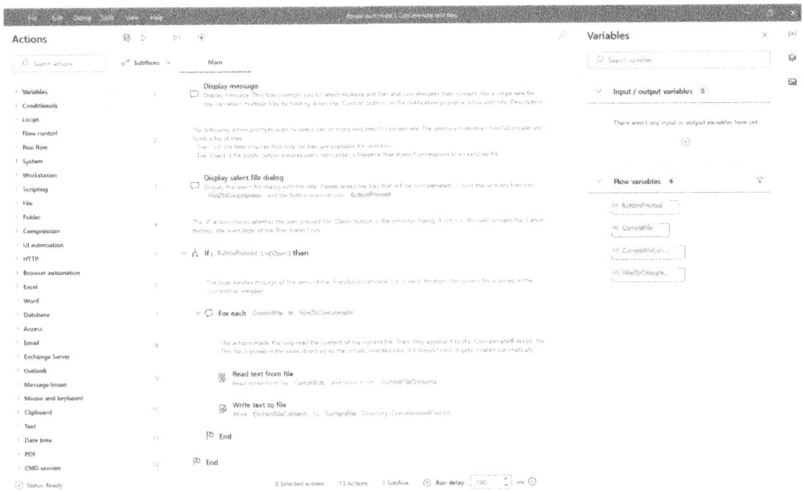

Figure 3.11 Power Automate script sample.

Figure 3.12 Create folders and files.

Building an RPA Script in Power Automate

Power Automate is Microsoft's RPA tool and is just one of many software packages in the area. It is a tool selected by many accountants due to its integration with Microsoft Office products, including Excel. Power Automate also ships free with Windows 11, making it an inexpensive and relatively easy software solution for nonprogrammers. Power Automate has a desktop version and a cloud version. For purposes of this chapter, we will be using the desktop version. The cloud version will integrate with Microsoft 365 cloud applications.

The flow will create PDF files of all the Word documents in a folder. Before starting, create a folder that contains all the letters that you want to convert and safe to PDF files. Name the folder Letters Also, create a subfolder named PDF as shown Figure 3.12. In this case, there are three letters to convert. We will create the script to convert all files in the folder to PDF.

When you start the desktop version of Power Automate, you will see this first welcome screen as shown in Figure 3.13. To create a new flow, select the button in the upper right corner.

To create the new flow, give it a Flow name. In this case, use CreatePDF and select Create as shown in Figure 3.14.

Once the flow is created, the main screen will appear. On the right side, you will see the Actions. In the middle, you will see the main workflow area and the variables on the right.

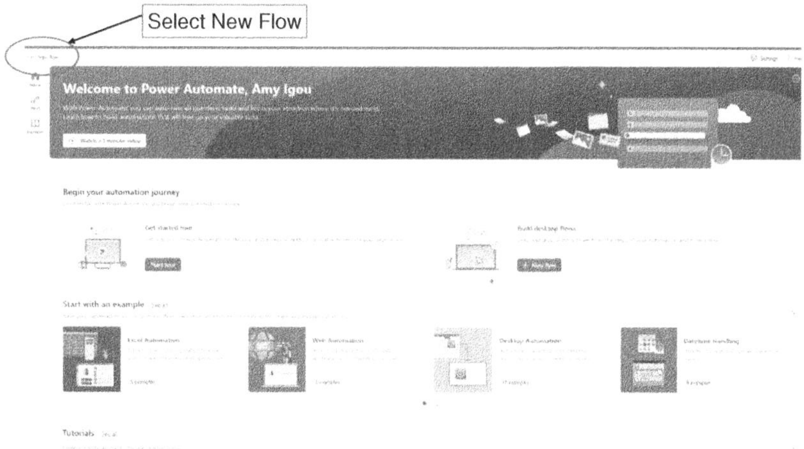

Figure 3.13 Power Automate welcome screen.

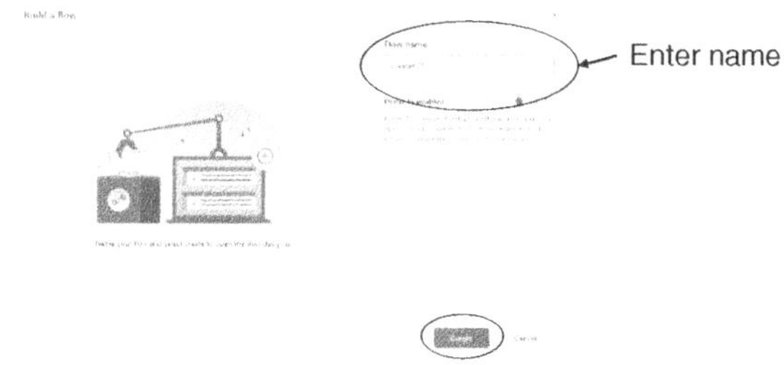

Figure 3.14 Name the flow.

To add a step to the flow, drag it from the Actions on the left to the Main area in the middle. The first action to add is to **Get files in folder** by dragging the action to the main area, as shown in Figure 3.15.

Each added action to the flow can be edited to specify details for the actions. For example, in this case, you need to identify which folder to retrieve the files. Select the three dots on the right of the action to get to the options and select **Edit** to display the pop-up box shown in Figure 3.16. Enter the path to the Word documents you wish to convert to PDFs. In this case, the documents are in a folder called Letters. Rather than typing the path, you can click on the folder icon to navigate to the correct path. This step creates a variable, **Files**, which contains a list of all the files in the folder.

Since the flow should work for any number of files in the folder, add a **For each** action, which is found under Loops. Change the options **For each** step by clicking the three dots to display the dialog box in Figure 3.17. Then click on the {x} button to select %Files%. This denotes the variable named **Files** created in the previous step.

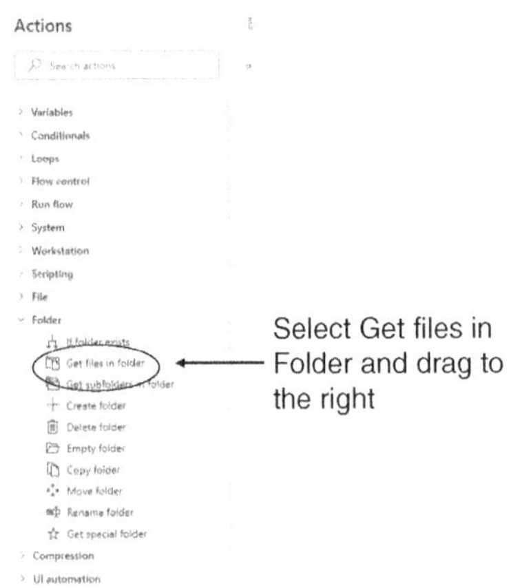

Figure 3.15 Add Get files in folder.

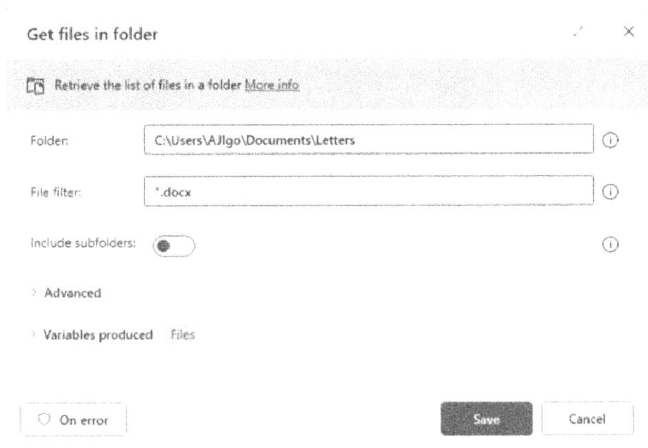

Figure 3.16 Get files dialog box.

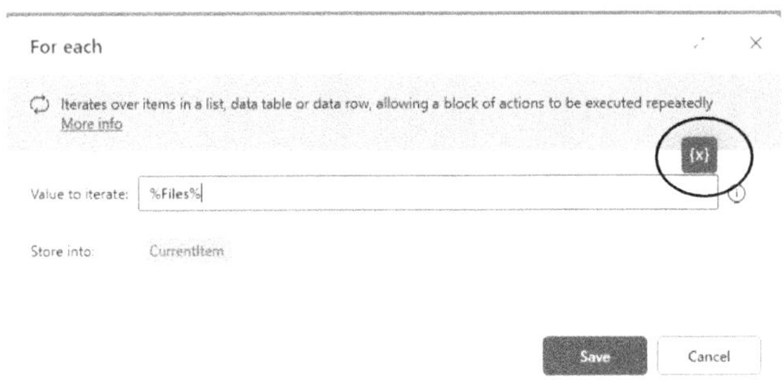

Figure 3.17 For each step options.

The remaining actions should be added between the **For each** and the **End** step that were previously added in the prior step.

Add the following actions from the left sidebar in the order listed here.

- Launch Word
- Get file path part
- Set variable
- Save Word
- Close Word

To find the action, use the search at the top of the actions. Your flow should look similar to Figure 3.18.

Now, you need to add the details for each action by clicking on the three dots. Each of the specific dialog boxes is shown in the following directions.

Figure 3.18 Actions added to For each loop.

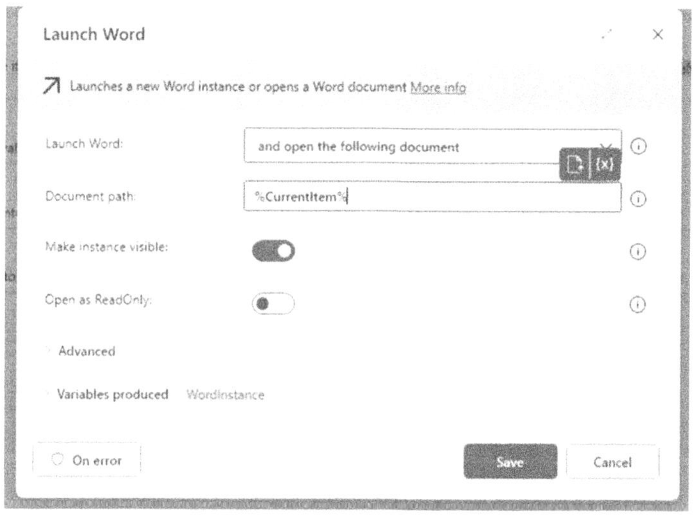

Figure 3.19 Launch Word options.

Launch Word. Select "open the following document" using the drop-down menu for the first option. Then, use the {x} to select %CurrentItem% to denote the current file from the list. Make the rest of the changes as shown in Figure 3.19.

Get File Path Part. Sets the file path and creates variables for the directory, FileName, FileNameNoExtension. Select %CurrentItem% for the File Path as shown in Figure 3.20.

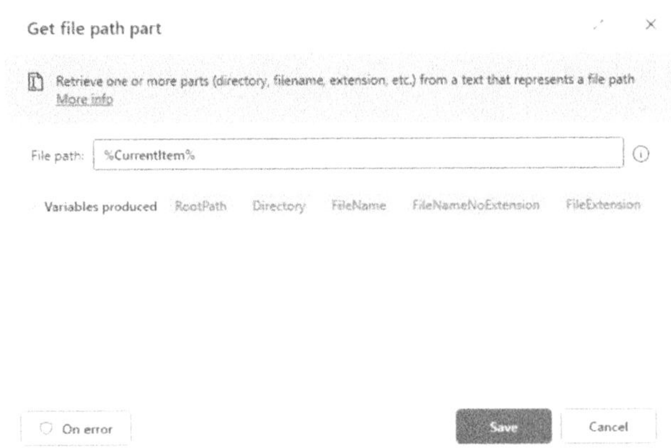

Figure 3.20 Get file path.

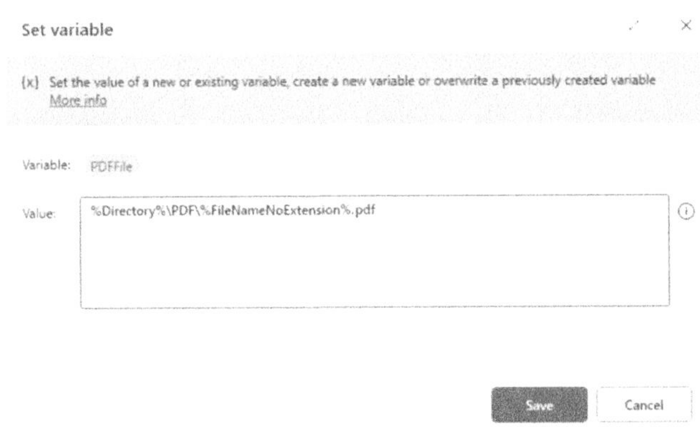

Figure 3.21 Set variable.

Set Variable. This step is going to create the entire path with the file name for the new PDF file. The variable is named PDFFile and add the statement **%Directory%\PDF\%FileNameNoExtension%.pdf** in the Value as shown in Figure 3.21. This will keep the path and the file name the same but change the extension to PDF.

Save Word. This step converts the Word document to a PDF document. Change the options as shown in Figure 3.22.

Close Word. This step closes the current Word document. Since no changes were made to the document, it will not be saved. Change the settings as shown in Figure 3.23.

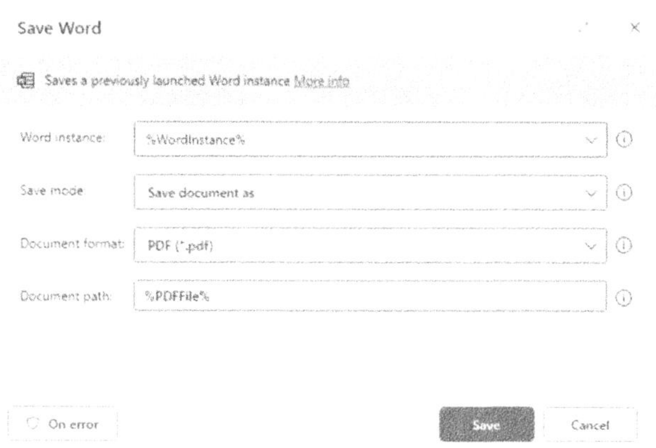

Figure 3.22 Save Word.

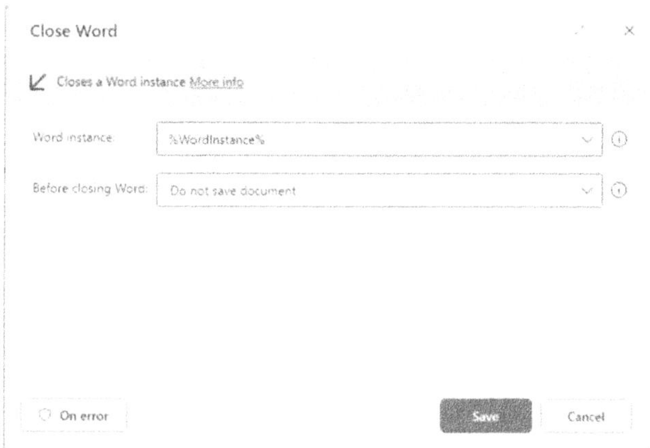

Figure 3.23 Close Word.

Key Terms

abnormal loss Losses that exceed the anticipated levels of normal loss.
allocation Apportioning costs through the use of a formula.
assignment Apportioning of costs achieved by using a physical mechanism that tracks the amount of cost to be redistributed.
cost driver An operating activity that is common to the products or services the business produces that correlates with costs.

cost object An item for which the business tracks costs.
invoice A document given to a customer by a vendor that displays the charges for goods or services purchased.
job order cost sheet A document used in a job order cost system that businesses use to record all cost associated with a specific job.
job order costing system A system of product costing that is most suitable for businesses that are concerned with identifying and calculating specific costs and assigning the costs to specific products or services.
materials request form A document that indicates which inventory items and their quantities are desired by production and the production job to which the inventory should be assigned.
normal loss Losses which fall within an expected tolerance level during production.
overhead Costs that are indirectly associated with a product or service.
purchase order A document given to a vendor by a customer that indicates the types, quantities, and prices of goods the customer intends to purchase.
source documents Physical documents used to assign costs.
timecard A document that captures time worked by an employee.

LEARNING ACTIVITY SOLUTIONS

Learning Activity 3.1

Transaction	*Period or Product*	*Product Cost Category*
Pay factory workers for the week	*Product*	*Direct Labor*
Hire a repair person to fix a factory machine	*Product*	*Overhead*
Pay for raw materials	*Product*	*Direct Materials*
Office supplies	*Period*	*N/A*

Learning Activity 3.2

1. *Del Dente Food Processing*
2. *Jessen LLP Attorneys at Law X*
3. *Americo Oil Refining*
4. *Elwood's Custom Wood Cabinetry X*
5. *Tyron's Chicken Processing Plant*

Learning Activity 3.3

Information	*Source Document*
1. Agreed upon purchase price for goods *2. Amount of material to be moved from raw material storage to production* *3. Start and stop time worked* *4. Vendor charges for goods and services* *5. Quantity of goods purchased from a vendor*	*Invoice* *4. Vendor charges for goods and services*
	Purchase Order *5. Quantity of goods purchased from a vendor* *1. Agreed-upon purchase price for goods*
	Material Requisition Form *2. Amount of material to be moved from raw material storage to production*
	Timecard *3. Start and stop time worked*

Learning Activity 3.4

$\$200{,}000/20{,}000\,DLH = \$10.00\,per\,direct\,labor\,hour$

Learning Activity 3.5

Direct material	*$2,000*
Direct labor (200 × $20)	*4,000*
Manufacturing overhead applied (200 × $10)	*2,000*
Total cost	*$8,000*
Units produced	*÷ 500*
Cost per unit	*$16.00*

Learning Activity 3.6

Direct material	*$19,600*
Direct labor	*6,000*
Overhead applied ($20/DLH × 1,000 DLH)	*20,000*
Total cost	*$45,600*
Units produced	*÷ 6,000*
Cost per unit	*$ 7.60*

Learning Activity 3.7

A. Work-in-Process—Job #115	*$120,000*	
Raw Material Inventory		*$120,000*
Work-in-Process—Job #115	*$ 55,000*	
Direct Labor		*$ 55,000*
Work-in-Process—Job #115	*$103,125*	
Manufacturing Overhead (1,375 Hours × $75.00)		*$103,125*
B. Work-in-Process	*$278,125*	
Finished Goods		*$278.125*
C. Cash	*$ 64,000*	
Accounts Receivable	*$256,000*	
Revenue		*$320,000*
Finished Goods	*$278,125*	
Cost of Goods Sold		*$278,125*
D. Profit = $41,875		
E. Raw Material	*$ 2,800*	
Loss from Defects	*$ 2,200*	
Work-in-Process—Job #116		*$ 5,000*

Review Questions

1. A company that produces unique products would likely uses a __________ costing system, while a company that produces homogeneous products would likely use a __________ costing system. **(Learning Objective 1)**
   a. job order; process
   b. process; job order
2. A ________ can be the basis for allocating overhead costs in a job order costing system. **(Learning Objective 2)**
   a. cost driver
   b. formula
   c. both

3. The amount of overhead that is applied to a production job in a job order costing system is commonly computed by multiplying the ________________ and the __________________. **(Learning Objective 2)**
   a. estimated cost driver usage; actual overhead rate
   b. estimated cost driver usage; predetermined overhead rate
   c. actual cost driver usage; actual overhead rate
   d. actual cost driver usage; predetermined overhead rate
4. The amount of loss from an abnormal scrapping of defective raw material would be computed using the following formula: ________________. **(Learning Objective 3)**
   a. amount paid for the associated raw material
   b. the salvage value of the associated raw material
   c. the amount paid for the associated raw material minus the salvage value
   d. the salvage value of the associated raw material minus the amount paid for the raw material
5. Cost for a production job in a job order costing systems are recorded on the **(Learning Objective 4)**
   a. Job Cost Ticket.
   b. Job Order Cost Sheet.
6. The journal entry associated with the completion of a production job would involve a debit to ________ and a credit to _________. **(Learning Objective 5)**
   a. debit to Work-in-Process, and a credit to Finished Goods
   b. debit to Finished Goods, and a credit to Work-in-Process
   c. debit to Work-in-Process, and a credit to Manufacturing Overhead Control
   d. debit to Manufacturing Overhead Control, and a credit to Work-in-Process

Short Exercises

S:3-1 (Learning Objective 1)

Job order costing is more suitable to companies that make heterogeneous products or perform heterogeneous services, while process costing is more suitable for firms that make more homogeneous products or services. Indicate which of the listed companies would more likely use a job order costing or process costing system.

	Job Order Costing	Process Costing
1. Engineering firm		
2. Oil refinery		
3. Bread making factory		
4. Custom home builder		
5. Foundry		

S:3-2 (Learning Objectives 2 and 4)

Job order costing systems are facilitated by various documents. Answer the following questions:

a. The total value of costs entered onto job cost sheets for incomplete jobs at the end of a reporting period is equal to what inventory value?
b. What document indicates which raw material should be pulled from the inventory warehouse and used in production?
c. What source document records what job employees work on?

Exercises

E:3-3 (Learning Objective 2)

H&R Construction uses a job order costing system and applies manufacturing overhead to its products on the basis of direct labor hours. The business made the following annual estimates:

Direct labor hours	18,000
Overhead costs	$252,000

H&R incurred 300 labor hours on job #804 and 170 labor hours on job #805 during the month of April.

Requirements

a. Compute the predetermined overhead rate.
b. Compute the total amount of overhead applied to production jobs #804 and #805 in April.

Problems

P:3-4 (Learning Objectives 2 and 4)

Heartland Lawn Tractor Corp builds garden tractors for residential use. Heartland builds tractors in batches and uses job order costing to account for the cost of each batch. Production job #802, for 100 tractors, was started in January and completed in February. January's costs included $42,000 of raw material, and $20,000 and $32,000 of overhead costs. Heartland's February activity is as follows:

Material	$24,000 of raw material was requisitioned on materials request #408 and issued from inventory to job #802.	
	$10,000 worth of indirect material was requisitioned and issued for use on job #802.	
Labor	Total direct labor hours worked producing the tractors	420 hours
	Total indirect labor hours worked	80 hours
Other Information	The labor rate for a laborer is $25.00 per hour and the factory overhead rate is $40.00 per direct labor hour, the allocation basis.	

Requirements

Complete parts a through g on the job order cost sheet for job #812.

Job Order Cost Sheet

Job Number: 802

Start Date: January 20XX

Completion Date: February 20XX

Direct Material			Direct Labor				Overhead			
							Allocation			
Date	Source	Amount	Date	Time	Rate	Amount	Date	Base	Rate	Amount
1-31-20XX	MRQ 212	$42,000	1-31-20XX	800 Hours	$25.00	$20,000	1-31-20XX	800 Hours	$40.00	$32,000
2-28-20XX	MRQ 408	(a)	2-28-20XX	420 Hours	$25.00	(b)	2-28-20XX	420 Hours	$40.00	(c)

Total Job Costs		
	Direct Material	(d)
	Direct Labor	(e)
	Overhead	(f)
	Total Cost	(g)

P:3-5 (Learning Objective 5)

Wilson Custom Manufacturing has two jobs in process, Job #888, Job #889. Data for the two jobs is as follows:

	Job #888	Job #889
Total Units Produced	1,000 units	1,200 units
Beginning Work-in-Process	$200,000	
Current Period Activity and Costs		
Raw Material	$ 28,000	$100,000
Direct Labor Hours	500	375
Direct Labor	$ 15,000	$ 11,250

Predetermined Overhead Rate: $50.00 per direct labor hour.

Requirements

a. Compute the costs applied to job #888 and record the journal entries to apply the raw material, direct labor, and overhead costs to job.
b. Assume job #888 is completed. Make the journal entry to move the cost of the job to finished goods.
c. Assume 10 of the units from job #888 are sold for $400 each in cash. Record the journal entry to record the sale and associated cost.
d. Assume 50 of the units from job #888 were found to be defective after they had been moved to finished goods. They were removed from finished goods and sold for $60 in cash each for scrap. Record the journal entry for the scrap transaction.

P:3-6 (Learning Objectives 3 and 5)

Natural Remedies Cosmetics, a leading cosmetics manufacturer, discovers that a batch of work-in-process (WIP) tubes of eyeliner is defective. The defective tubes are scrapped, but the tubes are eligible to be sold for salvage on a second-hand cosmetics website, "Minetoyours." Here are the details of the transaction:

- The company had 2,000 defective WIP tubes of eyeliner.
- The cost incurred for each WIP tube of eyeliner was $3.
- The salvage value of each defective WIP tube of eyeliner was $0.50.

Requirements

a. Compute the total amount taken out of work-in-process due to scrapping the defective tubes of eyeliner.
b. Compute the total salvage value of defective tubes of eyeliner.
c. Compute the difference between the amount taken out of work-in-process and the salvage value, representing the loss incurred from scrapping the defective tubes of eyeliner.
d. Record the journal entry to account for the scrap transaction and salvage.

Technology, Analytics, and Artificial Intelligence

T:3-7 Create an RPA bot using Power Automate

Each week, you spend significant time opening each timecard in Excel and merging the data into another spreadsheet. The task is critical to calculate the direct labor costs for each job, but it is very time-consuming and actually boring.

The workers store a timecard for each day in a central folder called TimeCards. You would like to create an RPA bot to simplify the task and merge the data with the press of a button.

The RPA script will read the information from each file in TimeCards folder. You want the bot to work whether there are 2 or 100 files in the folder. You will open the file for each timecard file in the folder. Copy the information in the "TimeSheet" range to the next available row in the Template.xlsx file. Then close the time card file and save and close the Template.xlsx file.

Steps

a. **File preparation:** Download the needed files from the course website. Place the files in a folder called TimeCards on your local hard drive. Move the Template.xlsx file to another folder. For example, you can move Template.xlsx to C:\documents\ and the individual timecards to C:\documents\TimeCards.
b. **Understanding the flow:** Draw a simple flowchart to determine the steps for the bot. This will help you create the bot using the RPA software.
c. **Additional preparation:** To be sure you know the steps, you can ask one of the GenAI tools how to create this RPA bot in the Power Automate desktop version.
d. **Create the bot:** Watch the provided video on the course website if needed.
e. **Run the bot:** Watch the bot work and create a new file.

CHAPTER 4

Process Costing

Learning Objectives

4.1 Describe how a firm uses a process costing system to identify the equivalent units of production.
4.2 Explain how a firm computes the equivalent units of production using a process costing system.
4.3 Explain how a firm computes the cost per equivalent unit of production using a process costing system.
4.4 Identify how a firm assigns costs to units in a process costing system.
4.5 Record the journal entries associated with a process costing system.

Accounting in Life

Pixabay / Pexels / Public Domain

Canning is a food preservation method that involves sealing food in jars or cans and then heating them to destroy any microorganisms that can cause spoilage. It's a process that has been used for centuries to extend the shelf life of perishable foods like fruits, vegetables, and meats.

While canning may be considered a thing of the past, it still holds value in certain situations. For example, home canning remains popular among individuals who enjoy preserving their own foods, especially in regions where access to fresh produce is limited or seasonal. Additionally, canned foods continue to be a staple in emergency preparedness kits and relief efforts, as they offer long shelf life and stability without the need for refrigeration. During the COVID-19 crisis, canning experienced a resurgence in popularity for several reasons including food security concerns, interest in self-sufficiency, supply chain disruptions, and economic considerations.

Dating jars when canning is a simple type of accounting practice that is essential for food safety and effective troubleshooting if a batch goes bad. Without dating, it would be impossible to identify one jar from the next.

Let's Review

In the previous chapter, you learned that accountants use job order costing to allocate costs to specific products or services. They track direct materials, direct labor, and overhead costs associated with each job. Job order costing enables accountants to accurately calculate the cost of each job which aids cost control and pricing decisions.

LEARNING ACTIVITY 4.1

Match the following descriptions with the correct terms: direct materials, direct labor, overhead costs, job order costing.

a. The cost of labor directly associated with the production of a specific job, such as wages for workers directly involved on an assembly line.
b. The cost of materials specifically identified and used in producing a particular job.
c. A costing method used by accountants to allocate costs to unique products or services.
d. Indirect costs incurred during the production process that cannot be easily traced to specific jobs, such as supplies, utilities, rent, and depreciation.

Businesses typically choose one of two systems for distributing product costs to finished goods: a *job order costing system* or a *process costing system*. In the previous chapter we examined *job order costing*, which is used when business want to keep track of unique products or services. In this chapter, we examine a *process costing system*. Businesses with homogeneous products use a *process costing system* to identify, calculate, and assign costs.

How Do Companies with Homogeneous Products Use Process Costing to Identify Costs?

Learning Objective 4.1

Describe how a firm uses a process costing system to identify the equivalent units of production.

A **process costing system** is a system of product costing that averages total production costs across the total number of units produced. Generally, businesses that use a process costing system produce large quantities of homogenous products using homogenous processes. Consequently, they are not concerned with identifying, calculating, and assigning costs to *specific* jobs, products, or services. Food processors or oil refineries are examples of the types of businesses that use process costing systems. They make large volumes of similar products using consistent processes on each unit produced.

LEARNING ACTIVITY 4.2

Select the businesses that would most likely use a process costing system.

a. Del Dente Food Processing ______

b. Jessen LLP Attorneys at Law ______

c. Americo Oil Refining ______

d. Elwood's Custom Wood Cabinetry ______

e. Tyron's Chicken Processing Plant ______

Accounting in Business

Creameries, like other businesses that produce large volumes of homogeneous products, use a form of process costing. To illustrate, let's look at Hansen's Dairy, a vertically integrated family farming operation in Hudson, Iowa, which offers a wide range of products through Hansen stores in Iowa's Cedar Valley and in grocery stores throughout the region. The Hansen family started farming in Hudson in 1864, with the seventh generation growing up on the farm today. The Hansen brothers opened a creamery in the 2000s to add value to the milk produced by the farm's livestock.

Hansen's Creamery produces skim, 1%, whole and chocolate milk, along with cream, butter, ice cream, cheese curds and more. Hansen's signature *Creamline* milk comes directly from Hansen's closed herd of purebred Holstein Cows.

Milk production starts with daily cow milking utilizing vacuum pressure. The milk then travels to a bulk tank where it is first cooled and then is trucked directly to the plant. At the plant, the milk is pasteurized, bottled, and immediately shipped to stores.

For Hansen's Dairy, identifying the cost of *each* gallon of milk is impractical, if not impossible, and unnecessary. Instead, process costing captures the cost of all the materials and processes in a batch and divides the cost by the number of units produced to get unit cost, or in Hansen's case, gallons of milk. "Costs and quality are monitored on a daily basis, as markets can change so frequently, and issues constantly arise that can affect the products and ultimately the business. We, as owners, are the primary labor force, which can allow for better awareness of most situations. A detailed annual review of the business financial data is performed to aid in our future decision-making," says Blair Hansen.

For Hansen's Dairy, cost control and high quality are paying sweet rewards.

Charlotte May / Pexels / Public Domain

Source: Author Interview with Blair Hansen, owner Hansen's Dairy.

Unit Product Cost

Unit product cost is production costs divided by production quantities as expressed by the following formula presented in Figure 4.1:

$$\text{Unit Cost} = \frac{\textbf{Sum of Actual Production Costs}}{\textbf{Production Quantity (in Units)}}$$

Figure 4.1 Unit product cost formula.

The numerator in the unit cost formula is the sum of production costs. It can be expressed as actual direct materials, actual direct labor, and actual or allocated overhead costs depending on which variable the company chooses to use in the computation. The denominator in the unit cost formula represents all production for the measurement period.

The Production Cost Report

Companies that use process costing prepare a **production cost report** to summarize the physical flow and cost flow of goods. The production cost report does the following:

1. Summarizes the flow of physical goods
2. Computes the output in terms of an equivalent unit of production
3. Computes the cost per equivalent unit of production
4. Assigns costs to units completed and work-in-process inventory

Let us consider Mott's Creamery, a dairy that, like Hansen's Dairy, produces skim, 1%, whole, and chocolate milk, along with other products. Mott's produces approximately four million gallons of milk annually from its herd of 2,000 Holstein cows, which includes approximately 600,000 gallons of whole milk. Let's look at the computation of a production cost report for whole milk produced at Mott's dairy processing plant Figure 4.2. The processing plant had the following data for the month of July:

	Units (Gallons)
Work-in-process on July 1 (100% raw material has been added and is 20% converted)	2,000
Gallons started during July	50,000
Work-in-process on July 31 (90% of raw material has been added and is 40% converted)	1,500
	Costs (Dollars)
July 1 work-in-process	$ 2,400
Direct materials used in July	$30,000
Direct labor costs in July	$26,000
Manufacturing overhead allocated in July	$43,000

Note: Direct material and conversion costs are added evenly during the production period and units are produced in a first-in, first-out manner.

Figure 4.2 Mott's dairy processing plant activity and costs for July.

The Physical Flow of Goods

The first step in the production cost report is to measure the physical flow of units and distinguish the units by type:

- Units that were in process at the beginning of a production period
- Units started during the period
- Units completed during the period
- Units that remain in work-in-process inventory at the end of a production period

Let us continue the Mott's Creamery example and examine the data illustrated in Figure 4.1. There were 2,000 gallons of whole milk in progress at the beginning of July, and an additional 50,000 gallons were started during the month. The production cost report must *account for* all 52,000 gallons. The data shows that of the 52,000 gallons to account for, 1,500 remained in process on July 31. Assuming a constant flow of production where the units in process at the beginning of July were completed before new gallons were started, the 2,000 gallons in process on July 1 were completed by July 31. The 1,500 gallons in process at the end of July would, therefore, come from the 50,000 gallons started in July. Thus, the 50,000 gallons started in July could be split into 48,500 gallons started and fully completed in July, and 1,500 gallons started but remaining in work-in-process on July 31. To summarize, there were 2,000 gallons in work-in-process inventory that were completed during the period, 48,500 gallons started and completed during the period, and 1,500 gallons in ending work-in-process, therefore accounting for all 52,000 gallons. Figure 4.3 shows the gallons (or units) that the creamery must account for, and gallons accounted for.

Units to Account For	
	Gallons
Work-in-process on July 1 (All raw material has been added and is 20% converted)	**2,000**
Gallons started during July	**50,000**
Gallons (units) to account for	**52,000**
Gallons Accounted for	
Work-in-process on July 1 (100% of raw material has been added and is 20% converted)	**2,000**
Gallons started and completed during July 31	**48,500**
Work-in-process on July 31 (80% of raw material has been added and is 40% converted)	**1,500**
Gallons (units) accounted for	**52,000**

Figure 4.3 Units to account for and units accounted for.

LEARNING ACTIVITY 4.3

Berry Frozen Foods, an organic food processor in Waterloo, Iowa, freezes and packages frozen fruits for supermarkets in the upper Midwest. Berry purchases fruits from regional farmers, sorts and inspects the fruit for quality, cleans the fruit, cryogenically flash freezes the fruit, and then packages and distributes the fruit to grocers throughout the region. Berry Frozen Foods utilizes a process costing system for its processing operations. Berry adds all direct materials (fruit) at the beginning of the process and adds conversion costs proportionally as it inspects, cleans, freezes, and packages the fruit. Berry's production quantities for July are presented here:

	Units (Packages)
Work-in-process inventory on July 1 (70% complete as to conversion costs)	100,000
Units started during July	140,000
Work-in-process inventory on July 31 (20% complete as to conversion costs)	20,000

Required: Compute Berry's units to account for during the month of July and separate the value into work-in-process inventory on July 1, inventory started and completed during July and ending work-in-process on July 31.

a. Work-in-process inventory on July 1: ______________

b. Inventory started and complete in July: ______________

c. Ending work-in-process on July 31: ______________

d. Total inventory units to account for in July: ______________

How Does a Firm Compute the Units Produced?

Learning Objective 4.2

Explain how a firm computes the equivalent units of production using a process costing system.

If businesses completed all production, start to finish, during the measurement period, they could merely count units produced. In reality, it is rare for a company to complete all production, start to finish, during a reporting period. Thus, companies must convert production data into an estimate of whole units produced. **Equivalent units of production** are an estimate of fully completed units that could have been produced by the resource inputs applied during a reporting period. To determine equivalent units of production, businesses do the following:

1. Count the physical units that are partially complete at the beginning and end of a reporting period.
2. Convert the count of partially completed units to the equivalent number of whole units the business could have produced with the effort put in to finish those that entered the period partially complete and get those that were started but not finished during the period to their current stage of partial completion.
3. Add that estimate to a count of units that it started and fully completed during the period.

Computing equivalent units of production requires estimations of the degree to which in-process units are complete. The following example provides a simple illustration of how equivalent units are computed assuming that of the 52,000 gallons that were in production during July, 1,500 remained in ending work-in-process and they are 40% converted.

$$\text{Equivalent Units of Production: } 50{,}000 + (1{,}500 \times 40\%) = 50{,}600 \text{ Gallons}$$

Businesses typically calculate equivalent units for both raw materials placed into production and the conversion of those raw materials. Equivalent units are further separated into the three categories of units accounted for in Figure 4.2:

1. Equivalent whole units that could have been produced with the resources used to finish units that entered the recording period partially complete
2. Whole units that were started and completed during the recording period
3. Equivalent whole units that could have been produced with the resources used to get units that are partially complete at the end of the reporting period to their current stage of completion

Equivalent Units for Materials

The business must consider the three categories of units to compute the equivalent units for raw material placed into production:

1. Looking at Figure 4.4 the first category consists of the 2,000 gallons in production on July 1. All the material was in process on July 1, so no additional (or 0%) of the remaining material is added. Thus, the equivalent gallons (or units) worth of raw material added to the units that started July in work-in-process is zero.
2. The second category consists of 48,500 gallons that were started and completed in July. Since the units were started and fully completed, all the material (100%) was added to production in July, resulting in 48,500 equivalent units of raw material.

3. The third category consists of 1,500 gallons that were started but not completed. Ninety percent of the raw material has been added to production. Thus, the equivalent units of material for the third category are (1,500 × 80%) 1,200 units.

Based on this analysis, the total equivalent units worth of raw material placed into production is 49,700 as shown in Figure 4.4.

Equivalent Units for Conversion

Computing the equivalent units for conversion is a similar process. Let's look at the data in Figure 4.4 to illustrate.

1. The first category consists of the 2,000 gallons in production on July 1. Those gallons entered July 20% complete; thus 80% of the remaining conversion needed to finish those gallons took place in July, resulting in (2,000 × 80%) 1,600 equivalent units worth of conversion effort in July.
2. The second category consists of 48,500 gallons that were started and completed in July. Since the gallons were started and fully completed, all of the conversion (100%) is assumed to have taken place in July, resulting in 48,500 equivalent units worth of conversion effort.
3. The third category consists of 1,500 gallons that were started but not completed. The units are 40% converted at the end of July, resulting in equivalent units of conversion for the third category of (1,500 × 40%) 600 units.

Based on this analysis, the total equivalent units (or gallons) worth of conversion in July is 50,700 gallons. Figure 4.5 illustrates the equivalent units worth of conversion that took place in July.

	Units Accounted For	Current Effort	Equivalent Units
Work-in-process on July 1 (All raw material has been added and is 20% converted)	2,000	0%	0
Gallons started and completed during July 31	48,500	100%	48,500
Work-in-process on July 31 (80% of raw material has been added and is 40% converted)	1,500	80%	1,200
Equivalent units of raw material put into production			49,700

Figure 4.4 Equivalent units raw materials.

	Units Accounted For	Current Effort	Equivalent Units
Work-in-process on July 1 (All raw material has been added and is 20% converted)	2,000	80%	1,600
Gallons started and completed during July 31	48,500	100%	48,500
Work-in-process on July 31 (80% of raw material has been added and is 40% converted)	1,500	40%	600
Equivalent units of conversion			50,700

Figure 4.5 Equivalent units of conversion.

LEARNING ACTIVITY 4.4

Let us expand on Learning Activity 4.3 regarding Berry Frozen Foods, an organic food processor in Waterloo, Iowa, that freezes and packages frozen fruits for supermarkets in the upper Midwest. Recall, Berry purchases fruits from regional farmers, sorts and inspects the fruit for quality, cleans the fruit, cryogenically flash freezes the fruit, and then packages and distributes the fruit to grocers throughout the region. Berry Frozen Foods utilizes a process costing system for its processing operations. Berry adds all direct materials (fruit) at the beginning of the process and adds conversion costs proportionally as it inspects, cleans, freezes, and packages the fruit. Berry's units to account for in July as calculated in Learning Activity 4.3 are presented here:

	Units (Packages)
Work-in-process inventory on July 1 (70% complete as to conversion costs)	100,000
Units started and completed during July	120,000
Work-in-process inventory on July 31 (20% complete as to conversion costs)	20,000
Total units to account for	240,000

Part A: Berry's equivalent units for direct materials for July using the FIFO method is:

Part B: Berry's the equivalent units of conversion for July using the FIFO method is:

How Does a Firm Compute the Cost of Units Produced?

Learning Objective 4.3
Explain how a firm computes the cost per equivalent unit of production in a process costing system.

Compute Cost per Equivalent Unit of Production

Now that we have computed the equivalent units of production for material and conversion, we can utilize those values to compute the cost per equivalent unit produced by dividing those values into material and conversion costs incurred during the period. We will use the first-in, first-out (FIFO) method to account for costs.[1] The FIFO method follows the physical flow of material and conversion and captures the equivalent unit activity during the current reporting period as accurately as possible based on completion percentage estimates.

To calculate the cost per equivalent unit of production using the FIFO method, *only* include current period material and conversion costs. The business divides current period material and conversion costs by the equivalent units of production for raw materials and conversion to arrive at the cost per equivalent unit of production (EUP).

Cost per EUP direct materials = Current direct materials costs / EUP for direct materials

Cost per EUP conversion = Current conversion costs / EUP for conversion

Let us continue with the Mott's Creamery example. The cost of raw material added to production in July was $30,000. To calculate the cost per equivalent unit of production for direct materials, we will divide the total current cost ($30,000) by the equivalent units of direct materials calculated above (49,700 EUP). We calculate the cost per equivalent unit of direct material for July as follows:

Cost per EUP direct materials = Total direct materials costs / EUP direct materials
= $30,000 / 49,700 EUP
= $0.60 / EUP

Conversion to costs for July such as labor and overhead expenditures amount to $69,000. The business computes costs per EUP for conversion by dividing the current cost ($69,000) by the 50,700 equivalent units of conversion computed above. We calculate the cost per equivalent unit of conversion for July as:

Cost per EUP conversion = Total conversion costs / EUP conversion
= $69,000 / 50,700 EUP
= $1.36 / EUP

[1]There are other methods, but they are outside the scope of this text.

LEARNING ACTIVITY 4.5

Continuing the Berry Frozen Food exercise, assume Berry incurred the following costs during July:

	Current Period Costs
Raw material costs for July	$ 70,000
Conversion costs for July (Direct Labor $80,000; Overhead $35,500)	$115,500

Assuming equivalent units of production for material is 140,000 and for conversion is 154,000, the cost per equivalent unit of production for both material and conversion are:

How Does a Firm Assign Costs to Units Completed and Work-in-process?

Learning Objective 4.4
Identify how a firm assigns costs to units in a process costing system.

The last step in the production cost report is to assign costs to units in work-in-process. This is accomplished by multiplying the ending work-in-process inventory balance in equivalent units by the material and conversion cost per equivalent units of production.

$$\text{Costs in Ending WIP} = \text{Ending WIP EUP} \times \text{Cost / EUP}$$

To determine the cost of raw materials in ending work-in-process at Mott's Creamery, we multiply the material balance of 1,200 equivalent units of production by the cost per equivalent unit of $0.60 resulting in $720 of raw material in ending work-in-process. Multiplying the conversion balance of 600 units by the cost per equivalent unit of $1.36 results in $816 of conversion costs in ending work-in-process. Taken together, the total balance in ending work-in-process is $1,536. Figure 4.6 illustrates the ending work-in-process balance at July 31.

Computing Costs Transferred Out

The business uses the total balance in ending work-in-process to determine the costs transferred out to finished goods or another processing department. We will assume goods in work-in-process are transferred to finished goods in our examples here. The computation for costs of goods transferred out is:

$$\text{Cost Transferred Out} = \text{Beginning WIP} + \text{Raw Material and Conversion Cost} - \text{Ending WIP}$$

Continuing the Mott's Creamery example and assuming the July 1 (beginning) cost of work-in-process is $1,744, costs for raw material placed into production is $30,000, the cost of conversion is $69,000 in July, and ending work-in-process inventory is $1,536, the cost transferred from work-in-process to finished goods during July amounted to $99,208. We compute that figure by adding the material and conversion costs of $30,000 and $69,000 to the beginning work-in-process balance of $1,744 and then subtracting the July 31 ending work-in-process balance of $1,536. Figure 4.7 illustrates the costs transferred to finished goods in July.

Figure 4.8 shows the completed production cost report for Mott's Creamery in July.

Figure 4.9 shows the flow of costs for Mott's Creamery from raw material and conversion costs, to finished goods.

The July 31 work-in-process inventory balance at Mott's Creamery

	Material	Conversion
July 31 work-in-process (in units)	1,200	600
Cost per equivalent unit of production	x $0.60	x $1.36
July 31 work-in-process	$ 720	$ 816
July 31 total work-in-process	$1,536	

Figure 4.6 Ending work-in-process.

Cost Flow Schedule (in millions)	
July 1 work-in-process	$ 1,744
Raw material costs incurred in July	+30,000
Conversion costs incurred in July	+69,000
July 31 work-in-process ($720 + $816)	– 1,536
Costs transferred to finished goods in July	$99,208

Figure 4.7 Costs transferred to finished goods.

Units Accounted For

	Units
Work-in-process on July 1 (All raw material added and is 20% converted)	2,000
Gallons started and completed during July 31	48,500
Work-in-process on July 31 (80% of raw material added and is 40% converted)	1,500
Gallons (units) accounted for	52,000

Equivalent Units

	Units	Current Effort	Equivalent Units
Work-in-process on July 1	2,000	0%	0
Gallons started and completed during July 31	48,500	100%	48,500
Work-in-process on July 31	1,500	80%	1,200
Equivalent units of raw material put into production			49,700
Work-in-process on July 1	2,000	80%	1,600
Gallons started and completed during July 31	48,500	100%	48,500
Work-in-process on July 31	1,500	40%	600
Equivalent units of conversion			50,700

Cost per Equivalent Unit of Production

	Material	Conversion
Current period production costs	$30,000	$69,000
Equivalent units of production	49,700	50,700
Cost per equivalent unit of production	$ 0.60	$ 1.36

	Material	Conversion
July 31 work-in-process (in units)	1,200	600
Cost per equivalent unit of production	x $ 0.60	x $ 1.36
July 31 work-in-process	$ 720	$ 816

Costs Transferred Out

July 1 work-in-process	$ 1,744
Raw material costs incurred in July	+30,000
Conversion costs incurred in July	+69,000
July 31 work-in-process ($720 + $816)	– 1,536
Costs transferred to finished goods in July	$99,208

Figure 4.8 Production cost report—EUP.

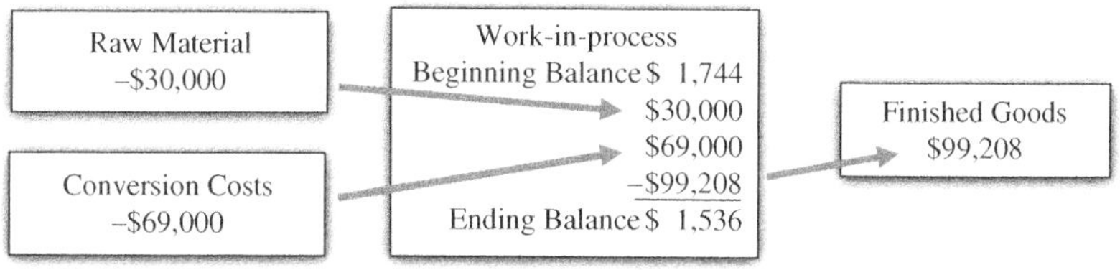

Figure 4.9 Costs flow for Mott's Creamery.

LEARNING ACTIVITY 4.6

Continuing the Berry Frozen Food exercise, assume Berry entered July with a balance of $65,000 in work-in-process inventory. Berry's equivalent units of production for July were as follows:

	EUP for	
	Material	Conversion
Units that were in process on July 1	0	30,000
Units that were started and completed in July	120,000	120,000
Units in ending inventory on July 31	20,000	4,000
Equivalent whole units of production	140,000	154,000

Current period material and conversion costs were $70,000 and $115,500 respectively, and cost per equivalent unit of production were $0.50 for material and $0.75 for conversion. Compute the costs of goods transferred from work-in-process to finished goods for July.

How Are Process Costs Recorded in the Financial Accounting System?

Learning Objective 4.5
Record the journal entries associated with a process costing system.

When utilizing a process costing model, the process of making journal entries involves systematically recording the costs associated with material and conversion directly into work-in-process and then calculating the work-in-process balance at the end of a reporting period to identify the amount that should be moved to finished goods. The journal entries follow the flow of costs displayed previously in Figure 4.7. Here is a step-by-step guide illustrated with a working example for Mott's Creamery:

Step 1: Record Direct Materials and Conversion Costs During the month of July, Mott's placed $30,000 worth of raw material into production and incurred $69,000 of conversion costs. Depending on the organization and the production processes, raw material may be purchased and initially posted into a raw material inventory account and then moved to work-in-process (much like we did in Chapter 3), or the costs might go right into work-in-process if the organization doesn't keep raw material storage. In the case of Mott's Creamer, let's assume that because their raw materials are perishable, they are posted directly into work-in-process when purchased. Let's also assume the raw material purchases were made on account. The journal entry to record the transactions and issue the $30,000 of material into production is as follows:

Work-in-process	$30,000	
Accounts Payable		$30,000

Conversion costs would be treated similarly. In the Mott's example, the company incurred $69,000 of conversion costs made up of $26,000 of labor and $43,000 of overhead. Let's assume the wages and overhead are both placed on account, wages payable and accounts payable, respectively. The journal entry to record the transactions for the incurrence of direct labor is as follows:

Work-in-process	$26,000	
Wages Payable		$26,000

The journal entry to record the transactions for the incurrence of overhead costs is as follows:

Work-in-process	$43,000	
Accounts Payable		$43,000

Step 2: Record Costs Transferred from Work-in-process to Finished Goods The second step involves reconciling the ending work-in-process balance estimated using the process costing calculations illustrated in Figure 4.4 to compute the amount of product that was completed and should be moved to finished goods as illustrated in Figure 4.5. In the example the work-in-process balance on July 1 was $1,744. Direct material cost of $30,000 and conversion cost of $69,000 were recorded during July, and the ending work-in-process balance was $1,536 (see Figure 4.4). As a result, $99,208 is moved from work-in-process to finished goods as illustrated in Figure 4.5. The journal entry to move the cost from work-in-process to finished goods is as follows:

Finished Goods	$99,208	
Work-in-process		$99,208

LEARNING ACTIVITY 4.7

Continuing the Berry Frozen Food exercise, record the following journal entries:

a. Post the costs in Learning Activity 4.5 into work-in-process. Assume raw material has already been purchased and is moved from raw material inventory, direct labor costs are credited to wages payable, and overhead costs are paid on account as well.
b. Move the appropriate costs calculated in Learning Activity 4.6 from work-in-process to finished goods.

Technology, Analytics, and AI

Self-service business intelligence software[2] (SSBI) can put advanced analytics at your fingertips. These tools are designed tool that integrates visualize data using a user-friendly graphical interface that makes data analysis accessible without requiring extensive technical expertise. Microsoft's Power BI is an SSBI tool integrates seamlessly with a wide range of data sources, including spreadsheets and databases, and as a result, can be a useful singular platform for analyzing, visualizing, and presenting information. Power BI allows for the creation of visualizations, interactive dashboards, and real-time analytics, thereby improving the managerial accountant's capabilities for turning data into information to drive informed decision-making.

Mikael Blomkvist / Pexels / Public Domain

[2] Dzuranin, A., Geertz, G., and Leek, M. (2023). *Data and analytics in accounting*. Hoboken, NJ: Wiley.

For managerial accountants, Power BI offers significant benefits as it allows for the integration of financial and operational data, and financial and nonfinancial, making it a powerful tool for providing a holistic view of company operations. By complex data into more user-friendly formats, Power BI allows accountants to present information in formats that are easily understood by stakeholders.

Let's use Power BI to create our own digital dashboard to analyze process costing information related to gasoline production at Clear Flow Petroleum. We can use Power BI to quickly develop visuals to help us gain important insights. The costs include raw crude oil, chemicals, additives, direct labor, overhead, utilities, and maintenance. Our visual dashboard will feature two charts: a donut chart showcasing the total cost composition and a clustered column chart comparing raw material costs with conversion costs. Let's see how it's done.

Let's start by opening up Power BI and importing our Clear_Flow_Petroleum_Data included with your chapter as shown in Figure 4.10.

Once you have imported the Clear_Flow_Petroleum_Data, check the Production_and_Cost_Data tab as illustrated in Figure 4.11 and then click "Load" at the bottom of the screen to use the January production cost data from Clear Flow.

Before developing our dashboard, we need to clean our data. You should use consistent column formatting without special characters or extra spaces, cells should be filled with values (e.g., "0" for numbers or "N/A" for text). You should also remove totals, subtotals, and merged

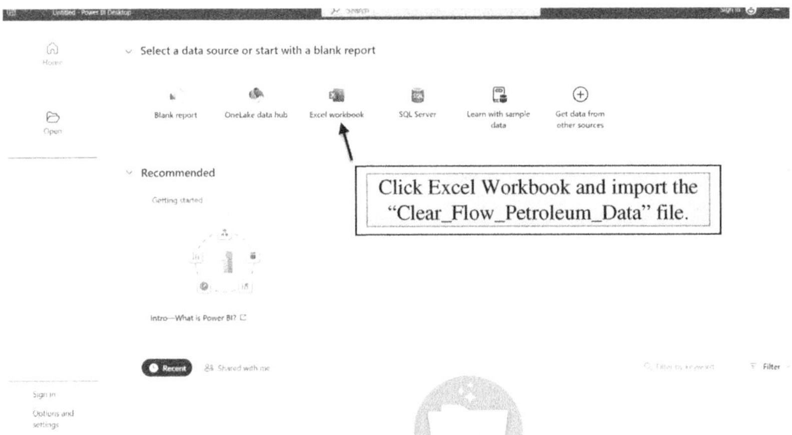

Figure 4.10 Import the data.

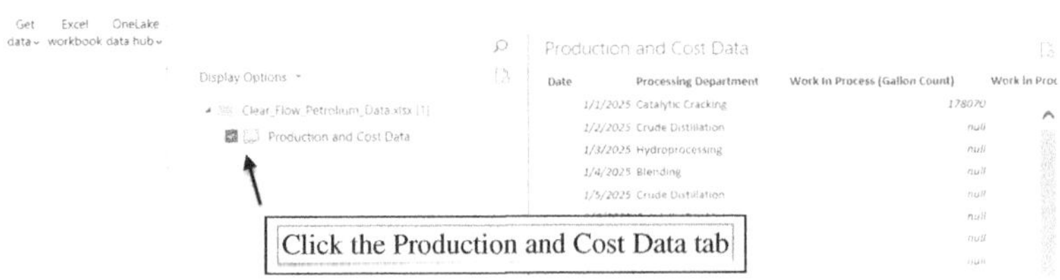

Figure 4.11 Selecting the data sheet.

cells; Power BI calculates these automatically and dynamically. Your data should be organized in columns, and each column should not have special formatting like bold text or colors. The data should be absent of special characters in data values and maintain consistent units across columns. More complex datasets can be separated into normalized tables, which is outside the scope of this text. This set of data includes column totals. Let's clean the data by removing the column totals. We do that by clicking "Transform data" and then clicking "Remove Rows" in the pop-up box as shown in Figure 4.12. Click "Remove Bottom Rows" and enter 1, and then click OK. You can then click the X in the top right corner of your pop-up screen. A box will appear asking, "Do you want to apply your changes now?" Click "Yes."

You can now insert a donut chart by and select the various production costs including the raw crude oil, chemicals and additives, direct labor, overhead, utilities, and maintenance. The default includes the sum of each of these columns of cost data as shown in Figure 4.13. The resultant chart illustrates the amount of total costs attributable to each cost category as well as the percentage of the total cost.

You may want to adjust the size and location of the chart in your dashboard in a manner that suits you. We extended the visual across the dashboard and changed the title to "Total Production Cost Breakdown" as shown in Figure 4.14.

You can now do the same process to create the clustered column chart comparing raw material costs with conversion costs. Select the Sum of Raw Crude Oil Input ($) and the Sum of Total Conversion Costs data. Rename your chart title to "Raw Crude Costs Versus Conversion Costs." Turn on the data labels under the Visuals and move the Legend by clicking on Legend,

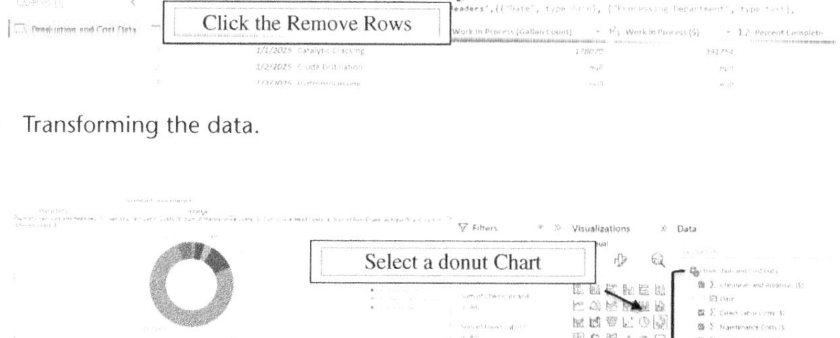

Figure 4.12 Transforming the data.

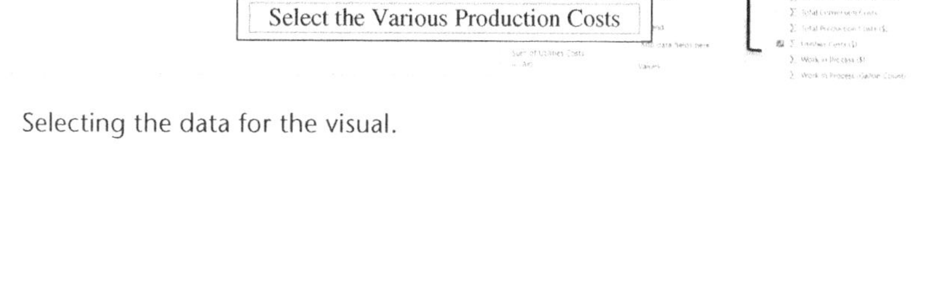

Figure 4.13 Selecting the data for the visual.

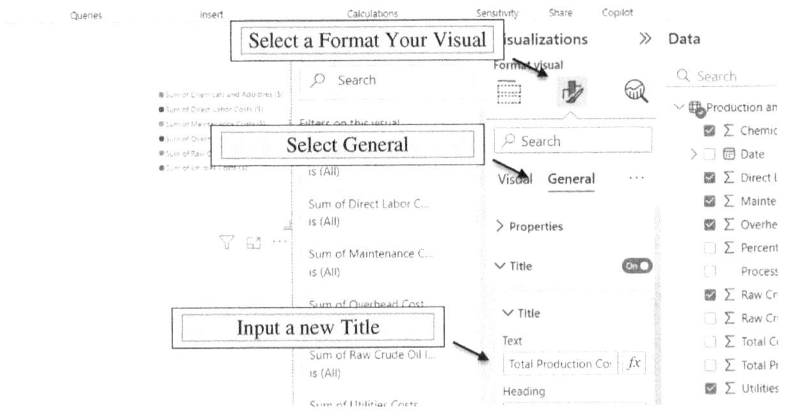

Figure 4.14 Formatting the visual.

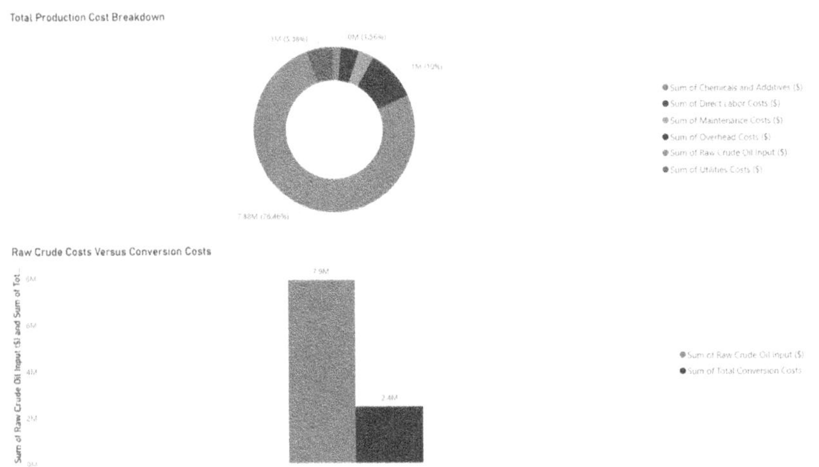

Figure 4.15 Production costs dashboard.

Options, and selecting Center Right under the Visuals tab. Your completed Production Cost Dashboard for Clear Flow Petroleum might look like Figure 4.15.

While this was a simple introductory example of Power BI, it demonstrates the software's potential for improving managerial accountant's job function and productivity. Power BI offers almost unlimited possibilities for creating dynamic dashboards, enabling advanced analysis and interpretation of data across various use cases. Practice your skills by giving Learning Activity 4.8 a try.

LEARNING ACTIVITY 4.8

Develop an additional visualization of your choice for Pure Flow Petroleum.

Key Terms

equivalent units of production (EUP) An estimate of fully completed units that could have been produced by the resource inputs applied during a reporting period.
process costing system A system of averaging total production costs over the total number of units produced.
production cost report A report prepared that summarizes the physical flow and cost flow of the goods in a process costing system.
self-service business intelligence software Software that enables users to independently analyze and visualize data through intuitive, no-code tools.

LEARNING ACTIVITY SOLUTIONS

Learning Activity 4.1

a. *Direct Labor*
b. *Direct Material*
c. *Job order costing*
d. *Overhead costs*

Learning Activity 4.2

a. Del Dente Food Processing ___*X*___
b. Jessen LLP Attorneys at Law ______
c. Americo Oil Refining ___*X*___
d. Elwood's Custom Wood Cabinetry ______
e. Tyron's Chicken Processing Plant ___*X*___

Learning Activity 4.3

a. Work-in-process inventory on July 1: ___*100,000*___
b. Inventory started and complete in July: ___*120,000*___
c. Ending work-in-process on July 31: ___*20,000*___
d. Total inventory units to account for: ___*240,000*___

Learning Activity 4.4

Part A: Berry's equivalent units for direct materials for July using the FIFO method:

		Current Effort	Equivalent Units
Raw material added to units in work-in-process on July 1	100,000	0%	0
Raw material added to units started and completed during July	120,000	100%	120,000
Raw material units left in work-in-process on July 31	20,000	100%	20,000
Equivalent whole units of raw materials put into production:			140,000

Part B: Berry's the equivalent units of conversion for July using the FIFO method:

		Current Effort	Equivalent Units
Conversion to finish units in work-in-process on July 1	100,000	30%	30,000
Conversion to units started and completed during July	120,000	100%	120,000
Conversion of units left in work-in-process on July 31	20,000	20%	4,000
Equivalent whole units of conversion effort:			154,000

Learning Activity 4.5

	Material	Conversion
July costs	$70,000	$115,500
July equivalent units of production	140,000	154,000
Cost per equivalent unit of production	$ 0.50	$ 0.75

Learning Activity 4.6

	EUP	Cost/EUP	Total Cost
July 31 work-in-process (material)	20,000	$ 0.50	$ 10,000
July 31 work-in-process (conversion)	4,000	$ 0.75	$ 3,000
Total July 31 work-in-process			$ 13,000

July 1 work-in-process	$ 25,000
Current material cost	70,000
Current conversion cost	115,500
July 31 work-in-process	13,000
Cost of goods transferred to finished goods	$197,500

Learning Activity 4.7

a.	*Work-in-process*	*185,500*	
	Raw material inventory		*70,000*
	Wages payable		*80,000*
	Work-in-process		*35,500*
b.	*Finished goods*	*197,500*	
	Work-in-process		*197,500*

Learning Activity 4.8

Solutions will vary.

Review Questions

1. A company that produces unique products would likely uses a __________ costing system, while a company that produces homogeneous products would likely use a __________ costing system. **(Learning Objective 1)**
   a. job order; process
   b. process; job order
2. What is an estimate of fully completed units that could have been produced by the resource inputs applied during a reporting period called? **(Learning Objective 2)**
   a. Units produced
   b. Equivalent units of production
   c. Converted units
   d. None of these
3. Computing the cost per equivalent unit of product divides __________ by the equivalent units of production. **(Learning Objective 3)**
   a. budgeted direct costs
   b. budgeted direct and indirect costs
   c. current direct costs
   d. current direct and indirect costs
4. You compute the costs in work-in-process for a process costing system by multiplying __________ times __________. **(Learning Objective 4)**
   a. ending units work-in-process; cost per unit
   b. ending equivalent units of production in work-in-process; cost per equivalent unit
   c. Either one is acceptable.

Short Exercises

S:4-1 (Learning Objective 1)

Job order costing is more suitable to companies that make heterogeneous products or perform heterogeneous services while process costing is more suitable for firms that make more homogeneous products or services. Indicate which of the listed companies would more likely use a job order costing or process costing system.

	Job Order Costing	Process Costing
1. Engineering firm		
2. Oil refinery		
3. Bread making factory		
4. Custom home builder		
5. Foundry		

S:4-2 (Learning Objective 1)

Which of the following are true about process costing and job order costing?

a. Only job order costing use three inventory accounts—Raw Materials Inventory, Work-in-process Inventory, and Finished Goods Inventory.
b. Only job order costing tracks direct materials, direct labor, and overhead.
c. Process costing assigns costs to various processes whereas job order costing assigns costs to jobs.
d. All of the these are true.

S:4-3 (Learning Objective 2)

If a firm that uses process costing has 50,000 physical units on hand, and those units are 25% complete. How many equivalent units would be on hand?

S:4-4 (Learning Objective 3)

Mountain Scents soap company enters the month of December with 1,000 bars of its high-quality lavender soap in process and 40% complete. Mountain Scents completed the bars of soap in December, started another 4,000 bars, and had 500 bars left at the end of December that were also 40% complete. Mountain Scents spent $2,400 on processing costs in the current period.

Requirements

a. How many equivalent units did Mountain Scents process?
b. What is the cost per equivalent unit?

S:4-5 (Learning Objective 4)

Café Frais Coffee Roasters had $4,000 of costs in work-in-process at the beginning of January. Café Frais spent $12,000 on coffee beans and another $8,000 on conversion costs during January. Café's work-in-process at the end of January was $5,000. What was the value of coffee that Café Frais transferred to finished goods in January?

Exercises

E:4-6 (Learning Objective 2)

Butter Brand Bread Company utilizes a process costing system for its commercial bakery where they produce enriched white bread. Butter Brand's production quantities for December are presented here:

	Units (Loaves)
Loaves-in-process on December 1	80,000
Loaves started during December	220,000
Loaves-in-process on December 31	60,000

Requirement

Compute and enter Butter Brand's units to account for during the month of December and separate the value into work-in-process inventory on December 1, inventory started and completed during December, and ending work-in-process on December 31.

Loaves-in-process on December 1: ________________
Loaves started and completed in December: ________________
Loaves-in-process on December 31: ________________
Total loaves to account for in December: ________________

E:4-7 (Learning Objective 3)

Daylight Milling Company mills whole grains into 16-oz. packages of breakfast cereal. Daylight adds 100% of the direct material into production at the beginning of the process and conversion costs are incurred proportionally as the cereal is milled. Daylight's units to account for (in pounds) for the month of February are presented next. The pounds in beginning inventory were 70% converted from raw material at the start of the period, and the pounds in ending inventory were 15% converted.

	Units (Pounds)
Work-in-process inventory on February 1 (70% converted)	6,000
Units and completed in February	175,000
Work-in-process inventory on February 28 (15% converted)	7,000

Requirements

a. Compute the equivalent units of raw material put into production during February.
b. Compute the equivalent unites of conversion incurred in in February.

E:4-8 (Learning Objective 4)

Continuing the Daylight Milling Company problem from E4-7, assume Daylight's beginning inventory totaled $7,200. Also assume Daylight put the equivalent of 182,000 pounds of grain into production and converted 177,850 equivalent units of grain into cereal. The total raw current period raw material costs incurred were $131,040, and the total conversion costs were $71,140. Finally, Daylight's ending equivalent units of raw material amounted to 7,000 pounds, and Daylights equivalent units of conversion in ending inventory amounted to 1,050 pounds.

Requirements

a. Compute the cost per equivalent unit for raw material and conversion.
b. Compute the cost of ending work-in-process in February.
c. Compute the cost of goods transferred out during February.

E:4-9 (Learning Objective 5)

a. Refer to E:4-8 and record the journal entry for part c.

Problems

P:4-10 (Learning Objectives 1 and 2)

Syntex Bio-Fuels utilizes a process costing system for its processing operations. Syntex adds all direct materials at the beginning of the process and adds conversion costs proportionally as it produces the fuel products. Syntex's units to account for in April are presented next. The gallons in beginning inventory were 60% converted from raw material at the start of the period, and the gallons in ending inventory were 30% converted.

	Units (Packages)
Work-in-process inventory on April 1 (60% complete as to conversion costs)	1,000,000
Units started during April	2,600,000
Work-in-process inventory on April 30 (30% complete as to conversion costs)	1,200,000

Requirements

a. Compute the number of units started and completed during April.
b. Compute Syntex's equivalent units for direct materials for April using the FIFO method.
c. Compute Syntex's equivalent units of conversion for April using the FIFO method.

P:4-11 (Learning Objectives 3 and 4)

Continuing the Syntex Bio-Fuels exercise, assume Syntex entered July with a balance of $1,440,000 in work-in-process inventory. Syntex's equivalent units of production for July are shown in the following table.

Equivalent Units of Production For	Material	Conversion
Units that were in process on July 1	0	400,000
Units that were started and completed in July	2,400,000	2,400,000
Units in ending inventory on July 31	1,200,000	360,000
Equivalent whole units of production	3,600,000	3,160,000

Current period material and conversion costs were $2,880.000 and $3,160,000, respectively, and cost per equivalent units of production were 3,600,000 gallons for material and 3,160,000 for conversion.

Requirements

a. Compute the cost per equivalent unit of production (EUP) for material and for conversion.
b. Compute the costs of goods transferred from work-in-process to finished goods for July.

P:4-12 (Learning Objective 5)

Continuing the Syntex Bio-Fuels exercise, record the appropriated journal entries for the following:

Requirements

a. Record the journal entry to account for the issuance of raw material and conversion costs into work-in-process. Raw material is purchased just-in-time and rather than being stored in a warehouse, it enters directly into production when it arrives at the fuel processing plant. Conversion costs are 20% labor and 80% overhead. Labor is recorded to wages payable and overhead costs are paid on account.
b. Record the journal entry to move costs from work-in-process to finished goods.

Technology, Analytics, and Artificial Intelligence

T:4-13 (Technology, Analytics, and Artificial Intelligence)

As the managerial accountant for Smooth and Sweet Yogurt, you are responsible for analyzing and presenting production cost data using Power BI. Production costs consist of milk, additives and cultures, direct labor, and overhead costs.

Required
Create production cost expenditure chart using the data in the Smooth_and_Sweet_Yogurt_Data file utilizing Power BI.

CHAPTER 5

Activity-based Costing

Learning Objectives

5.1 Identify the differences between traditional costing and activity-based costing and when organizations should consider using activity-based costing.
5.2 Identify the benefits and limitations of using an activity-based costing approach.
5.3 Identify the steps in activity-based costing approach.
5.4 Calculate costs using a traditional costing model and an activity-based model.
5.5 Illustrate the cost differences between traditional costing and activity-based costing models.
5.6 Describe activity-based management.

Accounting in Life

Mikhail Nilov / Pexels / Public Domain

Misuse of credit cards can have negative consequences for people who carry a balance. But suppose you can pay off your credit card monthly. In that case, a credit card can be a useful tool for tracking expenses and managing a personal budget. Credit card companies offer detailed monthly statements that categorize expenditures into categories and give users an overview of their spending habits. Categories might include typical reoccurring expenses like insurance, utilities, and maybe even rent, along with categories for items like food and restaurants, entertainment, and health and fitness. Reviewing monthly statements lets you identify trends and areas where you might be overspending. Using a credit card's tracking features can help you manage your finances and stay within your budget.

Let's Review

Recording costs accurately and efficiently is the first step in cost control. In Chapters 3 and 4, we learned to assign costs to products using job order and process costing systems. Job order costing systems are most effective for companies that offer unique products or services, such as a construction contractor or an accounting firm, where understanding the costs of each unique item is necessary. Process costing systems are most effective for companies that make large volumes of homogeneous products, such as an oil refinery or a food processing company, where there are limited benefits from tracking costs to individual items.

LEARNING ACTIVITY 5.1

Bertrand and Bertrand P.C. is a law firm that specializes in real estate and property law. Their clients are typically municipalities, government agencies, trust departments, and abstract and title companies. Shellenberger Heating and Cooling is a heating, ventilation, and cooling contracting company that specializes in large commercial projects. Voltary International is a global manufacturer of heating, ventilating, and cooling products. Voltary has six factories around the globe with each factory specializing in a particular product line. Which form costing methodology would each company likely use?

a. Bertrand and Bertrand, Job Order; Shellenberger, Job Order; Voltary, Job Order
b. Bertrand and Bertrand, Job Order; Shellenberger, Job Order; Voltary, Process
c. Bertrand and Bertrand, Process; Shellenberger, Job Order; Voltary, Job Order
d. Bertrand and Bertrand, Job Order; Shellenberger, Process; Voltary, Job Order

How Can Businesses Improve Accuracy in the Costing of Products or Services?

Learning Objective 5.1
Identify the differences between traditional costing and activity-based costing and when organizations should consider using activity-based costing.

Often, the most difficult part of computing accurate product or service costs is determining the amount of overhead that should be assigned to products or services, or the cost object. This is particularly true in diversified companies with diverse products that consume overhead costs in different ways. For example, manufacturing organizations have changed over time from labor-intensive production to using automation, robotics, and technology to replace the human element, increase productivity and quality, and to reduce cost. Similarly, service companies and professional service firms are shifting to more and more automation through the use of robotic process automation and artificial intelligence to handle many of the more mundane tasks in providing services, and sometimes not so mundane tasks.

The costing systems we have discussed so far utilize a normal costing mechanism (discussed in Chapter 2) that relies on developing a predetermined overhead rate to allocate overhead costs to products or services. The predetermined overhead rate is computed by dividing total overhead costs by the total cost driver activity to arrive at the overhead rate per measure of activity. We commonly use direct labor hours or machine hours as the cost driver. We then allocated overhead to products or services by multiplying the predetermined overhead rate by the cost driver activity consumed when producing the product or service. This is an efficient way to distribute overhead costs. But what if the company produces products or services that do not use labor "or" machine time, but use both labor "and" machine time, and each product uses varying amounts of labor and machine time? In that case, utilizing a singular overhead rate based on either labor or machine time would not be reflective of the actual overhead consumed when producing the particular products or services. Activity-based costing aims to remedy this conundrum.

Activity-based costing (ABC) is a costing method that allocates overhead to multiple activity cost pools and assigns the activity cost pools to products and services by means of cost drivers. In ABC, an **activity** is any event, action, transaction, or work that incurs cost when producing a product or providing a service. An **activity cost pool** is a collection of the total overhead costs for a given activity. Activity-based costing can be used in conjunction with other costing methods and is quite commonly used with job order costing. A cost driver is any factor or activity that has a direct cause-effect relationship with the resources consumed.

We have identified that businesses with products and services that vary in complexity and consumption of internal processes and activities should consider using an activity-based costing approach. In addition, a number of factors may signal that a business should consider using an activity-based costing approach. Those factors include producing a wide range of product lines and services, the business is vertically integrated, or managers manually calculating the real cost of products and services outside the company's accounting information system.

LEARNING ACTIVITY 5.2

Match the appropriate cost method with the following businesses. Each cost method can be used more than once.

Business	Cost Method
_____ Oil Refinery	A. Traditional Costing
_____ Diversified Manufacturer	B. Activity-Based Costing
_____ Professional Consulting Firm	
_____ Auto Repair Shop	
_____ Food Processor	

What Are the Strengths and Weaknesses of Activity-based Costing?

Learning Objective 5.2
Identify the benefits and limitations of using an activity-based costing approach.

The primary benefit of activity-based costing is that it separates costs into more cost pools, which can lead to better transparency as to what contributes to the cost of each activity. This creates an opportunity for improved cost control and, ultimately, better decision-making as products and services can be assigned costs for the particular activities they consume. Although activity-based costing systems have the potential for better cost data than traditional cost systems, there are limitations. Activity-based costing can be expensive to implement and manage as there is more information to track and more information to update periodically. Management accountants must balance the cost to track the information with the accuracy (Figure 5.1). Activity-based costing also relies on the use of cost allocation. In an activity-based costing system, overhead costs are spread to the various activity cost pools through reallocation. In some instances, identifying a cost driver for the allocations can be difficult, leaving the potential for allocations to be somewhat arbitrary or based on partial information. As a result, the selected activity cost driver for a particular cost pool must have a logical relationship to the costs in cost pool.

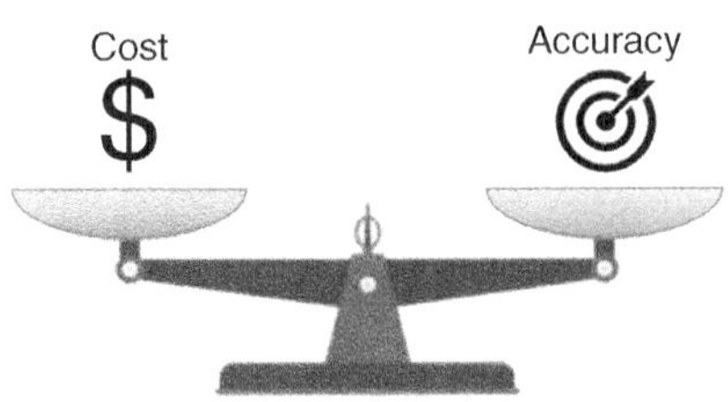

Figure 5.1 Cost versus accuracy comparison.

LEARNING ACTIVITY 5.3

SH Cosmetics manufactures natural cosmetics products and sells direct to consumers through commissioned sales representatives. SH manufactures a number of different types of cosmetics products, but there are five primary activities used for producing all of their cosmetics.

Required: Match the appropriate cost driver with each activity. A cost driver can be used more than once.

Activities	Cost Drivers
_____ Material Purchasing	A. Labor Hours
_____ Formulation and Machine Setup	B. Machine Hours
_____ Manual Mixing and Production	C. Raw Material Part Numbers Ordered
_____ Automated Packaging	D. Batches
_____ Inspection and Testing	

What Are the Elements of Activity-based Costing?

Learning Objective 5.3
Identify the steps in activity-based costing approach.

Activity-based costing allocates costs to products and services by splitting overhead costs into multiple overhead cost pools through allocation. Then, the overhead from the cost pools is assigned to products and services using cost drivers that serve as a proxy for the amount of each activity that was used by each product or service. Specifically, activity-based costing involves the following five steps:

1. Identify the major activities involved in manufacturing products or performing services. Each major activity becomes a cost pool.
2. Allocate expected overhead costs to the appropriate activity cost pools.
3. Identify the cost drivers that correlate with costs in each cost pool and the expected volume of the cost driver in the period.
4. Compute the **activity-based overhead rate** for each cost pool by dividing the overhead allocated to each cost pool by the expected cost driver volume over the period.

$$\begin{array}{c}\text{Estimated Overhead Per Activity}\\ \div\\ \text{Expected Use of Cost Driver Per Activity}\end{array} = \text{Activity-based Overhead Rate}$$

5. Assign overhead costs from each cost pool to products and services by multiplying the activity-based overhead rate times the cost-driver usage when producing the product or service.

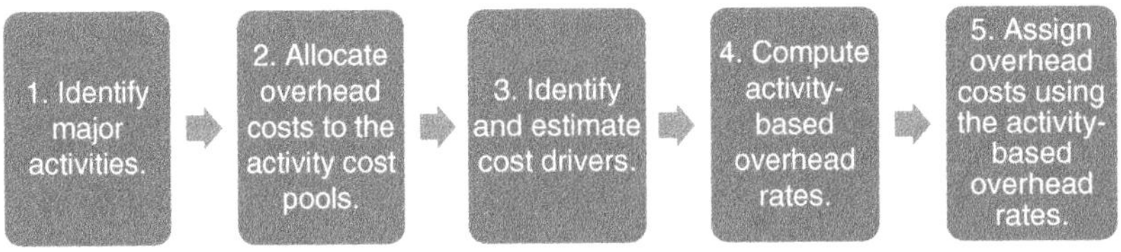

Figure 5.2 Steps in activity-based costing.

The expected overhead costs and cost driver volume are typically estimated during the annual budgeting process. Figure 5.2 shows the five steps involved in the activity-based costing method.

LEARNING ACTIVITY 5.4

SH Cosmetics has the following expected activities and costs associated with the production of cosmetics. The expected use of the cost driver for each activity cost pool is also listed.

Cost by Activity	**Cost Drivers**
$100,000 Material Purchasing	400 Raw Material Part Numbers Ordered
$150,000 Formulation and Machine Setup	250 Batches
$200,000 Manual Mixing and Production	20,000 Labor Hours
$500,000 Automated Packaging	2,000 Machine Hours
$50,000 Inspection and Testing	250 Batches

Required: Compute the activity-based overhead rate for each activity.

How Do Businesses Implement Activity-based Costing?

Learning Objective 5.4
Calculate costs using a traditional costing model and an activity-based costing model.

Implementing an activity-based costing model can result in more accurate indirect (overhead) cost allocation to finished products or services. In some cases, the differences between a traditional costing model and an activity-based costing model can be negligible. However, in some cases, the differences can be quite different. If the traditional model does not accurately reflect the consumption of indirect costs in the production of products or services, decision-making can be negatively affected. Figure 5.3 illustrates the traditional and activity-based costing models.

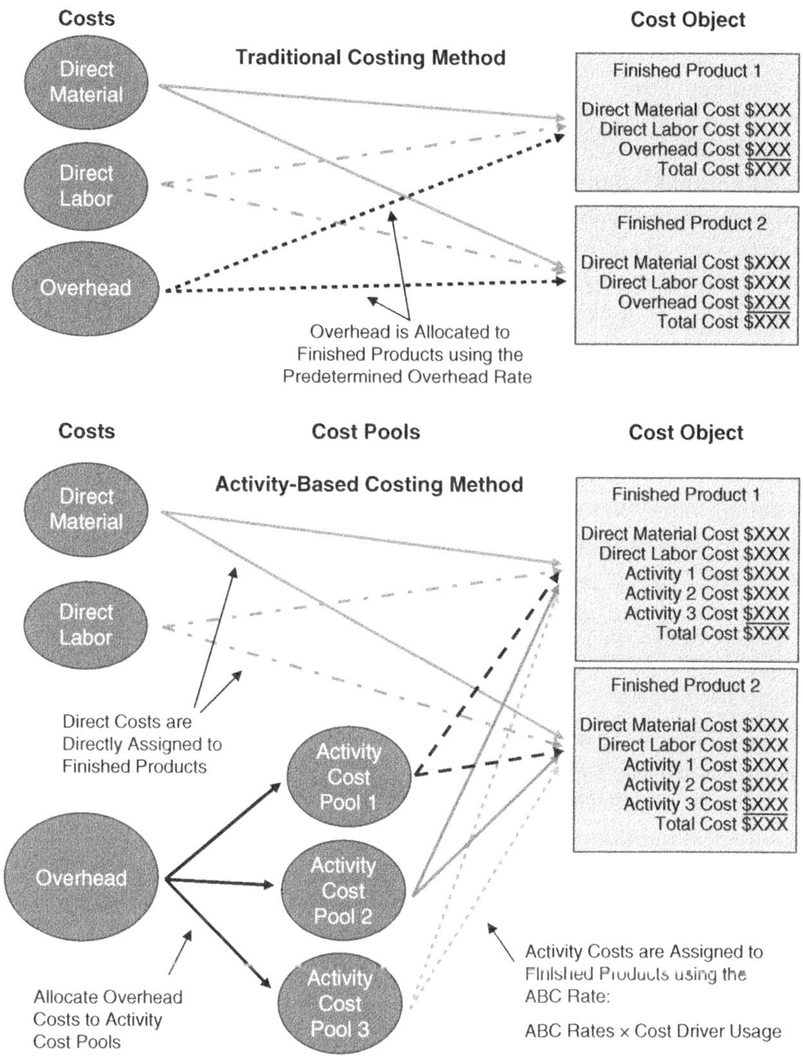

Figure 5.3 Traditional costing model versus activity-based costing model.

Let us look at data for JJ's Window and Glass Company. JJ's specializes in two product categories, automotive glass and structural glass. JJ's sells its automotive glass to auto body shops and glass repair shops and its structural glass to construction companies and developers. Although both products use similar raw materials and some of the same processes, automotive glass goes through additional steps, including a laminating process where a plastic layer is sandwiched between glass layers, and molding the glass into shape to fit a particular automobile. The additional processes to produce the automotive glass require the use of specialty equipment, which is unnecessary when manufacturing structural glass. Let us examine data related to the two glass products at JJ's Window and Glass (see Figure 5.4).

Let us first compute the cost per unit of auto glass and structural glass using a normal costing method where annual overhead is applied to products using a predetermined overhead rate based on direct labor hours (see Figure 5.5).

Now, let us consider additional information, such as the differences in the manufacturing processes between auto glass and structural glass, and utilize an ABC approach to costing the two products. First, JJ's Window and Glass Company's controller identifies three primary activities in the production of glass products: (1) Layering and Laminating; (2) Molding; and (3) Cutting and Sizing. In evaluating the relationship between overhead costs and each activity, the controller allocates the $2,000,000 of estimated overhead to the three cost pools in

Product	Direct Labor Hours per Unit	Annual Production	Total Direct Labor Hours
Auto Glass	0.5	5,000 units	2,500
Structural Glass	0.75	10,000 units	7,500
			10,000

Additional information regarding the products:

Auto Glass requires $150 in direct materials per unit; Structural Glass requires $100 direct materials per unit

Direct labor cost is $25 per hour

Total annual overhead costs are $2,000,000

Total direct labor hours is 10,000 hours

Figure 5.4 JJ's Window and Glass product cost data.

Overhead Cost Per Hour	$\frac{\$2,000,000}{10,000 \text{ Hours}}$ =	$200 per hours
	Auto Glass	**Structural Glass**
Direct Material Per Unit	$150.00	$100.00
Direct Labor Per Unit		
$25.00 × 0.5 Hours	$ 12.50	
$25.00 × 0.75 Hours		$ 18.75
Overhead		
$200 × 0.5 Hours	$100.00	
$200 × 0.75 Hours		$150.00
Total Cost Per Unit	$262.00	$268.75

Figure 5.5 JJ's Window and Glass cost per unit using a traditional costing method.

the following manner. First, $1,00,000 of the overhead is directly related to equipment and building space used for layering and laminating; $500,000 of the overhead is directly related to equipment and building space used for molding; and $200,000 is related to equipment and building space used to support cutting and sizing operations. The remaining $300,000 in overhead relates to shared costs related to employee training, supervision, and other miscellaneous expenses. The controller allocates those costs based on the amount of employee time dedicated to the three activities and splits the cost by allocating $100,000 to layering and laminating, $50,000 to molding, and $150,000 to cutting and sizing. Figure 5.6 illustrates the cost allocation in the first step in ABC costing.

JJ's Window and Glass uses machine hours and direct labor hours to allocate costs from the activity cost pools to products. Machine hours is the cost driver for Layering and Laminating and Molding, and direct labor hours serves as the cost driver for cutting and sizing. Figure 5.7 illustrates the cost drivers for each activity.

LEARNING ACTIVITY 5.5

Data for two of SH Cosmetics' products, Lip Gloss and Eye Shadow

Product	Direct Labor Hours per Unit	Annual Production	Total Direct Labor Hours
Shimmer Lip Gloss	0.04	25,000 units	1,000
Smoky Eye Shadow	0.02	10,000 units	2,000
			3,000

Additional information regarding the products:

Shimmer Lip Gloss uses $0.25 in direct materials per unit; Smoke Eye Shadow requires $0.50 of direct materials per unit. Direct labor cost is $25 per hour. Total annual overhead costs for all products amount to $100,000 and total labor hours for all products is 2,000.

Required: Compute the cost of Shimmer Lip Gloss and Smoky Eye Shadow using a traditional cost method that assumes direct labor hours is the cost.

Layering and Laminating	$1,100,000
Molding	$ 550,000
Cutting and Sizing	$ 450,000
Total Overhead Costs	$2,000,000

Figure 5.6 Reallocating overhead to cost pools.

Activity Cost Pools	Cost Driver (Activity Measure)
Layering and Laminating	Machine hours
Molding	Machine hours
Cutting and Sizing	Direct labor hours

Figure 5.7 JJ's Window and Glass cost drivers per activity cost pool.

	Expected Activity		
Activity Measure	**Auto Glass**	**Structural Glass**	**Total**
Machine hours	2,000	500	2,500
Direct labor hours	2,500	7,500	10,000
		Auto Glass	**Structural Glass**
Layering and Laminating			
$1,100,000 × (2,000 MH ÷ 2,500 MH)		$ 880,000	
$1,100,000 × (500 MH ÷ 2,500 MH)			$220,000
Molding			
$550,000 × (2,000 MH ÷ 2,500 MH)		$ 440,000	
$550,000 × (500 MH ÷ 2,500 MH)			$110,000
Cutting and Sizing			
$450,000 × (2,500 DLH ÷ 10,000 DLH)		$112,500	
$450,000 × (7,500 DLH ÷ 10,000 DLH)			$337,500
Total Overhead Cost Allocated		$1,432,500	$667,500
Total Units of Production		÷ 5,000 Units	÷ 10,000 Units
Overhead Cost Per Unit		$ 286.50	$ 66.75

Figure 5.8 JJ's Window and Glass overhead cost allocation using the activity-based costing method.

JJ's Window and Glass expects to incur 2,000 machine hours and 2,500 direct labor hours producing auto glass during the year, and 500 machine hours and 7,500 direct labor hours producing structural glass. Using the activity-based costing approach, the company uses machine hours and direct labor as the basis for allocating the costs of layering and laminating, molding, and cutting and sizing to the auto glass and structural glass product. Figure 5.8 illustrates the expected cost driver activity when producing 5,000 panes of auto glass and 10,000 panes of structural glass and the overhead costs allocated to each product using the activity-based costing approach. The allocation of costs results in $1,432,500 allocated to auto glass. Dividing that by 5,000 panes of glass equals an overhead cost of $286.50 per pane of glass. The allocation of costs results in $667,500 allocated to auto glass. Dividing that by 10,000 panes of glass equals an overhead cost of $66.75 per pane of glass.

	Auto Glass	Structural Glass
Direct Material Per Unit	$150.00	$ 100.00
Direct Labor Per Unit		
$25.00 × 0.5 Hours	$ 12.50	
$25.00 × 0.75 Hours		$ 18.75
Overhead per Unit	$288.50	$ 66.75
Total Cost per Unit	$449.00	$185.50

Figure 5.9 JJ's Window and Glass cost per unit using the activity-based costing method.

To compute the cost per unit using the activity-based costing approach, combine the material, direct labor, and overhead costs per unit. The estimated cost of a pane of auto glass using the activity-based costing method is $449.00, and the cost of a pane of structural glass is estimated to be $185.50. Figure 5.9 illustrates the cost calculation using the activity-based costing method.

LEARNING ACTIVITY 5.6

SH Cosmetics had the following overhead cost pools and expected activity when producing Shimmer Lip Gloss and Smokey Eye Shadow products.

Cost Pool	Cost Driver	Total Cost
Special Processing	Machine Hours	$ 30,000
Assembly	Direct Labor Hours	$ 60,000
Purchasing	Part Numbers Ordered	$ 8,000
Inspection and Testing	Batches	$ 2,000
Total		$100,000

	Expected Activity		
Activity Measure	Lip Gloss	Eye Shadow	Total
Machine hours	2,000	3,000	5,000
Direct labor hours	1,000	200	1,200
Parts Numbers Ordered	25	25	50
Batches Produced	20	30	50

Required: Using the data above and from Learning Activity 5.5, compute the cost per unit for the Shimmer Lip Gloss and Smokey Eye Shadow using the activity-based costing method.

What Are the Consequences of Using a Less Accurate Costing Model?

Learning Objective 5.5
Illustrate the cost differences between traditional costing and activity-based costing models.

In our JJ's Window and Glass Company, there are significant differences between the cost of panes of glass when using a traditional costing methodology that allocates overhead costs based on one cost driver, direct labor hours in our example, versus using an activity-based costing methodology that allocates overhead into multiple cost pools and allocates the costs from the cost pools using different cost drivers for each pool. In our example, the estimated cost of a pane of auto glass is $262.50 using the traditional costing method and $449.00 using the activity-based costing method. The cost of a pane of structural glass is $268.75 using the traditional costing method versus $185.50 using the activity-based costing method.

The accuracy that can be gained from implementing an activity-based costing method can lead to improved decision-making. Let us illustrate by considering the impact on pricing decisions. Let us assume the company desires a 30% gross margin on products. Using a traditional costing approach, the company prices a pane of auto glass at $341.25 and a pane of structural glass at $349.38. Using the activity-based costs, a pane of auto glass would sell for $583.70, whereas a pane of structural glass would sell for $241.15.

The difference in pricing is significant and may influence sales dramatically, which could result in lost sales, lower margins, and maybe even bankruptcy. For example, if the company set its prices using the traditional costing approach, the cost of auto glass would be quite low in the marketplace at an average of $341.25 per pane. That might result in a high sales volume for auto glass, but would it result in profits? Likely not. In fact, JJ's Window and Glass might lose money on every pane of auto glass sold. When we recomputed the cost of the glass products using the activity-based approach, we found that the cost of a pane of auto glass is more accurately $449.00 per pane. As a result, selling panes of glass for $341.25 per unit would result in a *loss of $107.75* for every pane of glass sold. This could be catastrophic for JJ's Window and Glass Company.

LEARNING ACTIVITY 5.7

In Learning Activities 5.5 and 5.6 you were required to compute the cost per unit for SH Cosmetics' Shimmer Lip Gloss and Smokey Eye Shadow using a traditional costing methodology and the activity-based costing method.

Required: Compare the cost of each product using the traditional versus the activity-based costing methods and discuss the implications of any differences.

How Can Activity-based Costing Improve Cost Control?

Learning Objective 5.6
Describe activity-based management.

Activity-based management (ABM) is the process of reducing cost through removing non-value-added activities and leaving only valued added activities that advance a product or service toward a state of completion. Activity-based management focuses on reducing costs to the end customer as it emphasizes efficiency, organization, and productivity. Activity-based management is a natural extension of activity-based costing because activity-based costing identifies various activities and tracks the associated costs, making activity-based management easy to implement and conduct.

Theoretically, value-added activities change, alter, or advance a product or service toward a state of completion. Examples of value-added activities in a production environment include activities like fabricating, assembling, painting, packaging and shipping. They also include engineering and design work to develop products. Non-value-added activities include activities that add cost, but do not alter, improve, or advance the product, such as moving material and inventory around the warehouse or factory, maintenance and repair work, and inspections. In a service industry, value-added activities involve those that are directly related to providing customer service. For example, in a tax preparation business, reviewing client information and preparing the tax return would be considered value-added activity, whereas inputting or transferring data from client intake forms or filing and storing documents would be considered non-value added. Tax preparers formerly used paper-based intake forms where clients would write important figures which would later be entered into tax software by a clerical worker. Most tax service firms have eliminated the non-value-added step of transferring client data from paper-based forms into their tax software, which reduces time and cost.

LEARNING ACTIVITY 5.8

Consider the activities that were identified for SH Cosmetics in Learning Activity 5.3.

Required: Identify which of the following activities are value-added or non-value-added by marking the value-added items (VA) and the non-value-added (NVA).

Activities

_____ Material Purchasing

_____ Formulation and Machine Setup

_____ Manual Mixing and Production

_____ Automated Packaging

_____ Inspection and Testing

Technology, Analytics, and AI

Activity-based costing requires additional analysis by management accountants as they frequently monitor each activity's cost drivers and overhead rates. One simple method is to create a visual dashboard for the managers to monitor the actual and applied costs in their respective area or department. Let's create a dashboard for Precision Gearworks, a manufacturer that creates three gears: performance, industrial, and transmission. They have tracked actual costs by the department and the applied costs by department and product.

Using the data *EOC Overhead_Cost_Allocation_Data.xlsx*, load the data into Power BI in the same manner as Chapter 4. Load both worksheets from the workbook. Before creating the visualizations, we should create a measure called Difference to determine if Precision Gearworks has either over or under allocated its costs. To create the measure, select **New Measure** from the Home toolbar, as shown in Figure 5.10.

Enter the following formula in the formula bar and click the green checkmark.

```
Difference = sum('Cost Allocation_Data'[Costs Applied])-sum('Actual Cost_
Data'[Debit Value ($)])
```

To enter the field names, such as Costs Applied, start typing the sheet name, and a selection pop-up will appear. Select the field name and continue typing the formula.

The first visualization we will add to the dashboard is a multi-row card. On this card, we will display the total actual costs and the total applied costs. To create this visualization, click the multi-card visualization card to display the card in the main area, as shown in Figure 5.11.

Figure 5.10 Home toolbar.

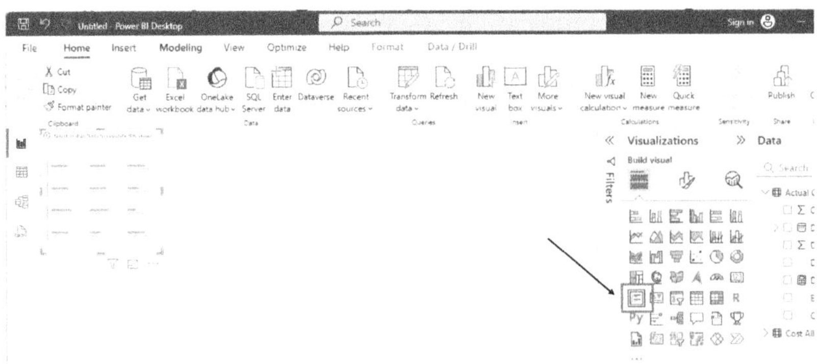

Figure 5.11 Select multi-row card visualization.

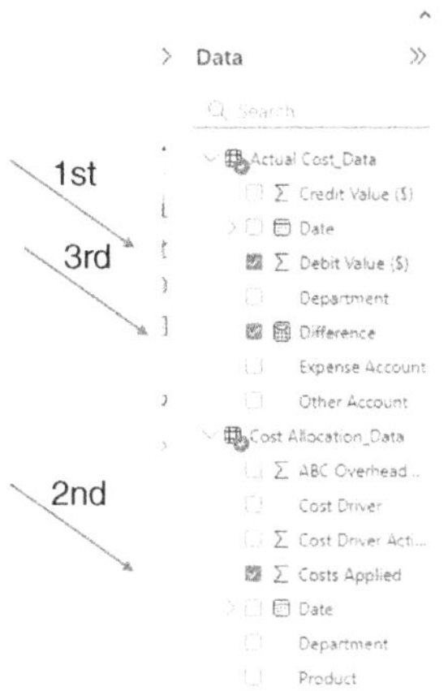

Figure 5.12 Select fields.

Figure 5.13 Multi-card visualization.

Click the fields in the order shown in Figure 5.12. This will display the total of those fields in the visualization as shown in Figure 5.13. Resize the visualization as you see fit.

Change the number format settings by selecting the Format area under visualizations and change the data format to Currency. Make any other changes as you wish. See Figure 5.14.

The next visualization will be a pie chart that breaks down the total applied costs by department. Select the pie chart icon from the list of visualizations. Drag Costs Applied to Values and Department to Legend to display the pie chart shown in Figure 5.15.

Before creating the final visualization, we need to create a relationship between the Department fields in the two tables. From the Modeling toolbar, select the Manage Relationships button as shown in Figure 5.16.

Select the New Relationship button at the top of the pop-up dialog box. Then, select the tables and appropriate columns as shown in Figure 5.17. Then click Save.

Figure 5.14 Change format.

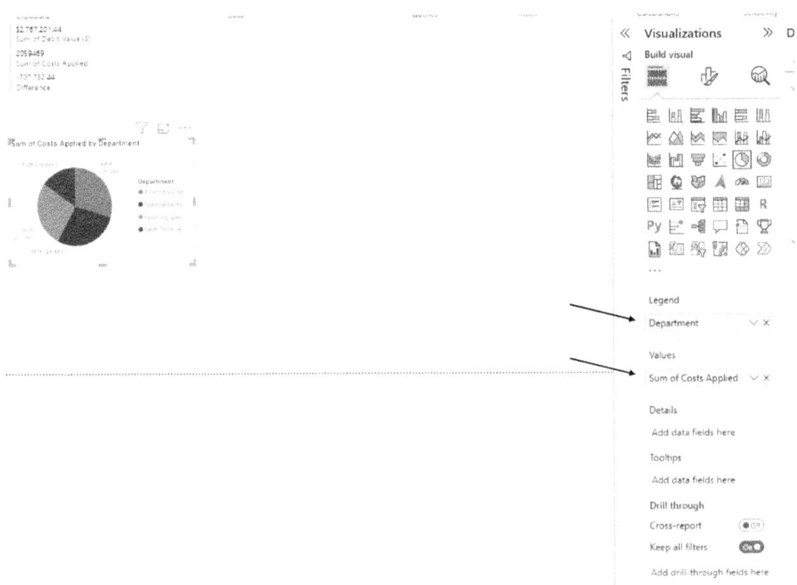

Figure 5.15 Pie chart.

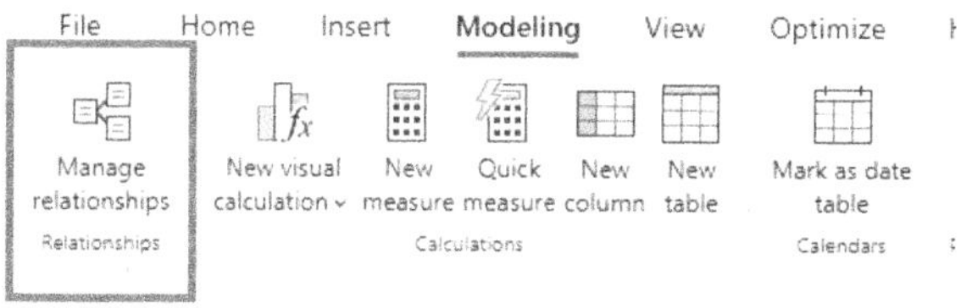

Figure 5.16 Manage relationships.

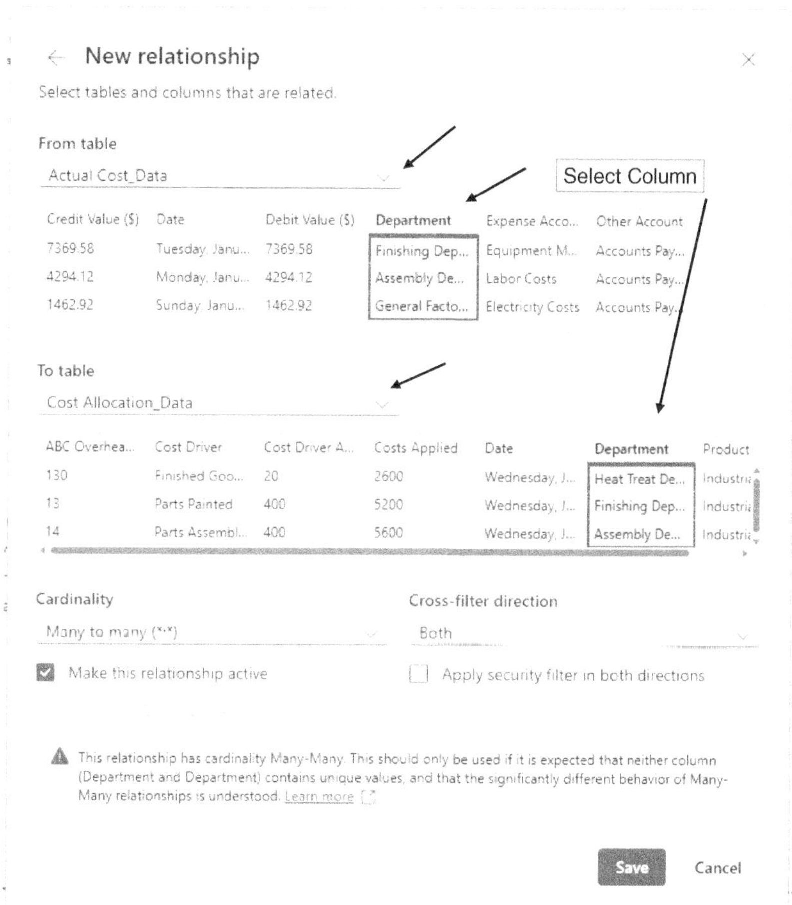

Figure 5.17 Change relationship settings.

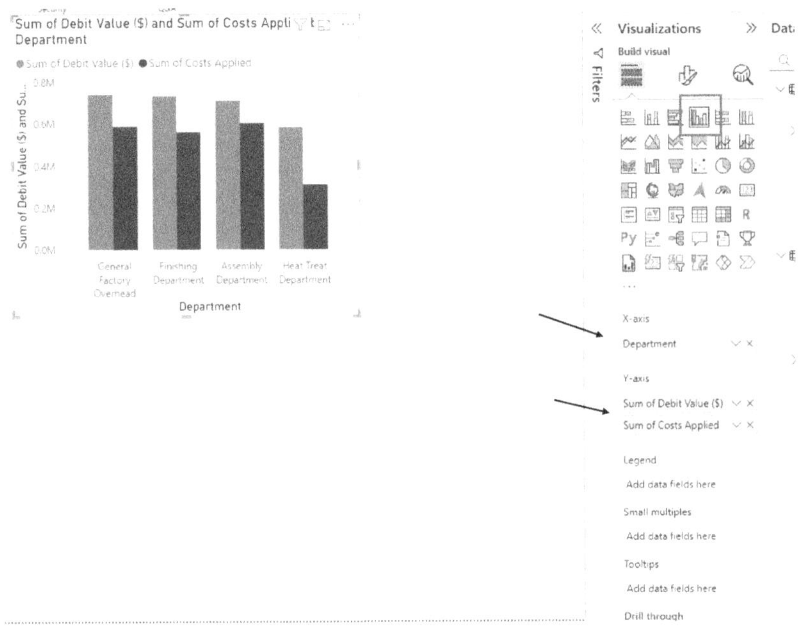

Figure 5.18 Create clustered bar chart.

The last visualization in the dashboard will be a cluster bar chart comparing the costs applied and the actual costs by department. Select the clustered bar chart from the visualizations. Drag Department to the x-axis and the Debit Value and Cost Applied to the y-axis as shown in Figure 5.18.

Format the chart as you wish to make it more usable.

Be sure to save your file with your dashboard.

Key Terms

activity-based costing (ABC) A costing method that allocates overhead to multiple activity cost pools and assigns the activity cost pools to products and services by means of cost drivers.
activity Any event, action, transaction, or work that causes the incurrence of costs when producing a product or providing a service.
activity cost pools A collection of the total overhead costs for a given activity.
activity-based overhead rate The result of dividing the overhead allocated to each cost pool by the expected cost driver volume over the period.
activity-based management (ABM) The process of reducing cost through removing non-value-added activities and leaving only valued added activities that advance a product or service toward a state of completion.

LEARNING ACTIVITY SOLUTIONS

Learning Activity 5.1

B

Learning Activity 5.2

__A__ Oil Refinery
__B__ Diversified Manufacturer
__B__ Professional Consulting Firm
__B__ Auto Repair Shop
__A__ Food Processor

Learning Activity 5.3

__C__ Material Purchasing
__B__ Formulation and Machine Setup
__A__ Manual Mixing and Purchasing
__B__ Automated Packaging
__D__ Inspection and Testing

Learning Activity 5.4

a. $\dfrac{\text{Material Purchasing Cost}}{\text{Part Numbers Ordered}}$ $\dfrac{\$100{,}000}{400}$ = *$45 per Order*

b. $\dfrac{\text{Formulation and Setup Cost}}{\text{Batches}}$ $\dfrac{\$150{,}000}{250}$ = *$600 per Batch*

c. $\dfrac{\text{Mixing and Production Costs}}{\text{Labor Hours}}$ $\dfrac{\$200{,}000}{20{,}000}$ = *$10 per Labor Hr.*

d. $\dfrac{\text{Automated Packaging Costs}}{\text{Machine Hours}}$ $\dfrac{\$500{,}000}{2{,}000}$ = *$250 per Machine Hr.*

e. $\dfrac{\text{Inspection and Testing Costs}}{\text{Batches}}$ $\dfrac{\$50{,}000}{250}$ = *$200 per Batch*

Learning Activity 5.5

Predetermined Overhead Rate

$$\frac{\text{Annual Overhead Costs } \$100{,}000}{\text{Expected Direct Labor Hours } 1{,}200 \text{ Hours}} = \$83.33 \text{ per direct labor hour}$$

Product Cost

	Lip Gloss	Eye Shadow
Direct Material	$0.25	$0.50
Direct Labor		
(0.04 hours × $25 per hour)	$1.00	
(0.02 hours × $25 per hour)		$0.50
Manufacturing Overhead		
(0.04 hours × $83.33 per hour)	$3.33	
(0.02 hours × $83.33 per hour)	____	$1.67
Total Cost per Unit	$4.58	$2.67

Learning Activity 5.6

Activity-based Overhead Rates

$$\frac{\text{Special Processing Cost}}{\text{Machine Hours}} \quad \frac{\$30{,}000}{5{,}000} = \$6 \text{ per Machine Hour}$$

$$\frac{\text{Assembly Cost}}{\text{Labor Hours}} \quad \frac{\$60{,}000}{1{,}200} = \$50 \text{ per Labor Hour}$$

$$\frac{\text{Purchasing Costs}}{\text{Part Numbers Ordered}} \quad \frac{\$8{,}000}{50} = \$160 \text{ per Part Number}$$

$$\frac{\text{Inspection and Test Costs}}{\text{Batches}} \quad \frac{\$2{,}000}{50} = \$40 \text{ per Batch}$$

Product Cost

	Lip Gloss	Eye Shadow
Direct Material	$0.25	$0.50
Direct Labor		
(0.04 hours × $25 per hour)	$1.00	
(0.02 hours × $25 per hour)		$0.50

Manufacturing Overhead		
Special Processing		
(2,000 hours × $6 per hour)/25,000	*$0.48*	
(3,000 hours × $6 per hour)/10,000		*$1.80*
Assembly		
(1,000 hours × $50 per hour)/25,000	*$2.00*	
(200 hours × $50 per hour)/10,000		*$1.00*
Purchasing		
(25 parts × $160 per hour)/25,000	*$0.16*	
(25 parts × $160 per hour)/10,000		*$0.40*
Inspection and Testing		
(20 batches × $40 per batch)/25,000	*$0.03*	
(30 batches × $40 per batch)/10,000	____	*$0.12*
Total Cost per Unit	*$3.92*	*$4.32*

Learning Activity 5.7

The activity-based costing approach resulted in a higher price of the eye shadow, which increased from $2.67 using the traditional costing approach, to $4.32 using the ABC approach. The primary cause for the difference is that production of eye shadow uses a majority of the special processing time and equipment. The overhead cost per tube of eye shadow amounts to $1.80, whereas the total overhead cost allocated to tube of eye shadow using the traditional approach amounted to $1.67. Alternatively, the cost of a tube of lip gloss declined from $4.58 per tube to $3.92 per tube. The cause of the decline is that the majority of the overhead for special processing is allocated to the eye shadow rather than the lip gloss when using the ABC approach.

Learning Activity 5.8

__*NVA*__ *Material Purchasing*
__*NVA*__ *Formulation and Machine Setup*
__*VA*__ *Manual Mixing and Production*
__*VA*__ *Automated and Packaging*
__*NVA*__ *Inspection and Test*

Review Questions

1. Companies commonly have difficulty computing accurate unit costs. **(Learning Objective 1)**
   a. True
   b. False
2. What factors have made costing products and services more difficult over time? **(Learning Objective 1)**
   a. Automation
   b. Robotics
   c. Artificial intelligence
   d. All of the above
3. What technologies help organizations manage more mundane tasks? **(Learning Objective 1)**
   a. Spreadsheets
   b. Robotic process automation
   c. Visualization tools
   d. Activity-based costing
4. The primary difference between activity-based costing systems and normal costing systems is the of multiple overhead cost pools in an activity-based system. **(Learning Objective 1)**
   a. True
   b. False
5. Any event, action, transaction, or work that causes the incurrence of cost when producing a product or service is called what? **(Learning Objective 1)**
   a. Action
   b. Activity
   c. Pool
   d. None of the above
6. A collection of the total overhead costs for a given activity is called what? **(Learning Objective 1)**
   a. Activity cost pool
   b. Action cost pool
7. Activity-based costing allocates overhead to multiple cost pools. **(Learning Objective 1)**
   a. True
   b. False
8. Activity-based costing assigns costs to products using a single cost driver. **(Learning Objective 1)**
   a. True
   b. False
9. Activity-based costing always results in more accurate costs. **(Learning Objective 2)**
   a. True
   b. False

10. What is a benefit of activity-based costing? **(Learning Objective 2)**
    a. Cost savings
    b. Better cost assignment
    c. Efficiency
    d. None of the above
11. What is a weakness of activity-based costing? **(Learning Objective 2)**
    a. Cost to implement
    b. Poor cost assignment
    c. More detailed costing
    d. All of the above
12. What is a benefit of activity-based costing? **(Learning Objective 2)**
    a. Better decision-making
    b. More cost pools
    c. Identifying multiple cost drivers
    d. All of the above
13. What is a weakness of activity-based costing? **(Learning Objective 2)**
    a. Use of cost allocations to cost pools
    b. Difficulty to identify multiple cost drivers
    c. Need to update and manage as the business changes
    d. All of the above
14. Activity-based costing is a tradeoff between _______ and ______. **(Learning Objective 2)**
    a. Cost; accuracy
    b. Allocation; assignment
    c. Single cost drivers; multiple cost drivers
    d. None of the above
15. What does the first step in implementing activity-based costing involve? **(Learning Objective 3)**
    a. Allocating costs to cost pools
    b. Identifying cost drivers
    c. Identifying major activities
    d. None of the above
16. What would an appropriate cost driver for automated processes most likely be? **(Learning Objective 3)**
    a. Labor hours
    b. Machine hours
    c. Batches
    d. Any of the above
17. The activity-based overhead rate is computed by dividing the ______________ by the ______________? **(Learning Objectives 3 and 4)**
    a. Actual overhead per activity; total cost driver usage per activity
    b. Estimated overhead per activity; expected cost driver usage per activity

18. What is the process of connecting overhead costs with products using the activity-based overhead rate? **(Learning Objective 3 and Learning Objective 4)**
    a. Allocation
    b. Assignment
19. In an activity-based costing system, overhead costs are __________ to overhead cost pools. **(Learning Objective 3 and Learning Objective 4)**
    a. Allocated
    b. Assigned
20. When implementing an activity-based costing system, how are material and labor handled? **(Learning Objective 4)**
    a. Allocated to finished products through activity-cost pools
    b. Directly assigned to finished products
21. What could be a consequence of using a traditional costing system when an activity-based costing system is applicable? **(Learning Objective 5)**
    a. Inaccurate product costs
    b. Poor pricing decisions
    c. Dysfunctional decision-making
    d. All of the above
22. Activity-based costing facilitates better cost control through ____________. **(Learning Objective 6)**
    a. Activity-based management
    b. Activity integration
    c. Cost driver minimization
    d. Mone of the above
23. Activity-based management is the process of reducing costs through removing non-value-added activities. **(Learning Objective 6)**
    a. True
    b. False
24. Why do value-added activities differ from non-value-added activities? **(Learning Objective 6)**
    a. Because they consume resources
    b. Because they advance the product or service toward a state of completion
    c. Because they involve material, labor or overhead in the production process
    d. All of the above are true.
25. Which of the following is most likely a value-added activity? **(Learning Objective 6)**
    a. Material purchasing
    b. Machine processing
    c. Inspections
    d. Machine setup

Short Exercises

S:5-1 (Learning Objective 1)

Match the appropriate cost method with the following businesses. Each cost method can be used more than once.

Business	Cost Method
_____ Dairy Farm	A. Traditional Costing
_____ Custom Manufacturer	B. Activity-Based Costing
_____ Accounting Firm	
_____ Large Electronics Manufacturer	

S:5-2 (Learning Objective 2)

Match the appropriate cost driver with each activity. A cost driver can be used more than once.

Activities	Cost Drivers
_____ Design	A. Labor Hours
_____ Packaging and Shipping	B. Machine Hours
_____ Inspections	C. Batches
_____ Assembly	
_____ Robotic Welding	

S:5-3 (Learning Objective 3)

Identify the appropriated cost driver for each activity and compute the activity-based overhead rated for each activity using the cost drivers.

Activity and Estimated Cost	Cost Driver and Estimated Usage
$1,000,000 Machine Processing	100 Batches
$2,000,000 Manual Assembly	100,000 Labor Hours
$250,000 Shipping	12,500 Machine Hours
$50,000 Inspection	50,000 Finished Good Items

S:5-4 (Learning Objective 4)

Shantell Manufacturing Corporation uses and activity-based costing method. Shantell has determined the following activity-based rates.

Machine Processing: $80 per Machine Hour
Manual Assembly: $20 per Labor Hour
Shipping: $5 per Finished Good Item
Inspection: $500 per Batch

Requirement
Compute the cost per unit of a product that is produced in 10 batches and uses 200 machine hours and 600 labor hours for 1,000 finished good units.

S:5-5 (Learning Objective 5)

In a typical cost flow, which of the following would be a reduction to Work-in-process Inventory?

a. The cost of raw material used in the production process
b. The application of overhead
c. The transfer of the cost of a finished production item
d. None of the above

S:5-6 (Learning Objective 6)

ReTreads specialty footwear manufactures sandals from recyclable materials and car tires. ReTreads has the following activities in the manufacturing process: raw material purchasing, material cutting and preparation, assembly and sewing, inspection, packaging, and shipping.

Requirement
Identify which of the following activities are value-added or non-value-added by marking the value-added items (VA) and the non-value-added (NVA).

Activities
_____ Material Purchasing
_____ Footbed forming
_____ Leather Cutting
_____ Leather Hole Punch
_____ Transferring Material-to-work in Process Storage
_____ Sewing
_____ Assembly
_____ Buckle Installation
_____ Test Sizing
_____ Packaging and Shipping

Exercises

E:5-7 (Learning Objective 1)

Describe the difference in the way overhead costs are allocated using a traditional cost system and an activity-based cost system.

E:5-8 (Learning Objective 2)

Describe the benefits and limitations of an activity-based cost system.

E:5-9 (Learning Objective 3)

List the five steps used to implement an activity-based cost system.

E:5-10 (Learning Objective 4)

ReTreads Premium Footwear manufactures and sells two models of sandals made from recycled materials. Cost data for ReTreads Premium Footwear products are as follows:

Product	Direct Labor Hours per Unit	Annual Production	Total Direct Labor Hours
The Woodruff	1.0	5,000 units	5,000
The Pine Hill	1.5	2,000 units	3,000
			8,000

Additional information regarding the products:

The Woodruff $6.00 in direct materials per unit; the Pine Hill requires $7.50 in direct materials per unit.

Direct labor cost is $25 per hour.

Total annual overhead costs amount to $240,000.

Requirement

Compute the predetermined overhead rate for ReTreads Premium Footwear. Total direct labor hours is the cost driver.

E:5-11 (Learning Objective 4)

ReTreads Premium Footwear manufactures and sells two models of sandals made from recycled materials. Cost data for ReTreads Premium Footwear products are as follows:

Product	Direct Labor Hours per Unit	Annual Production	Total Direct Labor Hours
The Woodruff	1.0	5,000 units	5,000
The Pine Hill	1.5	2,000 units	3,000
			8,000

Additional information regarding the products:

The Woodruff $6.00 in direct materials per unit; the Pine Hill requires $7.50 in direct materials per unit.

Direct labor cost is $25 per hour.

Total annual overhead costs amount to $240,000.

Requirement
Compute the cost of the Woodriff and the Pine Hill using a traditional cost method that assumes direct labor hours is the cost driver.

E:5-12 (Learning Objective 4)

ReTreads Premium Footwear manufactures and sells two models of sandals made from recycled materials. Cost data for ReTreads Premium Footwear products are as follows:

Product	Direct Labor Hours per Unit	Annual Production	Total Direct Labor Hours
The Woodruff	1.0	5,000 units	5,000
The Pine Hill	1.5	2,000 units	3,000
			8,000

Additional information regarding the products:

The Woodruff $6.00 in direct materials per unit; the Pine Hill requires $7.50 in direct materials per unit.

Direct labor cost is $25 per hour.

Total annual overhead costs amount to $240,000. The overhead costs are allocated to three cost pools as follows: $80,000 to the cutting and tooling department where costs are driven by machine hours; $120,000 to the assembly department where costs are driven by direct labor hours; and $40,000 to the packaging and shipping department, which also involves testing. Costs for the packaging and shipping department come about when batches are finished.

ReTreads had the following expected activity when producing the Woodruff and the Pine Hill.

	Expected Activity	
Activity Measure	The Woodruff	The Pine Hill
Machine hours	100	300
Direct labor hours	5,000	3,000
Batches Produced	50	30

Requirement
Compute the activity-based overhead rate for cutting and tooling, assembling, and packaging and shipping.

E:5-13 (Learning Objective 4)

ReTreads Premium Footwear manufactures and sells two models of sandals made from recycled materials. Cost data for ReTreads Premium Footwear products are as follows:

Product	Direct Labor Hours per Unit	Annual Production	Total Direct Labor Hours
The Woodruff	1.0	5,000 units	5,000
The Pine Hill	1.5	2,000 units	3,000
			8,000

Additional information regarding the products:

The Woodruff $6.00 in direct materials per unit; the Pine Hill requires $7.50 in direct materials per unit.

Direct labor cost is $25 per hour.

Total annual overhead costs amount to $240,000. The overhead costs are allocated to three cost pools as follows: $80,000 to the cutting and tooling department where costs are driven by machine hours; $120,000 to the assembly department where costs are driven by direct labor hours; and $40,000 to the packaging and shipping department which also involves testing. Costs for the packaging and shipping department come about when batches are finished.

ReTreads had the following expected activity when producing 5,000 units of the Woodruff and 2,000 units of the Pine Hill.

	Expected Activity	
Activity Measure	The Woodruff	The Pine Hill
Machine hours	100	300
Direct labor hours	5,000	3,000
Batches Produced	50	30

Requirement
Compute the cost of the Woodriff and the Pine Hill using an activity-based cost method.

E:5-14 (Learning Objective 5)

Explain how the implementation of activity-based costing can affect a company's pricing.

E:5-15 (Learning Objective 6)

Helix Metal Specialties Incorporate manufactures steel autobody components such as fenders and hoods. Helix contracted with Amos Automotive to produce 90,000 fenders over the next year. That includes production of 500 fenders daily in 250-unit batches. Production includes the following processing steps:

Receive Raw Material	30 min/Batch
Setup	30 min/Batch
Process (Punch & Press)	9 Sec/Fender
Move Processed Part to Paint	10 min/Batch
Paint	11 Sec/Fender
Pack and Ship	45 Sec/Fender

Requirement

Compute value-added and non-value-added time per day in minutes.

Technology, Analytics, and AI

T:5-16 Create Activity Costing Dashboard (Power BI)

Use the file *T5-41 Overhead_Cost_Allocation_Data.xlsx* to create the dashboard.

Smith Corp uses ABC costing to allocate costs from their three primary departments: Assembly, Painting, and Welding, in addition to General Overhead. Smith Corp manufactures two products, named A and B. The company uses various cost drivers to allocate costs and determines the overhead rates at the beginning of the year.

The manufacturing supervisor would like you to create a dashboard to compare the actual costs for the month of January to the costs applied using the overhead rates.

Build a dashboard that is similar to the one shown in the following figure.

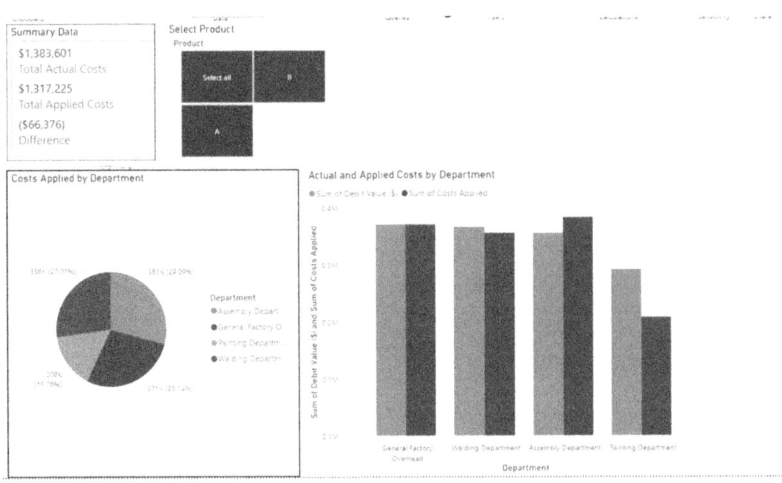

Specifications for the dashboard are as follows:

- The dashboard should include a multiple-line card that summarizes the total actual costs and the total applied costs.
- A pie chart should show the applied costs by department.
- A clustered column chart should compare the actual costs with the applied costs.
- A slicer for Product is used for the pie chart. Note: The actual costs are not tracked by product, so you do not want the slicer on any chart with actual costs.
- Another hint: For the actual costs, use the Debit Value column.
- Format the dashboard in any manner that looks professional or mimics the one shown in the chapter.

Questions to Answer

1. Have the costs been over- or underapplied?
2. What are the total actual costs?
3. For Product A, which department has the highest costs?
4. To which department were the costs underapplied by the greatest amount?

CHAPTER 6

Cost Behavior, the Cost Equation, and Cost-volume-profit Analysis

Learning Objectives

6.1 Describe fixed and variable costs and explain the concept of relevant range.
6.2 Explain the cost equation and use it to perform a cost-volume-profit analysis and compute the break-even point.
6.3 Compute sales required to achieve an earnings target and margin of safety with the break-even formula.
6.4 Use the cost equation to set pricing.
6.5 Explain the concept of operating leverage.
6.6 Describe mixed costs and use the high-low method to separate mixed costs into fixed and variable components of a cost equation.

Accounting in Life

Pixabay / Pexels / Public Domain

Variable costs are not always linear in the real world. For example, production workers typically become more efficient as their workday progresses but become less efficient later in the day or during extended periods of overtime after they become fatigued. You might equate it to a pitcher in baseball. Baseball statisticians scour through volumes of information for data that will help them manage their team more effectively. One question baseball managers have is, "When do you take out a starting pitcher?" A commonly used statistic to measure efficiency in modern-day baseball is OPS (batter on base plus slugging percentage), which measures how often a batter gets on base or hits the ball hard without getting on base. Pitchers are most effective at limiting batters' OPS after warming up and throwing 25 pitches. Still, their effectiveness starts to decline after 50 pitches when the pitcher becomes fatigued (see Figure 6.1).

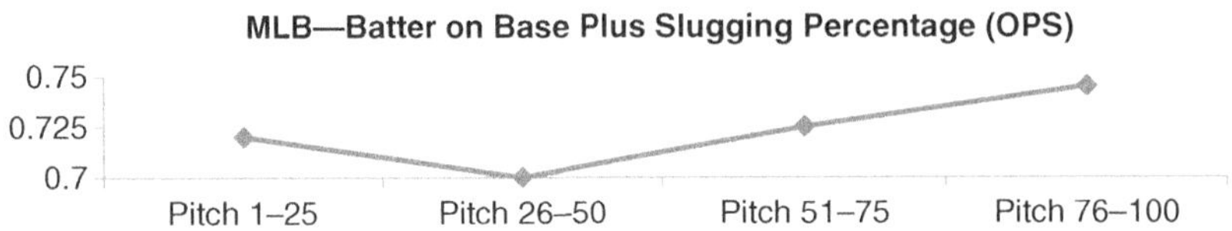

Figure 6.1 Batting percentage.

Let's Review

Judgment and decision-making related to planning, facilitating, and controlling operations often start with a good understanding of the cost of a firm's products or services. We learned in the last chapter that their relationship with the production of a product or service is one way to conceptualize costs. We defined direct costs as those that physically become part of a product or are directly associated with producing a product or performing a service. Indirect costs are costs that are necessary to produce a product or perform a service but are not physically part of the product or performance of the service itself. Indirect costs are commonly called overhead.

LEARNING ACTIVITY 6.1

For each cost listed, identify if it is direct or indirect in a factory.

1. Real estate taxes paid on the factory building.
   a. Direct
   b. Indirect
2. Health insurance costs for production employees.
   a. Direct
   b. Indirect

3. The salary of the production scheduler.
   a. Direct
   b. Indirect
4. The cost of wire used in circuit boards that are part of a product produced in the factory.
   a. Direct
   b. Indirect
5. The cost of shop supplies used to clean up the production area of the factory.
   a. Direct
   b. Indirect

How Do Businesses Identify and Account for Costs at Different Levels of Activity?

Learning Objective 6.1
Describe fixed and variable costs and explain the concept of relevant range.

In the previous chapter, we categorized costs based on their relationship with a product or service. We used that information to determine what products cost. However, the relationship between costs and products does not always stay the same as businesses produce or provide more or less service to customers, some costs remain constant, some costs vary, and some display both behaviors. Another useful way to conceptualize and categorize costs is by their relationship with business activity. In this section, we examine *fixed* and *variable costs.*

Fixed Costs

Fixed costs are costs that are constant, regardless of activity. For example, a production supervisor might be paid a monthly salary rather than an hourly wage. The monthly salary is a fixed cost because it does not change from period to period. The cost of equipment and assets are also considered fixed costs. Businesses usually expense assets over their useful life and that expense typically stays constant from month to month; thus, the cost of equipment is a fixed cost. Although total fixed costs remain constant, the amount of fixed costs attributable to each unit of output declines as a business produces more units. For example, if the **Ford Motor Company's** Dearborn Truck factory in Dearborn, Michigan, employs robots to assemble the Ford F150 pickup truck, the cost of the robots is spread across the trucks they assemble. The more they assemble, the more the costs are divided. Thus, the fixed cost per unit decreases as production increases and fixed cost per unit increases as production decreases. Figure 6.2 and Table 6.1 illustrate the cost behavior for fixed costs that remain constant regardless of the number of units produced and decline per unit as the number of units increases.

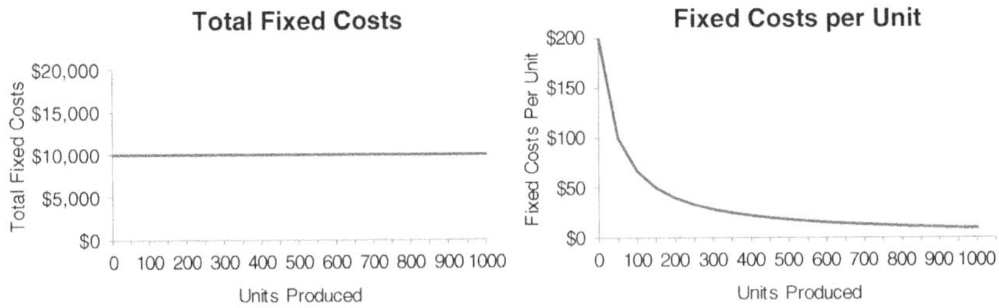

Figure 6.2 Total fixed cost and fixed cost per unit graphs.

Table 6.1 Total Fixed Cost and Fixed Cost per Unit Data

Total Fixed Costs	Number of Units Produced	Fixed Cost per Unit
$10,000	0 units	$10,000
10,000	50 units	$ 200
10,000	100 units	$ 100
10,000	1,000 units	$ 10

Remember this important fact about fixed costs: Total fixed costs remain constant, but fixed cost per unit decreases as more units are produced.

LEARNING ACTIVITY 6.2

Which statement is correct regarding fixed costs?

a. Total fixed costs increase as production decreases; fixed cost per unit stays constant as production decreases.
b. Total fixed costs stay constant as production decreases; fixed cost per unit increases as production decreases.
c. Total fixed costs stay constant as production decreases; fixed cost per unit decreases as production decreases.
d. None of the above is true.

Variable Costs

Variable costs are costs that fluctuate with business activity. For example, the hourly wage paid to assembly line workers is a variable cost. The cost of assembly line labor increases or decreases in correlation with changes in production. Employees might be sent home when production declines and recalled when the need for production returns. However, the number of labor hours needed to produce each unit of product is generally stable. Thus, the labor cost per individual unit stays constant. Variable costs per unit remain constant regardless of sales volume. For example, many college students elect to purchase a meal plan from their university. Is the cost of a meal plan a fixed or variable cost? The cost you pay for a meal plan is usually fixed as the plan offers a defined number of meals for one set price. How much more is the cost per meal on a meal plan if the student only eats half the meals during a semester? The cost per meal is twice as much if the student only eats half the meals. Figure 6.3 and Table 6.2 illustrate variable cost behavior. Total variable costs increase as units produced rise, as indicated by the upward slope. Variable cost per unit remains constant regardless of production volume, as indicated by the horizontal cost line.

Table 6.3 shows examples of diverse types of fixed and variable costs for a factory.

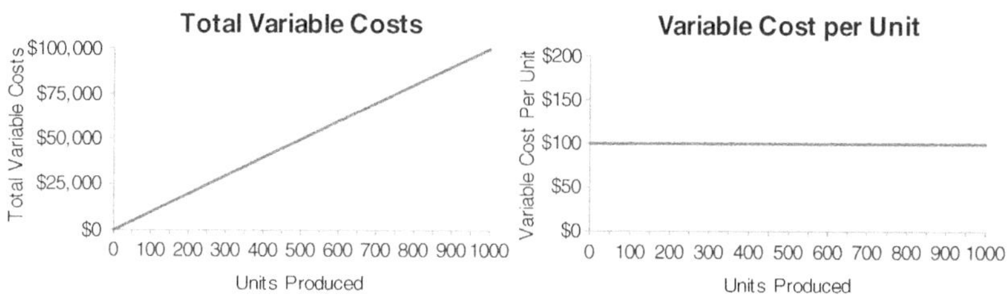

Figure 6.3 Total variable cost and variable cost per unit graphs.

Table 6.2 Total Variable Cost and Variable Cost per Unit Data

Number of Units Produced	Variable Cost per Unit	Total Variable Cost
0 units	$100	$ 0
50 units	100	$ 5,000
100 units	100	$ 10,000
1,000 units	100	$100,000

Table 6.3 Examples of Fixed and Variable Costs

	Definition	Examples
Fixed Cost	A cost that remains the same *in total*, regardless of changes over the relevant range.	Production supervisor's salary Depreciation Property taxes on factory
Variable Cost	A cost that increases or decreases *in total* in direct proportion to increases or decreases in the volume of activity.	Wages of line workers Raw materials

Remember this important fact about variable costs: Total variable cost fluctuates with changes in volume, but variable cost per unit remains constant.

LEARNING ACTIVITY 6.3

Which statement is correct regarding variable costs?

a. Total variable costs decrease as production decreases; variable cost per unit stays constant as production decreases.
b. Total variable costs stay constant as production decreases; variable cost per unit increases as production decreases.
c. Total variable costs stay constant as production decreases; variable cost per unit decreases as production decreases.
d. None of the above is true.

Relevant Range and Step Costs

Fixed and variable cost behavior holds within a range of production or business activity called the **relevant range**. For example, the cost of production equipment is typically fixed, but the equipment has limited production capacity. Consider the cost of robotics used in a factory setting. A robot can work 24 hours a day, seven days a week, but no more. Once customers demand more products than the robot can produce, the business must either refuse further sales or add another robot to create capacity. This is an example of **step costs**, which are costs that are constant within a range of activity but increase to a higher level once the range is exceeded. The fixed cost steps up from the cost of one robot to the cost of two. Fixed cost per unit also steps up as the new fixed cost is added to the existing fixed costs. The fixed cost per unit declines again as production volume increases. Figure 6.4 illustrates fixed cost behavior as it exceeds the relevant range and steps up. Notice that total fixed costs remain constant at a given level, whereas fixed costs per unit decrease as more units are produced.

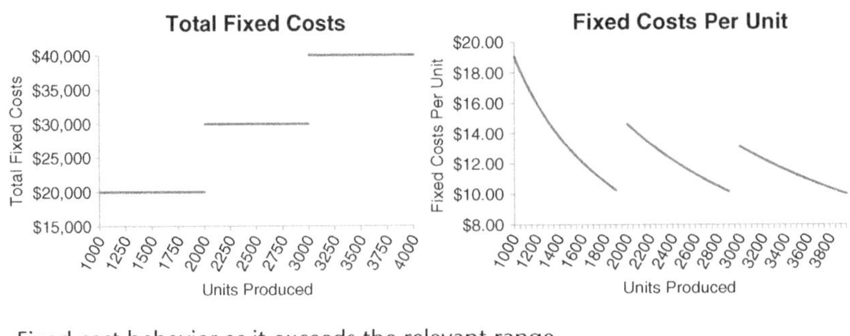

Figure 6.4 Fixed cost behavior as it exceeds the relevant range.

LEARNING ACTIVITY 6.4

Classify each of the following costs as either fixed or variable.

	Fixed, Variable
1. Depreciation of factory equipment	Fixed, Variable
2. Raw material	Fixed, Variable
3. Property taxes paid on a factory	Fixed, Variable
4. Component parts purchased from a vendor	Fixed, Variable
5. The CEO's salary	Fixed, Variable
6. Assembly line workers' wages	Fixed, Variable
7. Depreciation of office equipment	Fixed, Variable
8. Factory insurance	Fixed, Variable

How Do Businesses Use Fixed and Variable Costs to Manage Business Activity?

Learning Objective 6.2

Explain the cost equation and use it to perform a cost-volume-profit analysis and compute the break-even point.

Businesses analyze fixed and variable costs when making decisions. In this section, we look at how to calculate the total amount of a business's expenses, considering both fixed and variable costs.

Cost Equation

One of the most important tools for evaluating business performance is the cost equation. A **cost equation** is a mathematical function that companies use to predict the total amount of expenses that are associated with the sale and production of goods at a specified level. The cost equation is also an analytical tool that companies use to

- estimate costs and profits,
- determine at what level the company "breaks even" (the point when costs and profits are equal), and
- figure out how much the business must sell to meet an earnings target.

In the cost equation, total costs are depicted as total fixed costs plus the variable cost per unit times the units produced.

Fixed Costs + (Variable Cost per Unit × Units Produced) = Total Costs

Let us illustrate by looking at Sharp's Daylily Farm, a producer of fresh flowers for flower shops around their region. Sharp's daylilies have won awards around the country and are sold at a premium price of $0.48 per stem and in bundles of 100. Sharp's estimates a direct variable cost of $8 per bundle made up of direct labor to clip, prune, and package each bundle, the cost of the packaging; and the shipping fee. A large part of Sharp's costs is the cost of the property, greenhouses, and greenhouse equipment initially purchased at a price of $200,000, usable for 20 years, resulting in an annual fixed cost of $10,000 when the costs are spread over the useful life. Furthermore, Sharp's pays approximately $40,000 in fixed labor for an office manager each year. Sharp's total fixed cost is $50,000. If Sharps produced 5,000 bundles, the expected total costs are as follows:

Fixed Costs + (Variable Cost per Unit × Units Produced) = Total Costs
$50,000 + ($8 per Bundle × Bundles Produced) = Total Costs
$50,000 + ($8 per Bundle × 5,000) = $90,000

The fixed costs of $50,000 are composed of the $10,000 in annual costs for the property, greenhouse, and greenhouse equipment, along with the $40,000 for the office manager. The variable cost of $40,000 is composed of the variable cost of a bundle ($8), times the number of bundles produced (5,000).

Nikolay Danilov / Pexels / Public Domain

Cost-volume-profit Analysis

Businesses constantly monitor their costs and profits to track progress toward meeting objectives. In this section, we outline the analysis businesses undertake to make decisions about the product sales levels needed to cover costs and generate profit. Companies use the cost equation to perform cost-volume-profit analysis and compute a *break-even point.*

Cost-volume-profit (CVP) analysis is the study of the change in costs relative to the change in production volume. The **break-even point** is the sales level where total costs equal total sales dollars, and thus no profit is earned.

We begin with the assumptions that underpin cost-volume-profit analysis. Then, we will look at it graphically and calculate it with an equation. Several assumptions underlie cost-volume-profit analysis:

- Change in volume is the only factor that affects costs.
- Cost and revenue behave in a linear fashion.
- All costs are classified as either fixed or variable.
- All units produced are also sold.
- Sales mix remains constant when a company sells more than one product.

Cost-volume-profit Model

A cost-volume-profit graph illustrates a firm's cost structure and the break-even point. Examine the model in Figure 6.5 to learn about the key elements of the cost-volume-profit model and the underlying equation.

Associated Cost Equation: $500 + ($0.20 × Units Sold) = Total Cost

Cost-volume-profit Example with the Break-even Point

Let us look at another example using the automobile manufacturer we introduced in Chapter 2. The manufacturer wants to determine its break-even point. This analysis requires using cost-volume-profit analysis and developing an equation to calculate break-even.

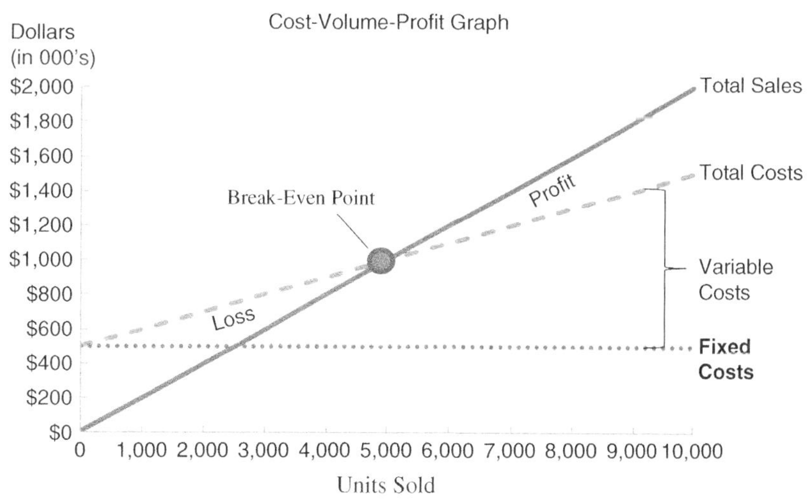

Figure 6.5 Cost-volume-profit model and equation.

During July, the manufacturer produced 10,000 cars. The manufacturer supplies each car it produces to dealers at a price of $20,000 per car. Total direct material cost and conversion cost (labor and overhead) incurred during the period were $43.75 million and $80.8 million, respectively. All the direct material is a variable cost, while $55.8 million of the conversion cost is variable. Variable conversion costs consist of direct labor and variable overhead, such as the variable electricity cost calculated earlier, supplies, maintenance, and repair, and other costs related to producing cars that vary with production and sales volume. The remaining $25 million of conversion cost is a fixed cost and consists of things like depreciation on the factory and factory equipment, salaries of production management and administration, insurance, and real estate taxes on the factory. The following table details the sales and cost information for the company:

	Total	Per Unit
Sales Price	$200 million	$20,000 per car
Variable Costs	99.55 million	9,955 per car
Fixed Costs	25 million	

To determine the break-even point for the automobile manufacturer, we will first need to create an equation that calculates total operating profit. Net sales revenue is the selling price per car multiplied by the number of cars sold during July. It amounts to $200 million ($20,000 per car × 10,000 cars). Fixed costs are $25 million.

$$\textbf{Net Sales Revenue} - \textbf{Fixed Costs} - \textbf{Variable Costs} = \textbf{Operating Profit}$$
$$(\$20{,}000 \textbf{ per car} \times 10{,}000 \textbf{ cars}) - \$25{,}000{,}000 - \textbf{Variable Costs} = \textbf{Operating Profit}$$
$$\$200{,}000{,}000 - \$25{,}000{,}000 - \textbf{Variable Costs} = \textbf{Operating Profit}$$

The equation requires variable cost data. Variable costs are $99.55 million for the 10,000 cars produced and consist of $43.75 million of direct material and $55.8 million of conversion cost. Since variable costs fluctuate with volume, it is important to compute the variable cost per unit. In July, $99.55 million in variable costs divided by 10,000 cars sold equals a total variable cost of $9,955 per car. Now that we have the variable costs data, we can complete the total operating profit equation. The operating profit for the manufacturer in July was $75,450,000, computed by subtracting the fixed costs ($25 million) and the variable costs ($99.55 million) from the net sales revenue of $200 million.

$$\textbf{Net Sales Revenue} - \textbf{Fixed Costs} - \textbf{Variable Costs} = \textbf{Operating Profit}$$
$$\$200{,}000{,}000 - \$25{,}000{,}000 - \$99{,}550{,}000 = \$75{,}450{,}000$$

With the operating profit information in hand, we have the inputs for the cost-volume-profit equation. The cost equation for the automobile factory is as follows:

Fixed Costs + Variable Cost per Unit (Units Produced) = Total Costs

\$25,000,000 + \$9,955 (Units Produced) = Total Costs

Total Costs

Net Sales Revenue – Fixed Costs – Variable Costs = Operating Profit

\$124,550,000

\$200,000,000 – \$25,000,000 – \$99,550,000 = \$75,450,000

\$20,000 × 10,000 Cars **\$9,955 × 10,000 Cars**

Computing the number of cars that need to be sold to break even requires using an expanded cost equation and *setting operating profit to \$0*. The break-even point in terms of unit quantity is approximately 2,489 cars (rounded to whole units) computed as follows:

Net Sales Revenue – Fixed Costs – Variable Costs	=	**Operating Profit**
(Price per Unit × Units Sold) –FC – (VC per Unit × Units Sold)	=	**Operating Profit**
(\$20,000 per Car × Cars Sold)–\$25,000,000 – (\$9,955 per Car × Cars Sold)	=	**\$0**
((\$20,000 per Car – \$9,955 per Car) × Cars Sold) – \$25,000,000	=	**\$0**
\$10,045 per Car × Cars Sold	=	**\$25,000,000**
Cars Sold	=	**\$25,000,000/\$10,045**
Cars Sold	=	**2,489 cars (rounded)**

Now that we know the break-even point in units, we can calculate the sales dollars required to break even. The sales dollars required to break even is the break-even units times the sales price (2,489 units × \$20,000), resulting in total break-even sales of \$49.78 million.

Sales Price per Unit × Break-even Units = Sales Dollars at Breakeven
\$20,000 per Car × 2,489 Cars = \$49,780,000

Breakeven is the point where total costs equal total revenues.

LEARNING ACTIVITY 6.5

Hudson Textiles expects to produce 500,000 garments during the next year. Sales and cost information are expected to be as follows:

Sales	$6,000,000
Variable costs	3,200,000
Fixed costs	1,960,000

Develop a cost equation and compute Hudson's break-even point in units and sales dollars.

1. Hudson's break-even point in garments sold is
   a. 500,000 garments.
   b. 350,000 garments.
   c. 240,000 garments.
   d. none of the above.
2. Hudson's break-even point in sales dollars is
   a. $4,200,000.
   b. $3,000,000.
   c. $1,240,000.
   d. none of the above.

Contribution Margin and the Contribution Margin Approach

Managers can use cost-volume-profit analysis to make decisions involving how much product needs to be sold to cover fixed costs and create a profit. One of the main metrics managers use is the contribution margin, the difference between net sales revenue and total variable costs. The **contribution margin** represents the amount remaining after deducting total variable costs from net sales that is available to pay for fixed costs; the amount remaining after covering fixed costs contributes to profit.

Net Sales – Variable Costs = Contribution Margin

To illustrate, recall the automobile manufacturer in the previous example. The company had the following sales and costs:

	Total	Per Unit
Sales Price	$200 million	$20,000 per car
Variable Costs	99.55 million	9,955 per car
Fixed Costs	25 million	

The contribution margin is $100.45 million ($200 million – $99.55 million) at 10,000 units sold.

Net Sales – Variable Costs	=	**Contribution Margin**
$200,000,000 – $99,550,000	=	**$100,450,000**

Contribution margin is particularly useful when it is computed on a per-unit basis and in a ratio. **Unit contribution margin** is the difference between net sales price per unit and the variable cost per unit. It is commonly used to evaluate incremental profits or potential profits from each additional unit sold. Contribution margin per unit for the automobile manufacturer is as follows:

Net Sales per Car – Variable Cost per Car	=	**Contribution Margin per Car**
$20,000 per Car – $9,955 per Car	=	**$10,045 per Car**

We can use contribution margin per unit to compute break-even sales in units. In the automobile manufacturer example, we divide total fixed costs of $25 million by the contribution margin per unit of $10,045 per car for a breakeven of approximately 2,489 cars. At a sales price of $20,000 per car, which equals $49,780,000 in total sales dollars.

Fixed Costs/Contribution Margin per Car	=	**Break-even Sales**
$250,000,000/$10,045	=	**2,489 Cars (rounded)**

Contribution margin ratio is the proportion of contribution margin to net sales revenue. To calculate the contribution margin ratio, divide the total contribution margin by the total net sales revenue or divide the contribution margin per unit by the net sales per unit. The contribution margin ratio for the automobile manufacturer is as follows:

Contribution Margin/Net Sales Revenue	=	**Contribution Margin Ratio**
$100,450,000/$200,000,000	=	**50.23% (rounded)**

Or

Contribution Margin per Car/Net Sales per Car	=	**Contribution Margin Ratio**
$10,045/$20,000	=	**50.23% (rounded)**

The **contribution margin ratio** is the percentage of each dollar of sales that is available to cover fixed costs and contribute to profit. It is useful for evaluating the relative performance of business activities of varied sizes and volumes. To illustrate, consider the 50.23% contribution margin ratio for an automobile that we calculated. What if the factory could produce an alternative car that sells for $30,000 with a contribution margin of $12,000 per car? The total contribution margin of $12,000 per car is greater than $10,045 per car, but the contribution margin of the alternative car is only 40% ($12,000/$30,000), suggesting the alternative car produces less profit per sales dollar than the car currently produced. An ultimate decision on which car would be more profitable to produce requires more information, but contribution margin ratio is the foundation for that decision. We will evaluate this type of decision-making further in Chapter 7.

We can also use the contribution margin ratio to calculate the break-even point in sales dollars. Dividing fixed costs by the contribution margin ratio will result in a break-even point in sales dollars. Dividing fixed costs of $25 million by the contribution margin ratio of 50.23% results in a break-even point of $49,780,000 in sales. This matches the result we found when we used the break-even formula earlier.

Fixed Costs/Contribution Margin Ratio	=	**Break-even Sales**
$250,000,000/50.23%	=	**$49,780,000 (rounded)**

Contribution margin is the difference between sales and variable costs. Products with a negative contribution margin should be avoided.

LEARNING ACTIVITY 6.6

Continuing the Hudson Textiles example, recall that Hudson expects to produce 500,000 garments during the next year. Expected sales and cost information are as follows:

Sales	$6,000,000
Variable costs	3,200,000
Fixed costs	1,960,000

a. Compute Hudson's contribution margin.
b. Compute Hudson's contribution margin per garment.
c. Compute Hudson's break-even point in garments using the contribution margin per garment.

ACCOUNTING IN BUSINESS

Cost control at Steffes, LLC.

At Steffes, LLC, cost control is crucial to managing the supply chain, and electric utility cost control is also the basis for marketing the company's line of electric thermal storage heating products. "Electric thermal storage (ETS) heating products store energy in the form of heat. Our ETS systems consume electricity when demand on the electrical grid is low.

The electricity is used to satisfy current heating needs and is stored to satisfy future heating needs when demand on the electrical grid is high," says Connie Aman, customer support manager. "Electric utilities commonly offer lower rates for consuming electricity at off-peak times or charge a rate for supplying enough electricity to meet a customer's demand needs. Our systems offer customers an opportunity to save money by using off-peak rates and controlling peak demand." By determining a potential customer's cost of electric consumption and demand, Steffes' sales personnel can create a cost equation that can be used to estimate total electrical costs for the customer after installing a Steffes ETS system. They can then compare current electricity costs against the estimate to show how much the customer would save if they purchased and installed a Steffes ETS heating system.

Ruvim / Pexels / Public Domain

Source: Author Interview with Jim Deichert, Business Unit Manager at Steffes, LLC.

How Do Managers Use Break-even Analyses to Facilitate Business Decisions?

Learning Objective 6.3
Use the break-even formula to compute the sales required to achieve an earnings target and margin of safety.

In this section, we look at how businesses use break-even analysis to inform decision-making. We focus on two concepts: *target profit* and *margin of safety*.

Target Profit

The calculation of target profit is one way that businesses use the break-even formula to make business decisions. **Target profit** is the profit that remains after deducting fixed and variable costs from net sales. The break-even formula is used to calculate target profit. Yet, rather than computing the point where total sales and total costs are equal, we calculate the point where total sales equal total costs *plus* target profit. This helps businesses identify sales needed to meet a profit objective.

$$\text{Net Sales} - \text{Fixed Costs} - \text{Variable Costs} = \text{Target Profit}$$

Let us illustrate using the automobile manufacturing company example. The company wants to determine how many cars it needs to sell to meet its target profit. Assume the company is targeting a profit of $30 million in July. The automobile company would compute the amount of sales needed to reach the target profit as net sales ($20,000 per Car × Cars Sold) less fixed costs ($25 million) less variable costs ($9,955 per Car × Cars Sold) equaling target profit of $30 million. After determining the target profit, the business determines the specific number of units required to meet this level. We show the calculation with the cost equation approach and contribution margin approach.

<u>Cost Equation Approach</u>

$$\left(\begin{matrix}\text{Sales Price per Car} \times \\ \text{Cars Sold}\end{matrix}\right) - \text{Fixed Costs} - \left(\begin{matrix}\text{Variable Cost per Car} \times \\ \text{Cars Sold}\end{matrix}\right) = \text{Target Profit}$$

$$\left(\begin{matrix}\$20{,}000 \text{ per Car} \times \\ \text{Cars Sold}\end{matrix}\right) - 25{,}000{,}000 - \left(\begin{matrix}9{,}955 \text{ per Car} \times \\ \text{Cars Sold}\end{matrix}\right) = \$30{,}000{,}000$$

$$\$10{,}045 \text{ per Car} \times \text{Cars Sold} = \$55{,}000{,}000$$

$$\text{Cars Sold} = \$55{,}000{,}000/\$10{,}045 \text{ per Car}$$

$$\text{Units Required to be Sold to Meet the Target Profit} = 5{,}475 \text{ Cars}$$

<u>Contribution Margin Approach</u>

$$\begin{aligned}\begin{matrix}\text{Units Required to be Sold to} \\ \text{Meet the Target Profit}\end{matrix} &= \frac{\text{Fixed Costs} + \text{Target Profit}}{\text{Contribution Margin per Car}} \\ &= \frac{\$25{,}000{,}000 + \$30{,}000{,}000}{\$10{,}045 \text{ per Car}} \\ &= 5{,}475 \text{ Cars}\end{aligned}$$

<u>Contribution Margin Ratio Approach</u>

$$\begin{aligned}\begin{matrix}\text{Sales Required to Meet} \\ \text{the Target Profit}\end{matrix} &= \frac{\text{Fixed Costs} + \text{Target Profit}}{\text{Contribution Margin Ratio}} \\ &= \frac{25{,}000{,}000 + \$30{,}000{,}000}{50.23\%} \\ &= \$109{,}496{,}317 \text{ (rounded)}\end{aligned}$$

ACCOUNTING IN BUSINESS

Setting Sales Targets at Hokulia Shaved Ice

David McBee / Pexels / Public Domain

At Hokulia Shaved Ice in Parker, Colorado, Owner Galen Hafla uses his understanding of cost behavior to estimate potential profit, set targets, and manage his workforce. "Most of my costs in the store are fixed and labor is my biggest expense. Each employee is paid an hourly wage during their shift, regardless of whether they sell any product. The costs of the shaved ice products themselves are relatively small and include the costs of the ice, syrup, cups, and spoons. There is a certain amount of profit margin in each shaved ice we sell. The more an employee sells during his or her shift, the more money I have available to cover his or her wages and contribute to paying for the store itself. Hopefully, there is something left for me after that."

Hafla sets sales targets for each shift in his store and communicates the targets with his shift workers. "First and foremost, I need to get foot traffic into my store," says Hafla. "Each shift, depending on the time of day, has a sales target, and employees are incentivized if they meet and exceed it."

Source: Author Interview with Galen Hafla, Owner of Hokulia Shaved Ice.

LEARNING ACTIVITY 6.7

Continuing the Hudson Textiles example, note that Hudson expects to produce 500,000 garments during the next year. The associated sales and cost information are as follows:

Sales	$6,000,000
Variable costs	3,200,000
Fixed costs	1,960,000

Compute how many units Hudson must sell to reach a target profit of $700,000.

Margin of Safety

Businesses also use cost-volume-profit analysis to determine a company's margin of safety or the difference between expected sales and break-even sales. **Margin of safety** represents the amount by which sales can decrease before the company fails to reach break-even. For managers, the margin of safety is a measure of risk.

Expected Sales – Break-even Sales = Unit Margin of Safety

Let us continue with the automobile manufacturer example and assume that expected sales are 3,110 cars, given a breakeven of 2,489 cars. The margin of safety is 621 cars.

Expected Sales – Break-even Sales = Unit Margin of Safety
3,110 Cars – 2,489 Cars = 621 Cars

This analysis suggests that sales could be 621 cars below expectations before the company would not break even. The margin of safety is also commonly converted into a percentage. The **margin of safety percentage** is the percentage by which sales could decrease before the company fails to break even. It is computed by dividing the unit margin of safety by the expected unit sales. The result is 20% (621/3,110).

Expected Sales		Break-even Sales		Unit Margin of Safety
3,110 Cars	–	2,489 Cars	=	621 Cars

Unit Margin of Safety		Expected Sales		Margin of Safety Percentage
621 Cars	/	3,110	=	20% (rounded)

Margin of safety measures risk as the percentage sales can fall before the firm fails to reach break-even sales using a given cost structure.

LEARNING ACTIVITY 6.8

Continuing the Hudson Textiles example, note that Hudson expects to produce 400,000 garments during the next year and the breakeven in sales is 350,000 garments.

a. Compute Hudson's margin of safety, in the number of garments if Hudson projects sales of 400,000 garments (or $4.8 million).
b. Compute Hudson's margin of safety percentage.

How Do Managers Use the Cost Equation to Set Selling Prices?

Learning Objective 6.4
Use the cost equation to set pricing.

Managers commonly use cost-volume-profit analysis to set sales prices. We learned that total sales are a function of both sales price and the quantity of items sold.

Total Sales = (Sales Price per Unit × Units Sold)

To use the sales computation within the cost equation to estimate the sales price needed to break even, or meet a desired level of earnings, we must estimate the number of units expected to be sold. Let us continue to illustrate using the automobile manufacturing company example and examine the effects of changes in sales price. Once again, assume that fixed costs are $25 million and variable costs are $9,955 per car. At what sales price will the company break even if it sells 6.250 cars? The break-even calculation using the cost equation approach is as follows:

<u>Cost Equation Approach</u>

Total Sales	–	**Fixed Costs**	–	**Variable Costs**	=	**Breakeven**
(Price per Car × Cars Sold)	–	**Fixed Costs**	–	**(Var. Cost per Car × Cars Sold)**	=	**Breakeven**
(Price per Car × 6.250)	–	**$25,000,000**	–	**($9,955 per Car × 6.250)**	=	**$0**
(Price per Car × 6.250)	–	**$25,000,000**	–	**($62,218,750)**	=	**$0**

Sales Price per Car × 6.250 Cars = $87,218,750
Sales Price per Car Required to Break Even = $87,218,750/6,250 Cars
Sales Price per Car Required to Break Even = $13,955 Cars

The company would have to sell its cars for $13,955 to break even. At what price would it need to sell the same amount of cars to make a profit of $20,000,000?

Cost Equation Approach

$$\left(\begin{matrix}\text{Price per Car} \times \\ \text{Cars Sold}\end{matrix}\right) - \text{Fixed Costs} - \left(\begin{matrix}\text{Var. Cost per Car} \times \\ \text{Cars Sold}\end{matrix}\right) = \text{Target Profit}$$

$$\left(\begin{matrix}\text{Price per Car} \times \\ 6{,}250\end{matrix}\right) - \$25{,}000{,}000 - \left(\begin{matrix}\$9{,}955 \text{ per Car} \times \\ 6{,}250\end{matrix}\right) = \$20{,}000{,}000$$

$$\left(\begin{matrix}\text{Price per Car} \times \\ 6{,}250\end{matrix}\right) - \$25{,}000{,}000 - (\$62{,}218{,}750) = \$20{,}000{,}000$$

Sales Price per Car × 6,250 Cars = $107,218,750
Sales Price per Car = $107,218,750/6,250 Cars
Sales Price per Car Required to Meet Target Profit = $17,155 Cars

Increasing the sales price to $17,155 from $13,955 will result in $20,000,000 in additional profit if the company continues to sell 6,250 cars. However, the sales price will usually influence the number of units a company sells. Thus, a company will usually try to optimize sales price and volume to reach the optimal profit.

The cost equation can be used to evaluate the effects of changes in sales price for a given sales volume. Since sales price can influence the number of units sold, businesses should optimize their pricing and volume to reach an optimal profit.

LEARNING ACTIVITY 6.9

ReTreads Premium Footwear, a manufacturer of sandals made from recycled materials, produces a model made with hemp uppers called the Wooderson. Each pair of Woodersons takes 1 hour to produce by a skilled artisan making $35 per hour. The raw material and variable overhead costs for a pair of Woodersons are $15 and $20 per pair, respectively. ReTreads' fixed costs associated with the Wooderson are $100,000.

a. How much does ReTreads need to charge per pair of Woodersons to break even, assuming it can sell 2,500 pairs?
b. How much must does ReTreads need to charge per pair of Woodersons to make a profit of $100,000, assuming it can sell 2,500 pairs?

ACCOUNTING IN BUSINESS

The iPhone Price Drop

Setting the right price is one of the most difficult and important decisions a firm can make. Reduced margins and lost profits are the result if a firm sets prices too low. On the other hand, customers may not purchase at all if prices are set too high. **Apple** surprised the world with the launch of the iPhone 11. Pressured by market competition, **Apple** launched the new model in September 2019 at a lower price than its predecessor. "Pricing for the iPhone 11, which we expect to be the highest-selling model by volume, was $50 below the iPhone XR that it replaced," said KeyBanc Capital analyst Andy Hargreaves. Apple hopes to generate enough additional sales to outweigh the revenue lost by the lower price.

Source: Maccardax, M. (2019). Apple iPhone pricing could trim margins, but 1.4 billion base remains compelling. *The Street* [online]. Available at: https://www.thestreet.com/investing/stocks/apple-iphone-pricing-could-trim-margins-but-1-4-billion-base-remains-compelling-15085804?puc=yahoo&cm_ven=YAHOO&yptr=yahoo

Is It Beneficial for a Business to Replace Variable Costs with Fixed Costs?

Learning Objective 6.5
Explain the concept of operating leverage.

The balance between fixed and variable costs is a critical decision that business managers make that affects operating leverage. **Operating leverage** is the degree to which a business increases profits when it increases sales or vice versa. The **degree of operating leverage ratio** is computed by dividing operating income by the total contribution margin.

$$\text{Degree of Operating Leverage} = \frac{\text{Contribution Margin}}{\text{Operating Income}}$$

Higher operating leverage usually means more risk, but that depends on a number of factors, including stability in the company's sales. Let us explore operating leverage in more detail.

Operating Leverage Ratio Calculation

Let us illustrate the degree of operating leverage ratio calculation using the automobile manufacturer example. Recalling the projected sales to meet the target profit was 3,110 cars, the sales price of each car is $20,000, variable costs are $9,955 per car, and fixed costs are $25 million. We compute the degree of operating leverage by first calculating the total contribution margin at the expected or targeted sales amount of $31,239,950 as follows: 3,110 cars times the contribution margin per car of $10,045. The next step is to divide that figure by operating profit of $6,239,950 (total contribution margin of $31,239,950 – fixed costs of $25,000,000). The result is 5.0064. Therefore, a $1 dollar change in sales will result in a $5.0064 dollar change in operating income.

$$\textbf{Degree of Operating Leverage} = \frac{\textbf{Contribution Margin}}{\textbf{Operating Income}}$$

$$= \frac{(\textbf{3,110 cars} \times \textbf{\$10,045 per car})}{\textbf{\$6,239,950}}$$

$$= \frac{\textbf{\$31,239,950}}{\textbf{\$6,239,950}}$$

$$= \textbf{5.0064 (rounded)}$$

Let us perform an analysis to test that conclusion. Recall that projected sales of 3,110 cars are expected to result in an operating profit of $6,239,950. Let's test the operating profit if we have sales that are 10% above the projection. Using the degree of operating leverage as a multiplier, we would expect that an increase in sales of 10% would result in a 50.064% increase in operating profit. If we compute profits at the 10% higher sales level, 3,421 cars or $68,420,000 in sales dollars, the results show a change in profits from $6,239,950 to $9,363,945, an increase of 50.064%, confirming our conclusion about the degree of operating leverage.

	Projected Sales (A) (3,110 Cars)	Percent Change	Projected Sales (B) (3,421 Cars)
Estimated Sales (Cars Sold × $20,000)	$62,200,000	10%	$68,420,000
Variable Costs (Cars Sold × $9,955)	30,960,050		34,056,055
Contribution Margin	31,239,950		34,363,945
Fixed Costs	25,000,000		25,000,000
Operating Income	$ 6,239,950	50.064%	$ 9,363,945

Increasing Operating Leverage

Organizations can increase their operating leverage ratio by replacing variable costs with fixed costs. For example, the automobile manufacturer might consider replacing manual labor with robotic labor. Robots require a large upfront investment, a fixed cost, but replace the variable cost of production labor. Since fixed costs remain constant, a company with more operating leverage will have greater increases in profits relative to increases in sales compared to a company with less operating leverage. Conversely, a company can have larger losses if sales decline. More leverage equals more risk, yet more risk can equal more reward. Companies in stable industries where sales are less likely to have large fluctuation are more likely to utilize additional operating leverage than companies in less stable environments.

Motor Group / Pexels / Public Domain

Operating Leverage Analysis

Let us illustrate the effects of operating leverage on the cost equation, breakeven, and potential profits and losses. Suppose the automobile manufacturer is considering investing in robotics to lower its variable production labor costs. Let us look at the cost equation at present and with the proposed changes. Figure 6.6 represents the status quo cost equation for the automotive manufacturer we have been using in our examples. The fixed costs are $25 million, variable cost per car is $9,955, and the break-even point is $49,780,000 in sales or 2,489 cars sold. Using the cost equation to estimate profits at sales levels of 1,000 and 9,000 units, we find an estimated *loss* of $14,955,000 at 1,000 units sold and an estimated *profit* of $65,405,000 at 9,000 units sold.

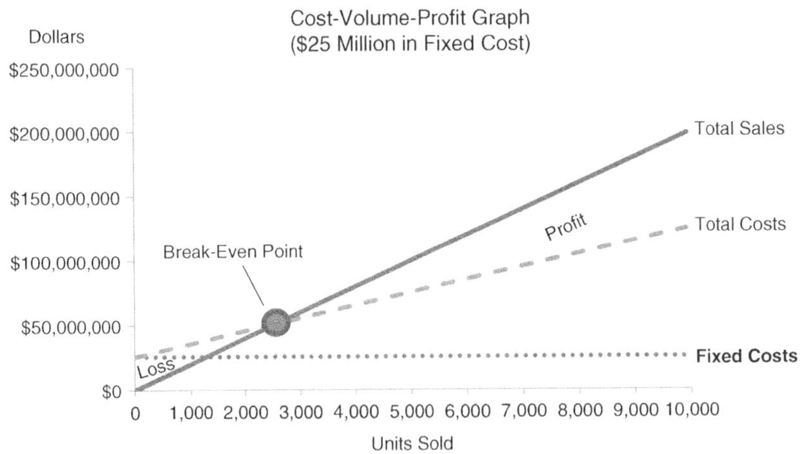

Figure 6.6 Cost volume profit graph at status quo.

Let's look at the Figure 6.6 calculations:

Break-even Point

Fixed Costs + Variable Cost per Car (Cars Sold) = Sales Price per Car (Cars Sold)
$25,000,000 + ($9,955 per Car × Cars Sold) = ($20,000 per Car × Cars Sold)
Break-even Point = 2,489 Units = 2,489 ($20,000) = $49,780,000

Potential Profit (or Loss) at 1,000 Cars Sold

Total Sales Revenue – Fixed Costs –Variable Costs = Profit (Loss)
($20,000 per Car × 1,000 Cars) – $25,000,000 –
($9,955 per Car × 1,000 Cars) = ($14,955,000)

Potential Profit (or Loss) at 9,000 Units Sold

Total Sales Revenue – Fixed Costs –Variable Costs = Profit (Loss)
($20,000 per Unit × 9,000 Units) – $25,000,000 –
($9,955 per Unit × 9,000) = $65,405,000

Figure 6.7 represents the cost equation for the automotive manufacturer after investing an additional $25 million in robotics to replace much of the direct labor and manual conversion of raw material into finished cars. The $25 million investment doubles fixed costs from $25 million to $50 million. Therefore, let us hypothetically estimate that the variable cost per unit decreases by a factor of 2 after the investment, resulting in a variable cost per unit of $4,978. The resulting break-even point is $66,560,000 in sales, or 3,328 cars sold. Using the

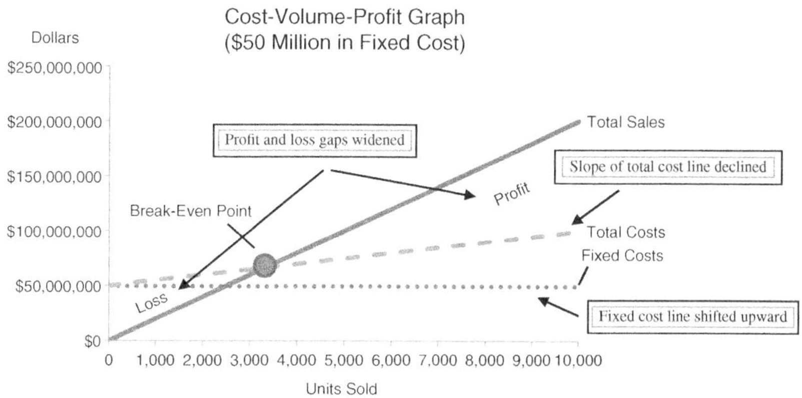

Figure 6.7 Cost-volume-profit graph after investment in robotics.

cost equation to estimate profits at sales levels of 1,000 and 9,000 units, we find an estimated *loss* of $34,978,000 at 1,000 units sold and an estimated *profit* of $85,198,000 at 9,000 units sold. If the company expects sales to be stable at or above the break-even point, it will likely choose to invest in robotics to increase the potential for larger profits.

Let's look at the Figure 6.7 calculations:

Break-even Point

Fixed Costs + Variable Cost per Car (Cars Sold) = Sales Price per Car (Cars Sold)
$50,000,000 + ($4,978 per Car × Cars Sold) = ($20,000 per Car × Cars Sold)
Break-even Point = 3,328 Units = 3,328 ($20,000) = $66,560,000

Potential Profit (or Loss) at 1,000 Cars Sold

Total Sales Revenue Fixed Costs –Variable Costs = Profit (Loss)
($20,000 per Car × 1,000 Cars) – $50,000,000 –
($4,978 per Car × 1,000 Cars) = ($34,978,000)

Potential Profit (or Loss) at 9,000 Cars Sold

Total Sales Revenue – Fixed Costs –Variable Costs = Profit (Loss)
($20,000 per Car × 9,000 Cars) – $50,000,000 –
($4,978 per Car × 9,000 Cars) = ($85,198,000)

When comparing the examples in Figures 6.6 and 6.7, the fixed cost line has shifted up from $25 million in Figure 6.6 to $50 million in Figure 6.7. This represents an increase in operating leverage. The company is leveraging the fixed cost to create capacity. The tradeoff is reduced variable costs per unit, which is represented by a reduction in slope in the total cost line in Figure 6.7. The gap between the fixed cost line and the total cost line represents variable costs, and in Figure 6.7, that gap has narrowed. As a result of the reduction in the slope of the total cost line, the gap between total costs and sales, which represents profit, increases. Thus, the figures show that the use of operating leverage has a potential reward via an exponential increase in profits as sales increase, but that comes with greater risk as potential losses also increase exponentially as sales decline. Because of this phenomenon, managers are generally cautious about making large investments in fixed costs when sales volume is volatile, and they tend to take advantage of leverage in situations where sales volume is more stable.

ACCOUNTING IN LIFE

Building Wealth with Leverage

In its basic form, leverage refers to purchasing an asset that returns more in profit than the asset costs. Many people use leverage to build wealth in the real estate market, but the practice can be risky. Consider an investor who purchases a $500,000 rental home using $100,000 of their own money and $400,000 borrowed from a bank. Assume the bank loan costs the investor 5% in interest annually. Let us also assume the home generates $20,000 per year in net rental income, and the value of the home increases by 5% per year or $25,000. The rental income and price appreciation result exceed the $20,000

Thirdman / Pexels / Public Domain

of interest cost on the borrowed money ($400,000 × 5%) by $25,000. Thus, the investor's return on his or her $100,000 investment would be $25,000 or 25%, not the 5% price increase. That is because the increase is based on the total home value, not the owner's equity percentage. By way of comparison, the average return on a stock market investment from 1926 to 2017 was 12%.[1] Thus, the investor has more than doubled the rate of return they could have made investing the $100,000 in the stock market. The amplification also works in reverse if home prices decline. Let's assume the home value declined by 5% (–$25,000) during the year. In that case the net rental income of $20,000 would not exceed the $20,000 in interest cost and the $25,000 price decline. The investor would lose $25,000 or 25% of their investment.

The degree of leverage in this example is 5. The effect of price changes on the investor's net worth is amplified by a factor of 5. From that perspective, a 20% increase in the value of the home can result in the investor doubling their money, while a 20% decrease would result in losing it all!

Businesses can use leverage to increase profitability. Greater leverage can equal greater returns. However, more leverage can also mean more risk and the potential for larger losses. Leaders aim to balance the risk versus reward of using leverage.

LEARNING ACTIVITY 6.10

The Dan Marshall Band plays at weddings, parties, and other events once or twice a month. They charge approximately $1,500 per 4-hour event. The band members have their own instruments, but they rent sound equipment and a trailer from a local music store for $500 for each gig, resulting in $1,000 in profit for each event. The band has enough requests to increase their number of performances to four gigs per month. They think it might be worth it if they invest in their own sound equipment and trailer for $25,000, which will be usable over the next 5 years.

[1] Source: S&P 500 Total Returns. Available at: https://www.slickcharts.com/sp500/returns

1. How much more would the band profit if they invested in the equipment and trailer rather than renting the equipment and trailer, assuming the band accepted a total of 240 gigs over the next 5 years?
   a. A decrease in profits of $45,000
   b. An increase in profits of $50,000
   c. An increase in profits of $95,000
   d. An increase in profits of $105,000
2. Compute the degree of operating leverage when purchasing the equipment and trailer.
   a. 0.8667
   b. 1.0746
   c. 1.5000
   d. 3.3374
3. Compute the degree of operating leverage assuming an increase in projected sales of 10%. Confirm the degree of operating leverages match.
   a. 0.8667
   b. 1.0746
   c. 1.5000
   d. 3.3374

What Do We Call Costs That Contain Both Fixed and Variable Elements?

Learning Objective 6.6
Describe the concept of mixed costs and use the high-low method to separate mixed costs and develop a cost equation.

Mixed costs contain both fixed and variable cost elements. For example, electric utility costs are usually mixed costs for a factory because factories typically must pay a fixed monthly fee for access to a certain amount of electrical capacity and a variable charge for the consumption of electricity. Thus, a factory's electrical bill will commonly consist of a charge for kilowatt capacity and a charge for electrical consumption measured in kilowatt hours. Table 6.4 shows the fixed and variable costs for a factory's electrical bill.

Use the High-Low Method to Separate Mixed Costs and Develop a Cost Equation

We have illustrated how the cost equation can be a powerful tool in evaluating business performance. Use of the cost equation requires a clear distinction between fixed and variable costs. As a result, mixed costs that have both fixed and variable components must be divided into their fixed and variable elements before being used in a cost equation.

Table 6.4 Factory Electric Bill: Fixed Versus Variable Costs

Kilowatt Hours (kWh) Used	Total Fixed Cost for KW Capacity	Cost per kWh	Total Variable Cost	Total Cost
0 kWh	$ 5,000	$ 10	$ 0	$ 5,000
500 kWh	$ 5,000	$ 10	$ 5,000	$ 10,000
5,000 kWh	$ 5,000	$ 10	$ 50,000	$ 55,000
1,000 kWh	$ 5,000	$ 10	$100,000	$ 105,000

LEARNING ACTIVITY 6.11

The following costs are mixed, true or false?

1. Raw material — True / False
2. Office Salaries — True / False
3. Assembly line workers' wages — True / False
4. Equipment lease with a base charge and charge for usage — True / False
5. Depreciation — True / False
6. Electric utilities in the factory — True / False

The **high-low method** is a common approach to dividing mixed costs into their fixed and variable elements mathematically. The high-low method requires knowledge of costs and production activity at two distinct levels of activity, usually a high and low level. We can attribute any difference in mixed costs at two levels of activity to a change in variable costs because, by definition, fixed costs do not change. To apply the high-low method, apply the following steps:

Step 1: Calculate variable cost per unit of activity by dividing the change in total mixed costs by the change in activity.

$$\frac{\textbf{(High Mixed Cost Total – Low Mixed Cost Total)}}{\textbf{(High Activity – Low Activity)}} = \textbf{Variable Cost per Unit}$$

Step 2: Compute total variable costs at either the high or low activity level with the variable cost per unit.

Variable Cost per Unit × Activity Level Unit Volume = Total Variable Costs

Step 3: Determine the fixed cost by subtracting the total variable cost from the total cost at the associated activity level.

Total Mixed Costs − Total Variable Costs = Total Fixed Costs

Step 4: Create the cost equation by combining the fixed and variable cost components.

Total Fixed Costs + (Variable Cost per Unit × Units Produced) = Total Cost

Let us look at an example of the automobile manufacturer introduced in Chapter 2. Large automotive factories consume sizable volumes of utilities such as electricity. Consumption spikes during peak production periods. Utility companies typically charge their industrial customers for total electrical consumption and electrical capacity needed during peak times. Consumption is usually measured in kilowatt-hours (kWh), while capacity is usually measured in kilowatts (KW). The electric company providing service to our automotive factory charges for both consumption and capacity. Imagine that you are an accounting manager responsible for determining fixed and variable charges to the factory. You could figure out the fixed and variable charges to the factory in terms of kilowatts and kilowatt-hours by closely examining monthly utility bills. However, it would be more relevant to managers to base those charges on measures that are related to the company, like car production volume. Therefore, you will convert total electrical costs into a fixed quotient and a variable quotient per car produced.

The total electricity costs and production volumes for January through June are listed in the following table. Begin by finding the high and low points. January had the highest production volume and May had the lowest production volume.

	January	February	March	April	May	June
Cars Produced	14,000	13,000	11,500	11,000	8,000	10,000
Utility Costs	$375,000	$320,000	$295,000	$260,000	$225,000	$240,000

Using the high and low points, we can determine the total fixed cost and total variable cost following these steps:

Step 1: Identify the highest and lowest level of activity and calculate the variable cost per unit.

$$\frac{\textbf{(High Mixed Cost Total} - \textbf{Low Mixed Cost Total)}}{\textbf{(High Activity} - \textbf{Low Activity)}} = \textbf{Variable Cost per Unit}$$

$$\frac{\textbf{Electricity Costs}}{\textbf{Car Production}} \quad \frac{(\$375{,}000 - \$225{,}000)}{(14{,}000 \text{ Cars} - 8{,}000 \text{ Cars})} = \textbf{\$25 of Electrical Costs per Car Produced}$$

Step 2: Calculate the total variable costs.

Variable Cost per Unit × Activity Level Unit Volume = Total Variable Costs

January: 14,000 Cars × $25 per Car = $350,000 Variable Utility Cost

June: 8,000 Cars × $25 per Car = $200,000 Variable Utility Cost

Step 3: Calculate the total fixed costs.

Total Mixed Costs – Total Variable Costs = Total Fixed Costs

	Total Electricity Costs	– Variable Cost	= Fixed Monthly Utility Cost
January:	$375,000	– $350,000	= $25,000
June:	$225,000	– $200,000	= $25,000

Step 4: Create the cost equation.

Total Fixed Costs + (Variable Cost per Unit × Units Produced) = Total Cost

$25,000 + ($25 per Car × Cars Produced) = Monthly Electricity Costs

This analysis shows that monthly electricity costs are $25,000. The automobile manufacturer can use the electricity cost equation for predicting electrical costs in future months. For example, if the business expects to produce 10,000 cars in July, estimated electricity costs are as follows:

25,000 + ($25 per car × 10,000 cars) = $275,000

When using the high-low method to separate mixed costs into their fixed and variable components, a change in mixed cost relative to a change in volume is attributable to variable costs only, as fixed costs, by definition, do not change.

LEARNING ACTIVITY 6.12

Hudson Textiles is a cut-and-sew manufacturing company specializing in high-end fashion products. Hudson prides itself on its detail and quality. Hudson uses dozens of commercial sewing machines in its 10,000-foot facility, and electricity needed to run the machines is a significant cost. Hudson's electrical bills blend demand and usage costs into one final monthly charge. Hudson's controller would like to better understand Hudson's electricity cost structure before working with production to reduce electrical costs. Hudson's electrical bills contain the following data for Hudson's electrical consumption and charges during the month with the highest and lowest consumption during the year:

	Electricity Consumed (in kWh)	Utility cost incurred (in Dollars)
Low month	152,000	$23,240
High month	90,200	$15,824

1. Compute Hudson's utility cost equation using the high-low method and the data provided. What is the variable cost per unit according to the cost equation?
   a. $0.12 per kWh
   b. $0.25 per kWh
   c. $0.30 per kWh
   d. None of the above
2. What is the fixed cost in Hudson's cost equation?
   a. $3,000
   b. $5,000
   c. $8,000
   d. None of the above
3. If Hudson averages 110,000 kWh in electricity consumption per month, what are electrical costs per month?
   a. $12,500
   b. $18,200
   c. $24,000
   d. None of the above

Technology, Analytics, and Artificial Intelligence

As an alternative to using the high-low method to develop cost models, companies can use statistics and machine learning. The high-low method is a simple mathematical function that only uses two data points to split the mixed costs for use in developing the cost equation. More robust methods are available, namely, least squares regression analysis, also called linear regression.

Least squares regression analysis is a statistical technique that is a foundational element of machine learning and artificial intelligence. Least squares regression analysis is a form of supervised learning used to find the relationship between two variables, an independent and dependent variable. An **independent variable** is a known variable that, when changed, causes changes in another variable. An independent variable is commonly called a predictor variable as it is used as the basis for predicting the value of another variable. When performing least squares regression in a business setting, the independent variable is usually an activity that influences cost. A **dependent variable** is an unknown variable that is predicted by one or more independent variables. The dependent variable is commonly a cost when performing least squares regression analysis in a business setting where business activity influences costs.

Least squares regression analysis produces a **regression line** and corresponding equation. The regression line or line of best fit, which, when drawn from a set of training data observations on x and y coordinates, minimizes the sum of the squared vertical differences between the observation points and the regression line. Check out this video to learn more about linear regression:

https://www.youtube.com/watch?v=CtsRRUddV2s

Now, let us look at an example. Examine the cost and production data for Zesta Travel Trailers in Figure 6.8. When plotted on an x-y chart, the training data points slope upward and to the right, indicating that an increase in units produced results in an increase in production costs. The regression line is the line of best fit that minimizes the sum of the squared deviations between the regression line and the data points.

Note, the least square regression analysis generates a regression line (or line of best fit) that minimizes the value of the *squared* differences between the data points and the regression line. Using the *raw* differences is not feasible because it would always result in a value of zero.

Month	Units Produced	Total Production Costs
January	1,500	$38,515,400
February	1,000	$36,750,555
March	2,000	$41,850,500
April	1,750	$39,485,555
May	1,650	$38,548,596
June	1,255	$36,781,889
July	2,150	$42,586,850
August	1,925	$41,578,555
September	1,500	$41,000,252
October	1,900	$41,457,856
November	1,950	$39,548,955
December	1,850	$40,458,764

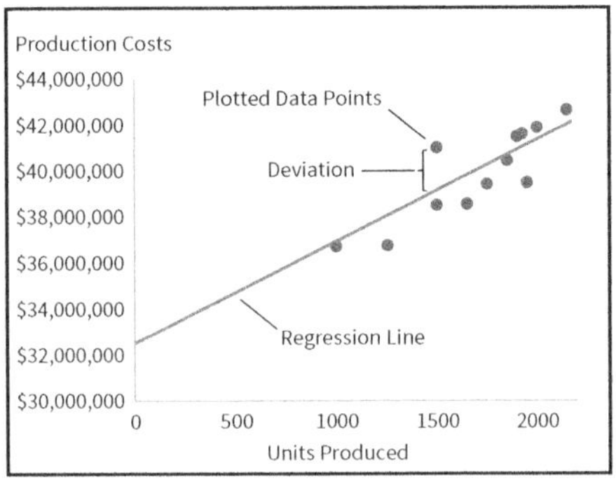

Figure 6.8 Regression line for Zesta Travel Trailers.

LEARNING ACTIVITY 6.13

Indicate if the following factors are most likely to be an independent (predictor) variable or a dependent (outcome) variable:

1. Utility Costs	Dependent / Independent
2. Units Produced	Dependent / Independent
3. Number of Employees	Dependent / Independent
4. Labor Costs	Dependent / Independent
5. Machine Run Time	Dependent / Independent

Use Least Squares Regression Analysis to Develop a Cost Equation in Microsoft Excel

We can use least squares regression analysis to develop an equation for the regression line (or line of best fit). The line of best fit can be depicted by a linear cost equation written as $y = b + m(x)$ where:

y = The value of the dependent variable
x = The value of the independent variable
b = Fixed cost
m = Variable cost per unit

The cost equation for Zesta Travel Trailers discussed in Figure 6.14 is as follows:

$$y \quad = \quad \text{b} \quad + \quad m \quad (x)$$

$$\text{Total Production Costs} = \$31{,}408{,}091.89 + \$4{,}976.34\ (\text{Units Produced})$$

Developing the cost equation through manual computation is quite complex. Fortunately, modern spreadsheet applications, like Microsoft Excel, have built in functions that can perform regression analysis and give us the cost equation with just a few clicks. let's start by looking at annual production and production cost data for Zest Travel Trailers, presented in Figure 6.9.

To perform a regression analysis in Microsoft Excel, you must first click on the Data tab. Underneath the Data tab, you will find an option on the far right to perform Data Analysis; click it. Figure 6.10 illustrates how to access the data analysis function in Microsoft Excel.

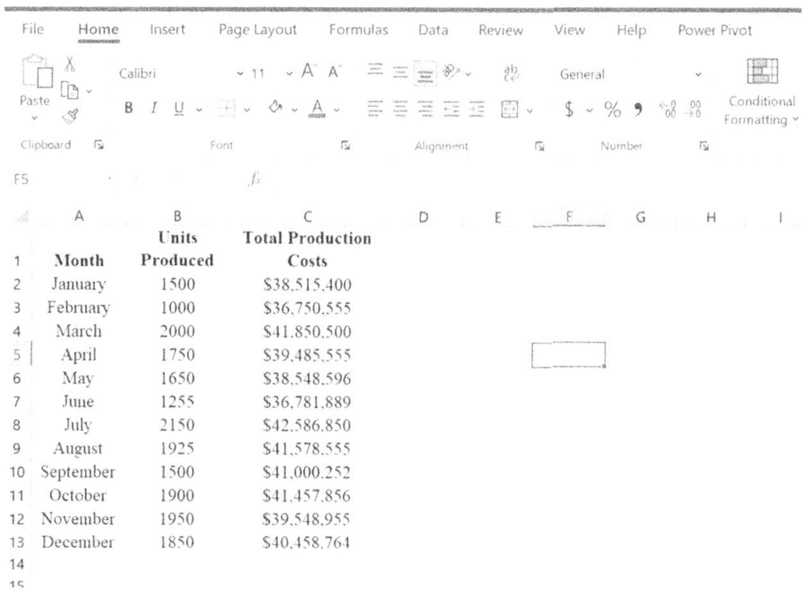

Month	Units Produced	Total Production Costs
January	1500	$38,515,400
February	1000	$36,750,555
March	2000	$41,850,500
April	1750	$39,485,555
May	1650	$38,548,596
June	1255	$36,781,889
July	2150	$42,586,850
August	1925	$41,578,555
September	1500	$41,000,252
October	1900	$41,457,856
November	1950	$39,548,955
December	1850	$40,458,764

Figure 6.9 Regression data for Zesta Travel Trailers.

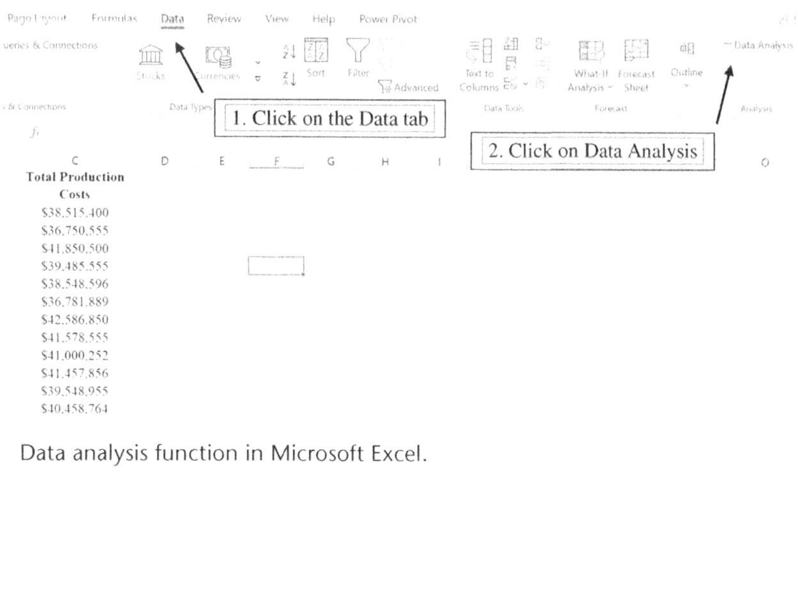

Figure 6.10 Data analysis function in Microsoft Excel.

If Data Analysis is not an option underneath your Data tab, you must turn on the Analysis ToolPak by clicking *File*, then *Options*, then *Add-Ins*, then *Go* (next to Manage Excel Add-Ins), then click the checkbox next to Analysis ToolPak, then click *OK*.

After selecting Data Analysis under the Data tab, you will have options to perform several statistical analyses. Scroll down until you find regression. Highlight it and click *OK*. Figure 6.11 illustrates.

The regression box will open and give you options to input your data. Start by inputting the Y range by highlighting the total production costs for the preceding year as shown in Figure 6.12.

The next step is to input the independent variable observations, or units produced in this case. Input the X range by highlighting the units produced for the preceding year as shown in Figure 6.13 and then click *OK* to calculate the results.

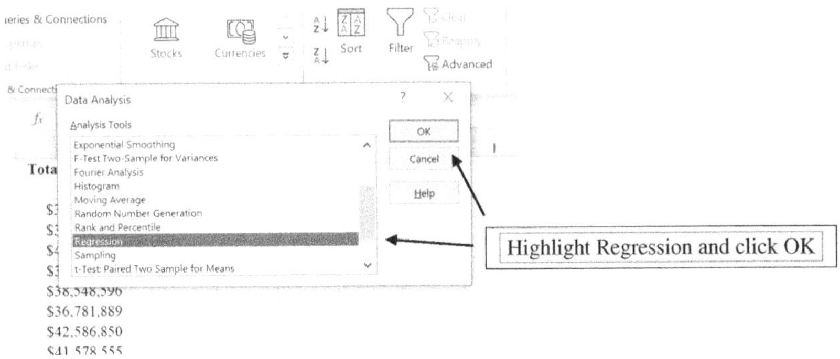

Figure 6.11 Statistical functions under the Data Analysis tool option.

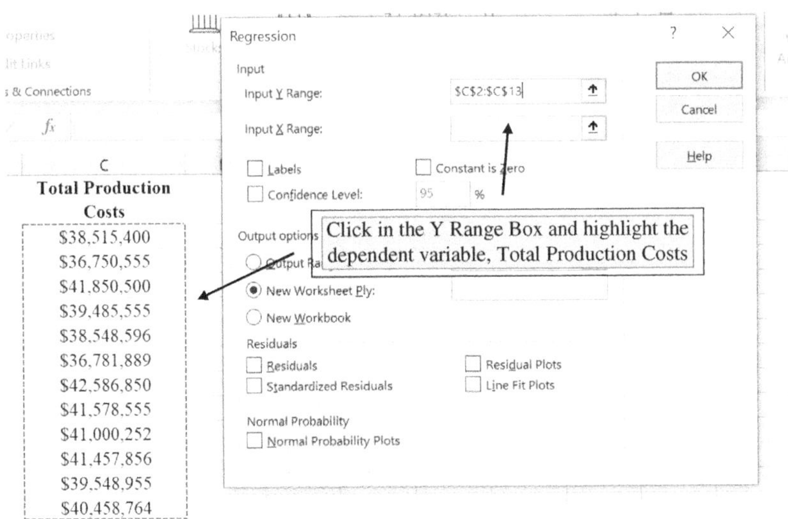

Figure 6.12 The observed dependent variable data.

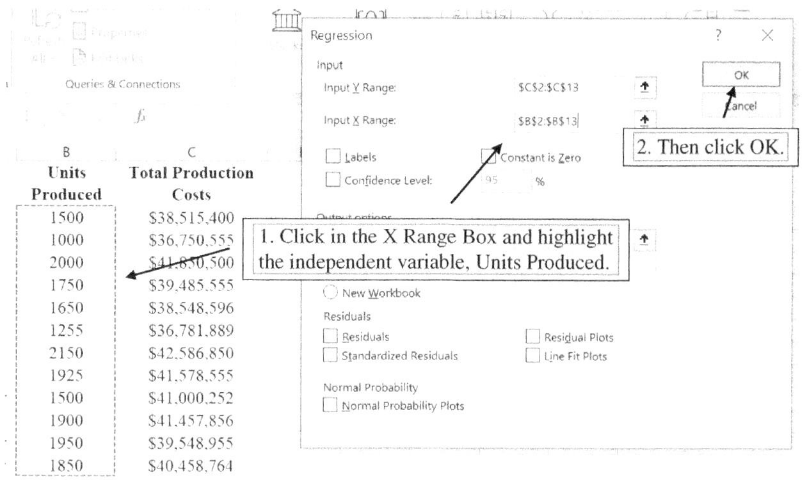

Figure 6.13 The observed independent variable data.

The Summary Output from the regression performed on the data from Zesta Travel Trailers is presented in Figure 6.14. The summary describes the predictive value of the model, it includes an ANOVA table which describes the statistical significance of the model, and it provides information about fixed and variable costs to be used in the resultant cost equation. All are described in detail next.

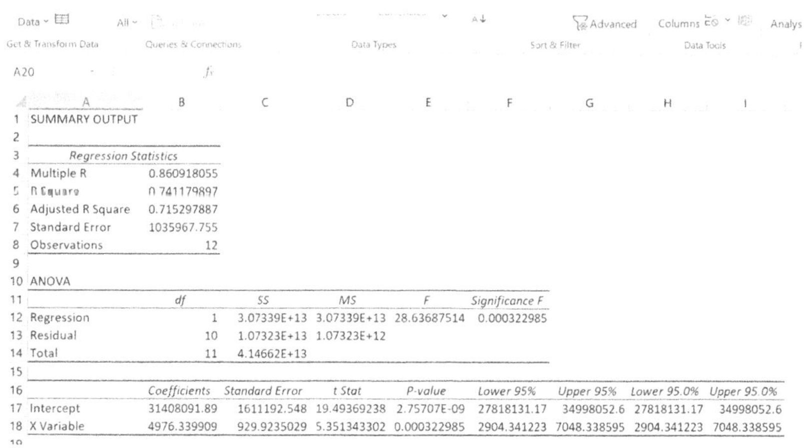

SUMMARY OUTPUT

Regression Statistics	
Multiple R	0.860918055
R Square	0.741179897
Adjusted R Square	0.715297887
Standard Error	1035967.755
Observations	12

ANOVA

	df	SS	MS	F	Significance F
Regression	1	3.07339E+13	3.07339E+13	28.63687514	0.000322985
Residual	10	1.07323E+13	1.07323E+12		
Total	11	4.14662E+13			

	Coefficients	Standard Error	t Stat	P-value	Lower 95%	Upper 95%	Lower 95.0%	Upper 95.0%
Intercept	31408091.89	1611192.548	19.49369238	2.75707E-09	27818131.17	34998052.6	27818131.17	34998052.6
X Variable	4976.339909	929.9235029	5.351343302	0.000322985	2904.341223	7048.338595	2904.341223	7048.338595

Figure 6.14 The regression output for Zesta Travel Trailers.

Figure 6.15 illustrates the Regression Statistics given in the Summary Output. Let us focus our attention to two important statistics: the Multiple R (or Correlation Coefficient) and the R Square (or Coefficient of Determination). The **correlation coefficient** is a measure of the strength of the relationship between two variables, and it represents the amount the *y* variable (production costs) changes relative to a change in the *x* variable (units produced). The correlation coefficient of 0.861 (Rounded) indicates that a one-unit change in units produced has a corresponding change of 0.861 in production costs. The **coefficient of determination** is a measure of the amount of the change in the dependent (*y*) variable (production costs) that can be described by the change in the independent (*x*) variable (units produced). The remainder of the change in the dependent variable is described by other independent variables or error. The R square of 0.741 (rounded) suggests that approximately 74.1% of the change in production costs is explained by the change in units produced. Other factors explain the remaining 25.9%.

The most important number to evaluate on the ANOVA table is the significance F. The **significance F** represents the probability that relationships between the variables would be found by chance. The significance F of 0.000322985 given in Figure 6.16 suggests there is a 0.03% probability that relationships of the magnitude that are observed in the data would happen by chance.

The final and perhaps most important figures in the summary output are the coefficient values of the intercept and the *x* variable. The intercept represents is the intercept in the equation for the line of best fit. It is also the fixed cost in the cost equation. The *x* variable represents the slope of the line of best fit. It also represents the variable cost per unit in the cost equation. Any mixed production costs are automatically separated into fixed and variable elements. Figure 6.17 shows an intercept (or fixed cost) of 31,408,091.89 and an *x* variable (or variable cost per unit) of 4,976.339909. Thus, the cost equation is as follows:

$$\text{Production Cost} = \$31{,}408{,}091.89 + \$4{,}976.34\ (\text{Units Produced})$$

It is important to note that regression analysis will always produce a line of best fit. It is also important to note that a line of best fit may not be useful for practical purposes even when strong statistical relationships exist. For example, a negative intercept would suggest a negative fixed cost, which we know is not possible. Thus, data analysts must exercise professional judgment when evaluating the results of regression analysis.

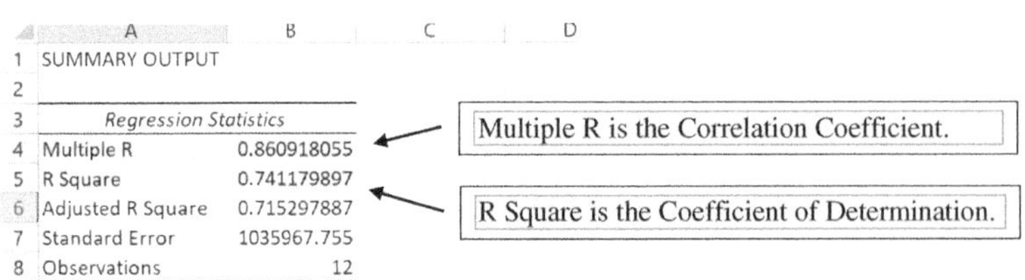

	A	B
1	SUMMARY OUTPUT	
2		
3	*Regression Statistics*	
4	Multiple R	0.860918055
5	R Square	0.741179897
6	Adjusted R Square	0.715297887
7	Standard Error	1035967.755
8	Observations	12

Figure 6.15 Correlation coefficient and coefficient of determination for the cost model.

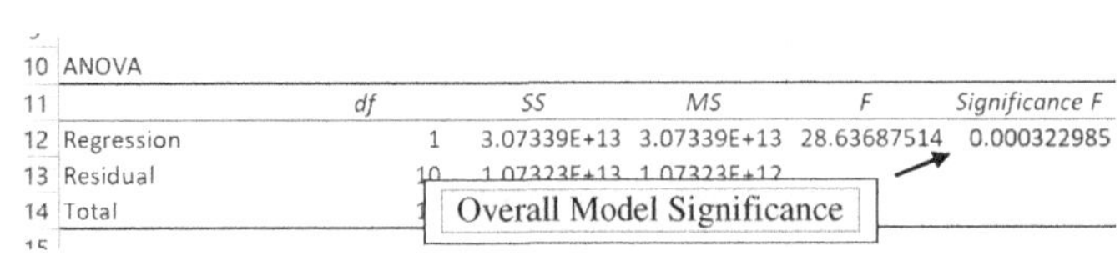

10	ANOVA					
11		*df*	*SS*	*MS*	*F*	*Significance F*
12	Regression	1	3.07339E+13	3.07339E+13	28.63687514	0.000322985
13	Residual	10	1.07323E+13	1.07323E+12		
14	Total	1[illegible]	[illegible]			

Figure 6.16 Cost model significance for Zesta Travel Trailers.

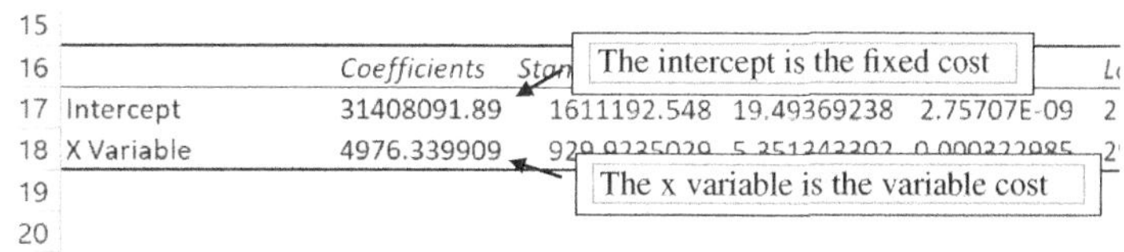

Figure 6.17 The resultant cost model for Zesta Travel Trailers.

Linear regression is a powerful tool for predicting cost behavior patterns, and computers can help businesspeople make computations quick and easy. However, people are ultimately responsible for the decisions, and computers make mistakes. For example, when using regression to predict future expenses, it is important that training data comes from similar conditions to those expected in the future. Data analysts making the computations must take care when selecting and cleaning the training data to ensure they are relevant.

LEARNING ACTIVITY 6.13

Determine the cost structure for utilities at the automobile manufacturer illustrated in the chapter. Assume utility costs are correlated with production. Use the following data to find the appropriate equation for utility costs. Use the least squares method to find your solution.

	Cars Produced (Independent Variable)	Utility Costs (Dependent Variable)
January	14,000	375,000
February	13,000	320,000
March	11,500	295,000
April	11,000	260,000
May	8,000	225,000
June	10,000	240,000

1. Complete the cost equation for utility costs using summary output from the Excel regression function: Utility Costs = __$6,120.22__ + ________ (Cars Produced)
   a. $13.23
   b. $24.86
   c. $48.00
   d. None of the above

2. What is the coefficient of determination?
   a. –0.833
   b. 0.833
   c. –0.902
   d. 0.902
3. Is the equation useful for predicting utility costs? Yes or No

Key Terms

fixed costs A cost that remains the same *in total*, regardless of changes the volume of activity.
variable costs A cost that increases or decreases *in total* in direct proportion to increases or decreases in the volume of activity.
relevant range The range of production in which fixed and variable cost behavior holds.
step costs Costs that are constant within a range of activity but increase to a higher level once the range is exceeded.
cost equation A mathematical function that companies use to predict the total amount of expenses that are associated with the sale and production of goods at a specified level.
cost-volume-profit The study of the change in costs relative to the change in production volume.
break-even point The sales level where total costs equal total sales dollars and thus no profit is earned.
contribution margin The amount remaining after deducting total variable costs from net sales that is available to pay for fixed costs and contribute to profit.
unit contribution margin The difference between net sales price per unit and variable cost per unit.
contribution margin ratio The percentage of each dollar of sales that is available to cover fixed costs and contribute to profit.
target profit The profit that remains after fixed and variable costs have been deducted from net sales.
margin of safety The amount by which sales can decrease before the company fails to reach breakeven.
margin of safety percentage The percent by which sales could decrease before the company fails to reach breakeven.
operating leverage The degree to which a business increases profits when it increases sales or vice versa.
degree of operating leverage ratio Operating income divided by the total contribution margin.
mixed costs A cost that has both fixed and variable components.
high-low method An approach to dividing mixed costs into their fixed and variable elements mathematically.
independent variable A known variable that, when changed, causes changes in another variable.

dependent variable An unknown variable that is predicted by one or more independent variables.
regression line The regression line, or line of best fit, is a line that when drawn over a set of observations on x and y coordinates, minimizes the sum of the squared vertical differences between the observation points and the regression line.
correlation coefficient Measures the strength of the relationship between two variables and represents the amount the y variable changes relative to a change in the x variable.
coefficient of determination Measures of the amount of the change in the dependent (y) variable that can be described by the change in the independent (x) variable.
significance F Represents the probability that relationships between the variables would be found by chance.

LEARNING ACTIVITY SOLUTIONS

Learning Activity 6.1

1. *b*
2. *b*
3. *b*
4. *a*
5. *b*

Learning Activity 6.2

b. *Total fixed costs stay constant as production decreases; fixed cost per unit increases as production decreases.*

Learning Activity 6.3

a. *Total variable costs decrease as production decreases; variable cost per unit stays constant as production decreases.*

Learning Activity 6.4

1. *Fixed*
2. *Variable*
3. *Fixed*
4. *Variable*
5. *Fixed*
6. *Variable*
7. *Fixed*
8. *Fixed*

Learning Activity 6.5

a. 350,000 garments
b. $4,200,000

Computations:

Sales Price per Garment: $6,000,000/500,000	=	$12.00 *per Garment*
Variable Cost per Garment: $3,200,000/500,000	=	$ 6.40 *per Garment*
Fixed Costs + *Variable Costs*	=	*Total Costs*
$1,960,000 + $3,200,000	=	$5,160,000
Cost Equation: *Fixed Costs* + (*Variable Cost per Unit* × *Units Sold*)	=	*Total Costs*
$1,960,000 + ($6.40 *per Garment* × *Garments Sold*)	=	*Total Costs*

Breakeven in Units:

Net Sales Revenue–Fixed Costs–Variable Costs	=	*Operating Profit*
(*Sales Price per Unit* × *Units Sold*)–*Fixed Costs*–(*Variable Cost per Unit* × *Units Sold*)	=	*Operating Profit*
($12.00 *per Garment* × *Garments Sold*)–$1,960,000–($6.40 *per Garment* × *Garments Sold*)	=	$0
($5.60 *per Garment* × *Garments Sold*)–$1,960,000	=	$0
($5.60 *per Garment* × *Garments Sold*)	=	$1,960,000
Garments Sold	=	$1,960,000/5.60
Garments Sold	=	350,000
Breakeven in Dollars: 350,000 *Garments* × $12.00 *per Garment*	=	$4,200,000

Learning Activity 6.6

a. *$2,800,000*

Sales	–	*Variable Cost*	=	*Contribution Margin*
$6,000,000	–	$3,200,000	=	$2,800,000

b. *$5.60*
Sales Price per Garment: $6,000,000/500,000 = $12.00 *per Garment*
Variable Cost per Garment: $3,200,000/500,000 = $ 6.40 *per Garment*
Contribution Margin per Garment: $12.00 – $6.40 = $5.60 *per Garment*

c. *350,000 Garments*

Fixed Costs		*Contribution Margin Per Garment*		*Breakeven*
$1,960,000	/	$5.60	=	350,000 *Garments*

Learning Activity 6.7

\$475,000

$$\begin{aligned} \textit{Sales Price per Garment}: \$6{,}000{,}000/500{,}000 &= \$12.00 \textit{ per Garment} \\ \textit{Variable Cost per Garment}: \$3{,}200{,}000/500{,}000 &= \$\ 6.40 \textit{ per Garment} \end{aligned}$$

$$\begin{array}{rcccccc} \textit{Target Sales} & = & \textit{Variable Costs} & + & \textit{Fixed Costs} & + & \textit{Target Profit} \\ \$12.00\ (\textit{Garment}) & = & \$6.40\ (\textit{Garments}) & + & \$1{,}960{,}000 & + & \$700{,}000 \\ \$5.60\ (\textit{Garment}) & = & & & \$1{,}960{,}000 & + & \$700{,}000 \end{array}$$

$$\textit{Garments} = \frac{\$2{,}660{,}000}{\$5.60 \textit{ per Garment}} = 475{,}000 \textit{ Garments}$$

Learning Activity 6.8

a. *50,000 Garments*

$$\begin{array}{ccccc} \textit{Projected Sales} & - & \textit{Break-even Sales} & = & \textit{Margin of Safety} \\ 400{,}000 \textit{ Garments} & - & 350{,}000 \textit{ Garments} & = & 50{,}000 \textit{ Garments} \end{array}$$

b. *12.5%*

$$\begin{array}{ccccc} \textit{Margin of Safety} & / & \textit{Projected Sales} & = & \textit{Margin of Safety Percentage} \\ 50{,}000 \textit{ Garments} & / & 400{,}000 \textit{ Garments} & = & 12.5\% \end{array}$$

Learning Activity 6.9

a. *\$110*

$$\begin{array}{rcr} (\textit{Unit Price} \times \textit{Units Sold}) - \textit{Fixed Costs} \\ -(\textit{Var Cost per Unit} \times \textit{Units Sold}) & = & \textit{Breakeven} \\ (\textit{Unit Price} \times 2.500) - \$100{,}000 \\ -((\$35 + \$15 + \$20) \times 2{,}500) & = & \$0 \\ \textit{Unit Price} \times 2{,}500 - \$100{,}000 - (\$70 \times 2{,}500) & = & \$0 \\ \textit{Unit Price} \times 2.500 & = & \$275{,}000 \\ \textit{Unit Price Required to Break Even} & = & \$275{,}000/2{,}500 \\ \textit{Unit Price Required to Break Even} & = & \$110 \textit{ per Pair} \end{array}$$

b. *$150*

$$\begin{aligned}
(\textit{Unit Price} \times \textit{Units Sold}) - \textit{Fixed Costs} - (\textit{Var Cost per Unit} \times \textit{Units Sold}) &= \textit{Target Profit}\\
(\textit{Unit Price} \times 2.500) - \$100{,}000 - ((\$35 + \$15 + \$20) \times 2{,}500) &= \$100{,}000\\
\textit{Unit Price} \times 2{,}500 - \$100{,}000 - (\$70 \times 2{,}500) &= \$100{,}000\\
\textit{Unit Price} \times 2.500 &= \$375{,}000\\
\textit{Unit Price Required} &= \$375{,}000/2{,}500\\
\textit{Unit Price Required to Meet Target Profit} &= \$150 \textit{ per Pair}
\end{aligned}$$

Learning Activity 6.10

1. a

<u>*Renting the equipment and trailer*</u>

		Price	–	Cost of Equipment and Trailer	=	Profit per Gig
Profit Per Gig	=	$1,500	–	$500	=	$1,000

$$\textit{Total Profit} = \$1{,}000 \textit{ per Gig} \times 240 \textit{ Gigs} = \$240{,}000$$

<u>*Purchasing the equipment and trailer*</u>

		Price	–	Cost of Equipment and Trailer	=	Profit per Gig
Profit per Gig	=	$1,500	–	$0	=	$1,500

$$\textit{Total Profit Before Investment} = \$1{,}500 \textit{ per Gig} \times 240 \textit{ Gigs} = \$360{,}000$$

$$\textit{Total Profit After Cost of Investment} = \$360{,}000 - \$25{,}000 = \$335{,}000$$

$$\textit{Increase in Profits} = \$335{,}000 - \$240{,}000 = \$95{,}000$$

2. b

$$\begin{aligned}
\textit{Degree of Operating Leverage} &= \textit{Contribution Margin/Operating Income}\\
&= \$360{,}000/\$335{,}000\\
&= 1.0746
\end{aligned}$$

3. b

	Projected Sales (240 Gigs)	Percent Change	Projected Sales (B) (264 Gigs)
Estimated Sales (Gigs × $1,500)	*$360,000*	*10%*	*$396,000*
Variable Costs (Units Sold × $0)	*0*		*0*
Contribution Margin	*360,000*		*396,000*
Fixed Costs	*25,000*		*25,000*
Operating Income	*$335,000*	*10.746%*	*$371,000*

Degree of Operating Leverage = 10.746%/10% = 1.0746

Learning Activity 6.11

1. *False*
2. *False*
3. *False*
4. *True*
5. *False*
6. *True*

Learning Activity 6.12

1. a

Variable Cost per Unit Computation:

$$\textit{Electricity Costs} \quad \frac{(\$23{,}240\text{–}\$15{,}824)}{(152{,}000\ kWh\text{–}90{,}200\ kWh)} = \$0.12\ \textit{per Car kWh}$$

2. b

Variable Cost per Unit Computation:

$$\textit{Electricity Costs} \quad \frac{(\$23{,}240\text{–}\$15{,}824)}{(152{,}000\ kWh\text{–}90{,}200\ kWh)} = \$0.12\ \textit{per Car kWh}$$

3. b

Estimated Monthly Electrical Cost: \$5,000 + (\$0.12 *per kWh* × 110,000 *kWh consumed*) = \$18,200

Learning Activity 6.13

1. *Dependent*
2. *Independent*
3. *Independent*
4. *Dependent*
5. *Independent*

Learning Activity 6.14

1. b
2. d

Utility Costs = __\$6,120.22__ + __24.86__ (*Cars Produced*)

3. *Yes*

SUMMARY OUTPUT									
Regression Statistics									
Multiple R	0.949937019								
R Square	0.90238034								
Adjusted R Square	0.877975425								
Standard Error	19556.21014								
Observations	6								
ANOVA									
	df	*SS*	*MS*	*F*	*Significance F*				
Regression	1	14141051913	14141051913	36.97535274	0.003696717				
Residual	4	1529781421	382445355.2						
Total	5	15670833333							
	Coefficients	*Standard Error*	*t Stat*	*P-value*	*Lower 95%*	*Upper 95%*	*Lower 95.0%*	*Upper 95.0%*	
Intercept	6120.218579	46687.5737	0.131088812	0.90203379	-123505.2669	135745.7041	-123505.267	135745.7041	
Cars Produced	24.86338798	4.088877918	6.080736201	0.003696717	13.5108429	36.21593306	13.5108429	36.21593306	

Review Questions

1. Which of the following statements accurately describe fixed costs and the concept of relevant range? **(Learning Objective 1)**
   a. Fixed costs remain constant regardless of the level of business activity, and they include expenses like production supervisor salaries and equipment costs.
   b. Fixed costs vary directly with the level of business activity, such as the cost of raw materials used in production.
   c. Fixed costs per unit increase as production increases and decrease as production decreases.
   d. Fixed costs only apply to labor expenses and not to equipment or other assets.
2. Which of the following best describes variable costs? **(Learning Objective 1)**
   a. Variable costs remain constant regardless of changes in production volume.
   b. Variable costs fluctuate with business activity and change in correlation with production levels.
   c. The cost of a meal plan for college students is an example of a variable cost.
   d. Variable costs per unit increase as production volume decreases.
3. Which of the following best describes step costs? **(Learning Objective 1)**
   a. Step costs remain constant regardless of production levels.
   b. Step costs increase continuously with each additional unit produced.
   c. Step costs are constant within a range of activity but increase to a higher level once the range is exceeded.
   d. Step costs per unit increase as production volume increases.
4. Fixed costs remain constant within the relevant range, but increase in steps when the production capacity is exceeded. **(Learning Objective 1)**
   a. True
   b. False
5. Which of the following best describes the cost equation? **(Learning Objective 2)**
   a. The cost equation is used to calculate the selling price of goods.
   b. The cost equation helps predict total expenses associated with a specified level of production and sales.
   c. The cost equation is only used to estimate fixed costs in a business.
   d. The cost equation ignores variable costs and focuses solely on fixed costs.
6. The cost equation is used to estimate costs and profits, determine the break-even point, and figure out the sales needed to meet an earnings target. **(Learning Objective 2)**
   a. True
   b. False
7. Which of the following is NOT an assumption underlying cost-volume-profit analysis? **(Learning Objective 2)**
   a. Change in volume is the only factor that affects costs.
   b. Cost and revenue behave in a linear fashion.
   c. All costs are classified as either fixed or variable.
   d. Sales mix remains constant when a company sells more than one product.

8. The break-even point is the sales level at which total costs equal total sales dollars, resulting in no profit. **(Learning Objective 2)**
   a. True
   b. False
9. What is the contribution margin in cost-volume-profit analysis? **(Learning Objective 2)**
   a. The difference between total sales revenue and total variable costs
   b. The difference between fixed costs and total variable costs
   c. The difference between total sales revenue and fixed costs
   d. The difference between total variable costs and net sales revenue
10. What is the purpose of calculating target profit using the break-even formula in cost-volume-profit analysis? **(Learning Objective 3)**
    a. To determine the optimal production level
    b. To calculate the break-even point
    c. To identify the sales needed to meet a profit objective
    d. To estimate total variable costs
11. Margin of safety is the amount by which expected sales can exceed break-even sales, and it is also expressed as a percentage indicating the risk level for managers. **(Learning Objective 3)**
    a. True
    b. False
12. What does the degree of operating leverage ratio indicate? **(Learning Objective 5)**
    a. The percentage increase in sales needed to cover fixed costs
    b. The ratio of variable costs to fixed costs
    c. The degree to which a business increases profits when it increases sales
    d. The total profit margin for a given level of sales
13. Which of the following is an example of a mixed cost? **(Learning Objective 6)**
    a. Raw material
    b. Office salaries
    c. Assembly line workers' wages
    d. Electric utilities in the factory
14. The high-low method requires knowledge of costs and production activity at two distinct levels, typically a high and low level, to separate mixed costs into their fixed and variable elements. **(Learning Objective 6)**
    a. True
    b. False

Short Exercises

S:6-1 (Learning Objective 1)

Match the cost behavior description with the correct term:

a. Costs that are constant, regardless of activity level
b. Costs that are constant within a range but increase to a higher level once the range is exceeded
c. Costs that fluctuate with changes in activity level
d. The range of production or business activity where fixed and variable costs behave predictably

Terms

_____ Fixed Costs
_____ Variable Costs
_____ Relevant Range
_____ Step Costs

S:6-2 (Learning Objective 2)

Vanetta Farms wants to understand its costs and profits for the upcoming season. Here are the details:

- Fixed Costs
  - Property, greenhouses, and equipment: $10,000 per year
  - Office manager's salary: $40,000 per year
  - Total Fixed Costs: $50,000 per year
- Variable Costs
  - Direct variable cost per bundle: $8
  - Expected production: 5,000 bundles

Which of the following correctly calculates the total costs for Vanetta Farms if they produce 5,000 bundles?

a. $40,000
b. $50,000
c. $90,000
d. $100,000

S:6-3 (Learning Objective 3)

ABC Manufacturing Company wants to calculate the target sales needed to achieve a profit of $50,000. Here are the details:

- Fixed Costs: $100,000
- Variable Costs: $20 per unit
- Selling Price per unit: $100

Calculate the target sales volume ABC Manufacturing Company needs to achieve a profit of $50,000.

S:6-4 (Learning Objective 4)

Saul's Insoles, a manufacturer of high-quality insoles made from recycled materials, produces a model made with organic cotton called the ComfortStep. Each pair of ComfortSteps takes 1.5 hours to produce by a skilled artisan making $30 per hour. The raw material and variable overhead costs for a pair of ComfortSteps are $10 and $25 per pair, respectively. Saul's Insoles' fixed costs associated with the ComfortStep are $80,000.

a. How much does Saul's Insoles need to charge per pair of ComfortSteps to break even, assuming it can sell 3,000 pairs?
b. How much must Saul's Insoles charge per pair of ComfortSteps to make a profit of $90,000, assuming it can sell 3,000 pairs?

S:6-5 (Learning Objective 5)

Elegant Ensembles, a tailor shop, provides custom tailoring services for weddings dresses and other garments. They charge approximately $50 per hour for their services. The shop currently rents a sewing machine for $200 per month, resulting in $1,000 in profit per month for 25 hours of service. The shop has enough demand to increase its hours of service to 100 hours per month. The shop is considering investing in its own sewing machine for $7,500, which will be usable over the next 5 years. Compute the degree of operating leverage when purchasing the sewing machine.

S:6-6 (Learning Objective 6)

Brownstone Footwear is a manufacturer specializing in premium leather shoes. Brownstone prides itself on its attention to detail and quality. Brownstone uses dozens of commercial machines in its 8,000-square-foot facility, and the electricity needed to run the machines is a significant cost. Brownstone's electrical bills blend demand and usage costs into one final monthly charge. Brownstone's controller would like to better understand Brownstone's electricity cost structure before working with production to reduce electrical costs. Brownstone's electrical bills contain the following data for Brownstone's electrical consumption and charges during the month with the highest and lowest consumption during the year:

Production (in Units)	Utility cost incurred (in Dollars)
Low month: 120,000	$20,000
High month: 75,000	$13,000

Determine the cost equation for Brownstone's utility costs using the high-low method.

Exercises

E:6-7 (Learning Objective 2)

Orion Wire Products wants to understand its costs and profits for the upcoming season. Here are the details:

- Fixed Costs
  - Land, equipment, and infrastructure: $8,000 per year
  - Manager's salary: $32,000 per year
  - Total Fixed Costs: $40,000 per year
- Variable Costs
  - Direct variable cost per box of wire: $6
  - Expected production: 6,000 boxes

What is the total cost for Orion if it produces 6,000 boxes?

E:6-8 (Learning Objective 3)

Pacific Ocean Supply wants to calculate the target sales for its new line of Deep Blue scuba masks needed to achieve a profit of $40,000. Here are the details:

- Fixed Costs: $80,000
- Variable Costs: $15 per unit
- Selling Price per Unit: $75

Calculate the target sales volume Pacific needs to achieve a profit of $40,000.

E:6-9 (Learning Objective 4)

Miles City Medical Devices, a manufacturer of high-quality medical devices, produces a model called the HealthMonitor. Each HealthMonitor takes 2.5 hours to produce by a skilled technician making $28 per hour. The raw material and variable overhead costs for a HealthMonitor are $14 and $30 per device, respectively. Miles City Medical Devices' fixed costs associated with the HealthMonitor are $75,000.

a. How much does Miles City Medical Devices need to charge per HealthMonitor to break even, assuming it can sell 2,000 devices?
b. How much must Miles City Medical Devices charge per HealthMonitor to make a profit of $60,000, assuming it can sell 2,000 devices?

E:6-10 (Learning Objective 5)

Frank's Flower Emporium, a flower shop, provides custom floral arrangements for events and daily orders. They charge approximately $50 per arrangement. The shop currently rents a flower cooler for $200 per month, resulting in $1,200 in profit per month for 30 arrangements. The shop has enough demand to increase their arrangements to 120 per month. They are considering investing in their own flower cooler for $8,000, which will be usable over the next 5 years. Compute the degree of operating leverage when purchasing the flower cooler.

E:6-11 (Learning Objective 6)

Tecktronics Inc., a tech company specializing in high-end electronic devices, prides itself on its cutting-edge technology and innovation. Tecktronics uses numerous high-powered servers in its 10,000-square-foot facility, and the electricity needed to run the servers is a significant cost. Tecktronics' electrical bills blend demand and usage costs into one final monthly charge. Tecktronics' controller would like to better understand the company's electricity cost structure before working with production to reduce electrical costs. Tecktronics' electrical bills contain the following data for electricity consumption and charges during the month with the highest and lowest consumption during the year:

Production (in Units)	Electricity Cost Incurred (in Dollars)
Low month: 100,000	$30,000
High month: 60,000	$18,000

Determine the cost equation for Tecktonics's electricity costs using the high-low method.

Technology, Analytics, and AI

T:6-12 Describe and Discuss ERP

After developing the regression model, you find the R^2 value to be 0.75.

1. What does an R^2 value of 0.75 tell you about how well the model fits the data?
2. What does the R^2 value of 0.75 say about the relationship between the independent and dependent variable?
3. If another independent variable is added to the model, how might it affect the R^2 value?

T:6-13 Linear Regression in Excel

Determine the cost structure for cell phone customers at Horizon Wireless. Assume data usage is correlated with costs. Use the following data to find the appropriate equation for cell phone costs. Use the least squares method to find your solution.

	Data Usage in Gigabytes (Independent Variable)	Cell Phone Costs (Dependent Variable)
January	14.2	$620
February	13.6	$604
March	22.5	$756
April	16.9	$724
May	12.3	$592
June	13.3	$601

1. Complete the cost equation for utility costs using summary output from the Excel regression function: Cell Phone Costs = __–$17.00__ + ________ (Gigabytes)
   a. $1.02
   b. $0.66
   c. $0.12
   d. $0.04
2. What is the adjusted coefficient of determination?
   a. 0.803
   b. 0.837
   c. 0.937
   d. 0.980
3. Is the equation useful for predicting utility costs? Yes or No
4. how did you come to your conclusion in part 3?

CHAPTER 7

Relevant Data and Business Decision-making

Learning Objectives

7.1 Describe the business decision-making process and the concept of relevant data.
7.2 Explain how a business can maximize profits when resources are constrained.
7.3 Identify relevant data and calculate if a business should outsource production or the performance of services.
7.4 Identify relevant data and calculate if a business should accept or reject a special order.
7.5 Identify relevant data and evaluate business unit or product line performance.
7.6 Identify relevant data and evaluate if a business should retain or replace an asset.
7.7 Describe the concepts of sell or process further for single and joint product decisions.

Accounting in Life

Ketut Subiyanto / Pexels / Public Domain

Making career choices is never easy for anyone, let alone for college students with limited experiences outside the classroom. Analyzing relevant data when making career decisions is critical for making efficient and accurate choices that one can be confident in. When choosing a career path, relevant data might include job market trends, salary information, job satisfaction levels, and personal interests. This ensures that the chosen career is in demand, financially viable, and personally fulfilling.

Let's Review

Business decision-making often starts with an understanding of a firm's costs. We learned in the previous chapter on cost behavior to define costs by their relationship with changes in sales and production activity. Variable costs change in proportion to activity, and fixed costs do not. We combined fixed and variable costs to form a cost equation to evaluate business performance and determine things like how much a business needs to sell to break even or generate a profit. In this chapter, we will learn how companies can use sales, production activity, and cost information to make common business decisions.

LEARNING ACTIVITY 7.1

Tristan Miller is a professional cosmetologist who owns and operates Amor Salon and Spa. Tristan specializes in hairstyling. Tristan rents a small salon space at a high-traffic retail location for $750 per week and typically charges $80 for a haircut with hairstyling. Tristan uses approximately $5 of consumables such as hair spray, disposable towels, and neck liners on each hair styling appointment. If Tristan charges $80 per hairstyling, how many clients are needed in a four-week month to break even?

a. 37
b. 40
c. 150
d. None of the above

How Do Businesses Make Decisions?

Learning Objective 7.1
Describe the business decision-making process and the concept of relevant data.

For business leaders, the ability to make good decisions is critical. Consider these important decisions:

- Setting the price of a new product
- Deciding to outsource business operations rather than perform them in-house
- Selecting a vendor to purchase parts from
- Evaluating an employee's performance

Good decision-making is the difference between success and failure in the business world. Most business decisions are not routine and seldom follow established blueprints entirely. But, approaching decisions systematically can improve the chance of making the best choice. In this section, we provide an overview of the steps in the decision-making process and then examine the role of data analysis. See Figure 7.1 for the five steps in this process.

Business Decision-making Process

Let's take a closer look at each step.

1. *Detect and define the problem.* The most critical step is a clear identification of the problem and its boundaries.
2. *Determine the potential alternatives.* This step involves defining potential choices. For instance, suppose a company receives a large number of orders at one time but does not have enough capacity to fulfill all of them. What choices does the company have? The company could refuse orders above existing capacity or expand capacity.
3. *Evaluate and quantify the outcomes under each alternative.* Businesses commonly start evaluating alternatives by quantifying the financial consequences of each and compiling a tally of the incremental costs and revenues. However, it is not only about dollars and cents. Businesses weigh nonfinancial data as well, such as safety, quality, the environment, or its effect on the community.
4. *Make the decision.* Ultimately, decision-makers must weigh the potential outcomes and make a choice.
5. *Analyze and reflect on the results.* After making a choice, business leaders continue to monitor and reflect on the outcomes. That might result in the identification of a new problem if expected results are not achieved, initiating a new decision-making process.

Quantifying the financial outcomes of a business decision is only a starting point. Businesses must also consider important nonfinancial factors like safety, quality, reputation, the environment, and more before choosing a course of action.

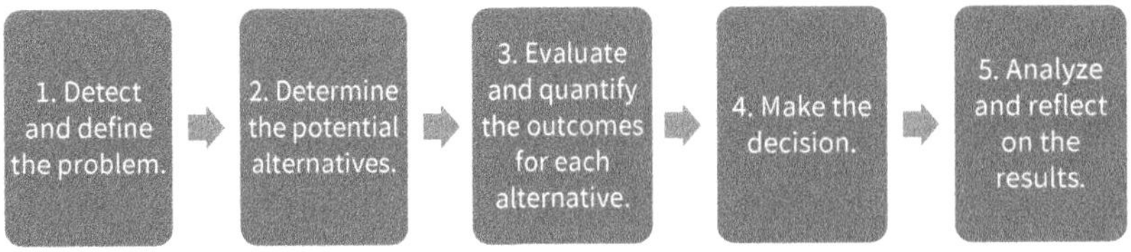

Figure 7.1 Steps in business decisions.

LEARNING ACTIVITY 7.2

Align the action with the step in the decision-making process to which it corresponds:

Step	Action
Step 1: Detect and define the problem.	A. Tally and compare incremental costs and revenues.
Step 2: Determine the possible alternatives.	B. Monitoring the outcomes.
Step 3: Evaluate and quantify the outcomes under each alternative.	C. A company's product cost is higher than the competition's product cost.
Step 4: Make the decision.	D. The company could continue to manufacture the product or outsource production to an overseas supplier.
Step 5: Analyze and reflect on the results.	E. Choosing one alternative over the other.

Which is the correct alignment of steps with actions?

a. A, C, E, B, D
b. C, D, A, E, B
c. B, D, C, E, A
d. All of the above

Incremental Analysis

To guide decision-making, business leaders rely on accountants to compile data and perform a quantitative analysis. Specifically, accountants examine the change in costs and revenues related to possible alternatives with **incremental analysis**, which illustrates expected financial results from alternative choices.

Incremental analysis is used to examine future decisions and illustrate expected financial results from alternative choices.

For example, suppose that Tristan Miller, the cosmetologist in the opening Learning Activity, is considering expanding services from hairstyling to also offer eyelash weaving and nail treatments. If there is strong demand for both of the new services, Tristan will have to decide which services to provide, considering time is limited. Tristan must consider how much time available to work each week. Tristan must also consider how much customer demand exists for each service and the potential profitability of each service.

Max Vakhtbovycn / Pexels / Public Domain

To perform incremental analyses, businesspeople gather data and information from many sources internally and externally to incorporate into an analysis. For example, Tristan might do the following:

- Estimate the potential profitability of new eyelash weaving and nail treatment services by researching the prices other spas charge and comparing those with the cost of materials she consumed when providing each service.
- Collect information from trade associations or local business support groups like her community's chamber of commerce to determine the volume of services her community demands and identify how many competitors there are.

The result of that analysis is a financial starting point. Next, businesses usually weigh nonfinancial factors. For example, Tristan might consider how enjoyable it is to provide each type of service. Tristan's enjoyment is an important nonfinancial factor. Figure 7.2 illustrates Tristan's decision-making process.

Relevant Data, Opportunity Cost, and Sunk Cost

The data used in an incremental analysis must be *relevant*. **Relevant data** are data that are changed or affected by selecting a particular course of action. For example, one relevant piece of information Tristan Miller must include in the analysis of adding the new product lines is the cost of new training and certification needed to obtain to perform the new services. The cost of training to be certified to perform eyelash weaving is typically around $1,000.

"*Change*" is the most important ingredient when deciding if a cost is relevant. If a business decision does not cause a particular cost to change, it is not relevant to that decision.

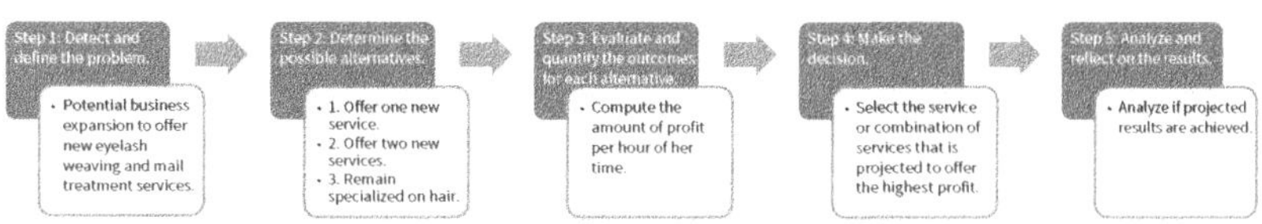

Figure 7.2 Tristan's decision-making process with incremental analysis.

Opportunity Cost

Another important piece of information to consider is **opportunity cost**, which is the lost benefits when electing to forgo a course of action. For example, if Tristan decides to pass on performing nail services and instead focus time on hairstyling and eyelash weaves, the potential money made from performing nail treatments is a lost opportunity, or opportunity cost.

Sunk Cost

Finally, it is possible that decision-makers erroneously incorporate information that is not relevant. Data that are commonly incorporated erroneously are *sunk costs*. A **sunk cost** is a cost that has already been incurred and cannot be affected further, regardless of the course of action. For example, what if Tristan had already completed a nail treatment certification course? The money spent on the nail treatment certification is already gone, and it will not be returned if Tristan decides not to perform nail treatments. What if Tristan will be required to spend money on continuing education courses *in the future* to maintain the certification necessary to perform nail treatment services? That future cost is relevant because it will be incurred *if* Tristan elects to sell nail treatments. It would *not* be relevant if Tristan elects to stop selling nail treatments.

LEARNING ACTIVITY 7.3

For each data item listed next, identify which elements are relevant.

A. A brewing company is considering developing a new type of beer. The company will be able to use existing equipment. When computing the profitability of the new type of beer, the cost of the existing equipment is ________.

B. A large public accounting firm offers a signing bonus to new hires. The firm is considering dismissing a new hire who has turned out to be unreliable after six months of work. When considering the cost of dismissing the employee, the signing bonus is ________.

C. An employee aiming for a promotion is considering the cost of tuition for attending graduate school, a requirement for the promotion. When considering the benefits of the promotion, the cost of tuition is ________.

D. A landscape business is considering expanding its services to include pool maintenance. The company will need to purchase special equipment to offer this new service. When computing the profitability of the pool maintenance service, the cost of the special equipment is ________.

E. A manufacturing firm is considering outsourcing some of its production to another company. This decision will allow the company to lease out the excess factory space. The amount of money received from the lease is ________.

Which items are relevant?

a. A, B, E
b. C, D, E
c. A, C, E
d. B, C, D

Relevance is determined by *change*. A piece of data is only relevant if it changes as a result of the decision.

Now that we have introduced the steps in decision-making and the role of analyzing costs, we turn to specific decision-making situations businesses encounter:

- Constrained resources
- Outsourcing production or performance of services
- Special orders
- Product line performance evaluation
- Asset replacement

How Do Businesses Choose Where They Will Spend Their Time and Money?

Learning Objective 7.2
Explain how a business can maximize profits when resources are constrained.

Scarce resources can be defined as business inputs with limited availability. Examples of resources that might be limited are skilled labor, machine time, factory space, or available raw materials. When a company has limited resources, management must decide how to use those resources most effectively. For example, scarce resources can result in a company choosing to limit sales of products or services.

Mike Bird / Pexels / Public Domain

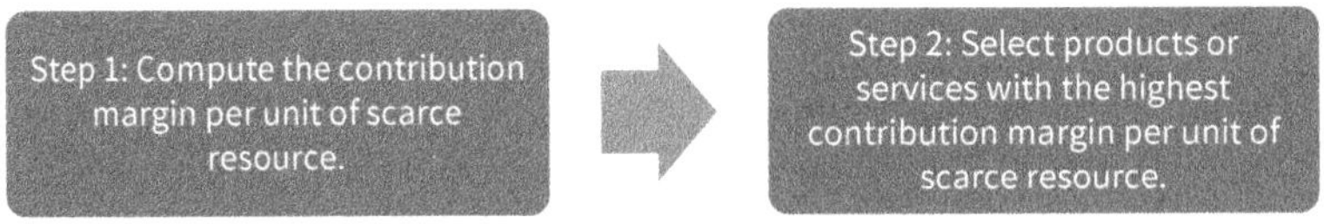

Figure 7.3 Profit maximization analysis.

Lithium, for example, is an important element of electric car batteries. However, the supply of lithium is scarce, which risks limiting the production of batteries. Without the batteries, car manufacturers may have to limit their production of electric vehicles.

The Decision-making Process: Maximizing Profit with Scarce Resources

When companies have limited resources, management usually performs an analysis of which products or services can provide the highest net income for each unit of scarce resource. Figure 7.3 outlines the steps accountants undertake to perform the analysis.

To perform step 1, the accountant divides the contribution margin per unit of each product by the number of units of the limited resource required to produce each unit of product:

$$\frac{\text{Contribution Margin per Unit of Product}}{\text{Units of the Limited Resource Needed to Produce the Product}}$$

Step 2 focuses on maximizing profits. The business should satisfy the demand for the products with the highest contribution margin per unit of scarce resource before those with lower contribution margins per unit of scarce resource.

Consider Kandice Jones, the owner of a small tax practice that focuses on tax returns for individuals, small businesses, and estates and trusts. Kandice made the decision to focus on preparing business tax returns for her customers and no longer offer to prepare individual tax returns or tax returns for estates and trusts to clients. The marketplace demands all three services, but after careful analysis, Kandice finds that preparing tax returns for business clients provides the most contribution per hour of her time. After finding that there is enough demand for business tax services to consume all of the available time, Kandice elects to specialize in business tax services and forgo opportunities to prepare tax returns for individuals, estates and trusts.

Remember, the contribution margin per unit is the difference between the net sales price per unit and the variable cost per unit.

$$\text{Net Sales per Unit} - \text{Variable Costs per Unit} = \text{Contribution Margin per Unit}$$

Example: Maximizing Profit with Scarce Resources

Let's explore how this process works by continuing our analysis of Tristan Miller's salon services business. Tristin's limited resource is time. In fact, time is a limited resource for anyone in a service business. Let's assume Tristan can devote 160 hours per month to providing client services such as hair care, nail treatments, or eyelash weaving. Let's also assume there is enough demand to consume 100 hours of Tristan's time per month on each of those services. In other

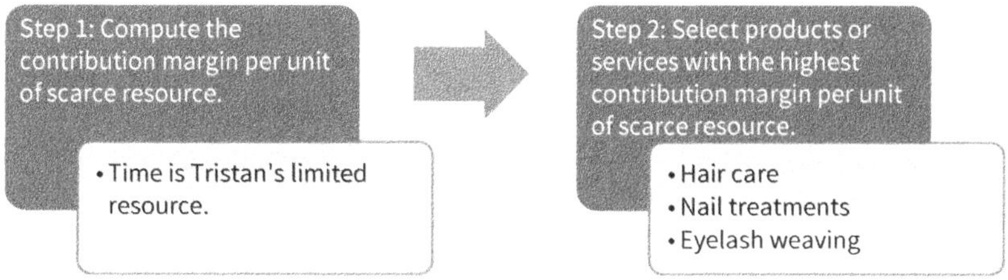

Figure 7.4 Tristan's profit maximization analysis.

words, Tristan has much more demand for services than time available. Figure 7.4 provides an overview of the steps in Tristan's profit analysis.

Consider the following data related to the three services:

	Hair Styling	Nail Treatments	Eyelashes
Selling price per instance	$80	$70	$150
Direct variable costs	5	12	60
Contribution margin	$75	$58	$ 90
Service time	1.5 hours	1 hour	2 hours

Taking into account the data related to the three services under consideration, where should Tristan allocate time to maximize profit?

Step 1: Compute the Contribution Margin Per Unit of Scarce Resource. The first step is to compute the contribution margin per unit of limited resource, Tristan's time. The computation of the contribution margin per hour for all three services is listed here:

	Hair Styling	Nail Treatments	Eyelashes
Contribution Margin per Unit	$ 75	$ 58	$ 90
÷ Service Time	÷ 1.5 hours	÷ 1 hour	÷ 2 hours
Contribution Margin per Hour	$50 per hour	$58 per hour	$45 Per Hour

Notice that eyelashes have the highest contribution margin *per unit* of $90 per set. However, eyelashes take 2 hours to weave into a client's existing lashes. That results in a contribution margin *per hour* of $45 per hour of time spent on lashes ($90/2 hours). Weaving a new set of eyelash extensions has the highest overall contribution margin *per unit* but takes the longest amount of time, resulting in the lowest contribution *per hour* of $45. Nail treatments, on the other hand, have the lowest total contribution *per unit* but take the shortest amount of time and have the highest contribution margin *per hour* of $58. These results reveal three important points:

1. Tristan would make the most money by satisfying customer demand for nail treatments.
2. Tristan can then provide hairstyling if if more time becomes available.
3. Tristan should only sell sets of eyelashes if there is additional time available after satisfying demand for nail treatments and hairstyling.

Step 2: Select Products or Services with the Highest Contribution Margin Per Unit of Scarce Resource. Based on this analysis, what sales mix will allow Tristan to maximize contribution margin? Tristan has demand for 100 hours of each service per month and only 160 available hours to devote to her clients. Tristan would maximize monthly profit by devoting 100 hours to nail treatments to satisfy the demand and devoting the remaining 60 hours of time to hair styling. The analysis indicates Tristan should not spend time selling and weaving in sets of eyelashes. Tristan's number of hours devoted to each service, or optimal sales mix, is as follows:

	Hair Styling	Nail Treatments	Eyelashes
Optimal Hours Devoted	× 60 Hours	× 100 Hours	× 0 Hours

The optimal sales mix would provide Tristan with $8,800 of contribution monthly. We compute Tristan's monthly contribution with the optimal number of hours devoted to each service, or sales mix, as follows:

	Hair Styling	Nail Treatments	Eyelashes
Contribution Margin per hour	$50 per hour	$58 per hour	$45
Optimal Hours Devoted	× 60	× 100	× 0
Total Monthly Contribution	$ 3,000	$ 5,800	$ 0
	$8,800		

ACCOUNTING IN BUSINESS

Choosing a Sales Mix

Brittney Dinardi operates **Wild Roots Studio** in Broadus, Montana. "I provide women's colors and cuts, men's cuts, kids' cuts, face waxing, protein treatments, and eyelash extensions," says Brittney. "Eyelash extensions and color services are most profitable," states Brittney, as they have the highest return per hour of her time, even though they take the longest to perform. Brittney stays busy with those services but fills in the gaps in her daily schedule with other services that take less time, like men's and kids' haircuts, each taking about 20 minutes. "I stay booked with those (eyelash extensions and women's colors), but it is also good to fill in smaller time slots with things like men's and kids' cuts." In the end, however, it isn't just about profit. "If you have full books, you are going to make a profit. I also choose to provide services I enjoy and am talented at doing," says Brittney.

Source: Author interview with Brittney Dinardi, Owner Wild Roots Studio.

LEARNING ACTIVITY 7.4

MC Aero Service is a small aviation business that provides air charter, air ambulance, air freight, and flight training services to customers in the mountain west. Gael Euker is MC Aero's owner and chief pilot. Gael employs one other pilot, and both are qualified to perform any of the services MC Aero offers. Federal Aviation Rules limit pilots to 1,000 hours of flight time per year, allowing MC Aero to perform 2,000 hours per year (1,000 hours × 2 pilots). Customer demand for MC Aero's services is as follows:

	Air Charter	Air Ambulance	Air Freight	Flight Training
Annual Customer Demand (in hours)	700	400	1,300	500

MC Aero charges customers a rate per hour of flight time. The hourly rate and associated hourly costs of providing each service are here:

	Air Charter	Air Ambulance	Air Freight	Flight Training
Sales Price per Hour of Flight Time	$500	$700	$400	$200
Average Fuel Cost per Hour	100	200	100	25
Average Pilot Cost per Hour	200	225	75	100
Other Variable Overhead per Hour	50	100	25	15

1. What is MC Aero's scarce resource?
   a. Hours of pilot flight time
   b. Fuel
   c. The airplanes
   d. The number of passengers
2. Compute the contribution margin per hour of flight time for each of MC Aero's services. Which has the highest contribution margin per hour?
   a. Air charter
   b. Air ambulance
   c. Air freight
   d. Flight training
3. Compute the optimal sales mix. How many hours should MC devote to air ambulance?
   a. 0
   b. 300
   c. 400
   d. 1,300

4. What is the total amount of contribution margin for MC Aero at the optimal sales mix?
   a. 0
   b. $260,000
   c. $340,000
   d. $375,000

Remember, a firm can maximize profit by choosing the sales mix that maximizes the contribution margin per scarce resource.

What Can Businesses Do When They Run Out of Capacity?

Learning Objective 7.3
Identify relevant data and calculate if a business should outsource production or the performance of services.

Suppose a business manufactures a product, sells services to customers, and provides internal services like payroll processing. Managers are considering outsourcing the production and performance of services to an external supplier. **Outsourcing** is purchasing a product or service from an external supplier that would otherwise be produced or performed in-house. In this section, we explain and illustrate the steps in evaluating outsourcing opportunities.

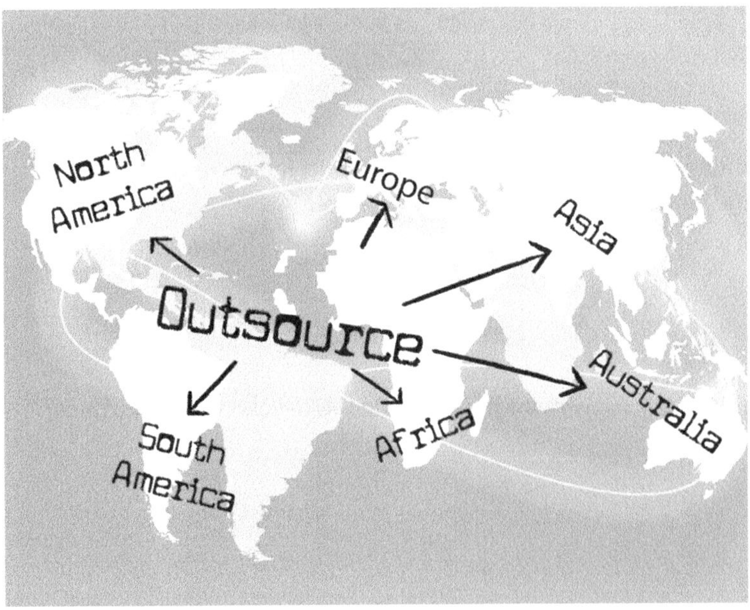

Jirehg / Pixabay

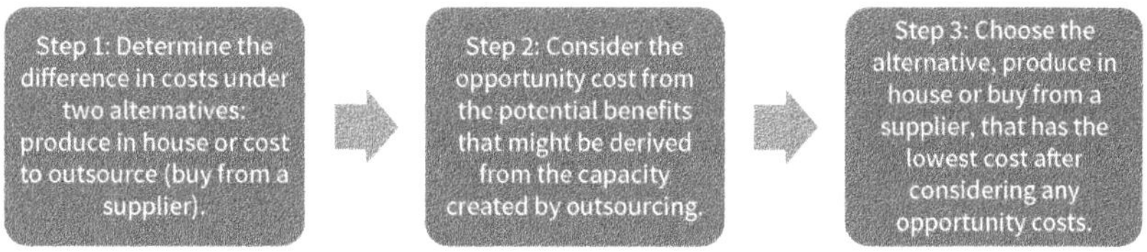

Figure 7.5 Evaluating outsourcing options decision-making process.

Decision-making Process: Evaluating Outsourcing Options

When evaluating an outsourcing opportunity, management follows the steps in Figure 7.5 to perform an analysis.

Recall that opportunity costs are benefits lost when a business elects to forgo a course of action. Electing to produce a product or perform a service in-house usually results in forgoing other opportunities that could be pursued with the capacity consumed. Companies evaluate decisions to outsource a product or service to an external supplier based on the current cost to make the product, vendor purchase price and quality, and opportunity cost.

Example: Evaluating Outsourcing Options

Let us look at an example related to the custom motorcycle manufacturer introduced in Chapter 2, Blackhawk Custom Cycles. When Blackhawk opened its business, it vowed to build every bike from scratch to the extent possible, including engines that Blackhawk assembles from raw components. Recently, Blackhawk has become concerned about costs and has started evaluating ways to improve its profitability. Valley Powertrain Specialties offered to produce and sell Blackhawk's 350cc engine for $985. Figure 7.6 provides an overview of the steps in analyzing Blackhawk's outsourcing decision.

Step 1: Determine the Difference in Costs Under the Two Alternatives. Blackhawk has decided to consider buying the engines from Valley rather than building them in-house. Blackhawk produces approximately 500 motorcycles and engines annually. The costs to produce the engines in-house are as follows:

	Cost per Engine	Total Engine Manufacturing Costs
Direct Materials	$350	$ 175,000
Direct Labor	$245	$ 122,500
Variable Overhead	$ 55	$ 27,500
Fixed Overhead		$ 100,000
Total Engine Manufacturing Costs		$ 425,000
Total Cost per Engine ($425,000)		$850 per unit

Initially, it appears that Blackhawk would be better off manufacturing the engine at a cost of $850 instead of purchasing them for $985 from Valley Powertrain. Would outsourcing change any of Blackhawk's fixed or variable costs? Further evaluation of Blackhawk's costs

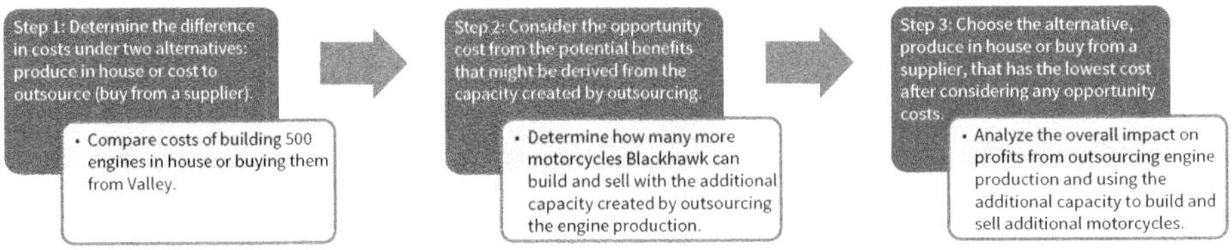

Figure 7.6 Blackhawk's outsourcing decision-making process.

reveals that $30,000 of its fixed overhead costs are directly associated with equipment used to build the engines, while the remaining $70,000 is associated with shop space and tools that are used on other production items in addition to the engines. If the company decides to purchase the engines instead of building them, fixed overhead costs would decrease by $30,000 because $70,000 of cost will remain and apply to more than just the engines. Considering this, the costs associated with making and buying the engines are as follows:

	Make	Buy	Profit Increase (Decrease)
Purchase Price			
($985 × 500 engines)	0	$492,500	$(492,500)
Direct Materials	$175,000	0	175,000
Direct Labor	122,500	0	122,500
Variable Overhead	27,500	0	27,500
Fixed Overhead	30,000	0	30,000
Total Incremental Cost	$355,000	$492,500	$(137,500)

The analysis summing the relevant costs, or costs that change if Blackhawk elects to purchase engines from Valley, shows a decrease in profits of $137,500 if Blackhawk elects to outsource and buy the engines. If Blackhawk discontinues engine production, it will no longer incur the costs of direct materials, direct labor, variable overhead, and $30,000 of fixed overhead. That totals to $355,000 of cost savings. However, Blackhawk will spend $492,500 purchasing the engines from Valley. Therefore, profit will decrease by $137,500 if Blackhawk purchases the engines. Another way to think about it is: Should Blackhawk spend $492,500 in order to save $355,000? Absolutely not!

Step 2: Consider the Possible Opportunity Cost from the Capacity Created by Outsourcing. Now, let us consider a potential opportunity that Blackhawk may undertake with the additional capacity created by outsourcing. Blackhawk has found that it can build and sell another 40 motorcycles at a profit of $3,500 per motorcycle with the additional capacity it would create by outsourcing the engine production to Valley. The additional $140,000 in profit (40 motorcycles × $3,500 profit per motorcycle) would be a lost opportunity (or opportunity cost) if Blackhawk continues to produce the engines in-house. Considering the cost of this opportunity, Blackhawk's cost of engines would be:

	Make	Buy	Profit Increase (Decrease)
Incremental Cost	$355,000	$492,500	$(137,500)
Opportunity Cost	140,000	0	$ 140,000
Total Revised Incremental Cost	$495,000	$492,500	$ 2,500

Further analysis reveals that Blackhawk would increase profits by $2,500 if it outsourced engine production and used the additional capacity to build and sell an additional 40 motorcycles. Outsourcing looks like a wise decision when the opportunity cost is considered.

However, once the economic impact of outsourcing is determined, firms must answer additional questions about other factors that are not so easily quantified, such as quality and timeliness. Firms will want to consider if the vendor can deliver a product or service of equivalent quality as produced in-house and if that product or service can be delivered or performed on time to not delay operations. Outsourcing decisions are important in business and consumer decisions, as the following example about hiring a lawn service illustrates.

Remember, when considering the economic impacts of outsourcing, choose the alternative that results in the lowest cost after considering the opportunity cost.

ACCOUNTING IN LIFE

Outsourcing to a Lawn Service

Have you ever considered hiring a lawn service? Many people outsource household duties like lawn care. When evaluating hiring a lawn service, a homeowner should consider the cost of a mower, gas, mower maintenance, and the value the owner places on other opportunities they might take advantage of when not mowing. Compare the sum of those values against the price of the lawn care service.

Let us look at the numbers. Assume the cost to hire a lawn service is $30 per weekly mowing. How does that compare to owning a mower and mowing oneself?

	Mowing Oneself	Lawn Service
Price of a Mower	$400.00	
÷ Life of the Mower (5 Years)	÷ 5	
Annual Cost of the Mower	$ 80.00	
Annual Mower Maintenance	60.00	
Annual Gallons of Gas (4 Gallons @ $3.00 Per Gallon)	12.00	
Total Cost	$152.00	
÷ Number of Mowings per Year	÷ 16	
Cost Per Mowing	$ 9.50	$30.00

A homeowner saves $20.50 per mowing by electing to purchase a mower and cut the grass on their own. The question still remains as to the value the homeowner places on the time lost mowing, which represents an opportunity cost. If the homeowner places a value of more than $20.50 on the time lost mowing, they should consider using the lawn service.

LEARNING ACTIVITY 7.5

ReTreads Premium Footwear Company prepared a cost summary for a pair of its Wooderson model sandals.

Direct Materials	$12
Direct Labor	23
Variable Overhead	3
Direct Fixed Overhead	10
Fixed Marketing Costs	7
Total Cost	$55

ReTreads intends to sell each pair for $100. ReTreads currently makes 5,000 pairs per year. Yang Zhou Industries has approached ReTreads and offered to manufacture the sandals for $50 per pair. Further analysis reveals that 40% of the direct fixed cost is related to rent on a building that it will still use for warehouse space if the sandals are made by ReTreads or outsourced to Yang Zhou Industries. In addition, the fixed marketing costs will remain if the company chooses to outsource or continue to manufacture the sandals.

1. Assume ReTreads has no other use for the facilities it is renting. How much more or less profit will ReTreads have if it accepts Yang Zhou's offer and outsources production? Should ReTreads accept Yang Zhou's offer?
   - **a.** Profit will increase by $10,000; accept Yang Zhou's offer.
   - **b.** Profit will increase by $30,000; accept Yang Zhou's offer.
   - **c.** Profit will decrease by $10,000; decline Yang Zhou's offer.
   - **d.** Profit will decrease by $30,000; decline Yang Zhou's offer.

2. Assume that if ReTreads outsourced to Yang Zhou Industries, ReTreads could sublet some of the building it is renting to another company for $4,000 per month. How much more or less profit will ReTreads have if it accepts Yang Zhou's offer and outsources production? Should ReTreads accept Yang Zhou's offer?
   a. Profit will increase by $15,000; accept Yang Zhou's offer.
   b. Profit will increase by $18,000; accept Yang Zhou's offer.
   c. Profit will decrease by $15,000; decline Yang Zhou's offer.
   d. Profit will decrease by $18,000; decline Yang Zhou's offer.

What Are the Consequences of a Discounted Price?

Learning Objective 7.4
Identify relevant data and calculate if a business should accept or reject a special order.

There are times when customers approach a business and ask to purchase a product at a lower price. Such requests often come with an offer of purchasing a large volume. Situations where a customer requests a product or service at a special price are commonly called **special orders**.

Decision-making Process: Special Orders

To evaluate special orders, businesses follow the steps outlined in Figure 7.7.

The significant issue that influences the cost of a special order is *capacity*. If the order can be filled using existing capacity, fixed costs do not change and are not relevant. Only variable costs are affected and are relevant.

Example: Special Orders

Consider **ReTreads Premium Footwear Company**. Let us assume ReTreads has capacity to produce 10,000 pairs of Wooderson sandals annually in its existing production facility, and it currently produces 5,000 pairs per year. ReTreads typically sells the Wooderson sandals at a sales price of $100 per pair. Shoe MD, a high-end retail shoe chain, has offered to purchase a one-time special order of 4,000 pairs of Wooderson sandals at a price of $45 per pair. This special order will be in addition to ReTreads' existing production of 5,000 pairs per year. Should ReTreads accept the special order? Figure 7.8 shows the steps ReTreads will follow in making this special-order decision.

Figure 7.7 Special order decision-making process.

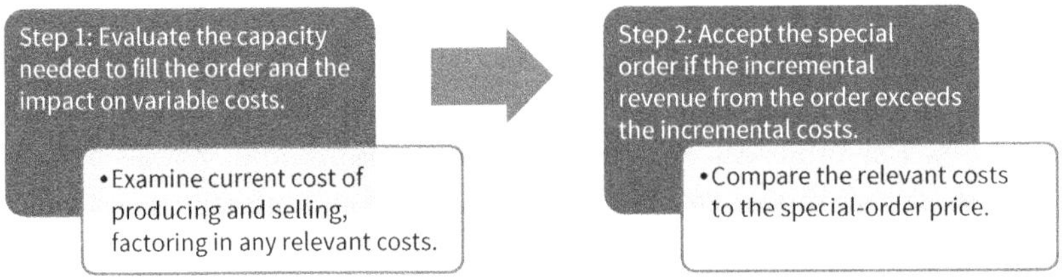

Figure 7.8 ReTreads' special order decision-making process.

Step 1: Evaluate the Capacity Needed to Fill the Order and the Impact on Variable Costs. The current cost of producing and selling Wooderson sandals are as follows:

Direct Materials	$ 12
Direct Labor	23
Variable Overhead	3
Direct Fixed Overhead	10
Fixed Marketing Costs	7
Total Cost	$ 55

ReTreads does not expect marketing costs to be affected by the special order. Shipping is normally paid by ReTreads' customers, but in this case, ReTreads will pay for shipping the product to Shoe MD at a cost of $1 per pair.

If ReTreads compares Shoe MD's offer of $45 per pair to their current total cost of $55 per pair, it would reject the order, potentially losing out on profit. A more careful analysis shows that the only costs affected by the special order are the direct material ($12 per pair), direct labor ($23 per pair), variable overhead ($3 per pair), and shipping costs ($1 per pair), amounting to a total cost of $39 per pair. Because Retreads can fill the order with existing capacity and marketing channels, fixed overhead and marketing costs are unchanged and not relevant.

Step 2: Accept the Special Order if the Incremental Revenue from the Order Exceeds the Incremental Costs. A comparison of the relevant costs of $39 per pair to the special order price of $45 per pair shows that ReTreads would make $24,000 in incremental profit if it accepted the special order as follows:

	Current Cost per Unit		Relevant Cost per Unit
Direct Materials	$12	*Relevant*	$12
Direct Labor	23	*Relevant*	23
Variable Overhead	3	*Relevant*	3
Direct Fixed Overhead	10	*Not Relevant*	0
Fixed Marketing Costs	7	*Not Relevant*	0
Total Cost	$55		$38

Shipping Cost	*Relevant*	1
Total Relevant Costs per Unit		$ 39
Special Order Price per Unit		$ 45
Relevant Cost per Unit		(39)
Profit per Unit		$ 6
Units Ordered		× 4,000
Incremental Profit		$ 24,000

Fixed costs are not relevant in the incremental analysis if production can take place within existing capacity. If an alternative would result in production outside capacity limits, fixed costs may increase if capacity is added through choices like the purchase of equipment.

LEARNING ACTIVITY 7.6

Rawlins Print Shop is a small family-owned business in San Marcos, Texas that specializes in printing fliers, brochures, business cards, and other commercial print media. Real Estate Associates (REA) is a real estate brokerage firm with offices in Austin and Round Rock. REA is planning an expansion into San Marcos and neighboring Lockhart. REA desires to do business locally and has approached Rawlins about printing 10,000 color brochures to be mailed out to homeowners in the region announcing the new business. The expansion is expensive, and REA has budgeted $7,500 for printing costs or $0.75 per brochure ($7,500/10,000 brochures). REA's marketing manager has asked if Rawlins would be willing to fill the order for that price.

Rawlins has the capacity to produce 250,000 brochures per year with its color printing equipment. Currently, Rawlins produces approximately 200,000 such brochures annually with the equipment being idle otherwise. Rawlins typically sells such brochures for $1.25 each and its annual costs are as follows:

Direct Materials	$0.50 per unit
Direct Labor	0.05 per unit
Variable Overhead	0.02 per unit
Fixed Overhead	0.15 per unit
Sales Commissions	4% of total sales
Shipping Costs	$1.00 per bundle of 100
Fixed Cost of Equipment	$12,000 per year
Fixed Advertising and Promotion	$10,000 per year

Other information: A sales commission will be paid to the sales manager at the time of the special order.

1. What significant factor should Rawlins consider when deciding which costs are relevant to its decision to accept the special order?
    a. Timeliness
    b. Capacity
    c. Quality
    d. Fixed costs
2. What is the increase or decrease in profit if Rawlins accepts the special order?
    a. ($100)
    b. ($22,100)
    c. $1,400
    d. $15,400

How Does a Company Evaluate the Performance of Different Business Lines?

Learning Objective 7.5
Identify relevant data and evaluate business unit or product line performance.

Evaluating the performance of business units or lines of products and services (referred to as simply *business units* hereafter) can be a complex task. Many costs are shared between business units, such as the cost of equipment used on multiple products or internal services like maintenance or administration.

Decision-making Process: Evaluating the Performance of Different Business Lines

Costs that are not associated with a particular business unit and are shared across more than one business unit are called **common costs**. Common costs must be carefully considered when evaluating business unit performance. The evaluation requires the steps shown in Figure 7.9.

Figure 7.9 Evaluating business unit performance decision-making process.

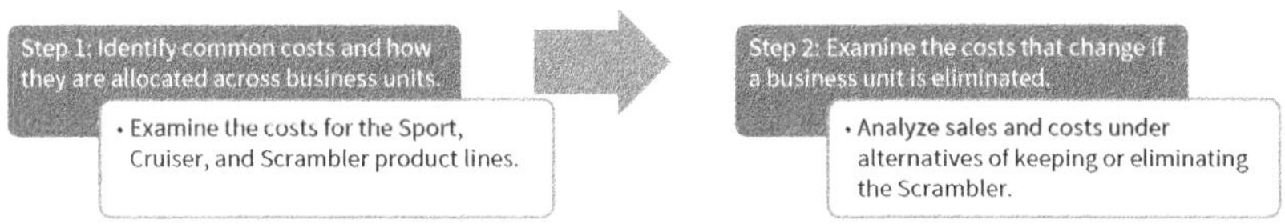

Figure 7.10 Blackhawk's business unit performance decision-making process.

Example: Evaluating the Performance of Different Business Lines

Let us illustrate with an example related to Blackhawk Custom Cycle, which we overview in Figure 7.10. In addition to the 350cc Sport motorcycle discussed earlier in the chapter, Blackhawk manufactures a 750cc Cruiser designed for long rides and highway travel and a 150cc Scrambler designed for both on and off-road use. Blackhawk is evaluating the performance of the three business lines.

Step 1: Identify Common Costs and How They Are Allocated Across Business Units. Let us start by examining the costs for each product line. Blackhawk's segmented income statement shows that the Scrambler model is the least popular and that the product is losing money.

The income statement separated by unit is as follows:

	Sport	Cruiser	Scrambler	Total
Sales	$4,000,000	$2,000,000	$ 900,000	$ 6,900,000
Variable Costs	(2,100,000)	(900,000)	(500,000)	(3,500,000)
Contribution Margin	1,900,000	1,100,000	400,000	3,400,000
Fixed Costs	(700,000)	(700,000)	(700,000)	(2,100,000)
Net Income (Loss)	$1,200,000	$ 400,000	$(300,000)	$1,300,000

On the surface, it appears the Scrambler is losing $300,000 annually, and eliminating the Scrambler would increase profits from $1,300,000 to $1,600,000. However, a closer evaluation of the fixed costs reveals that the $2,100,000 fixed costs are related to factory space, equipment, and administrative personnel that are common or shared by all product lines. Blackhawk allocates one-third of the common fixed costs ($700,000) to each of the products to arrive at the net income or loss for each product line. Blackhawk has identified that the elimination of a product will not reduce the fixed cost. If it eliminated the Scrambler, the Scrambler's $700,000 of fixed costs would be split evenly, $350,000, between each remaining model. Considering this, the elimination of the Scrambler will cost Blackhawk $400,000 in lost profits, reducing net income from $1,300,000 to $900,000. Blackhawk's new income statement without the Scrambler would be as follows:

	Sport	Cruiser	Total
Sales	$4,000,000	$2,000,000	$6,000,000
Variable Costs	(2,100,000)	(900,000)	(3,000,000)

Contribution Margin	1,900,000	1,100,000	3,000,000
Fixed Costs	(1,050,000)	(1,050,000)	(2,100,000)
Net Income (Loss)	$ 850,000	$ 50,000	$ 900,000

Step 2: Examine the Costs That Change if a Business Unit Is Eliminated. An examination of the sales and costs of the Scrambler under two alternatives, keep or eliminate, illustrates how profits change.

	Keep	Eliminate	Change
Sales	$ 900,000	$ 0	$ (900,000)
Variable Costs	(500,000)	0	500,000
Contribution Margin	400,000	0	(400,000)
Fixed Costs	(700,000)	(700,000)	0
Net Income	$(300,000)	$(700,000)	$(400,000)

Based on the analysis, Blackhawk decides to maintain the Scrambler.

A Better Way to Format a Segmented Income Statement

The best way to format an income statement segmented by product line or business unit is to separate any allocated common costs. A revised income statement for Blackhawk Custom Cycle with the common fixed costs separated into a separate column is as follows:

	Sport	Cruiser	Scrambler	Common Costs	Total
Sales	$4,000,000	$2,000,000	$ 900,000		$6,900,000
Variable Costs	(2,100,000)	(900,000)	(500,000)		(3,500,000)
Contribution Margin	1,900,000	1,100,000	400,000		4,400,000
Fixed Costs	0	0	0	$ (2,100,000)	(2,100,000)
Net Income (Loss)	$1,900,000	$1,100,000	$ 400,000	$(2,100,000)	$1,300,000

Identifying common costs is critical because common costs are usually unaffected if a business unit is added, eliminated, or changed. That is, common costs are not typically relevant in evaluating business units.

LEARNING ACTIVITY 7.7

DatCo Electronics Corporation is a computer software company that provides computer software for managing nonprofit businesses and software that helps companies manage employee expense reimbursement account balances. DatCo's financial manager segments the company's income statements by the two divisions (nonprofit and expense management). The company's segmented income statement for the two divisions for the year follows:

	Total	Nonprofit Division	Expense Management Division
Sales	$15,000,000	$10,000,000	$5,000,000
Variable Costs	(8,000,000)	(5,500,000)	(2,500,000)
Contribution Margin	7,000,000	4,500,000	2,500,000
Fixed Costs	(6,000,000)	(3,250,000)	(2,750,000)
Net Income (Loss)	$ 1,000,000	$ 1,250,000	$(250,000)

The president of DatCo is considering dropping the Expense Management Division since it has incurred a loss for the past year. Further analysis reveals that the direct fixed costs for the Nonprofit Division were $2,250,000 and $1,750,000 for the Expense Management Division. The other $2,000,000 in fixed costs are common to both divisions and were allocated evenly to both divisions. These costs would not be affected by the elimination of either division. What would the effect on net income be if DatCo eliminates the division?

a. $750,000
b. $1,000,000
c. ($750,000)
d. ($1,000,000)

How Do Businesses Use Data to Evaluate the Investment in New Equipment or Facilities?

Learning Objective 7.6
Identify relevant data and evaluate if a business should retain or replace an asset.

Fixed assets like equipment, machinery, or vehicles can become useless, worn, or costly to operate. In those cases, businesses must decide if it is economical to continue to use the asset or replace it with a new one.

Decision-making Process: Evaluating an Investment in New Equipment or Facilities

To evaluate the financial impact of continuing to use a fixed asset or replace it, businesses follow the steps in Figure 7.11.

Example: Evaluating an Investment in New Equipment or Facilities

Let us consider the following situation related to MC Aero to illustrate. MC Aero operates the Cessna 414 Chancellor, a twin-engine, eight-passenger airplane, for air ambulance and some of its air charter services. MC Aero's owner, Gael Euker, believes its current 414 Chancellor has higher operating costs than a new 414A Super Chancellor. The new 414A is faster, carries more cargo than the old model, and would help MC Aero obtain more business as a result. Figure 7.12 illustrates the steps in MC Aero's decision to invest in new equipment.

Joao Henrique Damiao de Oliveira / Pexels / Public Domain

Figure 7.11 Evaluating an investment in new equipment or facilities decision-making process.

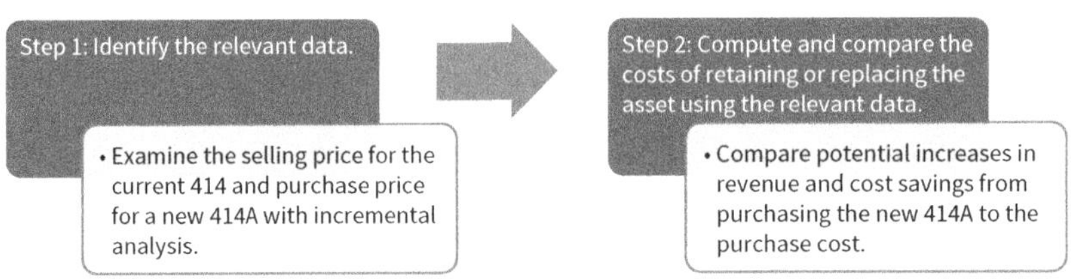

Figure 7.12 MC Aero's investment in new equipment decision-making process.

Step 1: Identify the Relevant Data. Gael has been offered $400,000 for his current 414 and can purchase a new 414A for $1,000,000. Other facts include the following:

Current 414 Chancellor	
Book Value	$250,000
Selling Price	$400,000
Remaining Useful Life	10 Years
Annual Revenue Generated	$600,000
Annual Variable Costs	$160,000
New 414A Super Chancellor	
Purchase Price	$1,000,000
Residual Value	$200,000
Useful Life	10 Years
Annual Revenue Generated	$650,000
Annual Variable Costs	$140,000

To reach a decision, MC Aero uses incremental analysis to evaluate the two options. An analysis of the data shows that the new 414A Super Chancellor will result in an incremental increase in revenue of $50,000 ($650,000 – $600,000) annually as the new airplane is faster and can haul more. But MC Aero must also consider other relevant data, such as cost savings.

Step 2: Compute and Compare the Costs of Retaining or Replacing the Asset Using the Relevant Data. To complete the analysis, MC Aero must consider potential increases in revenue and potential cost savings from purchasing the new Super Chancellor and compare that data with the cost of the new airplane. With the new 414A, MC Aero will be able to charge more and potentially accept trips the old plane cannot handle because of payload limits. Furthermore, the 414A Super Chancellor is more efficient, and expected operating cost savings amount to $20,000 annually ($160,000 – $140,000). Together, the additional revenue and operating cost savings amount to $70,000 annually ($50,000 + $20,000) or $700,000 ($70,000 × 10 years) over the life of the airplane. In addition, MC expects to generate $400,000 from the sale of the old 414. The new 414A will cost approximately $1,000,000, but MC will be able to sell it at the end of its 10-year life for a residual value of $200,000. Thus, the total net effect of replacing the current 414 with the new 414A is an increase in profits of $300,000 over the next 10 years as follows:

	Retain Current 414	Purchase New 414A	Profit Increase (Decrease)
Annual Revenue	$ 600,000	$ 650,000	$ 50,000
Annual Variable Operating Costs	(160,000)	(140,000)	20,000
Annual Contribution Margin	$ 440,000	$ 510,000	$ 70,000
Years in Service	× 10	× 10	× 10
Total Contribution Margin	$4,400,000	$5,100,000	$700,000

Cost of New Plane		(1,000,000)	(1,000,000)
Sale of the New 414A (at end of 10 years)		200,000	200,000
Sale of Current 414		400,000	400,000
Total Net Effect	$4,400,000	$4,700,000	$300,000

MC Aero decides to make the new investment in the 414A.

In the calculations, we did not use the book value of the current 414 ($250,000). The book value pertains to the original purchase of the current 414 and is a sunk cost. As discussed earlier, sunk costs have already been spent and will not be affected, regardless of the course of action taken. Therefore, it is not a relevant cost when determining if the company should retain or replace an asset.

ACCOUNTING IN LIFE

Deciding to Buy a New Car

Alex P / Pexels / Public Domain

An automobile is an expensive possession—and deciding to buy a new car can be a difficult decision. Is that shiny new car a worthwhile investment versus keeping an older car? The financial literacy publication *Money Under 30* points out that the decline in value is the bulk of the cost of car ownership, and cars decline more in value in their early years. The cost of fuel and maintenance is smaller in comparison, and the likely maintenance and fuel cost savings garnered from upgrading to a new car are very small. Thus, their conclusion is that owning an older car is cheaper. However, money isn't everything, as the inconvenience or safety concerns over a breakdown or the potential to switch to new electric car technology may outweigh the financial consequences for many people.

Source: https://www.moneyunder30.com/true-cost-of-owning-a-car

Compute and compare the costs of retaining or replacing the asset using the relevant data. Relevant data are the inflows and outflows that change due to the decision.

LEARNING ACTIVITY 7.8

VanWilder Corporation uses a wide range of equipment when manufacturing products, such as punch presses, laser cutting machines, robotic welders, and much more. Operations managers at VanWilder must weigh the costs of continuing to use older equipment against the cost of new equipment that may offer operating cost savings. VanWilder is considering upgrading one of its articulated robotic welders. Let us assume the following facts:

Old Welder		
	Book Value	\$2,000
	Selling Price	\$1,000
	Remaining Useful Life	5 Years
	Annual Variable Operating Costs	\$15,000
New Welder		
	Purchase Price	\$12,000
	Residual Value	\$4,000
	Useful Life	5 Years
	Annual Variable Operating Costs	\$10,000

VanWilder does not expect annual revenue of \$60,000 to change if it replaces the welder. Should VanWilder replace its welder with new equipment?

a. (\$10,000)
b. (\$6,000)
c. \$10,000
d. \$18,000

Should Businesses Sell Products As-is, Add More Features, or Split into Multiple Products?

Learning Objective 7.7

Describe the concepts of sell or process further for single and joint product decisions.

Businesses must make sell or process further decisions, which are decisions to either sell a product or continue to enhance it into a product of higher value or split it into multiple products. For example, oil refineries manufacture a number of products from crude oil ranging from kerosene-type jet fuel that requires limited refining to gasoline which requires much more processing. How does an oil refiner decide whether to sell jet fuel or continue to process it into gasoline? The decision-making process starts with comparing the difference between the incremental costs from the additional processing and the additional revenue that can be generated from selling a more refined product.

Single Product Decisions

Let us examine a situation where a business either sells a product as-is or enhances the product with further processing and sells it in the new condition at a higher price. Consider PureProtect Window and Door Company, a manufacturer of windows and doors for the residential home market. PureProtect currently sells its doors unpainted. PureProtect's management would like to know if it would be advantageous to the company to offer an option to have the doors factory painted as an additional charge to customers. The sales price and costs associated with painted and unpainted doors are as follows:

	Revenue and Expenses Per Door		
	Unpainted	Painted	Difference
Sales Price	$175	$225	$50
Manufacturing Costs	115	115	0
Painting Costs	0	35	(35)
Contribution Margin	$ 60	$ 75	$15

The relevant data are the incremental increase in the sales price per door and the incremental costs to paint each door. PureProtect would elect to add the option to paint doors if the incremental sales price exceeds the incremental cost. The sales price for painted doors increased from $175 for an unpainted door to $225 per painted door, for a difference of $50 per door. The additional painting costs amount to $35 per door. Thus, factory painting the doors would net PureProtect an additional $15 per door in contribution margin. Selling factory painted doors would be beneficial to PureProtect in this scenario.

LEARNING ACTIVITY 7.9

All-Out Aluminum Extrusion Company manufactures aluminum baseball bats. All-Out's marketing team believes the company could generate more revenue by offering and charging for customized painting options. All-Out's management has asked for an analysis of the incremental profitability of offering the custom painting option. The sales price and costs associated with traditional and customized bats are as follows. Input the difference between the traditional and custom painted bat columns and indicate if All-Out should offer the custom painting option to its customers:

	Revenue and Expenses Per Bat		
	Traditional	Custom	*Difference*
Sales Price	$150	$180	
Manufacturing Costs	85	85	
Traditional Painting Costs	6	0	
Custom Painting Costs	0	25	
Contribution Margin	$ 59	$ 70	

Should All-Out offer the custom painting option?

a. Yes

b. No

Joint Product Decisions

Let's now examine situations where a business either sells a product as-is or splits it into multiple products through further processing. We call products that are produced from a single set of inputs **joint products**. Gelato and skim milk are examples of joint products that are derived from whole milk. The **split-off point** is the point at which common inputs are split into joint products. In the case of whole milk, the split-off point is when the whole milk is allocated between skim milk and gelato products. Costs that occur before the split-off point are called **joint costs**, and they are irrelevant to the decision to sell the original input, in this case, whole milk, or process it further into skim milk and gelato. The decision is based on a comparison of the incremental costs that occur after the split-off point and the incremental increase in revenues generated by selling the skim milk and gelato compared to selling the whole milk without further processing.

ROMAN ODINTSOV / Pexels / Public Domain

	Values Related to 1 Gallon of Whole Milk	Values of the Products Produced from Further Processing 1 Gallon of Whole Milk		
		Skim Milk	Gelato	Total
Sales Price	$3.45	$2.75	$10.00	$12.75
Joint Production Costs	2.80			2.80
Additional Processing Costs	0.00			8.30
Contribution Margin	$0.65			$1.65

More Profitable

Figure 7.13 Joint Product Analysis.

Let us return to Mott's Creamery, a dairy farm that we introduced in Chapter 4. Mott's herd of 2,000 Holstein cows produces approximately four million gallons of milk each year. While some of the whole milk is bottled and sold, a little over half is further processed into skim milk and creamy, rich Italian gelato. Suzanne Mott manages the farm's finances and wants to evaluate the profitability of selling whole milk or further processing it into skim milk and gelato. Whole milk contains 4% milk fat that can be split off, resulting in fat-free skim milk and the milk fat that Mott's processes into gelato. Let us look at the analysis of the profitability of whole milk versus skim milk and gelato processed from the whole milk as shown in Figure 7.13.

You can see that skim milk and gelato come from whole milk, which costs $2.80 per gallon to produce and can be sold for $3.45 per gallon. This results in a contribution margin of $0.65 per gallon for whole milk sales. The $2.80 is a joint cost that is attributed to both the skim milk and gelato since whole milk is a common input for both products. The milk and milk fat from the whole milk are separated. The skim milk sells for $2.75 per gallon. The separated milk fat can be used to produce a gallon of gelato that can be sold for $10.00, but additional processing costing another $8.30 is necessary.

The total results show that a gallon of whole milk generates a contribution margin of $0.65. However, splitting the milk into skim milk and gelato generates a contribution margin of $1.65. Thus, splitting off the milk fat and creating skim milk and gelato would be more profitable to Mott's Creamery than just selling the whole milk.

The company must consider the incremental cost differences "and" the incremental difference in sales price. Any costs that occur prior to additional process or occur before the split-off point are part of all products and not relevant to the decision. Only additional processing costs and costs after the split-off point are relevant.

LEARNING ACTIVITY 7.10

Stanwick Farms, just outside Sleepy Eye, Minnesota, is a large producer of soybeans. Soybeans are a productive and valuable crop in the upper Midwest, and with market prices up, Stanwick nets about $4.00 per bushel at a price of $14.50 per bushel and the average cost to farm at $10.50 per bushel. Lloyd Stanwick, owner and operator of Stanwick Farms, is considering adding value to his soybean operation by investing in equipment to process the soybeans into soy oil and soy meal. A 60-pound bushel of soybeans can be processed into 10.7 pounds (or 1.4 gallons) of soybean oil that has a variety of uses, such as cooking oil and cosmetics, along with 48 pounds of soy meal used as feed for livestock. The current price for soybean oil is $4.85 per gallon, and the price for meal is approximately $0.25 per pound. The cost of processing soybeans into soybean oil and soybean meal is approximately $3.00 per bushel. Input the correct values in the following chart below and then answer the questions:

	Values related to 1 Bushel of Soybeans	Values of the Products Produced from Further Processing 1 Bushel of Soybeans		
		Soybean Oil	Soybean Meal	Total
Sales Price	$14.50			
Joint Production Costs	10.50			
Additional Processing Costs	0.00			
Contribution Margin	$4.00			

Does processing soybeans into soybean oil and soybean meal generate more profit?

a. Yes

b. No

Technology, Analytics, and Artificial Intelligence

Using Generative AI

OpenAI's ChatGPT can take instructions from a user and perform intelligent operations, including performing incremental analyses. Can you use ChatGPT to answer problems from this chapter? Let's look at parts 2 and 3 of Learning Activity 7.4 and use ChatGPT to check our answers:

INCREMENTAL ANALYSIS USING CHATGPT

Professor

MC Aero Service is a small aviation business that provides air charter, air ambulance, air freight, and flight training services to customers in the mountain west. Gael Euker is MC Aero's owner and chief pilot. Gael employs one other pilot and both are qualified to perform any of the services MC Aero offers. Federal Aviation Rules limit pilots to 1,000 hours of flight time per year, allowing MC Aero to perform 2,000 hours per year (1,000 hours × 2 pilots). Customer demand for MC Aero's services is as follows:

Air Charter Air Ambulance Air Freight Flight Training
Annual Customer Demand (in hours) 700 400 1,300 500

MC Aero charges customers a rate per hour of flight time. The hourly rate and associated hourly costs of providing each service are below:

Air Charter Air Ambulance Air Freight Flight Training
Sales Price Per Hour of Flight Time $500 $700 $400 $200
Average Fuel Cost Per Hour $100 $200 $100 $25
Average Pilot Cost Per Hour $200 $225 $75 $100
Other Variable Overhead Per Hour $50 $100 $25 $15

Compute the contribution margin per hour of flight time for each of MC Aero's services. Which has the highest contribution margin per hour.

ChatGPT

To calculate the contribution margin per hour of flight time for each of MC Aero's services, we need to subtract the variable costs per hour from the sales price per hour.

Here are the contribution margins per hour for each service:

Air Charter: Sales Price Per Hour of Flight Time: $500 Variable Costs Per Hour: $100 (Average Fuel Cost) + $200 (Average Pilot Cost) + $50 (Other Variable Overhead)

Contribution Margin Per Hour = Sales Price Per Hour – Variable Costs Per Hour Contribution Margin Per Hour = $500 – ($100 + $200 + $50) = $150

Air Ambulance: Sales Price Per Hour of Flight Time: $700 Variable Costs Per Hour: $200 (Average Fuel Cost) + $225 (Average Pilot Cost) + $100 (Other Variable Overhead) Contribution Margin Per Hour = Sales Price Per Hour – Variable Costs Per Hour Contribution Margin Per Hour = $700 – ($200 + $225 + $100) = $175

Air Freight: Sales Price Per Hour of Flight Time: $400 Variable Costs Per Hour: $100 (Average Fuel Cost) + $75 (Average Pilot Cost) + $25 (Other Variable Overhead) Contribution Margin Per Hour = Sales Price Per Hour – Variable Costs Per Hour Contribution Margin Per Hour = $400 – ($100 + $75 + $25) = $200

Flight Training: Sales Price Per Hour of Flight Time: $200 Variable Costs Per Hour: $25 (Average Fuel Cost) + $100 (Average Pilot Cost) + $15 (Other Variable Overhead) Contribution Margin Per Hour = Sales Price Per Hour – Variable Costs Per Hour Contribution Margin Per Hour = $200 – ($25 + $100 + $15) = $60

Among MC Aero's services, the Air Freight service has the highest contribution margin per hour at $200.

Did ChatGPT get the right answer for part 2 of Learning Activity 7.4? It sure did! The service with the highest contribution margin per hour is Air Freight at $200 per hour. ChatGPT can take instructions from a user and perform intelligent operations, including preparing elements of an operating budget. Can you use ChatGPT to answer problems from this chapter? Let's look at part 3 of Learning Activity 7.4 and use ChatGPT to check our answers:

Professor

Compute the optimal sales mix. How many hours should MC devote to Air Ambulance?

ChatGPT

To compute the optimal sales mix and determine how many hours MC Aero should devote to Air Ambulance, we need to compare the contribution margin per hour and customer demand for each service.

Here is the contribution margin per hour for each service:

Air Charter: $150 Air Ambulance: $175 Air Freight: $200 Flight Training: $60

And here is the customer demand for each service:

Air Charter: 700 hours Air Ambulance: 400 hours Air Freight: 1,300 hours Flight Training: 500 hours

To find the optimal sales mix, we can calculate the total contribution margin for different combinations of services and choose the combination with the highest total contribution margin.

Let's calculate the total contribution margin for each combination:

Which combination produces the highest contribution margin and doesn't use more than 2,000 hours?

1. Air Charter + Air Ambulance + Air Freight + Flight Training: Total Contribution Margin = (700 * $150) + (400 * $175) + (1,300 * $200) + (500 * $60)
2. Air Charter + Air Ambulance + Air Freight: Total Contribution Margin = (700 * $150) + (400 * $175) + (1,300 * $200)
3. Air Charter + Air Ambulance + Flight Training: Total Contribution Margin = (700 * $150) + (400 * $175) + (500 * $60)
4. Air Charter + Air Freight + Flight Training: Total Contribution Margin = (700 * $150) + (1,300 * $200) + (500 * $60)
5. Air Ambulance + Air Freight + Flight Training: Total Contribution Margin = (400 * $175) + (1,300 * $200) + (500 * $60)

After calculating the total contribution margin for each combination, we can determine the optimal sales mix by choosing the combination with the highest total contribution margin.

Once we identify the optimal sales mix, we can determine how many hours MC Aero should devote to Air Ambulance by looking at the corresponding demand for Air Ambulance in that combination. The number of hours MC Aero should allocate to Air Ambulance would be equal to the customer demand for Air Ambulance in the optimal sales mix.

Please note that without the specific values used in the calculations, I cannot provide an exact optimal sales mix or the number of hours MC Aero should devote to Air Ambulance.

Did ChatGPT get the right answer for part 3 of Learning Activity 7.4? Almost! ChatGPT identified a number of possible combinations but is unable to account for the limitation in scarce resources, 2,000 hours, using the prompts provided in Learning Activity 7.4.

The generative AI platform, ChatGPT was a useful tool for checking answers in part 2 but did not produce a correct answer to part 3. In fact, it gave a series of combinations that it said did not exceed 2,000 hours when, indeed, they did. When AI reports incorrect answers but reports them as fact, it is called a **hallucination**. Hallucinations are a serious problem with large language AI models like ChatGPT. The only way for users to mitigate the negative effects of hallucinations is to understand the concepts themselves. In this example, AI served as a useful sanity check and actually got part 2 of Learning Activity 7.4 correct. Still, it cannot be trusted to solve the problem completely.

Using Machine Learning

Another tool accountants can use is machine learning. This is another form of AI, which analyzes historical data to help predict the future. Programmers are typically required to develop machine learning applications using either Python or other languages. We will use a no-code program called WEKA to experiment with machine learning to create a model for approving loans.

For this example, use the dataset LoanData.csv. This data was modified from loans made on LendingTree.com.[1] In this dataset, there are approximately 9,000 data lines. Each line has an indicator noting whether the loan was paid or not. The data were modified to show Paid or Not Paid in the *not.fully.paid* field. The fields in the file are as follows:

- Int. Rate—interest rate on the loan
- Installment—monthly payment amount
- Log.annual—logarithm of annual income
- DTI—debt to income ration
- FICO—credit score
- Days.with.cr line—# of days using credit line
- Revol. Util—utilization of revolving credit balance
- Inq.last.6mths—credit inquiries in the last 6 months
- Delinq.2yrs—delinquencies in the last 2 years
- Not.fully.paid—binary indicator of PAID or NOTPAID if the balance has been paid

We will build a classification model using WEKA. This free, easy-to-use machine learning program does not require the user to be able to program in Python or any other language. Classification is a form of supervised learning, meaning the data are labeled. In our case, this is the last field with paid or not paid. The labeled variable is known as a class and is the

[1] Original data can be downloaded at https://www.kaggle.com/datasets/itssuru/loan-data

variable that the model will try to determine. Machine learning will use various mathematical algorithms to determine relationships between the variables and how they affect the class or labeled variable.

To build the model, open the Weka application. The initial screen will look like Figure 7.14. On this screen, you will select Explorer.

From the Preprocess screen, select Open and select the LoanData.csv file as shown in Figure 7.15. Once the file opens, select Visualize All to show the distribution of the variables.

Figure 7.14 Weka initial screen.

Figure 7.15 Weka preprocess screen.

Review the attribute list on the Preprocess screen. To simplify the model, we want to only select 3–5 variables, plus not.fully.paid. Check the variables, you do not want to include and click on Remove as shown in Figure 7.16.

Select Classify from the menu at the top of the screen. You will select the options to run a classification algorithm on this screen. In the classifier, click on Choose, then select Functions > Logistic and then the Start button. We will leave all other settings as given.

See Figure 7.17 for the Classify screen. The program will divide the data between training data and testing data. The model will initially be built with the training data.

The output will be displayed on the right side of the screen. There are two important areas to review in Figure 7.18. The first is the Correctly and Incorrectly Classified Instances. Based on the data and the specific variables selected, 83.89% of the transactions were correctly identified, representing the number of correct predictions from the testing portion of the data. Although this is a relatively good model for predicting future loan repayment, a different

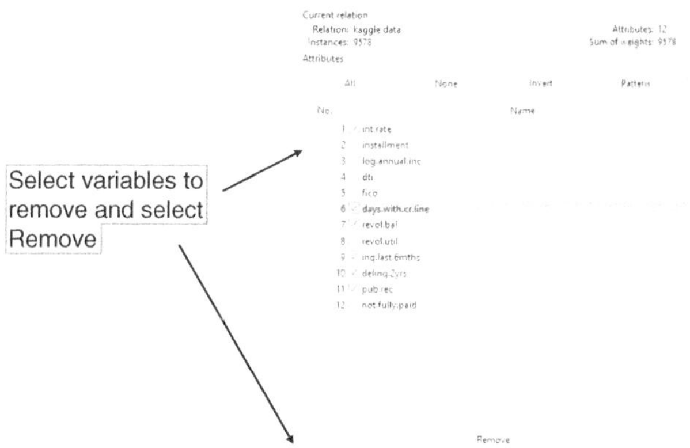

Figure 7.16 Weka select variables.

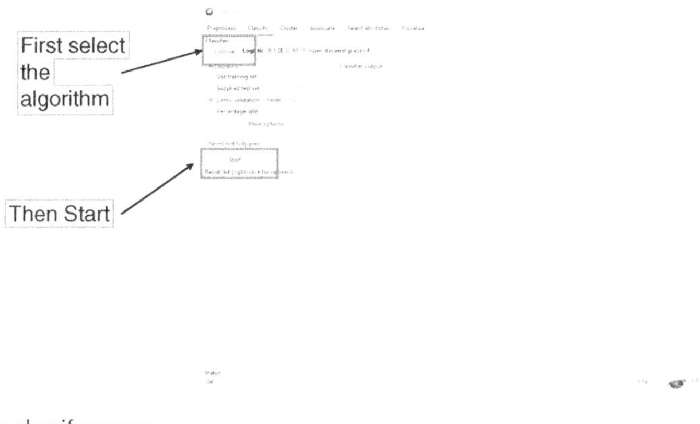

Figure 7.17 Weka classify screen.

```
=== Summary ===

Correctly Classified Instances        8035               83.8902 %
Incorrectly Classified Instances      1543               16.1098 %
Kappa statistic                          0.0221
Mean absolute error                      0.2556
Root mean squared error                  0.3582
Relative absolute error                 95.0294 %
Root relative squared error             97.7061 %
Total Number of Instances             9578

=== Detailed Accuracy By Class ===

                 TP Rate  FP Rate  Precision  Recall   F-Measure  MCC      ROC Area  PRC Area  Class
                 0.995    0.982    0.842      0.995    0.912      0.060    0.665     0.910     PAID
                 0.018    0.005    0.424      0.018    0.035      0.060    0.665     0.270     NOTPAID
Weighted Avg.    0.839    0.825    0.775      0.839    0.772      0.060    0.665     0.808

=== Confusion Matrix ===

    a    b   <-- classified as
 8007   38 |    a = PAID
 1505   28 |    b = NOTPAID
```

Figure 7.18 Classification output.

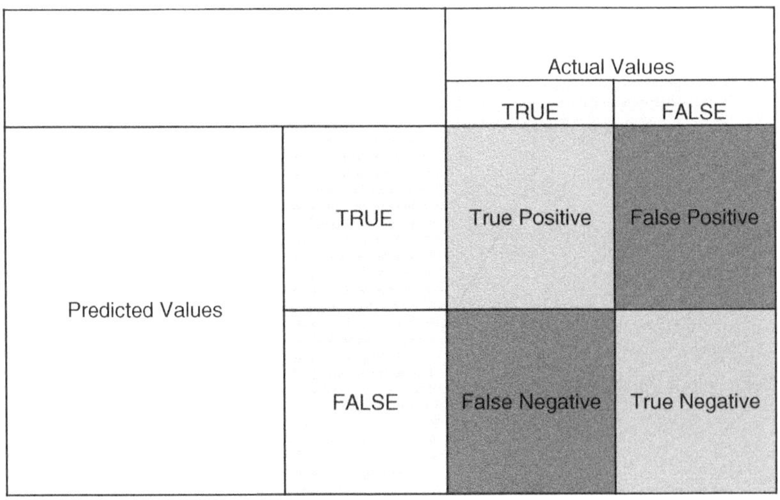

Figure 7.19 Confusion matrix sample.

selection of variables or algorithms may improve the model. It is difficult to find a good balance. A model too close to 100% may not work with future data because it is built too specifically for the input data. A model that is too low will not predict accurately enough.

The other key area is the confusion matrix. The matrix shows the breakdown of correctly identified loans as Paid and Not Paid. It also shows the number of each category incorrectly identified. See Figure 7.19 for an explanation of the confusion matrix breakdown.

To attempt to find a better model, return to the Preprocess screen and select the Undo button at the top of the screen. This will return all of the variables to the selection region. Select new variables to remove.

Finding the best possible model is sometimes a factor of trial and error. You may also consider the following algorithms to find a better algorithm. Keep in mind the difference in algorithms is how the relationships between data are calculated. Each uses different mathematical functions that you will learn as you study machine learning more in-depth.

Try one of the following algorithms from the Classify button:

- Bayes > naive bayes
- Meta > ADABoostM1
- Trees > RandomForest

Key Terms

incremental analysis Examination of the change in costs and revenues related to possible alternatives.
relevant data Data that are changed, or affected, by selecting a particular course of action.
opportunity cost The lost benefits when electing to forgo a course of action.
sunk cost A cost that has already been incurred and cannot be affected further, regardless of the course of action taken.
scarce resources Business inputs with limited availability.
outsourcing Purchasing a product or service from an external supplier that would otherwise be produced or performed in house.
special orders Situations where a customer requests a product or service at a special price.
common costs Costs that are not associated with a particular business unit and are shared across the more than one business unit.
joint products Products that are produced from a single set of inputs.
split-off point The point in which common inputs are split into joint products.
joint costs Costs that occur before the split-off point.
hallucination When AI reports incorrect answers but reports them as fact.

LEARNING ACTIVITY SOLUTIONS

Learning Activity 7.1

b

$$\begin{aligned}
\textit{Total Sales} &= \textit{Fixed Rent} + \textit{Variable Costs}\\
\$80.00\ (\textit{Clients}) &= \$3{,}000 + \$5.00\ (\textit{Clients})\\
\$75.00\ (\textit{Clients}) &= \$3{,}000\\
\textit{Clients} &= 40
\end{aligned}$$

Learning Activity 7.2

c

Learning Activity 7.3

b

Learning Activity 7.4

1. *a*
2. *c*

	Air Charter	Air Ambulance	Air Freight	Flight Training
Price per Hour of Flight Time	$500	$700	$400	$200
Fuel Cost per Hour	(100)	(200)	(100)	(25)
Pilot Hourly Labor Rate	(200)	(225)	(75)	(100)
Other Variable Overhead per Hour	(50)	(100)	(25)	(15)
Contribution Margin per Hour	$150	$175	$200	$ 60
Rank from Highest to Lowest Contribution Margin	3	2	1	4

3. *c*

	Air Charter	Air Ambulance	Air Freight	Flight Training	Total Hours Available
Annual Customer Demand (in hours)	700	400	1,300	500	2,900
Ranking by Contribution Margin	3	2	1	4	
Optimal Hours Devoted	300	400	1,300	0	2,000

To compute the optimal sales mix, MC would fulfill the demand from highest to lowest contribution margin per unit. That would result in fulfilling all of the demand for Air Freight and Air Ambulance, part of the demand for Air Charter, and none of the demand for flight training.

4. *d*

	Air Charter	Air Ambulance	Air Freight	Flight Training	Total Contribution Margin
Annual Hours Devoted	300	400	1,300	0	
Contribution per Hour	× $150	× $175	× $200	× $60	
Total Contribution Margin	$45,000	$70,000	$260,000	$0	$375,000

Learning Activity 7.5

1. *d*

	Make	Buy	Profit Increase (Decrease)
Purchase Price ($50 × 5,000 pairs)	$ 0	$250,000	$(250,000)
Direct Materials ($12 × 5,000 pairs)	60,000	0	60,000
Direct Labor ($23 × 5,000 pairs)	115,000	0	115,000
Variable Overhead ($3 × 5,000 pairs)	15,000	0	15,000
Direct Fixed Overhead ($10 × 5,000 pairs)	50,000	20,000	30,000
Total Incremental Cost	$240,000	$270,000	$ (30,000)

Note: Fixed marketing costs of $7 per pair of sandals is not affected by electing to make the sandals or outsource the production to Yang Zhou. Thus, it is not relevant and not included in the analysis. ReTreads should decline the offer from Yang Zhou. Total profit will decrease by $30,000.

2. *b*

	Make	Buy	Profit Increase (Decrease)
Incremental Cost	$240,000	$270,000	$(30,000)
Opportunity Cost ($4,000 x 12 Months)	48,000	0	48,000
Total Revised Incremental Cost	$288,000	$270,000	$ 18,000

ReTreads should accept Yang Zhou's offer because profit will increase by $18,000.

Learning Activity 7.6

1. *b*
2. *c*

	Current Cost per Brochure		Relevant Cost per Brochure
Direct Materials	$0.50		$0.50
Direct Labor	0.05		0.05
Variable Overhead	0.02		0.02
Fixed Overhead	0.15	Not Relevant	0.00
Sales Commission ($0.75 × 0.04)	4% of total sales		0.03
Shipping ($1.00 ÷ 100)	$1.00 per bundle of 100		0.01
Fixed Cost of Equipment	$ 12,000 per year	Not Relevant	0.00
Fixed Advertising and Promotion	$ 10,000 per year	Not Relevant	0.00
Total Relevant Cost per Brochure			$0.61

Special Order Price per Brochure	*$ 0.75*
Total Relevant Cost per Brochure	*(0.61)*
Profit Per Brochure	*$ 0.14*
Brochures Ordered	*× 10,000*
Incremental Profit (Loss)	***$ 1, 400.00***

Learning activity 7.7

c

	Nonprofit Division	Expense Management Division	Common Costs	Total
Sales	$10,000,000	$5,000,000		$15,000,000
Variable Costs	(5,500,000)	(2,500,000)		(8,000,000)
Contribution Margin	4,500,000	2,500,000		7,000,000
Fixed Costs	(2,250,000)	(1,750,000)	$ (2,000,000)	(6,000,000)
Net Income (Loss)	$ 2,250,000	$ 750,000	$ (2,000,000)	$ 1,000,000

DatCo would lose $750,000 of profit if it eliminated the Expense Management Division. Thus, eliminating the division would be a bad decision.

Learning Activity 7.8

d

	Retain Welder	Replace Welder	Profit Increase (Decrease)
Annual Revenue	$ 60,000	$ 60,000	$ 0
Annual Variable Operating Costs	(15,000)	(10,000)	5,000
Annual Contribution Margin	$ 45,000	$ 50,000	$ 5,000
Years in Service	× 5	× 5	× 5
Total Contribution Margin	$225,000	$250,000	$25,000
Cost of New Welder	0	(12,000)	(12,000)
Sale of the New (at end of 5 years)		4,000	4,000
Sale of Old Welder	0	1,000	1,000
Total Net Effect	$225,000	$239,000	$18,000

The analysis shows that the reduced operating costs over the 5-year life of the welders along with the proceeds from the sales of the welders outweigh the cost of purchasing the new welder by $16,000.

Learning Activity 7.9

a

	Revenue and Expense Per Bat		
	Traditional	Custom	Difference
Sales Price	$150	$180	$30
Manufacturing Costs	85	85	0
Traditional Painting Costs	6	0	6
Custom Painting Costs	0	25	(25)
Contribution Margin	$ 59	$ 70	$11

Learning Activity 7.10

a

		Values of the Products Produced from Further Processing 1 Bushel of Soybeans		
	Values related to 1 Bushel of Soybeans	Soybean Oil	Soybean Meal	Total
Sales Price	$14.50	$6.79	$12.00	$18.79
Joint Production Costs	10.50			10.50
Additional Processing Costs	0.00			3.00
Contribution Margin	$ 4.00			$ 5.29

Review Questions

1. Analyzing and reflecting are steps in the business decision process. **(Learning Objective 1)**
   a. True
   b. False
2. Data must change for it to be relevant for decision-making. **(Learning Objective 1)**
   a. True
   b. False
3. An opportunity cost is the price paid for an investment in an opportunity. **(Learning Objective 1)**
   a. True
   b. False

4. Which is an example of an opportunity cost? **(Learning Objective 1)**
   a. The price paid for a new piece of equipment
   b. Income that could be generated with capacity created by outsourcing a product or service
5. Is an opportunity cost relevant? **(Learning Objective 1)**
   a. Yes
   b. No
6. What is a sunk cost? **(Learning Objective 1)**
   a. A cost that has already been incurred.
   b. A cost that is tied to the outsourcing of services.
7. Is a sunk cost relevant? **(Learning Objective 1)**
   a. Yes
   b. No
8. What is a scarce resource? **(Learning Objective 2)**
   a. An input of limited availability
   b. A natural resource
9. How do managers maximize profits when resources are scarce? **(Learning Objective 2)**
   a. Sell the product with the highest margin per unit
   b. Sell the product with the highest margin per unit of scarce resource consumed
10. Which of the following would a company most likely consider outsourcing? **(Learning Objective 3)**
    a. Research and development of a new product
    b. Assembly of a product
11. What is the most important factor when considering the relevance of fixed costs in an outsourcing decision? **(Learning Objective 3)**
    a. The total fixed cost
    b. Capacity
12. Give an example of a nonfinancial factor that a company should consider when outsourcing. **(Learning Objective 3)**
    a. Quality
    b. Delivery time
    c. The supplier's human rights reputation
    d. All of the above
13. What is the most important factor when considering a special order? **(Learning Objective 4)**
    a. Total fixed costs
    b. Capacity
14. A company will usually except a special order when _______ _______ exceeds _______ _______. **(Learning Objective 4)**
    a. incremental revenue; incremental costs
    b. total capacity; total volume

15. Which is more likely to be an example of a common cost? **(Learning Objective 5)**
    a. A corporate-level human resources department
    b. The cost to develop a jig for welding components of a product
16. When evaluating an investment in new equipment or facilities, a firm can increase profits through increased ______, and decreased ______. **(Learning Objective 6)**
    a. volume; fixed cost
    b. revenue; cost
17. What are the two important elements of information when considering if a company should sell a product or further process it and sell it after? **(Learning Objective 7)**
    a. Incremental price change; incremental cost change
    b. Incremental volume; incremental capacity
18. What are examples of joint products? **(Learning Objective 7)**
    a. Lumber; firewood
    b. Lumber; particle board
19. Are joint costs usually relevant? **(Learning Objective 7)**
    a. Yes
    b. No

Short Exercises

S:7-1 (Learning Objective 1)

Which of the following is *not* a step in the business decision-making process?

a. Detect the problem.
b. Compare costs and expenditures.
c. Determine alternative courses of action.
d. Reflect on results.
e. All of these are steps in the decision-making process.

S:7-2 (Learning Objective 1)

Carolina Hernandez, a practicing CPA with a tax service in Coronado, California, is trying to determine if she should add financial planning services to her tax service. Carolina has identified the following costs associated with the financial planning business. Which is *not* relevant to deciding if the financial planning service will make Carolina a profit?

a. Costs to advertise the financial planning services
b. The salary of the existing administrative assistant
c. The cost of professional training on investing in annuities
d. The cost of a financial data subscription service
e. All of these costs are relevant to adding financial planning services.

S:7-3 (Learning Objective 1)

Donovan Smith was planning to tear down his old shed and build a new shed in his back yard. Which of the following would be relevant for Donovan?

a. The current price of lumber
b. The cost to tear down the old shed
c. The cost to build the old shed
d. The difference in the price of reusing the old foundation and building a new one
e. The cost of the wage he gives a laborer for helping him tear it down

S:7-4 (Learning Objective 2)

Tropical Twist Sorbet Sweets sells a variety of sorbet- and sherbert-based products including sorbet or sherbert cones, Hurricanes (a blended sherbert and candy treat), and Tropical Shakes. Tropical Twist is having difficulty getting enough weekly help to run its store, which is resulting in long lines. As a result, Tropical Twist is planning to reduce the number or product lines. Sales prices, variable costs, and production time are as follows:

	Cones	Hurricanes	Shakes
Sales Price Per Unit	$4.00	$7.50	$7.00
Variable Cost Per Unit	$2.50	$3.00	$3.50
Minutes to Prepare	2 min	4 min	3 min

Requirements

a. Which product line would most likely be discontinued?
b. Which product line is the most profitable?

S:7-5 (Learning Objective 3)

Preline Pump Company produces a part for one of its centrifugal pumps that has the following costs per unit:

Direct material	$ 6
Direct labor	3
Variable overhead	2
Fixed overhead	5
Total	$15

Win-Del Corporation can provide the part to Preline for $17 per unit. Preline has determined that 40% of its fixed overhead would be eliminated if it purchased the part from Win-Del. However, if Preline outsources the part, it can sublease the area it uses to produce the part for $50,000 per year. Preline currently produces 10,000 of the parts.

Requirements

a. By what margin is the choice more preferable?
b. Should Preline outsource the part?

S:7-6 (Learning Objective 4)

Westman Toy Company received a special order for 1,000 units of it Hi-Zee Boomerangs at a price of $10 each. Westman typically sells the product for $17 per Boomerang, and the costs for each Boomerang are as follows:

Direct material	$ 1
Direct labor	2
Overhead (75% fixed)	8
Total	$11

Assume that Westman has enough idle capacity to produce the 1,000 units.

Requirements

a. At what sales price would Westman break even on the special order?
b. Should Westman accept the special order?

S:7-7 (Learning Objective 5)

SteinWayz Trucking has two delivery territories: East and West. Financial information for the two territories is as follows:

	East	West
Sales	$1,420,000	$1,260,000
Direct costs:		
Variable	(705,000)	(440,000)
Fixed	(550,000)	(520,000)
Common costs	(300,000)	(200,000)
Net income (loss)	$(135,000)	$ 100,000

Management feels that the East territory is creating too much of a drain on the company and it should be eliminated. If the East delivery territory is eliminated, 50% of East's common costs would be eliminated; the rest would be reallocated to West.

Requirements

a. Should the East delivery territory be eliminated?
b. What would SteinWayz total net income (or loss) be if it eliminated East?

S:7-8 (Learning Objective 6)

JR Drilling Company is analyzing the following capital investment opportunity related to replacing a drilling rig it uses for residential drilling operations. The new rig will have a salvage value of $250,000 at the end of its useful life. Facts related to the opportunity are as follows:

Cost of the new rig	$2,500,000
Additional annual revenue generated by the new rig	$ 40,000
Annual expense savings generated by the new rig	$ 60,000
Useful life of the new rig	10 Years
Salvage value at the end of the useful life of the new rig	$ 250,000
Selling price of the old rig	$ 500,000
Remaining useful life of the old rig	10 Years
Salvage value at the end of the useful life of the old rig	$ 0

Requirements

a. Should JR replace the old rig with a new one?
b. How much more or less cash flow would JR have after replacing the old rig?

S:7-9 (Learning Objective 7)

Heidelberg Mining Company mines theromite, a product used in insulation and other industrial products. The joint cost of mining theromite amounts to $18 million dollars. Heidelberg is considering if the company should sell the raw theromite or further refine it and sell it as an industrial insulation product. The sales price and costs associated with theromite and the industrial insulation are as follows:

	Raw	Processed
Sales Price	$1,200	$6,500
Mining Costs	800	800
Processing Costs	0	5,500

Requirements

a. Should Heidelberg sell the raw theromite or process it further into industrial insulation?
b. How much more or less profit would Heidelberg make if it processed and sold the industrial insulation?

S:7-10 (Learning Objective 7)

Stacia Klemm owns and operates an orange grove that has been in her family for more than 100 years. Stacia can sell oranges for approximately $1.25 per pound in 20-pound boxes. She is considering investing in processing equipment to peel and package oranges in 8-ounce pouches and squeeze the peelings to produce an essential oil used in cosmetics. Two pounds of oranges produce three 8-ounce pouches and 4 ounces of essential oil. Sales prices and costs related to the products are as follows:

	Values related to 2 Pounds of Oranges	Values of the Products Produced from Further Processing 2 Pounds of Oranges		
		Three 8- oz. pouches	4 oz. oil	Total
Sales Price	$2.50	$1.50	$2.00	$3.50
Harvesting Costs	0.50			$0.50
Additional Processing Costs	0.00			$0.80

Requirements

a. Should Stacia further process the oranges?
b. How much more or less profit would Stacia make if she processed the oranges?

Exercises

E:7-11 (Learning Objective 1)

Everlasting Color manufactures long-lasting lip stains for the cosmetics industry. Lip stains, as compared to lip stick or lip gloss, have become popular because they stay on for 24 hours. Everlasting Color's processing is completely automated with capacity to produce 100,000 tubes of lip stain per month. Everlasting currently produces and sells 80,000 tubes per month with the following estimated cost per tube:

Raw material cost per tube	$0.85
Variable overhead cost per tube	$0.50
Allocated fixed overhead cost per tube	$1.00
Sales commissions per tube	$0.25

Requirements

a. What costs are relevant for computing the profit contributed by the sale of a tube of lip stain?
b. How much incremental profit would Everlasting Color make from selling 5,000 additional tubes of lip stain for $5 per tube?

E:7-12 (Learning Objectives 2 and 5)

Cane's Fishing and Tackle Company has three sales divisions: the soft plastics division, the lures and spinners division, and the fly-fishing division. Income statements for the three business divisions suggest that Cane's could be more profitable if it eliminated the fly-fishing division.

Cane's Fishing and Tackle Company
Income Statements for the Year 20XX

	Soft Plastics	Lures & Spinners	Fly Fishing
Sales	$500,000	$300,000	$270,000
Cost of Goods Sold	(225,000)	(170,000)	(233,000)
Gross Profit	275,000	130,000	37,000
Sales Commissions	25,000	15,000	13,500
Direct Management Costs	20,000	18,000	29,000
Common Management Costs	85,000	85,000	85,000
Net Income	$145,000	$ 12,000	($ 83,500)

Requirements

a. What would be the effect on overall profits if Cane's eliminated the fly-fishing division?
b. How could you arrange the income statement to more accurately reflect the performance of each division?

E:7-13 (Learning Objective 3)

O'Ryan Hose Company produces hoses for the automotive industry, and its basic line hose has the following costs to product per 100 unit batch:

Direct material	$120
Production Labor	30
Production Overhead	10
Allocated Facility Costs	50

NanKing Products could supply the hoses for $180 per 100 units.

Requirements

a. Should O'Ryan outsource to NanKing? What would be the effect on net income?
b. O'Ryan could use the capacity freed up by outsourcing to produce and sell a product to Genisis Automotive and generate $18,000 in gross margin. Considering this, should O'Ryan outsource, and what would be the effect on net income?

E:7-14 (Learning Objective 4)

Fatima's Fine Confectionaries and Chocolateria sells fine hand-made candies in its store in Cedar Falls, Iowa. Fatima normally sells her Holiday Turtles made of rich milk chocolate, caramel, and peanuts for $50 per box. She received an order for 200 boxes from Valley Bank for employee gifts. Valley asked if it could get better pricing. How much could Fatima sell the candy boxes to Valley Bank for if she wants to make $10 per box? The typical costs of each box are as follows:

Direct material	$ 8
Direct labor	18
Overhead (50% fixed)	14
Total	$40

Assume that Fatima has enough idle capacity to produce the 200 boxes.

Requirements

a. At what sales price would Fatima break even on the special order?
b. What price should Fatima set for Valley Bank if she wants to make $10 per box?

E:7-15 (Learning Objective 6)

Carlos Estevez's Coffee Company roasts fine coffees. Carlos is considering replacing its coffee roaster with a larger and more efficient model from Italy. Consider the following facts related to replacing the coffee roaster:

Cost of the new roaster	$500,000
Additional annual revenue generated by the new roaster	$ 40,000
Annual expense savings generated by the new roaster	($5,000)
Useful life of the new roaster	20 Years
Salvage value at the end of the useful life of the new roaster	$ 50,000
Current value of the old roaster	$ 25,000

Requirements

a. How much more or less profit would Carlos have after replacing the old roaster?
b. Should Carlos replace the old roaster with a new one?

E:7-16 (Learning Objective 7)

Aya owns a small aronia berry patch. Aronia berries are high in antioxidants and prized for their health benefits. Aya sells her berries in bulk from a van that she parks in strategic locations around town and at the weekend farmer's market. However, she is considering adding additional value to her berries by processing them into aronia berry smoothies. The sales price for a pound of berries in either bulk or smoothie form and costs are as follows:

	Bulk	Smoothie
Sales Price	$14	$22
Harvesting Costs	2	2
Processing and Packaging Costs	2	5

Requirements

a. How much more or less profit would Aya make if she processed and sold the berries into smoothies?
b. Should Aya sell bulk aronia berries or process them further into smoothies?

E:7-17 (Appendix A Learning Objective 2)

C-Valine Oil Company produces high-end specialty lubricants for the racing industry. C-Valine purchases crude oil and processes it into a heavy-weight gear oil for race cars. C-Valine can sell the gear oil as is, but the company is considering the value of processing it further into a highly refined transmission fluid that will also result in a byproduct that can be used for bearing grease. Sales prices and costs related to the gear oil, transmission fluid, and bearing grease are as follows:

	Price and Costs Related to a Quart of Heavy-weight Gear Oil	Values of the Products Produced from Further Processing 1 Quart of Heavy-weight Gear Oil		
		24 oz. Transmission Fluid	6 oz. Tube of Grease	Total
Sales Price	$16	$22	$4	$26
Processing and Packaging	5			$ 5
Additional Costs	0			$ 7

Requirements

a. How much more or less profit would C-Valine make from further processing?
b. Should C-Valine continue to sell the heavy weight gear oil as is, or further process it?

Problems

P:7-18 (Learning Objective 1)

Requirements

Select the correct answer for each of the following questions:

a. When are fixed costs less likely to be relevant in an outsourcing decision?
   i. The company has excess capacity.
   ii. The company is operating at full capacity.

b. Why are opportunity costs relevant?
   i. They change when a particular course of action is taken over another.
   ii. They do not change when a particular course of action is taken over another.

c. Why are sunk costs irrelevant?
   i. They change when a particular course of action is taken over another.
   ii. They do not change when a particular course of action is taken over another.

d. What factor is important to consider when evaluating step costs?
   i. Relevant range
   ii. Relevant value

e. What term best relates to relevant costs?
   i. Static
   ii. Changed

f. What time frame most reflects relevant costs?
   i. Past
   ii. Future

P:7-19 (Learning Objective 2)

RKM and Associates, Certified Public Accountants, is a small public accounting firm that provides three types of services to business clients: audit services, tax preparation services, and consulting services. To market its services, the company relies on radio and billboards for advertising. Information on the company's projected operations for the coming year are as follows:

	Audit	Taxes	Consulting
Revenue per billable hour	$150	$125	$200
Labor cost per hour	60	50	70
Material cost per hour	4	6	12
Variable travel and administrative costs per hour	12	1	15
Allocated fixed costs per year	200,000	300,000	500,000
Billable hours	15,000	20,000	10,000

Requirements

a. What is the firm's projected profit for the year at current operating levels?
b. Assuming the divisions can grow without affecting fixed costs, which division should the RKM try to grow and why?

P:7-20 Part A (Learning Objective 4)

Terry Peak Corporation is a manufacturer of rock-climbing hammers. Terry Peak has the capacity to produce 8,000 hammers per year due to limited space in its machining equipment.

Currently Terry Peak makes 6,000 units annually and sells them for $40 each. The costs are as follows:

Direct Material per Unit	$6.00
Direct Labor per Unit	$5.00
Variable Overhead per Unit	$6.00
Shipping and Packaging per Unit	$1.50
Sales Rep Commissions per Unit	$2.00
Fixed Manufacturing Overhead	$36,000 per year
Other Selling General & Administrative	$48,000 per year

Colorado Custom Equipment company offered to buy 1,000 hammers from Terry Peak for a price of $18 each. The Colorado order would pay out only 50% of the usual sales commission, and the shipping/packaging cost per unit would only be $0.50.

Requirement

a. What would be the increase/decrease in net profit if Terry took this order?

P:7-21 Part B (Learning Objective 3)

Refer to the information of about Terry Peak Corporation in P:13-20 Part A. Because of a labor shortage, Terry Peak wants to outsource all production. Expenses related to Selling/Commissions, General, and Administrative Expenses will remain. Vision Mountain Manufacturing has offered to produce the units and provide them to Terry Peak at a cost of $28.00 per unit. Terry Peak could also sublet its factory for $34,000 per year if it elects to buy the hammers from Vision.

Requirement

a. At the current volume of 6,000 units, how much more or less profit would Terry Peak make if it outsourced all production under this offer from Vision Mountain?
b. Would Terry Peak still accept the special order discussed in P13-20 Part A if it outsourced all production to Vista Mountain Manufacturing?

P:7-22 Part C (Learning Objective 6)

Refer to the information about Terry Peak Corporation in P:13-20 Part A. Terry Peak is now considering replacing some of its processing equipment with new and more efficient equipment. The new equipment will reduce the direct labor by $3.50 per hammer and the variable overhead by $1.50 per hammer and will increase the fixed overhead costs by $5,000.

Requirements

a. Without considering the special order, by how much would Terry Peak's profits change if it replaced the processing equipment?
b. How much would Terry Peak's profits change if it replaced the processing equipment and accepted the special order?

P:7-23 (Learning Objective 7)

Beatriz Cook owns and operates Beatriz's Baked goods, a company that produces frozen bread dough for bakeries. Beatriz thinks she can improve profitability if she processes her bread dough into other products or splits it into multiple products. Beatriz is considering several options:

1. Selling the bread dough frozen and in bulk, as she usually does.
2. Further processing the dough to make packaged frozen cinnamon rolls.
3. Splitting the 32 ounces of dough to produce 16 ounces of frozen pizza crusts and 16 ounces of frozen dinner rolls, both of which require minimal additional processing compared to producing cinnamon rolls.

The sales price and production costs for a 32-ounce package of Beatriz's raw dough, a package of cinnamon rolls that can be produced with 32 ounces of dough, and the pizza crusts and dinner rolls that can also be produced are as follows:

	Raw Dough	Cinnamon Rolls	Pizza Crusts	Dinner Rolls
Sales Price	$3.00	$9.00	$1.00	$4.00
Total Processing 32 Ounces of Raw Dough	1.50	1.50	1.50	1.50
Additional Processing	0.00	3.50	0.25	0.50
Total Packaging Costs	0.50	0.75	0.10	0.50

Requirements

1. How much more or less profit would Beatriz make if she produced the Cinnamon Rolls?
2. How much more or less profit would Beatriz make if she split the dough into Pizza Crusts and Dinner Rolls?
3. Which alternative should Beatriz choose? Why might she consider the other alternative?

Technology, Analytics, and AI

T:7-24 (Technology, Analytics, and Artificial Intelligence)

Peru Place Coffee, located in Cusco, Peru, is a prominent producer of coffee beans. Coffee is a valuable crop in the region, and with market prices high, Peru Place Coffee nets about $3.50

per pound at a selling price of $12.00 per pound, with an average cost to farm at $8.50 per pound. Juan Lopez, the owner and operator of Peru Place Coffee, is considering adding value to his coffee operation by investing in equipment to roast and grind the coffee beans into packaged ground coffee. A pound of green coffee beans can be processed into 1 pound of ground coffee. The current price for packaged ground coffee is $18.00 per pound. The cost of processing coffee beans into ground coffee is approximately $4.00 per pound.

Use ChatGPT to determine whether Juan should invest in the equipment to process the coffee beans into packaged ground coffee. Is ChatGPT correct?

T:7-25 (Technology, Analytics, and Artificial Intelligence)

The chief financial officer at Bando Industries would like to evaluate the profitability of its international division and potentially eliminate it since it is losing money. The company's segmented income statement for the domestic and international divisions for the year are as follows:

	Total	Domestic Division	International Division
Sales	$200,000,000	$140,000,000	$ 60,000,000
Variable Costs	(157,000,000)	(105,000,000)	(52,000,000)
Contribution Margin	43,000,000	35,000,000	8,000,000
Fixed Costs	(18,000,000)	(9,000,000)	(9,000,000)
Net Income (Loss)	$ 25,000,000	$ 26,000,000	$(1,000,000)

Further analysis reveals that the direct fixed costs for international and domestic divisions were approximately $5,000,000 apiece, and the rest of the fixed costs are allocated common costs that would not be affected by the elimination of either division. What would have been the total net income if Bando eliminated the international division? Should it be eliminated? Use ChatGPT to calculate the solution and determine if ChatGPT is correct.

T:7-26 (Technology, Analytics, and Artificial Intelligence)

Heritage Home Furnishings, a well-established furniture retailer, offers in-store financing to customers who need small loans to purchase furniture. Traditionally, the store's credit approval process relied on manual review by store associates using basic credit checks and customer-provided information. However, with an increasing number of customers applying for financing, the store has decided to implement machine learning (ML) to automate and optimize the approval process.

Steps:

1. Use Weka to upload the data T7-26 Credit_Approval_Data.xlsx. The data contain information about several customers that Heritage sold to over the last 5 years. The classification column is labeled Approved with the classes of NotApproved and Approved.
2. Determine 3–5 variables to include in the model. Pick those that you think would most likely determine if a loan should be approved or not.

3. Select one of the following algorithms for the classification:
   a. Trees > RandomForest
   b. Functions > Logistic
   c. Bayes > NaiveBayes
4. Review the output and answer the following questions. Try another option or variables if you want to see if you can get a better model.
   a. Which variables did you select, and why do you think they were most relevant to the decision?
   b. Are there any variables that should not be included into the model as they may cause bias or incorrect decisions?
   c. What was the percent accuracy you achieved?

CHAPTER 8

Capital Budgeting, Planning, and Decision-making

Learning Objectives

8.1 Describe how managers evaluate potential capital expenditures and identify the data relevant to making a choice.

8.2 Explain and apply the average rate of return method for evaluating and making capital budgeting decisions.

8.3 Explain and apply the payback method for evaluating and making capital budgeting decisions.

8.4 Summarize the time value of money concept.

8.5 Apply the time value of money concept to capital budgeting decisions.

8.6 Describe how managers account for risk and qualitative factors when making capital budgeting decisions.

Accounting in Life

Asad Photo Maldives / Pexels / Public Domain

Retirement may seem far off, but you will not have to save nearly as much if you start saving early because of the power of compounding. For example, if you start saving $100 a month at age 22 and save for 45 years, you would have just over $1 million at a retirement age of 67, assuming a 10% average rate of return on the investment. You would have invested a total of $54,000 over the 45 years but ended up with more than $1 million. If you were to wait until age 32 to start saving for retirement, you would have to save approximately $276 per month to reach the same value in your retirement account at age 67. Saving $276 per month for 35 years results in a total investment of $115,920, more than twice as much as you would have needed to invest if you had started early.

Let's Review

Business decision-making involves identifying the problem, determining alternative courses of action, computing expected results under each alternative, and making decisions. We learned in the last chapter that businesses evaluate alternatives by quantifying financial consequences. However, it is not all dollars and cents. Businesses also consider nonfinancial factors such as safety, quality, the environment, or impact on the community.

LEARNING ACTIVITY 8.1

For each situation and cost or revenue listed, indicate if the cost or revenue is relevant to the situation.

Situation	Cost or Revenue	Relevant or Not Relevant
1. A customer wants to purchase a large volume of manufactured merchandise at a discounted price. The order fits within the existing capacity.	The fixed cost of the manufacturing equipment	________
2. A business is considering outsourcing part of its production to another company, freeing up space to be used for other opportunities.	Revenue that could be generated from the extra space	________
3. A business owner is considering discontinuing a segment of business operations because it is losing money.	Costs shared by the discontinued business segment and other segments	________
4. A business owner is considering replacing an old piece of equipment with a new one because the old equipment is costing more than expected to repair and maintain. However, the old piece of equipment was incredibly expensive to purchase originally.	The original purchase price of the old equipment	________
5. A business owner is considering replacing an old piece of equipment with a new one.	Ongoing maintenance costs for the equipment	________

What Information Do Businesses Use to Identify Where to Invest Their Money?

Learning Objective 8.1

Describe how managers evaluate potential capital expenditures and identify the data relevant to making a choice.

Investments of capital into long-term fixed assets (capital assets) usually consume significant resources. Thus, businesses carefully evaluate potential investments in such assets. When a business acquires a capital asset by purchase or construction, it is making a **capital investment**. Managers use a process called **capital budgeting** to identify capital investment alternatives, evaluate each alternative, and then select the investments that produce the greatest return on the company's available investment resources.

Importance of Capital Investment Decisions

Capital investment decisions affect all businesses. Architects must consider if the purchase of specialized printers is worth the investment. Hospitals must consider if replacing older surgical equipment with a newer version will result in increased efficiencies and revenue. Boutique store owners must consider if purchasing new kiosks to display merchandise will result in increased sales. Every capital investment decision must be evaluated against the costs to implement and the resulting cash flow and net income. How do managers and owners make these decisions? They use data to perform capital budgeting analysis.

Data Relevance

We will look at several methods of capital budgeting analysis in this chapter. Keep in mind that the relevance of the data used in performing the capital budgeting analysis depends on the method used. Some methods compare the net income generated by the investment to the cost of the investment. In contrast, other methods compare the cash inflows generated by the investment to the cash outflows associated with making the investment. Table 8.1 shows the cash inflows and outflows associated with capital budgeting.

Businesses select capital investments that maximize either cash flow or maximize the difference between net income generated and the cost of the investment. Other relevant data for capital budgeting are the required rate of return, the marginal tax rate, and the duration of the investment. We will discuss these data sources in subsequent sections.

Table 8.1 Cash Flows and Capital Budgeting

Cash Inflows	Incremental increases in cash received from sales
	Incremental decreases in expenses
	Proceeds from the sale of old capital assets
	Proceeds from the sale of the new capital asset at the end of its life
	Tax savings triggered by the investment transaction
Cash Outflows	Initial cost of the capital investment
	Incremental increases in expenses
	Tax expenses triggered by the investment transaction

How Do Businesses Compare Net Income and the Cost of the Capital Investment When Making an Investment Decision?

Learning Objective 8.2
Explain and apply the average rate of return method for evaluating and making capital budgeting decisions.

The **average rate of return (ARR) method** compares the annual rate of return on a capital investment with the required rate of return that the company desires. The ARR method focuses on measuring the profitability of an investment. To apply the ARR method, follow these steps:

1. Determine the annual profit.
2. Determine the average annual rate of return on the investment.
3. Compare the annual rate of return to the required rate of return.

The **required rate of return** is the return a company desires from an investment. An investment that meets or exceeds the required rate of return is usually undertaken. Typically, the required rate of return, commonly called the company's cost of capital, is a combination of the interest rate charged for money borrowed plus the cost of equity capital (funds invested by shareholders). The cost of equity capital is a computation that combines the rate of return that could be garnered from a risk-free investment like US Treasury Bonds and the market rate of return such as the Standard and Poor's 500 stock index.

To illustrate, let's revisit the aviation firm, MC Aero, introduced in Chapter 7. MC Aero is a general aviation company that offers a range of services, from air ambulance services to air charter services, along with a flight school. Aero is considering adding a single-engine Cessna 172 Skyhawk airplane to use in its flight school. Apply the ARR method to evaluate this capital budgeting decision.

Arian Fernandez / https://www.pexels.com/photo/light-aircraft-flying-in-clear-kentucky-sky-30272216// last accessed March 13, 2025

The Skyhawk costs $280,000. MC Aero expects the airplane to generate $100,000 in sales annually. Annual operating costs include $10,000 for fuel, $5,000 for maintenance and inspections, $5,000 for insurance, and $16,000 for depreciation. The company's marginal tax rate is 25%. Aero expects the Skyhawk will have a **residual value** of $120,000 at the end of 10 years. At that point, it will be replaced. The first step is to compute the estimated annual profit (or net income) generated by the investment. The estimated annual sales and costs for the Skyhawk are as follows:

Sales		$100,000
Less Annual Operating Costs:		
Fuel	10,000	
Maintenance and Inspections	5,000	
Insurance	5,000	
Depreciation	16,000	36,000
Income Before Income Taxes		64,000
Income Tax Expense ($64,000 × 25%)		16,000
Net Income		$ 48,000

MC Aero's estimated annual profit from the investment in the Skyhawk is $48,000.

The next step is to determine the average annual rate of return on the investment. The annual return from the Skyhawk is calculated as follows:

$$\text{Annual Net Income} \div \text{Average Annual Investment}^* = \text{Annual Rate of Return}$$

$$\frac{^*\text{Original Cost of the Investment} + \text{Residual Value at the End of Useful Life}}{2}$$

The annual rate of return from the Skyhawk is

$$\$48{,}000 \div \$200{,}000^* = 24\%$$

$$^*\ \text{Average Annual Investment:} \frac{\$280{,}000 + \$120{,}000}{2}$$

The final step would be for MC Aero to compare the annual rate of return to the *required rate of return*. Suppose that MC Aero's required rate of return is 30%. In this case, MC Aero would choose *not* to purchase the Skyhawk because the annual rate of return (24%) is less than the required rate of return (30%). (See Figure 8.1.)

The annual rate of return method is simple to compute, but it has limitations:

1. It utilizes net income rather than actual cash flow.
2. It ignores the timing of returns and cash flow.

We will cover the effects of timing in the subsequent section on the *time value of money*.

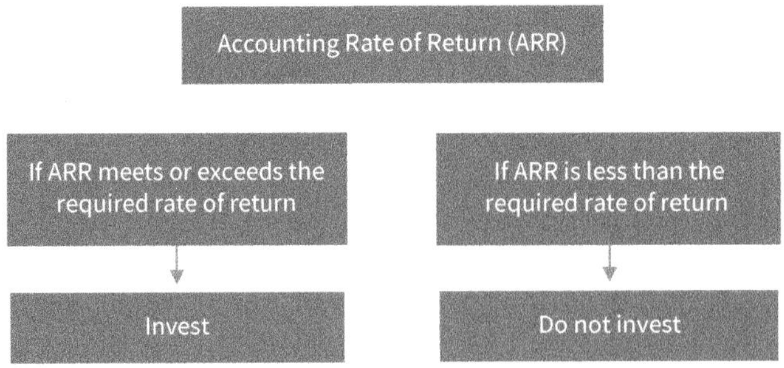

Figure 8.1 Accounting rate of return (ARR).

ACCOUNTING IN BUSINESS

Galen Hafla, owner of **Hokulia Shave Ice** in Parker, Colorado, was interested in expanding his business outside of his brick-and-mortar operation and purchasing assets that would allow him to be mobile and serve his shaved ice creations at swim meets, baseball and soccer tournaments, schools events, parties, and more. Hafla estimated he could generate $25,000 to $50,000 in additional sales annually if he were to invest in a mobile operation. He investigated two options offered by his franchise: a self-contained trailer or a tent-based configuration that requires setup at each event. "I elected to purchase the tent. The cost of the tent, mobile ice shavers, and other fixtures were cheaper than the trailer. However, the tent requires about two hours of additional labor to set up and take down at each event. But the tent allows me to locate my operation inside the event rather than in a parking lot. I've found that it gives me more sales opportunities and is safer for my customers, especially children. The added sales from the tent more than make up for the additional setup cost." Hafla is happy with the return he has made from the mobile operation. "We made about $6,000 in profit during our first year of mobile operation, nearly a 50% return on investment. Not bad. I expect sales and margins on mobile operations to go up next year now that we have experience. It has been a good investment."

Source: Author interview with Galen Hafla, owner of Hokulia Shave Ice

LEARNING ACTIVITY 8.2

Tristan Miller is considering adding a hydro massage bed to Amor Salon and Spa. The hydro massage bed costs $8,000. Tristan expects it to generate $3,000 in sales annually with only $500 in operating costs and $1,000 in depreciation annually. Tristan's marginal tax rate is 20%. Tristan expects the massage bed to be usable for 6 years and have a residual value of $2,000 at the end.

1. Compute the expected annual rate of return for the hydro massage bed.
2. Suppose Tristan's required rate of return is 12%. Should Tristan purchase the hydro massage bed?

Do Businesses Care How Long It Takes to Get a Return on Their Investment?

Learning Objective 8.3

Explain and apply the payback method for evaluating and making capital budgeting decisions.

Businesses do not operate on *profits*; they operate on *cash*. Capital investments consume cash, and business managers aim for cash in return from the investment. Other than the average rate of return method that focuses on net income, most methods for analyzing capital investments are based on cash flow. One such technique is the *payback method*. The **payback method** measures the amount of time it takes to generate a cash return that equals the cost of the initial investment.

The payback method divides the original cost of the investment by the expected annual cash inflow.

Original Cost of the Investment ÷ Expected Annual Cash Inflow = Payback Period

Let us look at MC Aero and its investment in the Cessna 172 Skyhawk. The relevant data related to the investment in the Skyhawk are as follows:

Original Purchase Price		$280,000
Residual Value at the End of Useful Life		120,000
Useful Life		10 years
Sales		$100,000
Less Annual Operating Costs:		
Fuel	$10,000	
Maintenance and Inspections	5,000	
Insurance	5,000	
Depreciation	16,000	36,000
Income Before Income Taxes		64,000
Income Tax Expense ($64,000 × 25%)		16,000
Net Income		$ 48,000

Rather than focusing on net income, the payback method is based on cash flow. The initial cash outflow for the investment is $280,000. The annual cash inflow is computed as follows:

Cash Sales		$100,000
Cash Expenses		
Fuel	$10,000	
Maintenance and Inspections	5,000	
Insurance	5,000	
Income Taxes	16,000	36,000
Annual Cash Inflow		64,000

The amount of time it takes for MC Aero to return the $280,000 investment in the Cessna 172 Skyhawk is computed as follows:

Original Cost of the Investment ÷ Expected Annual Cash Inflow = Payback Period

$280,000 ÷ $64,000 per year = 4.375 years

The payback method shows that it takes 4.375 years to recover the cash investment in the new Skyhawk. MC Aero should determine if this payback period is acceptable. Owners and managers often compare the payback period to a set amount of time, such as the useful life of the capital investment. In this case, MC Aero would choose to purchase the new Skyhawk because the payback period (4.375 years) is equal to or less than the useful life (10 years). (See Figure 8.2.)

The payback method is commonly used by businesses because it is simple to compute and incorporates cash flows rather than accounting net income. All else being equal, the shorter the payback period, the more attractive the asset. However, the payback method does not account for the *time value of money* or cash flows that occur after the payback period. Owners and managers, therefore, often use another method to evaluate if a capital investment should be approved.

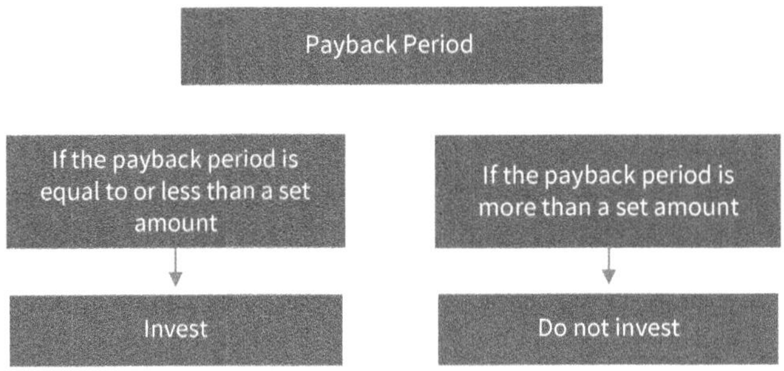

Figure 8.2 Payback period.

LEARNING ACTIVITY 8.3

Consider the addition of a hydro massage bed that Tristan Miller is planning to add to Amor Salon and Spa. The hydro massage bed costs $8,000. Tristan expects it to generate $3,000 in sales annually with only $500 in operating costs and an annual depreciation of $1,000. Tristan's marginal tax rate is 20%. Tristan expects the massage bed to be usable for 6 years and be worth $2,000 at the end of the useful life.

1. Compute the expected payback period for the hydro massage bed.
2. Assuming Tristan wants to recoup the initial investment within 6 years (the useful life of the hydro massage bed), should Tristan purchase the massage bed?

"Eighty-two percent of businesses that fail do so because of cash flow problems."[1] Profitable businesses can run short on cash if the operating cycle becomes long. The operating cycle is the time between a business's cash expenditures to pay for purchases or production of goods for sale and the collection of cash from selling the products. If it takes too long to recover the cost of a capital asset, businesses could experience a cash flow problem. This is why the payback period method is helpful in evaluating capital investment decisions.

How Do Businesses Account for the Timing of Cash Flows from an Investment?

Learning Objective 8.4
Summarize the time value of money concept.

Capital investments are typically used for long periods and thus generate a series of cash flows over time. The **time value of money** concept is based on the insight that cash received now is worth more than cash received in the future because cash received now can either be used to pay for things or invested. Thus, managers must consider the timing of cash inflows and outflows before making capital budgeting decisions.

Time Value of Money Assumptions

All time value of money techniques adopt the following assumptions:

1. Cash flows (or principal, p) are constantly reinvested at a static rate of return (or interest rate, i). In reality, however, a company may take cash flows from a project and set them aside rather than invest them, or invest them at a different rate of return than the investment being analyzed.
2. Cash flows occur at the end of the year over a number of periods (n). In a real-life situation, cash flows may come in sporadically over time.

[1] Mansfield, M. (2019). *Startup statistics—The numbers you need to know* [online]. Small Business Trends. Available at: https://smallbiztrends.com/2019/03/startup-statistics-small-business.html

Present Value, Future Value, and Compounding

The time value of money is based on the present value theory and the concepts of *present value*, *future value*, and *compounding*. **Present value** is the value of future cash flows in today's dollars. **Future value** is the value of a current investment at a date in the future based on an expected growth rate. The time value of money assumes that cash received today can be invested and is worth more than cash received in the future as a result of the investment returns. For example, consider a business that receives a cash inflow of $100 today. Also, assume that the business can invest the money at an interest rate of 10% annually. The $100 (the present value) would have a future value of $161.05 in 5 years. Let's look at the math. In 1 year, $100 would grow to $110 after earning $10 ($100 × 10%) in interest with a 10% rate of return. At the end of year 2, the $110 would grow by another 10% to $121. At the end of year 3 the $121 would grow by 10% to $133.10, then by 10% to 146.41 at the end of year 4, and finally by another 10% to $161.05 at the end of year 5.

Year	Interest Revenue	Ending Balance
Year 1	$100.00 × 10% = $10.00	$100.00 + $10.00 = $110.00
Year 2	$110.00 × 10% = $11.00	$110.00 + $11.00 = $121.00
Year 3	$121.00 × 10% = $12.10	$121.00 + $12.10 = $133.10
Year 4	$133.10 × 10% = $13.31	$133.10 + $13.31 = $146.41
Year 5	$146.41 × 10% = $14.64	$146.41 + $14.64 = $161.05

This process of interest being calculated on the principal and preceding accumulated interest is called **compounding**. Compound interest means that interest is calculated on the principal *and* on all previously earned interest. Figure 8.3 illustrates how $100 can grow to $161.05 in five years, with interest compounding at a rate of 10% annually.

Simple Interest Versus Compound Interest

An investment that earns compound interest is much better than an investment that earns *simple interest*. **Simple interest** means that interest is calculated only on the principal amount. For example, consider the $100 cash inflow invested at 10% for 5 years. Using simple interest, the investment only has a future value of $150 in 5 years because the interest revenue is only calculated on the principal amount (not the principal plus all previously earned interest).

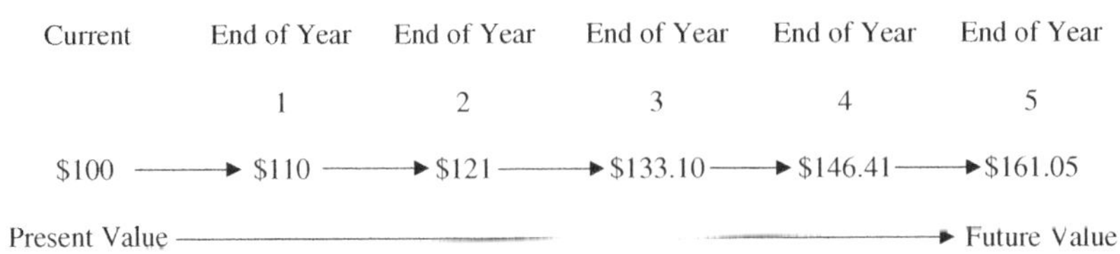

Figure 8.3 Compound interest of 100 at 10% over 5 years.

Year	Interest Revenue	Ending Balance
Year 1	\$100 × 10% = \$10	\$100 + \$10 = \$110
Year 2	\$100 × 10% = \$10	\$110 + \$10 = \$120
Year 3	\$100 × 10% = \$10	\$120 + \$10 = \$130
Year 4	\$100 × 10% = \$10	\$130 + \$10 = \$140
Year 5	\$100 × 10% = \$10	\$140 + \$10 = \$150

Over the life of the investment, the total amount of compound interest (\$61.05) is more than the total amount of simple interest (\$50). Most investments yield compound interest, so we will assume compound interest rather than simple interest, for the rest of this chapter.

Discounting

From the capital budgeting perspective, we are more likely to be concerned with computing the present value of future cash inflows rather than calculating the future value of a current investment. **Discounting** is the process of converting a future value to a present value. Discounting is a function of compound interest and time. The interest rate used to discount a future value to a present value is called the **discount rate**.

Let us look at our future value example from Figure 8.3 in reverse to illustrate. What is the present value of \$161.05 received 5 years from now, assuming we earn 10% if we invest the money? From that perspective, the present value is \$100. Let's look at the math and work backward from the future value by dividing the future value by 100% plus the discount rate. The discount rate is commonly set at the rate of return that can be achieved if the money was invested. Starting with \$161.05 in year 5, divide \$161.05 by 110% to arrive at \$146.41 in year 4. \$146.41 ÷ 110% is equal to \$133.10 for year 3. At year 2, \$133.10 ÷ 110% results in \$121. At the end of year one, \$121 ÷ 110% results in \$110. Finally, \$110 ÷ 110% is equal to the present value of \$100.

Year	Discount
Year 5	\$161.05 / (100% + 10%) = \$146.41
Year 4	\$146.41 / (100% + 10%) = \$133.10
Year 3	\$133.10 / (100% + 10%) = \$121.00
Year 2	\$121.00 / (100% + 10%) = \$110.00
Year 1	\$110.00 / (100% + 10%) = \$100.00

You can use a present value table that has already completed the mathematical steps or a financial calculator to compute the present value of a future cash inflow. We determine the present value (PV) factor from the table, Present Value of \$1 (Figure 8.4). The PV factor is located in the 10% column for 5 periods, which is 0.621. Multiplying \$161.05 by 0.621 (the percentage associated with a 10% compound interest rate for a period of five years) results in the present value of \$100.

Present Value of $1			
	Interest Rate (i)		
Periods (n)	10%	15%	20%
1	0.909	0.870	0.833
2	0.826	0.756	0.694
3	0.751	0.658	0.579
4	0.683	0.572	0.482
5	0.621	0.497	0.402
6	0.564	0.432	0.335
7	0.513	0.376	0.279
8	0.467	0.327	0.233
9	0.424	0.284	0.194
10	0.386	0.247	0.162

Figure 8.4 Present value of $1 table.

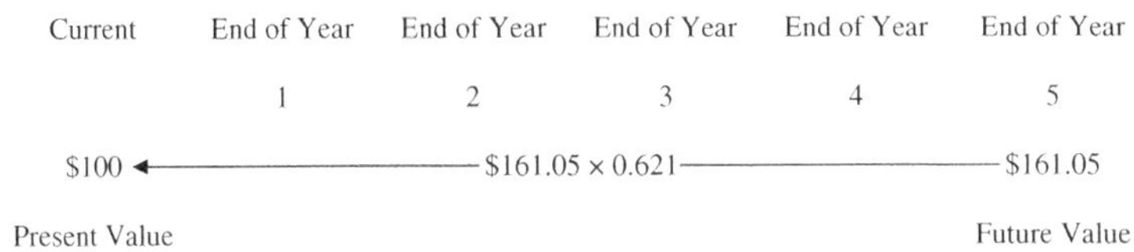

Figure 8.5 Present value of $1 timeline.

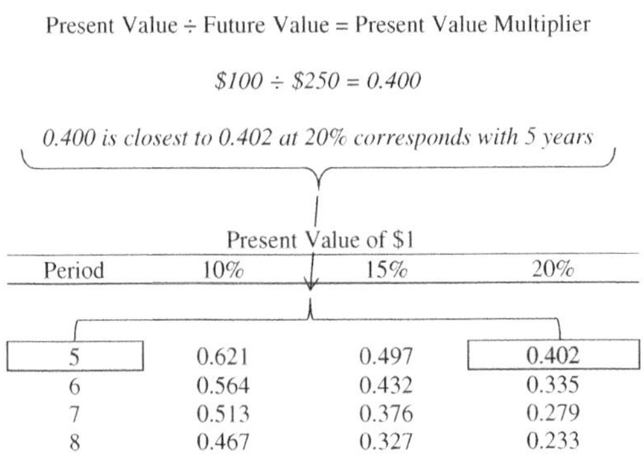

Figure 8.6 Present value multiplier year 5.

$$\text{Present value} = \text{Future value} \times \text{PV multiplier for } i = 10\%,\ n = 5$$

$$\$100 = \$161.05 \times 0.621$$

Figure 8.5 illustrates this solution with a timeline.

You can also use the present value table to compute how long an investment needs to be held at a particular interest rate to achieve an investment goal. How many years must a $100 investment (the present value) that returns 15% annually be held in order to generate a future value of approximately $250? (See Figure 8.6.)

It is also possible to use the table to estimate a needed rate of return to achieve an objective. For example, what interest rate must an investment return if the initial present value of the investment is $100 and the desired future value is $400 after 10 years? (See Figure 8.7.)

Present Value ÷ Future Value = Present Value Multiplier

$100 ÷ $400 = 0.250

0.250 at 10 years corresponds most closely with 0.247 at 15%

Present Value of $1			
Period	10%	15%	20%
7	0.513	0.376	0.279
8	0.467	0.327	0.233
9	0.424	0.284	0.194
10	0.386	0.247	0.162

Figure 8.7 Present value multiplier year 10.

LEARNING ACTIVITY 8.4

Answer the following questions using the present value of $1 table.

Present Value of $1

	Interest Rate (*i*)		
Periods (*n*)	**10%**	**15%**	**20%**
1	0.909	0.870	0.833
2	0.826	0.756	0.694
3	0.751	0.658	0.579
4	0.683	0.572	0.482
5	0.621	0.497	0.402
6	0.564	0.432	0.335
7	0.513	0.376	0.279
8	0.467	0.327	0.233
9	0.424	0.284	0.194
10	0.386	0.247	0.162

1. What is the present value of an investment that returns $100,000 at the end of 8 years with an expected rate of return of 15%?
2. How many years must a $5,000 investment that returns 10% annually be held in order to generate a future value of approximately $9,750?
3. What interest rate must an investment return if the company desires a present value investment of $1,000 and a future value of approximately $2,000 at the end of 5 years?

Annuities

Cash inflows from capital expenditures do not always come in one lump sum; they often come in a stream or series of cash flows over the life of the investment. A series of cash flows over time is called an **annuity**. For example, let's look at a series of cash receipts: $100 received annually for 5 years. Assuming we can invest at a rate of 10%, what is the present value of the stream of five consecutive $100 cash receipts? We will show two approaches:

1. Discount each cash receipt.
2. Use the present value of an annuity table.

Figure 8.8 illustrates how to compute the present value by discounting each cash receipt using the present value factor for $1 presented in Figure 8.3.

Another approach is to use a table that calculates the present value of an annuity. This approach only works if the cash flows are even (equal in amount and time period). The table in Figure 8.6 presents the value in which an annuity payment is multiplied by to arrive at the present value of the annuity. *Period* represents the number of consecutive cash flows.

In this example, we have five consecutive $100 cash inflows, a total of $500. We calculate the present value by multiplying the $100 times the present value of an annuity factor for five years. From Figure 8.9, the annuity PV factor is found in the 10% column at 5 periods, or 3.790.

$$\text{Present value} = \text{Amount of each cash flow} \times \text{Annuity PV factor for } i = 10\%, n = 5$$

$$\$379 = \$100 \times 3.790$$

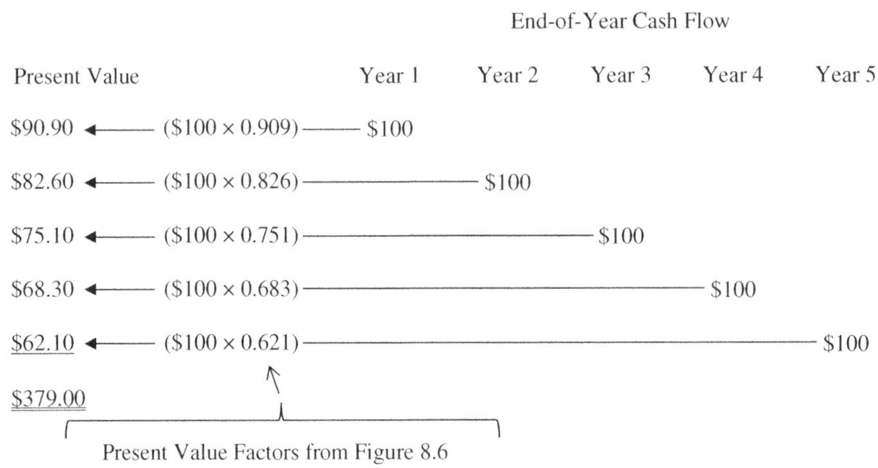

Figure 8.8 Discounting.

Present Value of an Ordinary Annuity of $1

Period	10%	15%	20%
1	0.909	0.870	0.833
2	1.746	1.626	1.528
3	2.497	2.283	2.106
4	3.170	2.855	2.589
5	3.790	3.353	2.991
6	4.355	3.785	3.326
7	4.868	4.160	3.605
8	5.335	4.487	3.837
9	5.759	4.772	4.031
10	6.145	5.019	4.192

Figure 8.9 Present value of an ordinary annuity of $1.

LEARNING ACTIVITY 8.5

Answer the following questions using the following present value of an ordinary annuity table.

Present Value of an Ordinary Annuity of $1

Period	10%	15%	20%
1	0.909	0.870	0.833
2	1.746	1.626	1.528
3	2.497	2.283	2.106
4	3.170	2.855	2.589
5	3.790	3.353	2.991
6	4.355	3.785	3.326
7	4.868	4.160	3.605
8	5.335	4.487	3.837
9	5.759	4.772	4.031
10	6.145	5.019	4.192

What is the present value of an investment that returns $10,000 annually for 7 years at a rate of 10%?

How Do Businesses Apply Time Value of Money Concepts?

Learning Objective 8.5
Apply the time value of money concept to capital budgeting decisions.

Neither the payback period method nor the accounting rate of return method recognizes the time value of money. That is, these methods fail to consider the *timing* of the net cash inflows that a capital asset generates. The *net present value method*, *present value index*, and the *internal rate of return* method overcome this weakness. These capital budgeting methods incorporate the concept of compound interest and the time value of money. Let's begin by discussing the net present value method.

The Net Present Value Method for Evaluating Capital Investments

The **net present value method** compares the present value of cash inflows from an investment to the amount invested. The amount invested (or invested capital) is netted with the present value of the cash inflows. The result is called the net present value. The cash inflows are discounted to the present value, or the date of the initial investment, using the desired rate of return for the investment or **hurdle rate**. Thus, the discount rate used in net present value calculations is the hurdle rate. The hurdle rate considers factors like the **cost of capital**, which is the interest rate charged by creditors for the use of their money on the investment, along with the riskiness of the investment, and how easily the investment can be liquidated if it does not produce as expected. If the net present value is positive, the investment returns a value that is greater than the hurdle rate, and the project is generally accepted.

Let's look at an example related to Hokulia Shaved Ice in Parker, Colorado. Assume the owner, Galen Hafla, is considering expanding his smoothie offerings to include blends that contain freshly squeezed juice. He is considering purchasing a continuous feed juice extractor for $4,000, and he expects the extractor will increase his smoothie cash revenue by $3,000 annually over the 3-year life of the machine. The relevant data are presented here:

Cost of the juice extractor	$4,000
Useful life	3 years
Hurdle rate	20%
Annual cash flow	$3,000

The net present value of the capital investment is calculated using the present value of $1 factors from Figure 8.3. The factors at 20% for one (0.833), two (0.694), and three (0.579) years, respectively, are used in the computation. The net present value is calculated as follows:

Year	Annual Cash Flow	Present Value of $1 Factor at 20% Discount Rate	Present Value of Annual Cash Flow
1	$3,000 ×	0.833 –	$2,499
2	3,000 ×	0.694 =	2,082
3	3,000 ×	0.579 =	1,737
	Total		$6,318
	Less cost of juicer		(4,000)
	Net present value		$2,318

The net present value of $2,318 represents the $9,000 ($3,000 × 3 years) of total future cash inflows discounted to current value ($6,318) using a rate of 20%, less the $4,000 outflow. *The positive net present value indicates that the investment is returning more than the hurdle rate of 20% and the investment should be undertaken.*

Since the juicer is expected to produce equal annual cash flows, we can also compute the net present value using the present value of an ordinary annuity factor from Figure 8.6. The factor at 20% and 3 years is 2.106. The net present value is calculated as follows:

Years	Equal Annual Cash Flows	Present Value of an Ordinary Annuity Factor at 20% Discount Rate for 3 Years	Present Value of Annual Cash Flows
3	$3,000 ×	2.106 =	$6,318
	Less cost of juicer		(4,000)
	Net present value		$2,318

Notice that the net present value is the same when using the present value of $1 factor for each year and adding the result of the present value of an ordinary annuity factor. The present value of an ordinary annuity factor for 3 years at a 20% discount rate is equal to the sum of the present value factors for years 1 through 3 at a 20% discount rate (0.833 + 0.694 + 0.579 = 2.106).

Although the net present value method is complex to calculate, it has several advantages. The net present value method is considered preferable to the average rate of return and payback methods because of the following differences:

1. It considers the time value of money. Money earned today is more valuable than money earned in the future, assuming it is invested. The net present value method assumes cash flows are invested.
2. The method considers cash flows over net income. Businesses operate on cash, not profits, so this method provides a realistic picture of the inflows and outflows of cash that come from a company's capital investment.
3. It can be used to compare multiple projects of different size and duration.

LEARNING ACTIVITY 8.6

Consider the hydro massage bed that Tristan Miller is planning to add to Amor Salon and Spa. The hydro massage bed costs $12,000, and Tristan expects it to generate $2,000 in annual cash flow for 8 years. Tristan expects a rate or return, or hurdle rate, of 10% for new ventures.

1. Compute the expected net present value for the hydro massage bed using the present value of an ordinary annuity table.

Present Value of an Ordinary Annuity of $1

Period	10%	15%	20%
1	0.909	0.870	0.833
2	1.746	1.626	1.528
3	2.497	2.283	2.106
4	3.170	2.855	2.589
5	3.790	3.353	2.991
6	4.355	3.785	3.326
7	4.868	4.160	3.605
8	5.335	4.487	3.837
9	5.759	4.772	4.031
10	6.145	5.019	4.192

2. Should Tristan purchase the hydro massage bed in this situation?

The Net Present Value Method with Uneven Cash Flows

The preceding examples related to Galen Hafla's purchase of a juicer at his Hokulia Shaved Ice franchise assumed equal annual cash flows of $3,000. It is more realistic to assume uneven cash flows since sales of the new smoothies may grow over time. Let's assume the same relevant data as the earlier example, but the cash flows are no longer a consistent $3,000 per year, and are $1,000 in year 1, $3,000 in year 2, and $5,000 in year 3.

Cost of the juice extractor	$4,000
Useful life	3 years
Hurdle rate	20%
Annual cash flow	$1,000 (Year 1); $3,000 (Year 2); $5,000 (Year 3)

Solving for unequal cash flows requires the use of three net present value factors for each year of the investment's life. Referencing present value of $1 factors from Figure 8.4, the factors are 20% for one (0.833), two (0.694), and three (0.579) years, respectively, in the computation. The net present value is calculated as follows:

Year	Annual Cash Flow	Present Value of $1 Factor at 20% Discount Rate	Present Value of Annual Cash Flow
1	$1,000 ×	0.833 =	$ 833
2	3,000 ×	0.694 =	2,082
3	5,000 ×	0.579 =	2,895
	Total		$5,810
	Less Cost of Juicer		(4,000)
	Net Present Value		$1,810

The net present value of $1,810 represents the $9,000 of total future cash inflows discounted to current value ($5,810) using a rate of 20%, less the $4,000 outflow. Notice that the present value of $5,810 is less than the present value of $6,318 in the preceding example, that assumed equal annual cash flows of $3,000 per year. The investment returns a cash flow of $9,000 in both situations, but the second example assumes a greater amount is returned in year 3 rather than year 1. The cash made in year 1 has a higher present value factor because it has been discounted less than the cash made in year 3. This is because of the assumption that the business will continually invest cash at a 20% rate of return. Cash obtained in year 1 would be invested for two more years than cash obtained in year 3.

LEARNING ACTIVITY 8.7

Let's take another look at the hydro massage bed Tristan Miller is planning to add to Amor Salon and Spa and assume the following cash flows over the next 8 years:

Year	Cash Flows
1	$5,000
2	4,000
3	2,000
4	1,000
5	1,000
6	1,000
7	1,000
8	$1,000

1. Assuming the hydro massage bed costs $12,000 and Tristan's hurdle rate is 10% for new ventures. Compute the expected net present value for the hydro massage bed using the present value of $1 table.

Present Value of $1

	Interest Rate (*i*)		
Periods (*n*)	**10%**	**15%**	**20%**
1	0.909	0.870	0.833
2	0.826	0.756	0.694
3	0.751	0.658	0.579
4	0.683	0.572	0.482
5	0.621	0.497	0.402
6	0.564	0.432	0.335
7	0.513	0.376	0.279
8	0.467	0.327	0.233
9	0.424	0.284	0.194
10	0.386	0.247	0.162

2. Should Tristan purchase the hydro massage in this situation?

ACCOUNTING IN LIFE

The decision to attend college is one of the biggest decisions a person makes in life. The Bureau of Labor and Statistics shows that the median college graduate's annual earnings exceed those of people with only a high school diploma by about $20,000 as shown in Figure 8.10. Undoubtedly, a Bachelor's degree is worth the investment. But what about a Master's degree? The median cost of tuition and fees for a Master's degree at a public university is around $15,000[2] annually, according to the National Center for Education Statistics. The median annual earnings for individuals with a Master's degree increases by $15,000 over those with a Bachelor's. But there is a hidden cost of attending a full-time master's program: wages forgone. The student loses out on an average of $65,000 in wages by attending a program that takes a year to complete. Thus, the total cost of obtaining a Master's degree full-time is approximately $80,000 ($15,000 + $65,000). Is it worth it?

[2] Source: COE—Annual Earnings by Educational Attainment.

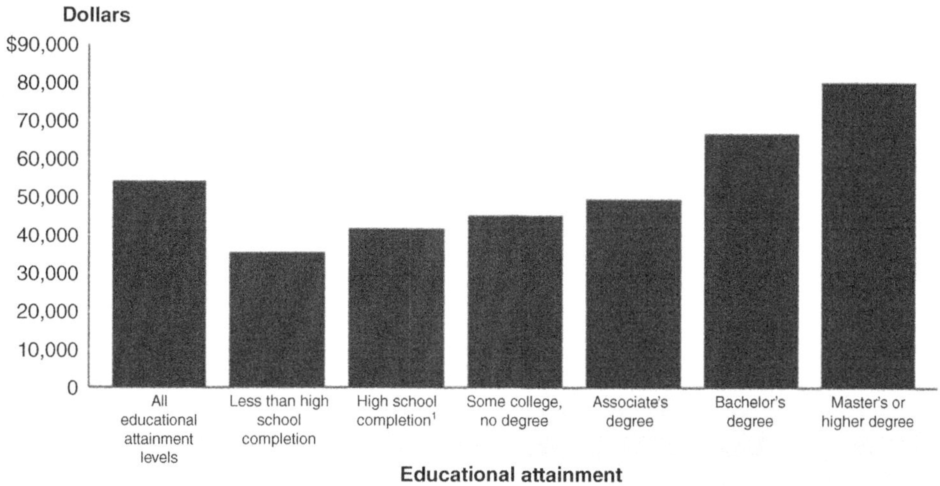

Figure 8.10 Annual earnings by educational attainment in 2022.[3]

The net present value of obtaining a Master's degree full-time would be computed as follows, assuming the degree holder worked for 30 years after obtaining the degree and using a 10% discount rate:

Years	Annual Wage Difference	Present Value of an Ordinary Annuity Factor at 10% Discount Rate for 30 Years	Present Value of Annual Cash Flows
30	$15,000 x	9.4269 =	$141,404
	Cost of the Degree		(80,000)
	Net present value		$61,404

The value of a Master's degree appears to be well worth the cost. Are you considering a program? Input the relevant data and see if it will pay off. Consider using the average return on a stock market investment of 12% as the discount rate:

Earnings with Bachelor's degree ____________ Years working ____________

Earnings with Master's degree ____________ Discount rate ____________

Cost of tuition and fees ____________

Net present value of the Master's degree ____________

[3]Source: US Bureau of Labor Statistics / public_domain.

Present Value Index

Businesses often do not have access to an unlimited amount of capital and must choose which investment alternatives to select to make the best use of available funds. The *present value index* can be used to rank capital investment proposals. The **present value index** is the total present value of the cash inflows provided by an investment divided by the amount invested.

$$\text{Present Value Index} = \frac{\text{Present Value of the Cash Inflows}}{\text{Amount Invested}}$$

To illustrate, the present value index of the juicer (using even cash flows) that Hokulia Shaved Ice is considering would be computed as follows:

$$\text{Present Value Index} = \frac{\$6{,}318}{\$4{,}000} = 1.5795$$

Hokulia's owner, Galan Hafla, could compare this with other investment options. Let us assume Hafla has $20,000 available to invest in new capital projects. He is considering adding the $4,000 juicer and the mobile operation discussed earlier for $12,000. He is also considering adding barista equipment at a cost of $5,000 and expanding his coffee operations. The expected net present value of the cash inflows from each investment is $6,318 for the juicer, $21,628 for the mobile operation, and $6,280 for the expanded coffee offerings. The present value index for the three investment opportunities is as follows:

	Juicer	Mobile Operation	Coffee
Present Value of Cash Inflows	$6,318	$21,628	$6,280
÷ Amount Invested	÷$4,000	÷$12,000	÷$5,000
Present Value Index	1.5795	1.8023	1.2600
Ranking	2	1	3

The present value index is the highest for the investment in mobile operation, suggesting that the project should be a top priority. The juicer is the second most profitable, with an index of 1.5795, and the coffee is the least profitable, with an index of 1.2600. Hokulia would get the best returns if it invested in the juicer and the mobile operation. That would consume $16,000 of total investment and return a net present value of $27,946.

LEARNING ACTIVITY 8.8

1. Let's take another look at the hydro massage bed Tristan Miller is planning to add to Amor Salon and Spa. The cost of the hydro massage bed is $12,000, and the present value of expected cash inflows is $12,199. What is the present value index?
2. Tristan could purchase a massage chair for $8,990, and the present value of expected future cash flows produced by the chair is $9,195. Which investment has the highest return on investment, the massage chair or the hydro massage bed?

Internal Rate of Return Method

Sometimes, it is helpful to know the exact rate of return an investment produces. That rate is called the **internal rate of return**. The **internal rate of return method** computes the rate of return necessary to get a net present value of zero for a series of cash flows at a given investment amount. We can approximate the internal rate of return using the Present Value of an Ordinary Annuity table (see Figure 8.6). To apply the internal rate of return method, use the following steps:

1. Compute the present value of an ordinary annuity factor by dividing the amount invested by the annual cash flow.
2. Find the closest present value of an ordinary annuity factor at the number of years of the useful life of the investment.
3. Identify the associated interest rate on the table, which is the internal rate of return.

To illustrate, let's look at the MC Aero example discussed previously. Recall that MC Aero was considering purchasing a Cessna 172 Skyhawk for a price of $280,000. The expected annual cash inflow was $56,000 for 10 years. We determine the present value of an ordinary annuity factor by dividing the amount invested by the annual cash flow:

$$\text{Present Value of Ordinary Annuity Factor} = \frac{\text{Amount Invested}}{\text{Annual Cash Flow}} = \frac{\$280{,}000}{\$56{,}000} = 5.000$$

Next, we look for the closest present value of an ordinary annuity factor at the 10-year useful life of the investment:

Present Value of an Ordinary Annuity of $1

Period	10%	15%	20%
1	0.909	0.870	0.833
2	1.746	1.626	1.528
3	2.497	2.283	2.106
4	3.170	2.855	2.589
5	3.790	3.353	2.991
6	4.355	3.785	3.326
7	4.868	4.160	3.605
8	5.335	4.487	3.837
9	5.759	4.772	4.031
10	6.145	5.019	4.192

The present value of an ordinary annuity factor of 5.019 at 10 years is the closest value to 5.000. The associated interest rate of 15% is the approximate internal rate of return.

LEARNING ACTIVITY 8.9

Assume the massage chair being considered by Tristan Miller for Amor Salon and Spa is expected to produce an annual cash flow of $2,745 for 5 years and costs $8,999. Use the present value of an ordinary annuity table to find the investment's internal rate of return.

ACCOUNTING IN BUSINESS

RDNE Stock project / Pexels / Public Domain

Capital budgeting doesn't just apply to the purchase of equipment or other capital assets. Ali Parrish is the Executive Director at **Iowa Heartland Habitat for Humanity** in Waterloo, Iowa. Since 1990, the Iowa Heartland Habitat for Humanity has been "dedicated to eliminating substandard housing through construction, rehabilitation, and preserving homes; by advocating for fair housing policies; and by providing access to resources to help families improve their shelter conditions." Over the years, Iowa Heartland Habitat for Humanity has grown from building singular homes for needy families to a multifaceted organization that includes home construction, home repair, transitional rental properties, and even a retail home improvement store called the ReStore. Ali uses capital budgeting methodologies to help her make decisions about growing the organization. "We incur significant startup costs when expanding," says Ali. "I may have to add personnel, and there may be training costs, office supplies and equipment, insurance, research expenses, licensing and permits, and a lot more. Before we added the ReStore, we had to compare the startup and ongoing costs with the revenue we expected it to generate."

Successful business growth requires careful consideration of cash in and cash out, whether that growth is through adding new machinery, adding employees, or expanding into new areas of business. Understanding capital budgeting is essential for any business leader.

Source: Author interview with Ali Parrish, Executive Director at Iowa Heartland Habitat for Humanity.

Do Other Factors Affect Capital Budgeting Decisions?

Learning Objective 8.6
Describe how managers account for risk and qualitative factors when making capital budgeting decisions.

We've looked at several capital budgeting methods. When making decisions, managers also consider risk and qualitative factors.

Risk

Managers account for various types of risk and uncertainty when using the present value method to evaluate capital investment opportunities. The types of risk and uncertainty include inflation, cash flow uncertainty, and lack of liquidity.

- Inflation—Inflation involves an increase in prices and a corresponding fall in purchasing power. Inflation can be accounted for in future cash flow projections or in an adjustment to the hurdle rate.
- Cash flow uncertainty—Managers usually add a premium to the hurdle rate to account for uncertainty in future cash flows.
- Lack of liquidity—Liquidity is defined as how easily an investment can be converted to cash. Since the performance of capital investments is not certain, managers favor investments they can more easily withdraw cash from, or liquidate. Investments that are more difficult to liquidate usually require a higher rate of return and a premium is added to the hurdle rate to account for the lack of liquidity.

Qualitative Factors

Quantitative analysis methods as we have examined, are usually the starting point for making decisions to invest capital. Important qualitative factors are difficult to assess quantitatively, but they should still be considered. Examples of qualitative factors include safety, quality, the environment, or impact on the community.

Recall our conversation with cosmetologist Brittney Dinardi in Chapter 7 where she stated, "I also choose to provide services I enjoy." What is the value Brittney places on doing work that she enjoys? In the preceding Hokulia example, what if Hafla's goal was to have a business that promotes a health-conscious lifestyle, and the addition of the juicer does that? What value should he place on that desire? One approach is to make a conservative estimate of the economic value the business places on qualitative factors and incorporate them into the net present value computation either through adjustments to the cash flow or the hurdle (discount) rate.

Incorporating Risk and Qualitative Factors

Let's reexamine Galen Hafla's investment in the juice extractor to illustrate how a business might incorporate risk and qualitative factors into its net present value analysis. The relevant data we used in our calculations are as follows:

Cost of the juice extractor	$4,000
Useful life	3 years
Hurdle rate	20%
Annual cash flow	$3,000

Following are Hafla's original net present value computation:

Year	Annual Cash Flow	Present Value of $1 Factor at 20% Discount Rate	Present Value of Annual Cash Flow
1	$3,000 x	0.833 =	$2,499
2	3,000 x	0.694 =	2,082
3	3,000 x	0.579 =	1,737
	Total		$6,318
	Less cost of juicer		(4,000)
	Net present value		$2,318

Let's revisit the data and incorporate inflation, risk, and uncertain qualitative factors.

1. Hafla is expecting a 5% inflation rate in his costs but doesn't expect to raise prices, which will impact his cash flow. He might revise his three-year cash flow estimate from $3,000 annually to $3,000 in year 1, $2,850 in year 2 ($3,000 minus 5%), and $2,708 in year 3 ($2,850 minus 5%).
2. When deciding on a hurdle rate, Hafla might consider the cost of money. He expects to take out a business loan for the juicer, and the interest rate on the loan is 10%. Hafla's hurdle rate should at least cover this cost of capital.
3. Hafla is also uncertain about his cash flow estimates and thus adds a 3% premium.
4. Hafla expects that if the addition of the juicer does not add cash flow, he won't be able to sell the juicer and recover some of his money, making it nonliquid (or not able to convert to cash). He adds a 4% premium to his hurdle rate for the lack of liquidity.

5. However, Hafla desires to add this health-conscious element and is willing to reduce his hurdle rate by 2%. Thus, Hafla uses a 15% (10% + 3% + 4% – 2%) hurdle rate to discount his future cash flows in his new net present value computation.

The relevant data are as follows:

Cost of the juice extractor	$4,000
Useful life	3 years
Hurdle rate	15%
Annual cash flow	$3,000 (Year 1)
	$2,850 (Year 2)
	$2,708 (Year 3)

Year	Annual Cash Flow	Present Value of $1 Factor at 15% Discount Rate	Present Value of Annual Cash Flow
1	$3,000 ×	0.870 =	$2,610
2	2,850 ×	0.756 =	2,154
3	2,708 ×	0.658 =	1,782
	Total		$6,546
	Less Cost of Juicer		(4,000)
	Net Present Value		$2,546

Notice the net present value has increased from $2,318 (no adjustment for risk) to $2,546. Although the expected annual cash flow has decreased due to inflation in costs, that decrease is more than offset by the reduction in the discount rate that Hafla was willing to accept to add this health-conscious element to his business.

LEARNING ACTIVITY 8.10

Describe how you might mitigate the effect of risk factors like inflation, uncertainty, or lack of liquidity in a net present value computation.

Technology, Analytics, and AI

Capital budgeting computations that incorporate time value of money principles can be performed quickly and accurately using built-in function in spreadsheet application packages like

Microsoft Excel. Excel includes functions for calculating present values, future values, net present values, and more. Time value functions in Excel include the following:

- pv—present value—the current value of a future sum of money given a specified rate of return
- fv—future value—the future value of a current sum of money given a specified rate of return
- rate—interest rate per period
- nper—number of periods
- pmt—number of payments per period (assuming an equal stream of annuity payments)
- type—indicates if payments are made at the beginning (1) or end (0) of the period
- npv—net present value—the current value of a stream of inflows and outflows given a specified rate of return

Following are examples of various problems covered throughout the chapter using Excel to solve them.

Present Value

Example: What is the present value of $161.05 received 5 years from now, assuming we earn 10% if we invest the money? See Figures 8.11 and 8.12. This would return a solution of approximately $100. In other words, it would take an investment of $100 at a rate of 10% to have $161.05 in 5 years.

Future Value

Example: What is the future value of $100 five years from now, assuming we invest the money and earn a 10% annual rate of return? See Figure 8.13. This would return a solution of approximately $161.05. In other words, an investment of $100 at a rate of 10% would return $161.05 in 5 years.

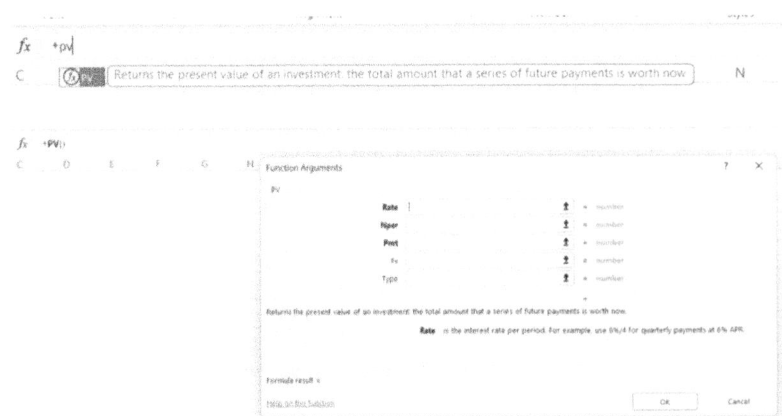

Figure 8.11 Time value in Excel.

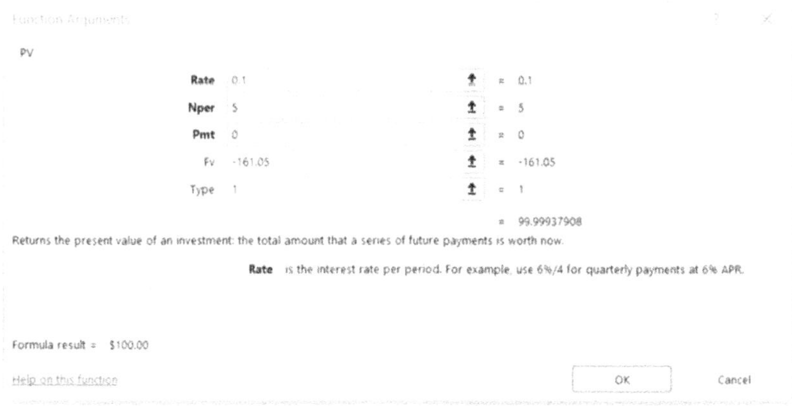

Figure 8.12 Present value in Excel.

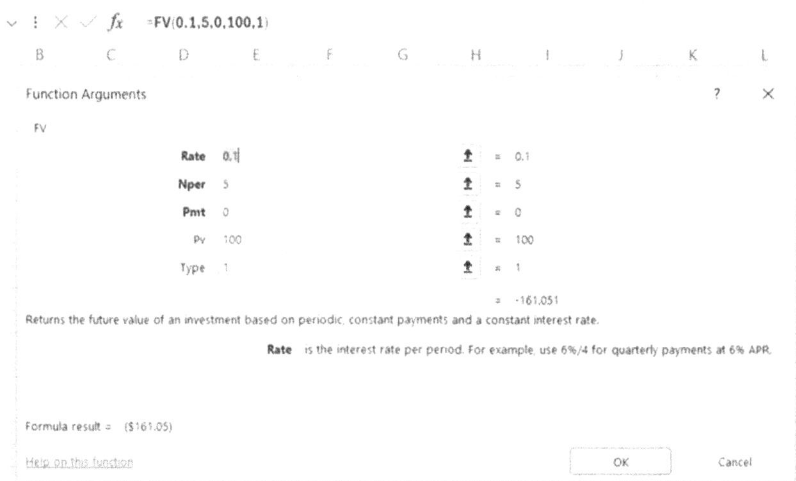

Figure 8.13 Future value in Excel.

Present Value of an Annuity

Example: What is the present value of the receipt of $161.05 at the end of each of the next 5 years consecutively, assuming an interest rate of 10%? See Figure 8.14. This would return a solution of approximately $416.98. In other words, an investment of $416.98 at a rate of 10% today would grow to the same value as investments of $100 at the end of each of the next 5 years.

Future Value of an Annuity

Example: What is the future value of the receipt of $100 at the end of each of the next 5 years consecutively, assuming an interest rate of 10%? See Figure 8.15. This would return a solution of approximately $671.56. In other words, annual investments of $100 at the end of each of the next 5 years at a rate of 10% would grow to $671.56 the end of 5 years.

Net Present Value

Example: What is the net present value of a $600 investment that results in the receipt of $161.05 at the end of 5 years consecutively, assuming an interest rate of 10%? The data are as follows:

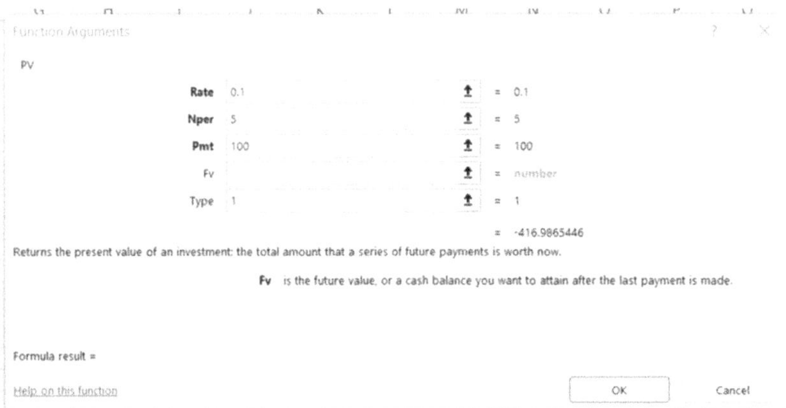

Figure 8.14 Present value of an annuity in Excel.

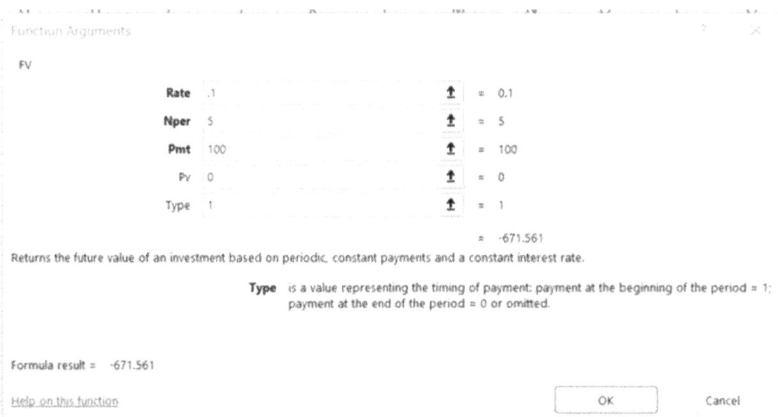

Figure 8.15 Future value of an annuity in Excel.

Figure 8.16 Net present value.

Cash flow	Date
($600.00)	01/01/2025
$161.05	12/31/2025
$161.05	12/31/2026
$161.05	12/31/2027
$161.05	12/31/2028
$161.05	12/31/2029

See Figure 8.16. This would return a solution of approximately $10.61. In other words, the net present value of a $600 investment that returns $161.05 over the next 5 years is $10.61. The positive net present value indicates the investment has a rate of return that is greater than 10% and would be viewed favorably.

Data Analysis Tools (Goal Seek)

The Goal Seek function in Excel is a useful tool used to find the necessary input value to achieve a specific goal or target. Goal seek is particularly useful for finding things like the break-even point, sales targets, or the investment or interest rate need to achieve an investment value or even the net present value. To use Goal Seek, you will need a formula with one cell that depends on another. For instance, in our case, the net present value is dependent on a discount rate, investment value, or annual cash flow. You can use any of those values as the value you will change to achieve a specified net present value. Let's look at the net present value example above. You might wonder what amount of investment would yield a "0" NPV given the cash flows and discount rate. In concept, you might think of that as the break-even investment value, taking the time value of money into account.

To perform the Goal Seek, go to the Data tab,

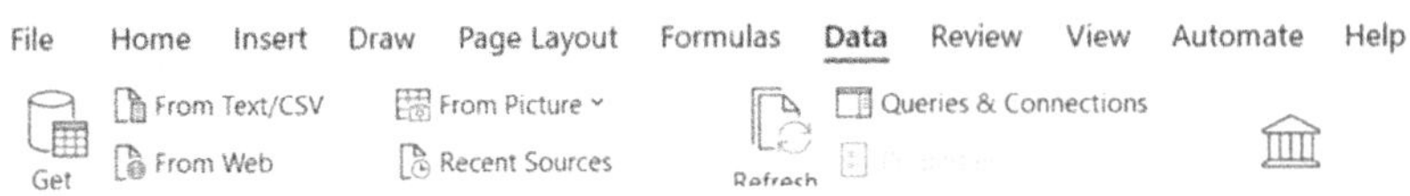

Then click on the Forecast group, then What-If Analysis, and then Goal Seek from the drop-down menu.

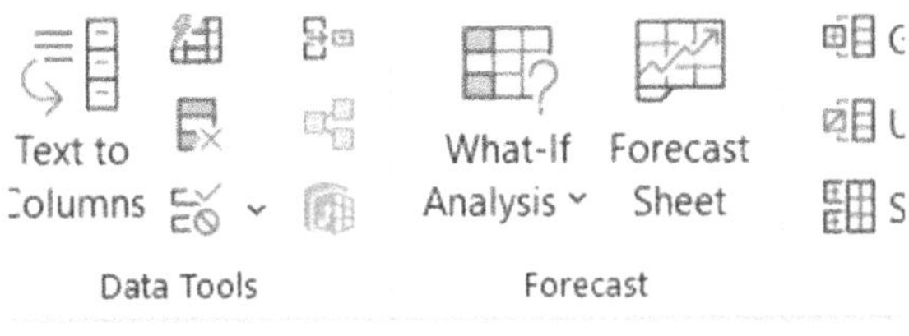

Then you can enter your parameters, Set Cell, To Value, and By Changing Cell. In our case we will Set Cell to D2 (the cell in which you have entered your XNPV formula), To Value to "0", by Changing Cell A2 (the first cash flow which represents the initial investment). Your initial investment was $600 in the original example. Once you have entered the data, click OK to run Goal Seek and get the solution.

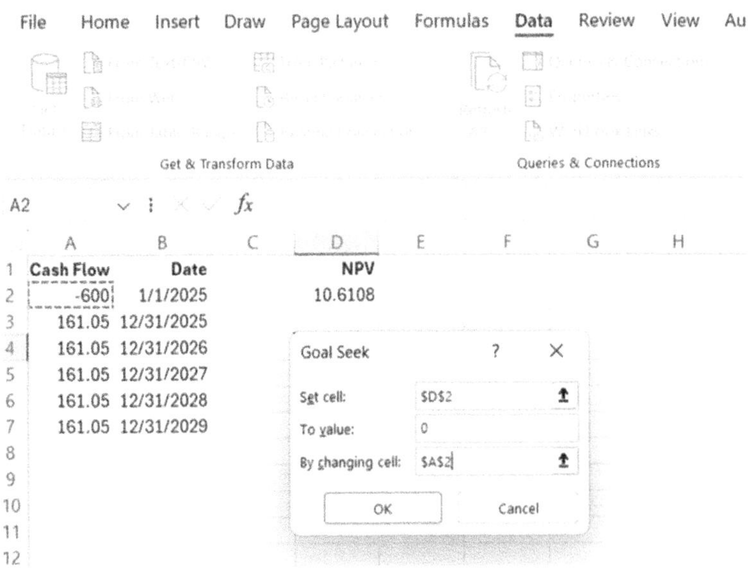

Your initial investment value will change to the value that results in a "0" NPV. In this case an initial investment (or cash outflow) of approximately $610.61 would result in a NPV of "0" given a 10% discount rate and annual cash inflows of $161.05 for 5 years.

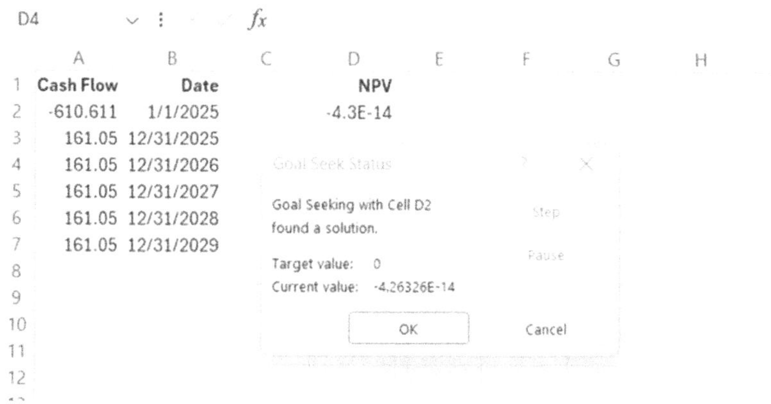

Goal Seek is a useful tool in Excel for determining the input needed to achieve a desired output. It allows you to automate the solving of various data analytical equations and optimization problems.

Key Terms

capital investment The acquisition of a capital asset.
capital budgeting A process where management identifies capital investment alternatives, evaluates the effect of each alternative, and selects the investments that produce the greatest return on the company's available investment resources.
average rate of return (ARR) method Compares the annual rate of return on the capital investment with a required rate of return the company desires.
required rate of return The return a company desires from an investment.
residual value The value of an asset after its useful life is surpassed.
payback method Measures the amount of time it takes to generate a cash return that equals the amount of the initial investment.
time value of money concept A concept that assumes that cash received now is worth more than cash received in the future.
present value The value of future cash flows in today's dollars.
future value The value of an investment at a date in the future based on an expected growth rate.
compounding The process of calculating interest on principal and preceding accumulated interest.
simple interest Interest calculated only on the principal amount.
discounting The process of converting a future value to a current value.
discount rate The interest rate used to discount a future value to a present value.
annuity A series of cash flows over time.

net present value method Compares the present value of cash inflows from an investment with the amount invested.
hurdle rate The desired rate of return for an investment.
cost of capital The interest rate charged by creditors and owners for use of their money on the investment.
present value index The total present value of the cash inflows provided by an investment divided by the amount invested.
internal rate of return The rate of return an investment produces.
internal rate of return method Computes the rate of return necessary to get a net present value of zero for a series of cash flows at a given investment amount.

LEARNING ACTIVITY SOLUTIONS

Learning Activity 8.1

1. *Not Relevant*
2. *Relevant*
3. *Not Relevant*
4. *Not Relevant*
5. *Relevant*

Learning Activity 8.2

1.

Sales		*$3,000*
Less Annual Costs:		
Operating Costs	*500*	
Depreciation	*1,000*	*1,500*
Income Before Income Taxes		*1,500*
Income Tax Expense ($1,500 × 20%)		*300*
Net Income		*$1,200*

The annual rate of return from the hydro massage bed is calculated as follows:

$$\$1,200 \div \$5,000^{*} = 24\%$$

$$\textit{Annual Net Income} \div \textit{Average Annual Investment}^{*} = \textit{Annual Rate of Return}$$

$$(\$8,000 + \$2,000)/2$$

$$\frac{\text{*Original Cost of the Investment + Residual Value at the End of Useful Life}}{2}$$

2. *Yes, Tonya should purchase the hydro massage bed because the annual rate of return (24%) meets or exceeds the required rate of return (12%).*

Learning Activity 8.3

1.
   The net income is computed as follows:

Sales		*$3,000*
Less Annual Costs:		
Operating Costs	*500*	
Depreciation	*1,000*	*1,500*
Income Before Income Taxes		*1,500*
Income Tax Expense		*300*
Net Income		*$1,200*

   The annual cash inflow is computed as follows:

Cash Sales		*$3,000*
Cash Expenses:		
Operating Expenses	*$500*	
Tax Expenses ($1,200 net income x 20% tax rate)	*300*	
Total Expenses		*800*
Annual Cash In-flow		*$2,200*

   The amount of time it takes for Tanya to return the $12,000 investment in the hydro massage bed is computed as follows:

Original Cost of the Investment ÷ Expected Annual Cash Inflow = Payback Period

$8,000 ÷ $2,200 per year = 3.64 years

2. *Yes, Tanya should purchase the hydro massage bed because the payback period (3.64 years) is equal to or less than the useful life (6 years).*

Learning Activity 8.4

1. *Present value = Future value × PV factor for i = 15%, n = 8*
$100,000 × 0.327 = $32,700

2. $5,000 ÷ $9,750 = 0.513 (0.513 at 10% corresponds with 7 years)

Present Value of $1

Period	10%	15%	20%
7	0.513	0.376	0.279
8	0.467	0.327	0.233
9	0.424	0.284	0.194
10	0.386	0.247	0.162

3. $1,000 ÷ $2,000 = 0.500 (0.500 at 5 years corresponds most closely with 0.497 at 15%)

Present Value of $1

Period	10%	15%	20%
5	0.621	0.497	0.402
6	0.564	0.432	0.335
7	0.513	0.376	0.279
8	0.467	0.327	0.233

Learning Activity 8.5

Present value = Amount of each cash flow × Annuity PV factor for i = 10%, n = 7
$10,000 × 4.868 = $48,680

Learning Activity 8.6

1.

Years	Equal Annual Cash Flows	Present Value of an Ordinary Annuity Factor at 10% Discount Rate for 8 Years	Present Value of Annual Cash Flows
8	$2,000 ×	5.335 =	$10,670
	Hydro Massage Bed Cost		(12,000)
	Net Present Value		$(1,330)

2. *No, the negative net present value suggests that the return on the hydro massager is less than the hurdle rate of 10%.*

Learning Activity 8.7

1.

Year	Annual Cash Flow	Present Value of $1 Factor at 10% Discount Rate	Present Value of Annual Cash Flow
1	$ 5,000	0.909	$ 4,545
2	4,000	0.826	3,304
3	2,000	0.751	1,502
4	1,000	0.683	683
5	1,000	0.621	621
6	1,000	0.564	564
7	1,000	0.513	513
8	1,000	0.467	467
	Total		$12,199
	Hydro massager cost		(12,000)
	Net present value		$ 199

2. *Yes, the positive net present value suggests that the return on the hydro massager is greater than the hurdle rate of 10%.*

Learning Activity 8.8

1.

$$\text{Present Value Index} = \frac{\$12{,}199}{\$12{,}000} = 1.0166$$

2. *The massage chair has the higher return on investment, as indicated by the present value index, calculated as follows:*

	Massage Bed	*Massage Chair*
Present Value of Cash Inflows	*$12,199*	*$9,195*
÷ Amount Invested	*÷$12,000*	*÷$8,999*
Present Value Index	*1.0166*	*1.0218*
Ranking	*2*	*1*

Learning Activity 8.9

$$\text{Present Value Annuity Factor} = \frac{\text{Amount Invested}}{\text{Annual Cash Flow}} = \frac{\$8{,}999}{\$2{,}745} = 3.278$$

Present Value of an Annuity Factor

Year	10%	15%	20%
1	.909	.870	.833
2	1.746	1.626	1.528
3	2.497	2.283	2.106
4	3.170	2.855	2.589
5	3.790	3.353	2.991
6	4.355	3.785	3.326
7	4.868	4.160	3.605
8	5.335	4.487	3.837
9	5.759	4.772	4.031
10	6.145	5.019	4.192

The computed present value of an annuity factor of 3.278 is close to 3.353, the annuity factor that corresponds to 15% for 5 years. Thus, the internal rate of return is approximately 15%.

Learning Activity 8.10

Mitigating the effects of risk factors like inflation, uncertainty, or lack of liquidity in a net present value computation requires a multipronged approach that adjusts both the data and the methodology used in the analysis, including the following:

Mitigating the effect of inflation involves (1) adjusting future cash flows to account for inflation, and (2) adjusting the discount rate to account for inflation.

Mitigating the risk of uncertain cash flows involves increasing the discount rate by adding a risk premium.

Mitigating the risk from a lack of liquidity involves (1) increasing the discount rate by adding a liquidity premium or (2) adjusting or delaying the timing of the cash flows.

These strategies can be used independently or in collaboration to provide a holistic approach to mitigating common risks to making a good business decision.

Review Questions

1. What process does a business use to identify, evaluate, and select capital investment opportunities? **(Learning Objective 1)**
   a. Capital budgeting
   b. Capital rationing
2. Businesses select capital investments that maximize cash flow. **(Learning Objective 1)**
   a. True
   b. False
3. A method for evaluating capital budgeting decisions that compares the annual rate of return on a capital investment with a required rate of return is the **(Learning Objective 2)**
   a. required rate of return method.
   b. average rate of return method.
4. The rate of return a company desires is called the **(Learning Objective 2)**
   a. desired rate of return.
   b. required rate of return.
5. The average rate of return method is limited because it uses accounting net income instead of actual cash flow. **(Learning Objective 2)**
   a. True
   b. False
6. A method for analyzing capital budgeting investments that divides the original cost of an investment by the expected annual cash flow is **(Learning Objective 3)**
   a. the payback method.
   b. the cost return method.
7. A limitation of the average rate of return method and the payback method is that they do not consider the time value of money. **(Learning Objective 3)**
   a. True
   b. False
8. The value of future cash flows in today's dollars is called **(Learning Objective 4)**
   a. present value.
   b. future value.

9. The concept of compounding involves calculating interest on the principal balance and the preceding accumulated interest. **(Learning Objective 4)**
   a. True
   b. False
10. Simple interest would result in more earnings than compound interest over time. **(Learning Objective 4)**
   a. True
   b. False
11. A(n) _______ is a series of cash flows over time. **(Learning Objective 4)**
   a. compound cash flow
   b. annuity
12. The net present value method compares the present value of cash inflows from an investment to the amount invested. **(Learning Objective 5)**
   a. True
   b. False
13. The _______ is equal to the desired rate of return on an investment. **(Learning Objective 5)**
   a. minimum rate
   b. hurdle rate
14. A company will usually accept a special order when _______ _______ exceeds _______ _______. **(Learning Objective 4)**
   a. incremental revenue; incremental costs
   b. total capacity; total volume
15. Which is more likely to be an example of a common cost? **(Learning Objective 5)**
   a. A corporate level human resources department
   b. The cost to develop a jig for welding components of a product
16. What is the interest rate charged by creditors and owners for use of their money on an investment called? **(Learning Objective 5)**
   a. The cost of credit
   b. The cost of capital
17. Risk factors that should be considered when using the present value method to evaluate capital investments include which of the following? **(Learning Objective 6)**
   a. Inflation
   b. Cash flow uncertainty
   c. Lack of liquidity
   d. All of the above
18. Qualitative factors that should be considered when making a capital investment decision include which of the following? **(Learning Objective 6)**
   a. Safety
   b. Quality
   c. Impact on the environment
   d. All of the above

Short Exercises

S:8-1 (Learning Objective 1)

Which of the following doesn't always represent cash inflows that could be caused by a capital investment decision?

a. Incremental increases in cash received from sales
b. Sale of old capital assets
c. Taxes
d. All of these always represent cash inflows

S:8-2 (Learning Objective 2)

Which of the following is not an element of the average rate of return method?

a. Determine the annual cash flow.
b. Determine the average annual rate of return on the investment.
c. Compare the average annual rate of return to a required return.
d. All of these are elements of the average annual rate of return method.

S:8-3 (Learning Objective 2)

Which of the following is a limitation of the average rate of return method?

a. It uses net income rather than cash flow.
b. It ignores the timing of returns and cash flows.
c. It ignores the residual value of investments.
d. Both a and b are limitations.
e. All of these are limitations.

S:8-4 (Learning Objective 3)

Which of the following is not a characteristic of the payback method of evaluating capital investments?

a. It uses net income rather than cash flow.
b. It ignores the timing of returns and cash flows.
c. It ignores the residual value of investments.
d. All of these are characteristics of the payback method.

S:8-5 (Learning Objective 4)

Time value of money is based on present value theory and which concept(s)?

a. Present value
b. Future value
c. Compounding
d. Time value of money incorporates all these concepts.

S:8-6 (Learning Objective 4)

What is the difference between simple interest and compound interest?

a. Simple interest is calculated only on the principal amount.
b. Compound interest is calculated on the principal amount and all previously earned interest.
c. Simple interest results in fewer earnings.
d. All of these are differences between simple and compound interest.

S:8-7 (Learning Objective 5)

What is the method that compares the present value of cash inflows from an investment with the amount invested?

a. The present value method
b. The net present value method
c. The compound interest method
d. None of these are correct.

S:8-8 (Learning Objective 5)

The present value index can be used to which of the following?

a. Select investments from a group of investment opportunities when resources are limited.
b. Identify the amount of return from a project relative to the size of the investment.
c. Both a and b are correct.
d. Neither a nor b are correct.

S:8-9 (Learning Objective 6)

Risk factors that should be considered when using the net present value method include which of the following?

a. Inflation
b. Liquidity
c. Cash flow uncertainty
d. All of these are risk factors.

S:8-10 (Learning Objective 6)

Identify at least two qualitative factors that should be considered before making an investment choice.

Exercises

E:8-11 (Learning Objective 2)

Stacy Grimes operates a lawn care business in Cedar Rapids, Iowa. Stacy is considering the addition of a new zero turn lawn mower to her business. The new lawn mower is $14,000, and Stacy expects it to generate $11,000 in sales annually with $3,400 in operating costs, and the lawn mower has a 5-year useful life with a $2,000 residual value at the end of its useful life. Stacy's marginal tax rate is 25%.

Requirement

Compute the expected annual rate of return for the lawn mower.

E:8-12 (Learning Objective 3)

Continuing example E:8-11 regarding Stacy Grimes and her evaluation of the addition of a new zero turn lawn mower to her business. The new lawn mower is $14,000, and Stacy expects it to generate $11,000 in sales annually with $3,400 in operating costs, and the lawn mower has a 5-year useful life with a $2,000 residual value at the end of its useful life. Stacy's marginal tax rate is 25%.

Requirement

Compute the expected payback period for investment in the lawn mower.

E:8-13 (Learning Objective 4)

Using the following present value table, compute the amount that would need to be invested in an investment account (the present value) at a compound interest rate of 10% for 10 years if an investor desired to have $500,000 at the end of 10 years.

Present Value of $1

	Interest Rate (i)		
Periods (n)	10%	15%	20%
1	0.909	0.870	0.833
2	0.826	0.756	0.694
3	0.751	0.658	0.579
4	0.683	0.572	0.482

Present Value of $1

	Interest Rate (*i*)		
Periods (*n*)	10%	15%	20%
5	0.621	0.497	0.402
6	0.564	0.432	0.335
7	0.513	0.376	0.279
8	0.467	0.327	0.233
9	0.424	0.284	0.194
10	0.386	0.247	0.162

E:8-14 (Learning Objective 4)

Using the present value of an ordinary annuity table below, compute the present value of an investment that would be needed if an investor desired to get $50,000 in cash flow from the investment for the next 5 years assuming the account had a compound interest rate of 15%.

Present Value of an Ordinary Annuity of $1

Period	10%	15%	20%
1	0.909	0.870	0.833
2	1.746	1.626	1.528
3	2.497	2.283	2.106
4	3.170	2.855	2.589
5	3.790	3.353	2.991
6	4.355	3.785	3.326
7	4.868	4.160	3.605
8	5.335	4.487	3.837
9	5.759	4.772	4.031
10	6.145	5.019	4.192

E:8-15 (Learning Objective 5)

Stacy Grimes is evaluating the possibility of investing in a new zero turn lawn mower for her lawn business. The relevant data are presented here:

Cost of the lawn mower	$14,000
Useful life	5 years
Hurdle rate	20%
Annual cash flow	$6,300

Requirement

Use the following present value of $1 table to compute the net present value of the capital investment.

Present Value of $1

	Interest Rate (i)		
Periods (n)	10%	15%	20%
1	0.909	0.870	0.833
2	0.826	0.756	0.694
3	0.751	0.658	0.579
4	0.683	0.572	0.482
5	0.621	0.497	0.402
6	0.564	0.432	0.335
7	0.513	0.376	0.279
8	0.467	0.327	0.233
9	0.424	0.284	0.194
10	0.386	0.247	0.162

E:8-16 (Learning Objective 5)

Let's revisit E8-15 and recompute the solution as an ordinary annuity and using the annuity table. Recall, Stacy Grimes is evaluating the possibility of investing in a new zero turn lawn mower for her lawn business. The relevant data are presented here:

Cost of the lawn mower	$14,000
Useful life	5 years
Hurdle rate	20%
Annual cash flow	$6,300

Requirement

a. Use the following present value of an ordinary annuity of $1 table to compute the net present value of the capital investment.
b. Compute the present value index for the investment

Present Value of an Ordinary Annuity of $1

Period	10%	15%	20%
1	0.909	0.870	0.833
2	1.746	1.626	1.528
3	2.497	2.283	2.106
4	3.170	2.855	2.589
5	3.790	3.353	2.991
6	4.355	3.785	3.326

Present Value of an Ordinary Annuity of $1			
Period	**10%**	**15%**	**20%**
7	4.868	4.160	3.605
8	5.335	4.487	3.837
9	5.759	4.772	4.031
10	6.145	5.019	4.192

E:8-17 (Learning Objective 6)

Let's revisit E8-15 and recompute the solution assuming a 10% rate of inflation. Recall, Stacy Grimes is evaluating the possibility of investing in a new zero turn lawn mower for her lawn business. The relevant data are presented here:

Cost of the lawn mower	$14,000
Useful life	5 years
Hurdle rate	20%
Annual cash flow	$6,300
Expected Inflation rate	10%

Requirement

Use the following present value of $1 table to compute the net present value of the capital investment.

Present Value of $1			
	Interest Rate (*i*)		
Periods (*n*)	**10%**	**15%**	**20%**
1	0.909	0.870	0.833
2	0.826	0.756	0.694
3	0.751	0.658	0.579
4	0.683	0.572	0.482
5	0.621	0.497	0.402
6	0.564	0.432	0.335
7	0.513	0.376	0.279
8	0.467	0.327	0.233
9	0.424	0.284	0.194
10	0.386	0.247	0.162

Problems

P:8-18 (Learning Objectives 2 and 3)

Lindsey's Leather Handbags and Accessories of Geneva-on-the-Lake, Ohio, makes leather handbags, purses, backpacks, and other accessories. Lindsey Stone, owner and CEO, would like to update the company's 10 leather sewing machines to new Juki DU-1181N heavy duty industrial sewing machines. The Juki is more versatile and can sew heavier grade leather than the old machines and would allow Lindsey to expand sales to other products requiring the use of such material. They are also more cost efficient. The purchase price for the new machines is $1,500 each after tax, and installation and setup costs are $5,000. Lindsey expects sales to grow by an average of $10,000 per year with only $2,000 in associated operational costs. Lindsey also expects to save $1,000 per year on the operational costs associated with existing products and the existing sewing machines. The machines have a 7-year useful life with a $250 residual value per machine at the end of their useful life. Lindsey's marginal tax rate is 30%.

Requirement

a. Compute the expected annual rate of return for the sewing machines.
b. Compute the expected payback for the sewing machines.

P:8-19 (Learning Objectives 4 and 5)

Let's revisit P:8-18 and the scenario centered around Lindsey's Leather Handbags and Accessories of Geneva-on-the-Lake, Ohio. Let's also consider the time value of money and assume a more conservative estimate of future cash flow will result in an inflow of $4,500 annually. If Lindsey requires a 15% rate of return on investments, would the new machines be a good choice? Use the following relevant data:

Cost of the Sewing Machines	$20,000
Useful life	7 years
Salvage Value	$0
Annual cash inflow	$4,500
Total cash inflow	$31,500

Requirement

a. Use the following present value of an ordinary annuity of $1 table to compute the net present value of the capital investment.

Present Value of an Ordinary Annuity of $1

Period	10%	15%	20%
1	0.909	0.870	0.833
2	1.746	1.626	1.528

Present Value of an Ordinary Annuity of $1

Period	10%	15%	20%
3	2.497	2.283	2.106
4	3.170	2.855	2.589
5	3.790	3.353	2.991
6	4.355	3.785	3.326
7	4.868	4.160	3.605
8	5.335	4.487	3.837
9	5.759	4.772	4.031
10	6.145	5.019	4.192

b. Compute the present value index for the investment.
c. Would Lindsey purchase the machines? Use your findings in parts a and b to explain why.

P:8-20 (Learning Objectives 4, 5, and 6)

Let's revisit P:8-19 and the scenario centered around Lindsey's Leather Handbags and Accessories of Geneva-on-the-Lake, Ohio. Let's assume the cash inflow generated by the investment will not be equal over time and the sewing machines can be salvaged. If Lindsey requires a 15% rate of return on investments, would the new machines be a good choice? Use the following relevant data:

Cost of the sewing machines		$20,000
Useful life		7 years
Salvage value		$ 2,500
Annual cash inflow	Year 1	$ 7,000
	Year 2	$ 6,000
	Year 3	$ 5,000
	Year 4	$ 4,000
	Year 5	$ 3,000
	Year 6	$ 2,000
	Year 7*	$ 4,500
	Total	$31,500

** Includes $2,500 salvage value.*

Requirement

a. Use the following present value of $1 table to compute the net present value of the capital investment.

Present Value of $1

	Interest Rate (*i*)		
Periods (*n*)	10%	15%	20%
1	0.909	0.870	0.833
2	0.826	0.756	0.694
3	0.751	0.658	0.579
4	0.683	0.572	0.482
5	0.621	0.497	0.402
6	0.564	0.432	0.335
7	0.513	0.376	0.279
8	0.467	0.327	0.233
9	0.424	0.284	0.194
10	0.386	0.247	0.162

b. Compute the present value index for the investment.
c. Would Lindsey purchase the machines? Use your findings in parts a and b to explain why.
d. If your conclusion differs from P8-19, explain why.

Technology, Analytics, and Artificial Intelligence

T:8-21 (Technology, Analytics, and Artificial Intelligence)

Let's revisit P:8-20 and the scenario centered around Lindsey's Leather Handbags and Accessories of Geneva-on-the-Lake, Ohio. Let's assume the cash inflow generated by the investment will not be equal over time and the sewing machines can be salvaged. If Lindsey requires a 15% rate of return on investments, would the new machines be a good choice? Use the following relevant data:

Cost of the Sewing Machines at 1/1/2025	$20,000
Useful life	7 years
Salvage Value at 12/31/2031	$2,500

Annual cash inflow	12/31/2025	\$ 7,000
	12/31/2026	\$ 6,000
	12/31/2027	\$ 5,000
	12/31/2028	\$ 4,000
	12/31/2029	\$ 3,000
	12/31/2030	\$ 2,000
	12/31/2031	\$4,500*
	Total	\$31,500

** Includes \$2,500 salvage value.*

Requirement

a. Use the XNPV function in Excel to compute the net present value of the capital investment. How does your answer compare to your answer in E:8-20?
b. Use the XNPV function in Excel to compute the net present value of the capital investment assuming a required rate of return of 18%. Would Lindsey make the investment in this scenario?

T:8-22 (Technology, Analytics, and Artificial Intelligence)

Use the Goal Seek function in Excel to find the investment in T:8-21 that results in a NPV of \$5,000.

CHAPTER 9

Planning and Budgeting for Business Operations

Learning Objectives

9.1 Describe the purpose of budgeting and the budget cycle.
9.2 Discuss how to plan for the preparation of a budget.
9.3 Describe how businesses use technology when budgeting.
9.4 Prepare the master budget for a manufacturing company.

Accounting in Life

Tima Miroshnichenko / Pexels / Public Domain
Source: https://www.nerdwallet.com/blog/finance/how-i-ditched-debt-the-budget-obsessive/

Preparing Your Personal Budget: Preparing a personal budget can be one of the best ways to keep yourself out of debt. An article titled "How I Ditched Debt: Become a Budget Obsessive," chronicles how Christine and Corbin Brown paid off $72,000 in debt. How did they do it? "I became a real stickler with the budget," Christine says. "I am somewhat obsessed with being under budget in each category, and I've found many ways to save money." Some of the strategies the Brown's recommend are to separate needs and wants and budget for important needs. This is helpful when "no" is the best choice.

Let's Review

We learned in the last chapter that businesses carefully plan for large capital investments through the use of capital budgeting. Large capital investments can include a significant piece of equipment, a building, or an entire business venture, among other things. Methods of capital budgeting include the average rate of return method, the payback method, the net present value method, and the internal rate of return method. The net present value and internal rate of return methods use time value principles to analyze if the value of cash inflows exceeds the value of cash outflows in present terms. The present value of a future cash inflow is discounted using a required rate of return, or hurdle rate. Ideally, businesses should pursue investments that exceed the hurdle rate. However, the amount of capital available is usually limited, so businesses select the investments that yield the largest return on the amount invested.

LEARNING ACTIVITY 9.1

Consider the following investment alternatives related to Tru's Taco Wagon. Tru can add only one more significant piece of equipment to her food truck due to limited space. She is considering a double-decker convection pizza oven that will allow for the addition of Taco Pizza and other pizza-related items to the menu, or a 12-gallon electric braising oven that will allow her to cook authentic beef Barbacoa and grow her business by selling specialty tacos and burritos. The pizza oven costs $12,000 and is expected to return $4,000 in net cash flow for each of the next 5 years. The braising oven costs $9,000 and is expected to return $2,400 in net cash flow for each of the next 5 years. Use the following present value of an annuity table to answer the following questions.

Present Value of an Annuity Multiplier

Year	10%	15%	20%
1	0.909	0.870	0.833
2	1.746	1.626	1.528
3	2.497	2.283	2.106

4	3.170	2.855	2.589
5	3.790	3.353	2.991
6	4.355	3.785	3.326
7	4.868	4.160	3.605
8	5.335	4.487	3.837
9	5.759	4.772	4.031
10	6.145	5.019	4.192

1. Compute the net present value for each investment, assuming a hurdle rate of 15%.
2. Compute the internal rate of return for each investment.
3. Which investment should Tru choose and why?

Why Do Businesses Prepare an Operating Budget?

Learning Objective 9.1
Describe the purpose of budgeting and the budget cycle.

In the last chapter, we introduced capital budgeting, the process where businesses evaluate and plan for large capital investments. In this chapter, we examine how businesses plan for operations and prepare an operating budget. An **operating budget** is a detailed projection of activities, revenues, and expenses over an operating cycle, typically a year. Businesses prepare operating budgets for several reasons:

1. Facilitating planning for resource needs
2. Providing a benchmark
3. Facilitating managerial control
4. Identifying internal efficiencies and inefficiencies
5. Assigning responsibility

Businesses usually establish an operating budget annually to help identify resource needs, enable managers and employees to coordinate operations, and set goals and benchmarks for comparison. Let us illustrate using Blackhawk Custom Cycles, the motorcycle manufacturer introduced earlier. Assume Blackhawk expects a significant increase in demand for its motorcycles in the upcoming year. Blackhawk's production manager requires notification of the impending increase in demand to ensure the shop is adequately equipped and staffed to handle the increased production. Without notification, inefficiencies may ensue, and ultimately, customers may suffer. For example, failure to plan for increased staff may result in

- existing staff working excessive overtime to keep pace with demand,
- less-efficient and lower-quality production performed during overtime hours as employees get fatigued, or
- increased costs as overtime wages are paid at a higher rate than regular wages.

These factors can result in a lower-quality product that is more costly to produce, ending in reduced profits. In addition, the production manager needs adequate time to acquire the necessary equipment and machine capacity to avoid bottlenecks and late delivery.

Budgets are useful tools for a manager to help their organization identify efficiencies and inefficiencies. Budgets can serve as a **benchmark** or standard against which to compare actual results. By comparing actual results with budgets, business managers can establish if operations are performing effectively.

In every size of business, budgets help business owners plan for business changes, anticipate revenues and expenses, and manage cash flow. In larger businesses, budgets can help draw the lines of responsibility. The preparation of an operating budget usually involves managers who are responsible for performance as well as employees from various areas of an organization. Involving employees facilitates communication and transparency of organizational plans and can motivate employees to buy-in to the plans.

How Do Businesses Plan an Operating Budget?

Learning Objective 9.2
Discuss how to plan for the preparation of the budget.

Budgeting involves strategic planning, a process where organizations set broad-based goals and objectives, priorities, and the course for future operations. Once they establish goals and objectives, businesses begin forecasting and preparing the budget. Businesses then compare the budget with actual business results and adjust operations if necessary. They may also adjust forecasts and budgets if necessary. Figure 9.1 shows the budget cycle process.

Budgeting requires scheduling and coordination between the various contributors in an organization. Managers typically oversee the preparation of a budget for their area of functional responsibility. A **master budget** is a combination of the functional-level budgets and incorporates a cash forecast and projected financial statements. The master budget includes schedules for sales, production of finished products, purchases of materials and supplies, direct labor and wages, overhead expenditures, capital expenditures, and selling and administrative expenses. During the budgeting process, the business combines those schedules to project cash flow, net income, and eventually, the balance sheet at the end of the budget period. Data from each of the budget schedules trickles down, so they must be completed sequentially. For example, sales drives production, which drives the need for direct material, direct labor, and manufacturing overhead, which when combined, constitute the cost of goods sold. Figure 9.2 displays the typical budget schedules, and the arrows represent the flow of data from one schedule to the next.

Figure 9.1 The budget cycle.

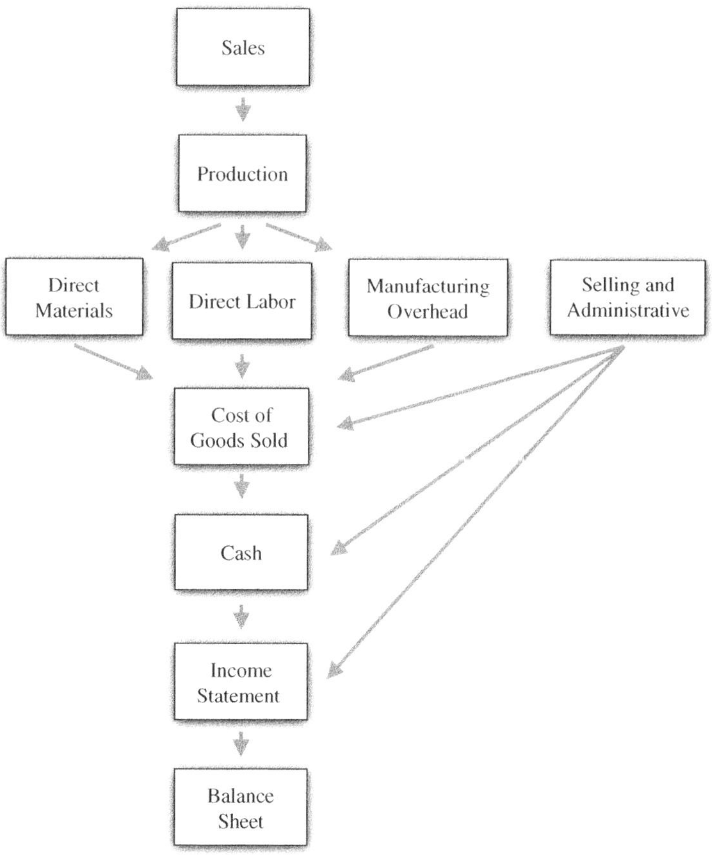

Figure 9.2 The master budget order.

LEARNING ACTIVITY 9.2

Which budget is the most difficult to compute but is most essential for accuracy?

a. The production budget
b. The sales budget
c. The overhead budget
d. The production budget

What Types of Software Do Businesses Use to Prepare a Budget?

Learning Objective 9.3
Describe how businesses use technology when budgeting.

Businesses commonly use spreadsheet applications when preparing budgets. A survey by the *Harvard Business Review* in 2016 shows that 90% of companies use spreadsheets for budgeting.[1]

Spreadsheet application software packages like Microsoft Excel or Google Sheets are ideally suited for preparing budgets because they are easily customizable and adaptable; they contain built-in computational and statistical functions; they can be integrated and combined; they are inexpensive; and they require limited training.

How Do Businesses Prepare Their Operating Budget?

Learning Objective 9.4
Prepare the master budget for a manufacturing company.

The master budget is prepared using the flow illustrated in Figure 9.2 and starts with the sales budget.

Sales Budget

All master budgets begin with sales. The sales budget estimates the quantity of goods or services a company expects to sell. The expected quantity is multiplied by the expected sales price per unit of product to compute expected sales in dollars.

$$\text{Expected Sales in Units} \times \text{Sales Price Per Unit} = \text{Budgeted Sales in Dollars}$$

[1] Harvard Business Review. (2016). *The new game plan for strategic planning.* Harvard Business Review Analytic Services Report.

The sales budget has a significant influence on the remaining budget: the remaining budgets cascade from the sales forecast, as illustrated in Figure 9.2. The sales forecast is particularly difficult to predict accurately and requires market research and knowledge of the customer base, the industry, market conditions, economic conditions, competitors, and more.

Let's look at an example related to Bob Willis Custom Wheel Company, a manufacturer of spoke wheels for motorcycles. Willis generally sells to custom motorcycle companies like Blackhawk Custom Cycle. Willis employs a full-time sales manager who prepares a quarterly sales forecast. Willis' sales budget is displayed in Figure 9.3. The sales budget is a function of projected unit sales times sales price per unit.

Bob Willis Custom Wheel Company
Sales Budget
Year Ending December 20XX

	Quarter				
	1	2	3	4	Year
Projected unit sales	1,000	1,200	1,600	1,000	4,800
Sales price per unit	× $200	× $200	× $200	× $200	× $200
Total projected sales	$200,000	$240,000	$320,000	$200,000	$960,000

Figure 9.3 Sales budget.

Production Budget

The production budget computes the number of units of a product to be produced. The production budget is based on the sales budget and desired inventory levels. The production budget is based on the formula in Figure 9.4.

Continuing with the Bob Willis Custom Wheels example, let us assume that Willis' desired ending inventory at the end of a particular quarter is 20% of the next quarter's expected production. The business wants to balance avoiding stocking out of products with having too much inventory on hand in case demand for the product declines. Critical assumptions like this when preparing a budget are made with input from essential personnel. Desired ending inventory is contingent on demand, production lead time, the carrying cost of inventory, inventory space, the cost of stocking out of product, and the flexibility of the production department. Figure 9.5 illustrates the Willis Wheels production budget.

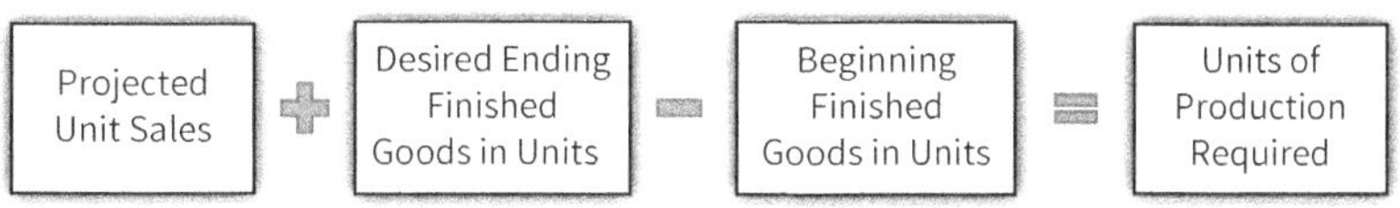

Figure 9.4 Production budget formula.

Bob Willis Custom Wheels

Production Budget

Year Ending December 20XX

	Quarter				
	1	2	3	4	Year
Projected unit sales (Figure 9.3)	1,000	1,200	1,600	1,000	
Add: Desired ending units[a]	240	320	200	240	
Less: Beginning units[b]	200	240	320	200[b]	
Production required	1,040	1,280	1,480	1,040	4,840

a. 20% of next quarter's sales.
b. First quarter of next year's production is projected at 1,200 units.

Figure 9.5 Production budget.

Willis' production budget begins with the budgeted sales for each quarter, 1,000, 1,200, 1,600, and 1,000 units, respectively. Willis desires to hold 20% of the next quarter's expected sales on hand at the end of a given quarter. Willis will enter the year with 200 wheels on hand. Based on those assumptions, Bob Willis Custom Wheels expects to produce 1,040, 1,280, 1,480, and 1,040 wheels in quarters 1 through 4 of the given year.

LEARNING ACTIVITY 9.3

Tristan Miller from Amor salon and spa has started an organization called Amor Artisan Hair Accessories. Tristan would ultimately like to generate enough profits to be able to donate aid to Latin American refugees by manufacturing hair accessories in Belize for sale in Tristan's salon and other salons in the region. Tristan invested $10,000 to start the operation but would like to prepare a budget for the first 3 months of operations in order to plan for resource needs and get an idea of how much money will be generated to give to refugees. Tristan's first product is a beaded leather hair band. Tristan plans to sell the bands at the salon at a wholesale price of $10 per band but expects that most of her sales will come from selling bands to other salons. Tristan plans to sell boxes of 20 bands to other salons at the same $10 price per band. Tristan is projecting to sell 2,000 bands every month during the first year. The first quarter sales budget is as follows:

Amor Artisan Hair Accessories
Sales Budget
Quarter Ending March 20XX

	January	February	March	Quarter
Projected unit sales	2,000	2,000	2,000	6,000
Sales price per unit	× $10	× $10	× $10	× $10
Total projected sales	$20,000	$20,000	$20,000	$60,000

As a new business venture, Tristan has no starting finished bands inventory, but desires to have at least 25% of the following month's finished goods on hand at the end of each month in case production is not as efficient as desired. Considering the sales of 2,000 bands per month and the desired ending inventory equaling 25% of monthly sales, compute the production budget for the first quarter:

Amor Artisan Hair Accessories
Production Budget
Quarter Ending March 20XX

Production Budget	January	February	March	Quarter
Sales, units				
Plus, target ending inventory, units				
Units required to meet sales and inventory needs				
Less beginning inventory, units				
Production needed				

Direct Materials Budget

After a business establishes the production budget, the next step is determining the needs for raw material inventory and purchasing raw materials. The direct material budget calculates material needs to meet production and maintain desired inventory levels (Figure 9.6). Desired ending inventory is contingent on demand, supplier lead time, the carrying cost of inventory, inventory space, the cost of stocking out, and stopping production. The business computes expected purchases for each component of direct materials. The formula to compute direct material purchases is shown in Figure 9.6.

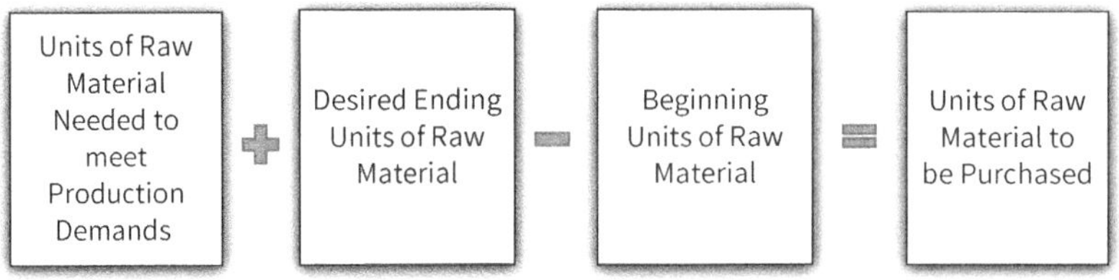

Figure 9.6 Direct material purchases formula.

Bob Willis Custom Wheels
Direct Material Budget
Year Ending December 20XX

	Wheel Spokes				
	Quarter				
	1	2	3	4	Year
Units to be produced[a]	1,040	1,280	1,480	1,040	
Linear feet of spoke wire per finished wheel	27	27	27	27	
Spoke wire required to meet production	28,080	34,560	39,960	28,080	
Add: Target ending inventory in linear feet[b]	5,184	5,994	4,212	4,212	
Total linear feet of spoke wire needed	33,264	40,554	44,172	32,292	
Less: Beginning inventory in linear feet	4,212	5,184	5,994	4,212	
Purchases needed (linear feet)	29,052	35,370	38,178	28,080	130,680
Cost per linear foot	$ 1.00	$ 1.00	$ 1.00	$ 1.00	$ 1.00
Total cost of purchases	$29,052	$35,370	$38,178	$28,080	$130,680

a. Next year's first quarter production is projected at 1,040 units.
b. 15% of next quarter's income required to meet production.

Figure 9.7 Direct material budget—wheel spokes.

Figures 9.7 and 9.8 illustrate the direct materials budgets for the two component parts that go into one of Bob Willis' Custom Wheels, Spokes and Rims. Let's start with the spokes. Willis desires to keep 20% of the next quarter's anticipated production on hand. Willis expects production of 1,040, 1,280, 1,480, and 1,040 apiece for the four quarters on its production budget. Those production figures serve as our starting point to estimate material purchases.

The direct material for wheel spokes comes in coils of steel wire. Each wheel requires 27 linear feet of spoke wire that is cut to the correct length for each spoke. The expected number of wheels produced, times the linear feet of wire needed per wheel, results in the amount of *wire needed to meet production*, 28,080, 34,560, 39,960, and 28,080 for the four quarters, respectively

	Wheel Rims				
	Quarter				
	1	2	3	4	Year
Units to be produced	1,040	1,280	1,480	1,040	
Linear feet of rim steel per finished wheel	5	5	5	5	
Rim steel required to meet production	5,200	6,400	7,400	5,200	
Add: Target ending inventory in linear feet	960	1,110	780	780	
Total linear feet of rim steel needed	6,160	7,510	8,180	5,980	
Less: Beginning inventory in linear feet	780	960	1,110	780	
Purchases needed (linear feet)	5,380	6,550	7,070	5,200	24,200
Cost per linear foot	$ 7	$ 7	$ 7	$ 7	$ 7
Total cost of purchases	$37,660	$45,850	$49,490	$36,400	$169,400

a. Next year's first quarter production is projected at 1,040 units.
b. 15% of next quarter's rim steel required to meet production.

Figure 9.8 Direct material budget—wheel rims.

(Line 3 in Figure 9.7). Bob Willis Custom Wheels also desires to hold 15% of the next quarter's expected production needs on hand at the end of a given quarter to avoid stockouts that might affect the production line. Given that assumption, the *target ending inventory* for the four quarters is 5,184, 5,994, 4,212, and 4,212, respectively. To illustrate the computation, the first quarter's target ending inventory of 5,184 is computed by multiplying the second quarter's wire required to meet production times 15% (34,560 × 15% = 5,184). The fourth quarter's target ending inventory is computed by multiplying next year's first quarter needs times 15%. The expected needs for the first quarter next year are 28,080 linear feet, listed in footnote b of the illustration. The target ending inventory for the fourth quarter is 28,080 × 15% = 4,212.

Total wire needed is computed in the fifth column and represents a sum of the wire needed to meet production and the wire needed to meet the target ending inventory. Total wire needed amounts to 33,264, 40,554, 44,172, and 32,292 for the four quarters, respectively. Finally, existing inventory must be considered before deciding on how much material should be purchased. Thus, we deduct *beginning inventory* from the *total wire needed* to arrive at the amount of *wire purchases needed*. Note, the beginning inventory for a particular quarter is equal to the ending inventory from the prior quarter.

Once we arrive at the purchases needed in linear feet, we multiply that figure by the cost per linear foot to compute the total cost of purchases. The total cost of spoke wire is estimated to be $29,052, $35,370, $38,178, and $28,080.

The other component in one of Bob Willis' Custom Wheels is steel used to form the outside rim of the wheels. Like the spoke wire, rim steel comes in coils and usage is measured in linear feet. Each wheel uses five linear feet of rim steel.

Figure 9.8 shows the direct materials budget for wheel rims. Let's start with the amount of rim steel required to meet production needs. The expected number of wheels produced times the linear feet of steel needed per wheel (5 linear feet) indicates that the amount of *rim steel required to meet production is* 5,200, 6,400, 7,400, and 5,200 linear feet for the four quarters, respectively (Line 3 in Figure 9.8). Like the spoke wire, Bob Willis Custom Wheels desires to hold 15% of the next quarter's expected production needs on hand at the end of a given quarter to avoid stockouts that might affect the production line. Given that assumption, *target ending inventory* for the four quarters is 960, 1,110, 780, and 780, respectively. The first quarter's target ending inventory of 960 is computed by multiplying the second quarter's steel required to meet production times 15% (6,400 × 15% = 960). The fourth quarter's target ending inventory is computed by multiplying next year's first quarter needs times 15%. The expected needs for the first quarter next year is 5,200 linear feet, listed in footnote b of the illustration. The target ending inventory for the fourth quarter is 5,200 × 15% = 780 linear feet.

Total steel needed is computed in the fifth row and represents a sum of the rim steel needed to meet production and the steel needed to meet target ending inventory. Total steel needed amounts to 6,160, 7,510, 8,180, and 5,980 for each of the four quarters, respectively. The business considers existing inventory before deciding how much material should be purchased. Thus, *beginning inventory* is deducted from the *total rim steel needed* to arrive at the amount of *purchases needed*. Note, the beginning inventory for a particular quarter is equal to the ending inventory from the prior quarter.

Once we arrive at the purchases needed in linear feet, that figure is multiplied by the cost per linear foot to compute the total cost of purchases. The total cost of rim steel per quarter is estimated to be $37,660, $45,850, $49,490, and $36,400, respectively.

Total raw material purchases is the sum of the cost or purchases from all inventory items. In this case, we need to consider the spoke wire from Figure 9.7 and the rim steel from Figure 9.7. The total direct material purchases budget is displayed in Figure 9.9.

Total cost of spoke wire purchases	29,052	35,370	38,178	28,080	130,680
Total cost of rim steel purchases	37,660	45,850	49,490	36,400	169,400
Total direct material purchases	$66,712	$81,220	$87,668	$64,480	$300,080

Figure 9.9 Total direct material purchases.

LEARNING ACTIVITY 9.4

Refer to the number of hairbands to be produced by Amor Artisan Hair Accessories in Learning Activity 9.3. Using the following estimated number of units to be produced and the direct material inventory assumptions, compute direct material purchases for the first quarter.

	January	February	March	Quarter
Finished Hairbands to be produced (in units)	2,500	2,000	2,000	6,500

Raw Material Inventory Assumptions

	Thread	Beads
Raw material items per finished goods unit	4 Lin. Ft.	50
Target ending inventory (% next quarter's production needs)	25%	10%
Cost per unit	\$ 0.25	\$ 0.04
Beginning raw material (linear feet)	2,500	31,250
Beginning raw material (dollars)	\$ 625	\$ 1,250

Use the following table to compute the leather banding purchases for the first quarter:

Amor Artisan Hair Accessories
Direct Material Budget
Quarter Ending March 20XX

	Leather Banding			
	January	February	March	Quarter
Finished hairbands to be produced				
Linear feet of leather				
Leather required to meet production				
Add: Target ending inventory in linear feet				
Total linear feet of leather needed				
Less: Beginning inventory in linear feet				
Purchases needed (in linear feet)				
Cost per linear foot				
Total cost of leather purchases				

Use the following table to compute the bead purchases for the first quarter:

	Beads			
	January	February	March	Quarter
Units to be produced				
Beads per finished hairband				
Beads required to meet production				
Add: Target ending inventory in beads				
Total beads needed				
Less: Beginning inventory in beads				

LEARNING ACTIVITY 9.4

Purchases needed (in beads)	
Cost per bead	
Total cost of bead purchases	

Use the following table to compute the total purchases for the first quarter:

Total cost of leather purchases	
Total cost of bead purchases	
Total direct material purchases	

Bob Willis Custom Wheels

Direct Labor Budget

Year Ending December 20XX

	1	2	3	4	Year
Units to be produced (from production budget)	1,040	1,280	1,480	1,040	4,840
Direct labor hours per unit	0.75	0.75	0.75	0.75	0.75
Direct labor hours required	780	960	1,110	780	3,630
Cost per direct labor hour	$ 25.00	$ 25.00	$ 25.00	$ 25.00	$ 25.00
Total direct labor cost	$ 19,500	$ 24,000	$ 27,750	$ 9,500	$ 90,750

Figure 9.10 Direct labor budget.

Direct Labor Budget

Production also triggers a need for direct labor as shown in Figure 9.10. The direct labor budget calculates time needed to meet production and the cost of the time. Key assumptions in the direct labor budget are the labor hours per finished unit and the average cost per labor hour. In our example, each spoke wheel requires 45 minutes or 0.75 hours of time to produce. Willis determines production time with the help of personnel in the production operations and product design departments. The firm's average labor rate for production workers is $25 per hour. That rate includes estimated wages, and associated costs for insurance benefits, taxes, and insurance. In this case, Willis pays production workers $20 per hour, but in addition to regular wages, Willis is obligated to pay for government taxes and insurance programs that amount to approximately 10% of wages or $2 per hour and Willis contributes approximately $3 per hour worked to pay for health insurance for each employee. Together, these costs amount to $25 per hour. These estimates are usually computed with the assistance from the human resources department.

LEARNING ACTIVITY 9.5

Refer to the number of hairbands to be produced by Amor Artisan Hair Accessories in Learning Activity 9.3. Using the following estimated number of units to be produced, and the direct labor assumptions, compute the direct labor budget for the first quarter.

	January	February	March	Quarter
Finished hairbands to be produced (in units)	2,500	2,000	2,000	6,500

Direct Labor Assumptions

Direct labor required per unit (in hours)	0.25 hours
Direct labor cost per hour	$ 3.00

Use the following table to compute the direct labor for the first quarter:

Amor Artisan Hair Accessories
Direct Labor Budget
Quarter Ending December 20XX

	January	February	March	Quarter
Units to be produced (from production budget)				
Direct labor hours per unit				
Direct labor hours required				
Cost per direct labor hour				
Total direct labor cost				

Manufacturing Overhead Budget

Production also requires overhead expenditures. Some overhead expenditures are fixed; others are triggered by production activity. The manufacturing overhead budget is a collection of expected overhead costs over a period. Let's look at the Bob Willis Custom Wheels example and build the manufacturing overhead budget. The following assumptions related to fixed and variable costs are critical to the preparation of the budget:

- Willis' factory consumes a significant amount of natural gas and electricity to heat and light the factory and operate machinery. Willis receives both fixed and variable charges for gas and electricity. Willis is charged $3,000 per quarter ($1,000 per month) from the public utility for access to both gas and electricity, and Willis is also charged gas and electrical consumption, which Willis estimates to cost approximately $0.75 per unit produced.

- Willis pays rent on its factory facility at a cost of $9,000 per quarter, budgets $22,500 per quarter for the production manager's salary, and depreciates equipment at a rate of $4,500 per quarter.
- Willis' machinery and equipment require maintenance and upkeep. Willis estimates the cost of such upkeep varies with production at a rate of $4 per unit produced.
- In addition to direct material, Willis consumes supplies and other indirect materials while producing wheels. Willis estimates that each wheel consumes $1.50 of indirect material.
- Finally, Willis performs a comprehensive inspection of every tenth wheel produced. The detailed inspection process takes about an hour at a rate of $25 per hour. Thus, the estimated inspection cost is $25 for every tenth wheel produced.

Willis' manufacturing overhead budget is displayed in Figure 9.11.

Bob Willis Custom Wheels
Manufacturing Overhead Budget
Year Ending December 20XX

	1	2	3	4	Year
Units produced	1,040	1,280	1,480	1,040	4,840
Fixed Costs					
Gas and electricity	3,000	3,000	3,000	3,000	12,000
Facility rent	9,000	9,000	9,000	9,000	36,000
Production manager salary	22,500	22,500	22,500	22,500	90,000
Depreciation	4,500	4,500	4,500	4,500	18,000
Total Fixed Costs	39,000	39,000	39,000	39,000	156,000
Variable Costs					
Gas and electricity	780	960	1,110	780	3,630
Maintenance	4,160	5,120	5,920	4,160	19,360
Indirect material	1,560	1,920	2,220	1,560	7,260
Inspection	2,600	3,200	3,700	2,600	12,100
Total Variable Costs	9,100	11,200	12,950	9,100	42,350
Total Overhead Costs	$ 48,100	$ 50,200	$ 51,950	$ 48,100	$198,350

Figure 9.11 Manufacturing overhead budget.

LEARNING ACTIVITY 9.6

Refer to the number of hairbands to be produced by Amor Artisan Hair Accessories in Learning Activity 9.3. Using the following estimated number of units to be produced and the manufacturing overhead assumptions, compute manufacturing overhead budget for the first quarter.

	January	February	March	Quarter
Finished Hairbands to be Produced (in Units)	2,500	2,000	2,000	6,500

Overhead Assumptions	
Storage costs per month	$ 350.00
Production supervisor wage	$ 400.00
Depreciation	$ 25.00
Indirect material cost per unit	$ 0.05
Inspection cost per batch	$ 10.00
Number of units produced per batch	500.00

Use the following table to compute overhead for the first quarter:

Amor Artisan Hair Accessories
Manufacturing Overhead Budget
Quarter Ending March 20XX

	January	February	March	Quarter
Fixed Costs				
Storage rent				
Production manager salary				
Depreciation				
Total Fixed Costs				
Variable Costs				
Indirect material				
Inspection				
Total Variable Costs				
Total Overhead Costs				

Cost of Goods Sold Budget

As Figure 9.12 illustrates, the cost of goods sold budget is formed from an accumulation of the direct materials, direct labor, and manufacturing overhead budgets. The first step in developing a cost of goods sold budget is to develop a schedule of the cost per unit, assuming the full absorption of the direct materials, direct labor, and manufacturing overhead costs into the units produced.

Full absorption costing is the concept of spreading all production costs across all of the units produced. We use full absorption costing when arriving at the cost to produce each unit, or per unit production cost. The per unit production cost is critical to computing the cost of goods sold budget as it is used to convert estimated ending inventory units computed in Figure 9.3 to budgeted inventory *in dollars* by multiplying the estimated ending inventory units by the per unit cost. The estimated per unit cost per wheel is $114.29 per wheel based on the following information:

- The total budgeted manufacturing overhead costs from the manufacturing overhead budget (Figure 9.11) amount to $198,350. We divide that figure by the budgeted production of 4,840 units from Figure 9.5 to calculate a budgeted manufacturing overhead cost per unit of $33.54.
- We determine the budgeted direct material cost per unit from the information used in the direct material budget (Figures 9.7 and 9.8) of 27 linear feet of spoke wire at a cost of $1 per foot and 5 linear feet of stainless rim steel at a cost of $7 per foot. This results in a budgeted direct material cost per unit of $62.
- We calculate the budgeted direct labor cost per unit from the information used in the direct labor budget (Figure 9.10). It is estimated to take approximately 0.75 hours to produce a wheel at an average labor rate of $25 per hour, resulting in a budgeted direct labor cost per wheel of $18.75.

Figure 9.13 displays the per unit cost schedule for Bob Willis' Custom Wheel Company.

The final step is determining the ending finished goods inventory value in Figure 9.14. To do so, we multiply the estimated total cost per finished wheel computed in Figure 9.13 by the desired ending finished goods inventory in units shown in Figure 9.5.

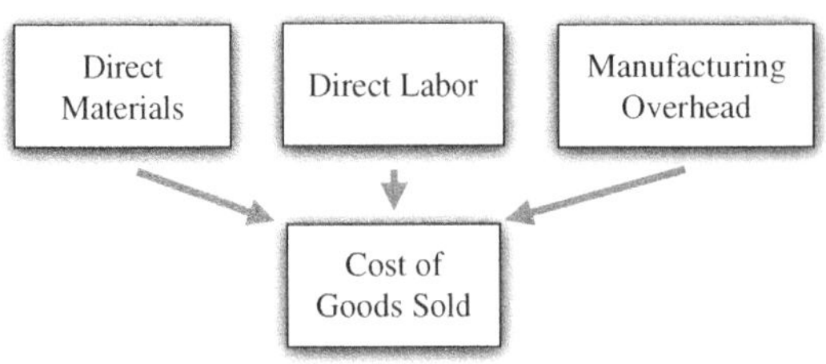

Figure 9.12 Cost of goods sold computation.

Bob Willis Custom Wheel Company Per Unit Cost Schedule Year Ending December 20XX						
	Cost		Units		Cost Per Unit	
Fixed Costs	156,000	÷	4,840	=		32.23
Variable Costs	42,350	÷	4,840	=		8.75
Total Overhead	$ 198,350	÷	4,840	=	$	40.98
Direct Material						62.00
Direct Labor						18.75
Estimated Total Cost Per Finished Wheel					$	121.73

Figure 9.13 Per unit cost schedule.

	Quarter			
	1	2	3	4
Desired ending units (from Figure 9.5)	240	320	200	240
Cost per finished wheel	121.73	121.73	121.73	121.73
Ending finished goods value (in dollars)*	29,216.00	38,954.00	24,346.00	29,216.00

**Rounded to the nearest whole dollar.*

Figure 9.14 Ending finished goods inventory value.

The ending finished goods value is an essential element of the cost of goods sold budget, the remainder of which is based on the formulas in the following cost of goods sold flow chart presented in Figures 9.15 through 9.19.

Computing Cost of Goods Sold

Computing the cost of goods sold for a manufacturing company requires the accumulation of data related to material purchases, labor costs, expenditures on manufacturing overhead, and inventory balances at both the beginning and ending of the period under consideration. In concept, cost of goods sold can be calculated by netting the change in finished goods inventory with the **cost of goods manufactured** during the period. Cost of goods manufactured is total manufacturing costs net of any change in manufacturing work-in-process during the period. **Work in process** consists of any product that is partially completed during the period. In the case of Bob Willis Custom Wheel Company, work-in-process would consist of the cost of spoke wire, rim steel, direct labor, and overhead expenditures

LEARNING ACTIVITY 9.7

The estimated total cost per finished hair band can be computed using the data from Learning Activities 9.3 through 9.6. Use the process displayed in Figure 9.13 and compute the estimated cost per finished band.

	Total Cost	Units	Cost per Unit
Fixed Costs			
Variable Costs			
Total Overhead			
Direct Material			
Direct Labor			
Estimated Total Cost per Finished Band			

LEARNING ACTIVITY 9.8

The ending finished goods inventory value for Amor Artisan Hair Accessories is based on the number of hair bands in ending inventory times the cost per finished hair band. Following the example in Figure 9.14, compute the estimated ending finished goods inventory for Amor Artisan Hair Accessories.

	January	February	March	Quarter
Desired ending units (from Learning Activity 9.3)				
Cost per finished Hair Band (from Learning Activity 9.7)				
Ending finished goods value (in dollars)				

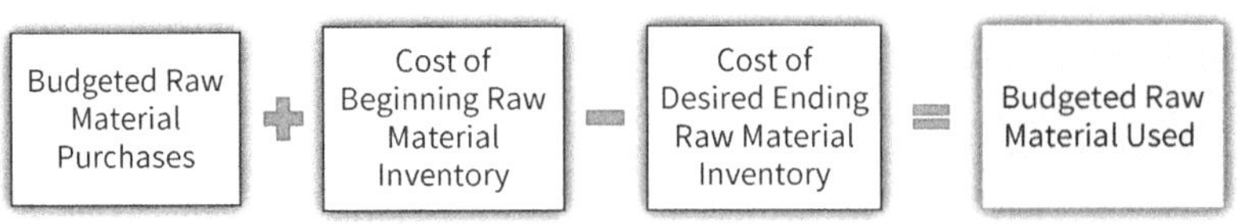

Figure 9.15 Raw material used formula.

made to wheels that are in the production process but are not finished and ready to sell to a customer. **Total manufacturing cost** consists of the raw material used, direct labor consumed, and manufacturing overhead costs incurred during a given period. Direct labor and manufacturing overhead costs can be taken directly from the direct labor (Figure 9.10) and manufacturing overhead budgets (Figure 9.11). **Raw material used** is the difference between raw material purchases and the change in raw material inventory.

Raw Material Used

Let us look at the calculation of raw material used by Bob Willis Custom Wheels. We can take Bob Willis' raw material purchases from the purchases budget (Figure 9.9). The raw material purchases value is netted with the change in raw material inventory, which is shown in Figure 9.15.

For the first quarter, for example, raw material purchases are $66,712. The desired ending raw material inventory of $11,904 is computed by using the data from the material purchases budget (Figures 9.4 and 9.5). The budgeted ending spoke wire inventory is 5,184 linear feet × $1 per linear foot, or $5,184 (Figure 9.7). The budgeted ending rim steel inventory is 960 linear feet × $7, $6,720 (Figure 9.8). Total budgeted ending inventory for the first quarter is $11,904 ($5,184 + $6,720). The budgeted beginning spoke wire inventory is 4.212 linear feet x $1 per linear foot, or $4,212 of wire inventory. The budgeted rim steel inventory is 780 linear feet × $7 per linear foot, or $5,460. Total budgeted ending inventory for the first quarter is $9,672 ($4,212 + $ 5,460). (See Figure 9.16.)

Total Manufacturing Cost

Raw material used becomes an element of the next key component in the cost of goods sold budget, total manufacturing cost. Total manufacturing cost is the sum of raw material used, plus current direct labor and manufacturing overhead. (See Figure 9.17.)

Willis' manufacturing costs are the sum of raw material used from Figure 9.16 plus direct material (Figure 9.10) and manufacturing overhead (Figure 9.11). For the first quarter, for example, budgeted raw material used is $64,480, plus $19,500 in direct labor and $48,100 in manufacturing overhead for the quarter, resulting in total manufacturing cost of $132,080 for the first quarter. (See Figure 9.18.)

	Quarter				
	1	2	3	4	Year
Raw Material Purchases	66,712	81,220	87,668	64,480	300,080
Add: Beginning Raw Material Inventory	9,672	11,904	13,764	9,672	9,672
Less: Ending Raw Material Inventory	11,904	13,764	9,672	9,672	9,672
Raw Material Used	$64,480	$79,360	$91,760	$64,480	$300,080

Figure 9.16 Budgeted raw material used.

LEARNING ACTIVITY 9.9

Amor Artisan Hair Accessories' raw material used is based on the raw materials purchased plus or minus the change in raw material inventory. Raw material purchases come from Learning Activity 9.4.

Total cost of leather purchases	2,375	2,000	2,125	6,500
Total cost of bead purchases	4,150	4,000	4,000	12,150
Total raw material purchases	$ 6,525	$ 6,000	$ 6,125	$ 18,650

It is necessary to add beginning raw materials, which is the opening material balance $1,850, from the initial $10,000 investment and can be found on the opening balance sheet. Ending raw material is computed using the raw material budget formed in Learning Activity 9.4. Ending raw material is the target ending inventory for each raw material item multiplied by the price per unit. Using this information and the following budget table, compute Amor Artisan Hair Accessories' raw material used for the first quarter.

Direct Material	January	February	March	Quarter
Raw Material Purchases				
Add: Beginning Raw Material Inventory				
Less: Ending Raw Material Inventory				
Raw Material Used				

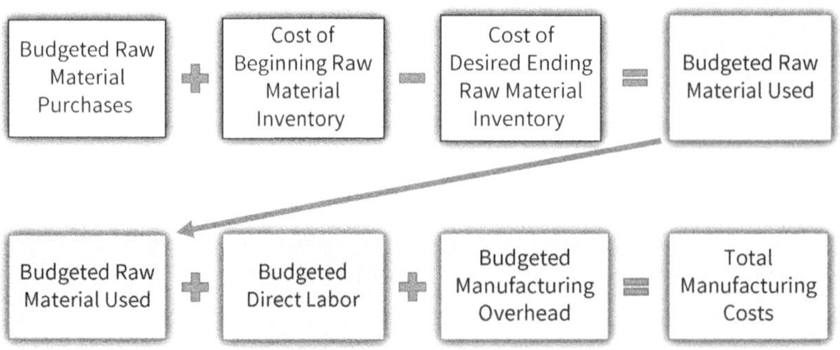

Figure 9.17 Total manufacturing cost formula.

	Quarter				
	1	2	3	4	Year
Raw Material Purchases	66,712	81,220	87,668	64,480	300,080
Add: Beginning Raw Material Inventory	9,672	11,904	13,764	9,672	9,672
Less: Ending Raw Material Inventory	11,904	13,764	9,672	9,672	9,672
Raw Material Used	$64,480	$79,360	$91,760	$64,480	$300,080
Direct Labor	19,500	24,000	27,750	19,500	90,750
Manufacturing Overhead	48,100	50,200	51,950	48,100	198,350
Total Manufacturing Costs	$132,080	$153,560	$171,460	$132,080	$589,180

Figure 9.18 Budgeted manufacturing costs.

LEARNING ACTIVITY 9.10

Compute the total manufacturing costs for Artisan Hair Accessories using the raw material used, direct labor, and manufacturing overhead previously calculated in Learning Activities 9.9, 9.5, 9.6, respectively.

	January	February	March	Quarter
Raw Material Used				
Direct Labor				
Manufacturing Overhead				
Total Manufacturing Cost				

Cost of Goods Manufactured

Total manufacturing costs become an element of cost of goods manufactured, which is composed of total manufacturing costs plus desired ending work-in-process, less beginning work-in-process for a given period (see Figure 9.19).

Let us look at the computation for the first quarter cost of goods manufactured for Bob Willis Wheel Company (Figure 9.20). The total cost of goods manufactured for the first quarter is $137,518. This comprised manufacturing cost of $136,544 plus desired ending work-in-process inventory of $3,895, less the expected beginning work-in-process inventory of $2,922. Work-in-process inventory is projected to be 10% of the budgeted finished goods inventory for the subsequent quarter (e.g., second quarter budgeted ending finished goods of $38,954 × 10% = $3,895). The 10% assumption is set by management, who would have

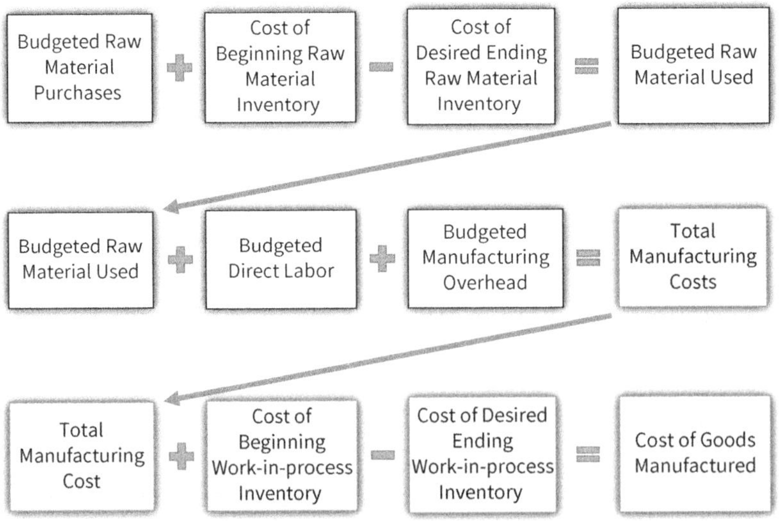

Figure 9.19 Cost of goods sold formula.

	Quarter				
	1	2	3	4	Year
Raw Material Purchases	66,712	81,220	87,668	64,480	300,080
Add: Beginning Raw Material Inventory	9,672	11,904	13,764	9,672	9,672
Less: Ending Raw Material Inventory	11,904	13,764	9,672	9,672	9,672
Raw Material Used	$ 64,480	$ 79,360	$ 91,760	$ 64,480	$300,080
Direct Labor	19,500	24,000	27,750	19,500	90,750
Manufacturing Overhead	48,100	50,200	51,950	48,100	198,350
Total Manufacturing Costs	$132,080	$153,560	$171,460	$132,080	$589,180
Add: Beginning Work-in-process Inventory	2,922	3,895	2,435	2,922	2,922
Less: Ending Work-in-process Inventory	3,895	2,435	2,922	2,922	2,922
Cost of Goods Manufactured	$131,107	$155,021	$170,973	$132,080	$589,180

Figure 9.20 Costs of goods manufactured.

a desire to keep inventory levels as low as possible while having enough safety stock in the case of inefficiency or other impediments to smooth production. Note, the beginning work-in-process is based on the same 10% assumption applied to the ending first quarter finished goods inventory of $29,216. The fourth quarter ending work-in-process of $2,922 is also based on the 10% assumption and also assumes next year's first quarter ending finished goods inventory will be the same as this year's, $29,216.

LEARNING ACTIVITY 9.11

Compute cost of goods manufactured for Artisan Hair Accessories using the total manufacturing costs computed in Learning Activity 9.10 and netted with the change in work-in-process inventory. Artisan expects work-in-process inventory to equal 10% of the desired ending finished goods balance for the period. Ending finished goods must be computed first. Use the ending finished goods (in units) from Learning Activity 9.3 and the cost per finished goods unit from Learning Activity 9.7.

	January	February	March	Quarter
Ending Finished Goods in Units				
Cost per Finished Goods Unit				
Ending Finished Goods in Dollars				

Also, compute the cost of goods manufactured using total manufacturing costs calculated in Learning Activity 9.10, the beginning finished goods taken from the beginning balance sheet, and the ending finished goods just calculated.

	January	February	March	Quarter
Total Manufacturing Cost				
Add: Beginning Work-in-Process Inventory				
Less: Ending Work-in-Process Inventory				
Cost of Goods Manufactured				

Cost of Goods Sold

Cost of goods manufactured becomes an element of cost of goods sold, which is composed of cost of goods manufactured plus beginning work-in-process, less desired ending work-in-process for a given period as shown in Figure 9.21.

Let us look at the computation for the first quarter cost of goods sold for Bob Willis Wheel Company (Figure 9.22). The total cost of goods sold for the first quarter is $125,891. This is composed of cost of goods manufactured of $131,107 plus beginning finished goods inventory, $24,000 from the company's balance sheet, minus desired ending finished inventory of $29,216. Beginning finished goods is taken from the company's beginning balance sheet. Desired ending finished goods is computed by multiplying the desired ending finished goods inventory from the production budget of 240 units (Figure 9.3) times the estimated total cost per finished wheel of $121.73 computed in Figure 9.10. The result is $29,216 (240 × 121.73).

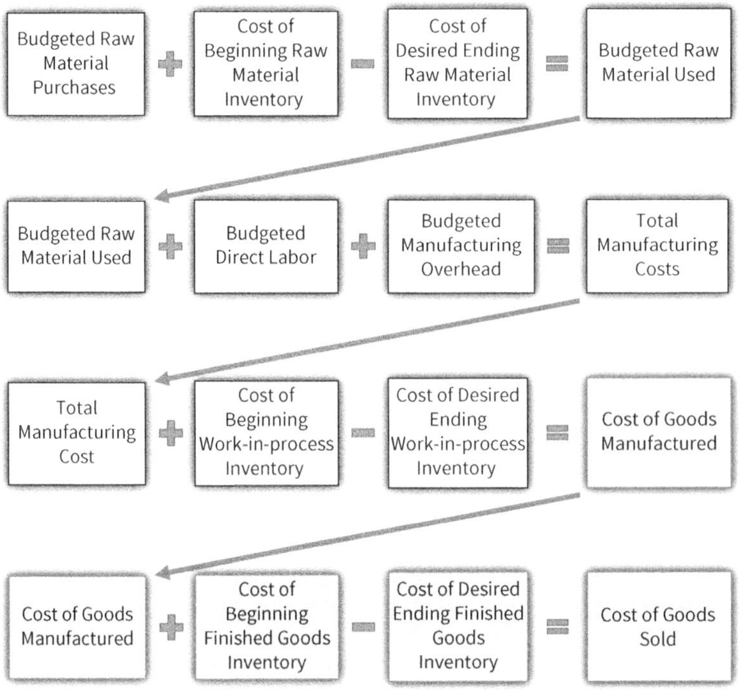

Figure 9.21 Cost of goods sold formula.

	Quarter				
	1	2	3	4	Year
Raw Material Purchases	66,712	81,220	87,668	64,480	300,080
Add: Beginning Raw Material Inventory	9,672	11,904	13,764	9,672	9,672
Less: Ending Raw Material Inventory	11,904	13,764	9,672	9,672	9,672
Raw Material Used	$64,480	$79,360	$91,760	$64,480	$300,080
Direct Labor	19,500	24,000	27,750	19,500	90,750
Manufacturing Overhead	48,100	50,200	51,950	48,100	198,350
Total Manufacturing Costs	$132,080	$153,560	$171,460	$132,080	$589,180
Add: Beginning Work-in-process Inventory	2,922	3,895	2,435	2,922	2,922
Less: Ending Work-in-process Inventory	3,895	2,435	2,922	2,922	2,922
Cost of Goods Manufactured	$131,107	$155,021	$170,973	$132,080	$589,180
Add: Beginning Finished Goods Inventory	24,000	29,216	38,954	24,346	24,000
Less: Ending Finished Goods Inventory	29,216	38,954	24,346	29,216	29,216
Cost of Goods Sold	$125,891	$145,282	$185,581	$127,211	$583,965

Figure 9.22 Costs of goods sold.

ACCOUNTING IN BUSINESS

Antoni Shkraba / Pexels / Public Domain

Which type of inventory is most valuable and least valuable from business and creditor perspectives? From a creditor's perspective, finished goods may be less valuable than raw materials.

A business cannot sell raw materials or work-in-process, so they are probably less valuable to have on hand than finished goods. From a creditor's perspective, such as a banker who has loaned a company money, extra finished goods are riskier to hold than extra raw materials because raw materials can usually be returned to a vendor for a refund if business slows. Undesirable finished goods might have to be deeply discounted to get customers to buy them, maybe even discounted below cost. From that perspective, finished goods inventory is undesirable to creditors.

LEARNING ACTIVITY 9.12

Compute cost of goods sold for Artisan Hair Accessories using the cost of goods manufactured and ending finished goods calculated in Learning Activity 9.10 along with the beginning balance sheet to capture the beginning finished goods value.

Cost of Goods Manufactured	
Add: Beginning Finished Goods Inventory	
Less: Ending Finished Goods	
Cost of Goods Sold	

Selling and Administrative Expense Budget

Organizational costs that are not associated with the product or service produced are included in a selling and administrative expense budget. That would include any costs other than direct material, direct labor, and overhead. Examples of costs that are part of the selling and administrative expense budget are the costs of the senior executives including the chief executive officer and the chief financial officer; the costs of the human resources department; and costs associated with office space, fixtures, and related depreciation that is not part of the production department. The costs of the sales department and the costs to ship finished goods are also included in selling and administration as they are not associated with the cost of producing the product or service but are associated with selling and getting the product or service to customers. The number and types of costs can be many and depend on the firm, but let us illustrate with the following details from Willis:

- Variable Selling and Administrative Costs: Sales commissions of 5% of the sales price for each unit are paid to sales personnel to provide an incentive. The cost of shipping each unit to customers is approximately $12 for each unit sold as well.
- Fixed Selling and Administrative Costs: Salaries for executive and administrative staff amount to $10,000 and $5,000 each month, respectively. The company plans to spend approximately $2,500 each month on advertising. Business insurance costs are approximately $1,500 per month and depreciation expense on equipment used in the office is $1,500 per month. (Note that depreciation costs for equipment used in production are included in the overhead budget.)

Figure 9.23 captures the selling and administrative budget for Bob Willis Custom Wheel Company.

LEARNING ACTIVITY 9.13

Compute the selling and administrative expense budget for Artisan Hair Accessories using the following assumptions.

Assumptions:

Freight Out Cost per 500 Unit Batch	$ 10
Monthly Office Salary	$500
Monthly Advertising	$300
Monthly Insurance	$ 50

Amor Artisan Hair Accessories
Selling and Administrative Budget
Quarter Ending March 20XX

	January	February	March	Quarter
Freight Out				
Office Salary				
Advertising				
Insurance				
Total Selling and Administrative Expenses				

Bob Willis' Custom Wheel Company
Selling and Administrative Budget
Year Ending December 20XX

	1	2	3	4	Year
Sales Commissions	10,000	12,000	16,000	10,000	48,000
Freight Out	12,000	14,400	19,200	12,000	57,600
Executive Salary	10,000	10,000	10,000	10,000	40,000
Office Salary	5,000	5,000	5,000	5,000	20,000
Advertising	2,500	2,500	2,500	2,500	10,000
Insurance	1,500	1,500	1,500	1,500	6,000
Depreciation	1,500	1,500	1,500	1,500	6,000
Total Selling and Administrative Expenses	$42,500	$46,900	$55,700	$42,500	$187,600

Figure 9.23 Selling and administrative budget.

Cash Budget

The cash budget is typically prepared after all sales and expense budgets have been prepared, and before the proforma income statement and balance sheet as shown in Figure 9.24.

The cash budget computes cash receipts and cash disbursements, the difference in period cash flow, which is summed with the beginning cash balance to arrive at an expected future balance. Let us look at the Bob Willis' Custom Wheel Company example starting with Figure 9.25.

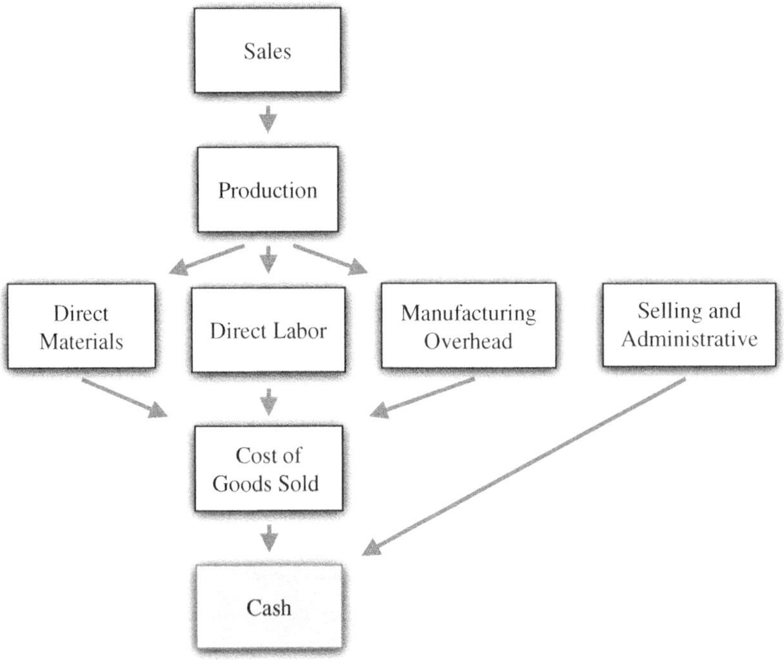

Figure 9.24 Flow into the cash budget.

	1	2	3	4	Year
Total Sales	200,000	240,000	320,000	200,000	960,000
Receipts from Current Month Sales	170,000	204,000	272,000	170,000	816,000
Receipts from Prior Month Sales	26,000	26,000	31,200	41,600	124,800
Cash Receipts	196,000	230,000	303,200	211,600	940,800

Figure 9.25 Cash receipts budget.

Cash Receipts

The first element of the cash budget is the cash receipts. The cash receipts budget sums anticipated receipts based on an assumption about the firm's collection pattern. The collection pattern is the expected rate in which sales are collected from customers under the assumption that some sales are made on account and payment is collected after the sale is made. Collection patterns are influenced by firms' credit policies, including any discounts it may offer for early payment or penalties for late payment. The collection pattern in our Bob Willis'

Custom Wheels example assumes that 85% of current quarter sales are collected during the current quarter. Of the 15% that remain, 13% are collected in the next quarter, and 2% go uncollected. For example, in the first quarter of our Willis' Custom Wheels example, sales are budgeted to be $200,000 (Figure 9.25). Our cash receipts budget assumes that 85% of the $200,000, or $170,000, is collected in the first quarter. Thirteen percent of the $200,000 is collected in the second quarter. Two percent goes uncollected. The first quarter's receipts also include collections from the fourth quarter of the prior year. The fourth quarter sales from the prior year were $200,000, resulting in $26,000 or 13% collected in cash in the first quarter. Thus, the total first quarter collections are $196,000, based on $170,000 from the first quarter sales plus $26,000 from the fourth quarter sales last year.

Cash Disbursements

Cash disbursements can be estimated in a number of ways. We elect to split cash disbursement into two facets in our working example: cash disbursement for purchases of raw materials and cash disbursements for all other expenses. We do so because cash disbursements for raw material purchases commonly make up a large percentage of a company's cash disbursements and companies commonly make arrangements to be able to put such purchases "on account" and

LEARNING ACTIVITY 9.14

Develop a cash receipts budget for Amor Artisan Hair Accessories. The collection pattern for Amor assumes that 50% of current month sales are collected during the current month. Forty-eight percent are collected in the next month, and 2% go uncollected. Since this was the first year of operations, there are no preexisting sales to collect.

The cash receipts budget requires a lookback to budget sales. Recall the budgeted sales given in Learning Activity 9.3:

	January	February	March	Quarter
Projected unit sales	2,000	2,000	2,000	6,000
Sales price per unit	$ 10.00	$ 10.00	$ 10.00	$ 10.00
Total projected sales	$ 20,000	$ 20,000	$ 20,000	$ 60,000

Compute the cash receipts budget using the budgeted sales data and associated assumptions:

Cash Receipts Budget	January	February	March	Quarter
Total Sales				
Receipts from Current Month Sales				
Receipts from Prior Month Sales				
Cash Receipts				

pay for them after goods are delivered. Our assumption is that 90% of the cost of the current quarter raw material purchases are paid in the current quarter, while the remaining 10% are paid in the following quarter. The first quarter's raw material purchases, $66,712, are taken directly from the purchases budget (Figure 9.9). That value is multiplied by 90% ($66,712 × 90%) to arrive at the payment for current purchases of $60,041. Prior quarter purchases are not given in the table but amounted to $65,000. Payments for prior quarter purchases are 10% of the $65,000 and amount to $6,500. Thus, the cash disbursements for raw material purchases in the first quarter were $66,541, the total of the payments for current quarter purchases ($60,041), and the payments for purchase made in the fourth quarter of the prior year ($6,500). Note, the second quarter's payments for prior quarter purchases amount to $6,671 or 10% of the first quarter purchases. Figure 9.26 shows the cash disbursement for raw material for Willis.

Other cash disbursements, including disbursements for payroll and other overhead and selling and administrative costs, are assumed to take place during the period in which the costs were incurred. The computation for other cash disbursements draws on the data from the

	Quarter				
	1	2	3	4	Year
Raw Material Purchases	$66,712	$81,220	$87,668	$64,480	$300,080
Payments for Current Purchases	60,041	73,098	78,901	58,032	270,072
Payments for Prior Quarter Purchases	6,500	6,671	8,122	8,767	30,060
Cash Disbursements for Raw Material Purchases	$66,541	$79,769	$87,023	$66,799	$300,132

Figure 9.26 Cash disbursement for raw material purchases.

LEARNING ACTIVITY 9.15

Develop a cash disbursement budget for raw materials purchases for Amor Artisan Hair Accessories. The payment pattern for Amor assumes that 55% of current purchases are paid immediately, while 45% are paid in the following month. Since this was the first year of operations, there are no preexisting purchases to pay for.

Cash Disbursements for Material Purchases	January	February	March	Quarter
Material Purchases				
Payments for Current Purchases				
Payments for Prior Month Purchases				
Cash Disbursements for Material Purchases				

labor budget (Figure 9.10), the manufacturing overhead budget (Figure 9.11), and the selling and administrative budget (Figure 9.23). The three budgets are summed, with any noncash expenses being excluded. Notice the manufacturing overhead budget included depreciation. That value is deducted from the cash disbursement budget because it is a noncash expense. The cash disbursement for depreciable items such as equipment is made when the item is purchased. Depreciation is also part of the selling and administrative budget and thus it is deducted. The first quarter's other cash disbursements include the sum of $19,500 of direct labor, manufacturing overhead of $48,100, and selling and administrative expenses of $42,500, less $4,500 and $1,500 of depreciation that was included in the manufacturing overhead and selling and administrative budgets. The resultant other cash disbusement for the first quarter is $104,100, as shown in Figure 9.27.

Other Cash Disbursements	1	2	3	4	Year
Direct Labor	19,500	24,000	27,750	19,500	90,750
Manufacturing Overhead	48,100	50,200	51,950	48,100	198,350
Less Manufacturing Overhead Depreciation	(4,500)	(4,500)	(4,500)	(4,500)	(18,000)
Selling and Administrative	42,500	46,900	55,700	42,500	187,600
Less Selling and Administrative Depreciation	(1,500)	(1,500)	(1,500)	(1,500)	(6,000)
Total Other Cash Disbursements	$104,100	$115,100	$129,400	$104,100	$452,700

Figure 9.27 Other cash disbursements.

LEARNING ACTIVITY 9.16

Develop a cash disbursement budget for direct labor, manufacturing overhead, and selling and administrative expenses for Amor Artisan Hair Accessories. Use the budgets prepared in Learning Activities 9.5 (direct labor), 9.6 (manufacturing overhead), and 9.13 (selling and administrative).

Other Cash Disbursements	January	February	March	Quarter
Direct Labor				
Overhead				
Less Overhead Depreciation				
Selling and Administrative				
Total other cash disbursements				

A final cash summary nets the cash receipts with the cash disbursements to arrive at a change in the cash balance for the period. That value is added to the beginning cash balance for the period to arrive at a new ending balance. For the first quarter, in our Bob Willis Custom Wheels example, cash receipts amounted to $196,000. Cash disbursements for raw material purchases amounted to $66,451, and other cash disbursements amounted to $104,100. The change in cash for the period is an increase of $25,359 (Figure 9.28). The change in cash of $25,359 is added to the beginning cash balance for the quarter of $205,000, taken from the beginning balance sheet (Figure 9.32), resulting in an ending cash balance for the first quarter of $230,359. The completed balance sheet (Figure 9.32) will be reviewed in detail in a later section.

Cash Budget Summary	1	2	3	4	Year
Cash Receipts	$196,000	$230,000	$303,200	$211,600	$940,800
Cash Disbursements for Material Purchases	(66,541)	(79,769)	(87,023)	(66,799)	(300,132)
Other Cash Disbursements	(104,100)	(115,100)	(129,400)	(104,100)	(452,700)
Change in Cash Balance	25,359	35,131	86,777	40,701	187,968
Beginning Cash Balance	205,000	230,359	265,490	352,267	205,000
Ending Cash Balance	$230,359	$265,490	$352,267	$392,968	$392,968

Figure 9.28 Cash budget summary.

LEARNING ACTIVITY 9.17

Develop a cash budget summary for Amor Artisan Hair Accessories. The beginning cash balance from the beginning balance sheet is $6,150. Use the cash receipts budget (Learning Activity 9.14), cash disbursements budget for material purchases (Learning Activity 9.15), and other cash disbursements (Learning Activity 9.16), and add the activity to the beginning cash balance to arrive at new cash balances for the first quarter.

Cash Budget Summary	January	February	March	Quarter
Cash Receipts				
Cash Disbursements for Material Purchases				
Other Cash Disbursements				
Change in Cash Balance				
Beginning Cash Balance				
Ending Cash Balance				

Projected Income Statement

The projected income statement is typically prepared after the cash budget and is based on the sales, cost of goods sold, and selling and administrative budgets as shown in Figure 9.29. Developing a projected income statement provides management insight into profitability and the effects of operational decisions.

Let us continue with the Bob Willis Wheel Company example in Figure 9.30 below. The first quarter's income statement consists of $200,000 of projected sales taken directly from the sales budget in Figure 9.2. The $200,000 consists of **gross sales**, not collections. Recall that on our cash budget we projected that cash collections from sales would amount to $196,000. The $4,000 difference is attributable to situations where customers do not pay for items they purchase. Those uncollectable sales are termed **bad debts**. They are deducted from total gross sales to arrive at the actual amount of **net sales** the company expects to collect. Cost of goods sold of $125,891, taken directly from the first quarter of the cost of goods sold budget (Figure 9.22), is deducted from net sales to arrive at a gross margin of $70,109. Selling and administrative expenses of $42,500, taken directly for the first quarter of the selling and administrative budget (Figure 9.23), is deducted from the gross margin to arrive at a net income of $27,609 for the quarter in Figure 9.30.

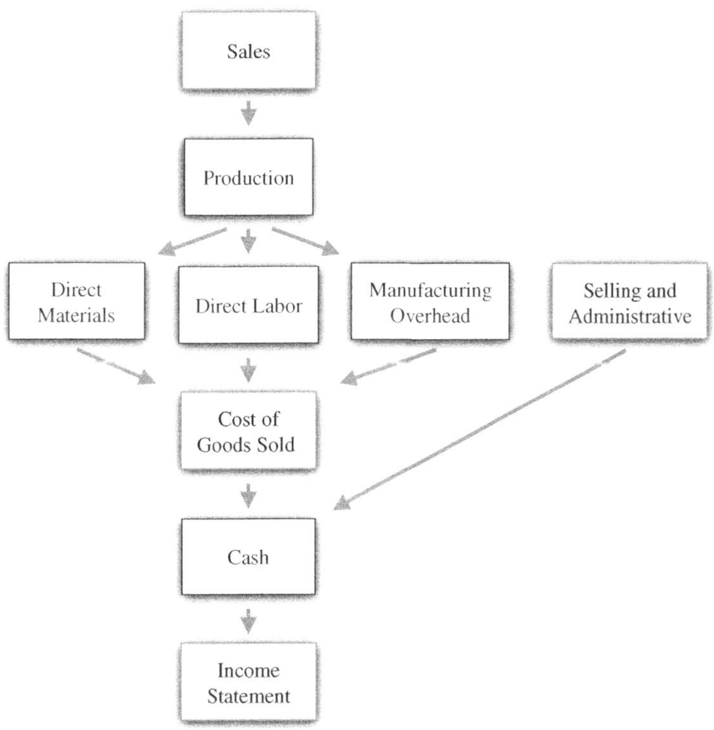

Figure 9.29 Flow into the income statement.

Bob Willis' Custom Wheel Company
Budgeted Income Statement
Year Ending December 20XX

	1	2	3	4	Year
Sales Revenue	$200,000	$240,000	$320,000	$200,000	$960,000
Bad Debts	(4,000)	(4,800)	(6,400)	(4,000)	(19,200)
Net Sales	196,000	235,200	313,600	196,000	940,800
Less: Cost of Goods Sold	(125,891)	(145,282)	(185,581)	(127,211)	(583,965)
Gross Margin	70,109	89,918	128,019	68,789	356,835
Selling and Administrative Expenses	(42,500)	(46,900)	(55,700)	(42,500)	(187,600)
Net Income	$ 27,609	$ 43,018	$ 72,319	$ 26,289	$169,235

Figure 9.30 Budgeted income statement.

LEARNING ACTIVITY 9.18

Prepare a budgeted income statement for Amor Artisan Hair Accessories. Use the data from the sales budget, cash receipts budget (Learning Activity 9.14), cost of goods sold budget (Learning Activity 9.12), and selling and administrative expense budget (Learning Activity 9.13).

Amor Artisan Hair Accessories
Budgeted Income Statement
Quarter Ending March 20XX

	January	February	March	Quarter
Sales Revenue				
Bad Debts				
Net Sales				
Less: Cost of Goods Sold				
Gross Margin				
Selling and Administrative Expenses				
Net Income				

Projected Balance Sheet

The final element of the operating budget is the projected balance sheet. Developing a projected balance sheet provides management insight into the firm's financial position. (See Figure 9.31.)

Let us continue with the Bob Willis Wheel Company example with the budgeted balance sheet in Figure 9.32.

Let's follow through and review the calculation for each line item that is highlighted in the first quarter balance sheet. First, that cash balance is taken straight from the cash budget (Figure 9.28). Accounts receivable is computed by adding the previous period's accounts receivable balance ($200,000) and first quarter sales from Figure 9.2 ($200,000), and then subtracting the first quarter cash collections from Figure 9.25 ($194,000) to result in a new accounts receivable balance of $206,000 for the first quarter.

We take first quarter inventory balances for raw material ($11,904), work-in-process ($3,895), and finished goods ($29,216) directly from the cost of goods sold budget in

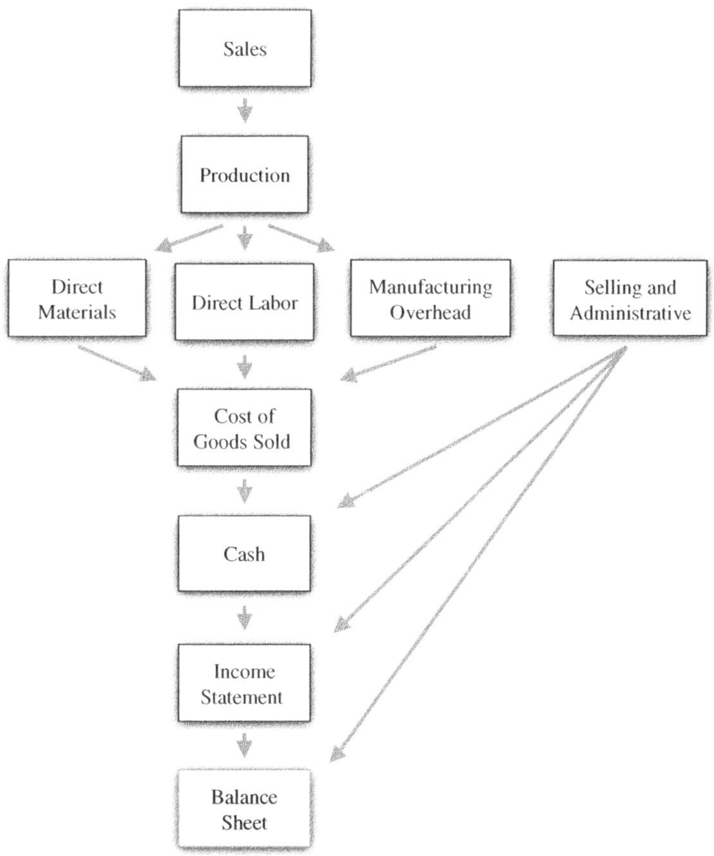

Figure 9.31 Flow into the balance sheet.

Figure 9.22. There were no capital expenditures; thus, the property plant and equipment (PP&E) did not change. Depreciation on the equipment of $4,500 was recorded on the manufacturing overhead budget in Figure 9.11 and $1,500 on the selling and administrative budget in Figure 9.23. That $6,000 is added to the beginning accumulated depreciation balance of $200,000 to result in a first quarter balance of $206,000. The total assets equal $769,374.

The only liability, accounts payable, is computed similarly to accounts receivable. Accounts payable is computed by adding the previous period's accounts payable balance ($200,000) and first quarter material purchases ($66,712), and then subtracting the first quarter cash disbursements from Figure 9.26 ($66,541) to result in a new accounts payable balance of $200,171 for the first quarter. The first quarter owner's equity balance is computed by adding the beginning balance of $541,594 and the first quarter net income of $27,609 from Figure 9.30. Adding the result of $569,203 to the accounts payable balance of $200,171 equals $769,374. That liability plus equity balance matches the total asset balance.

Bob Willis' Custom Wheel Company

Budgeted Balance Sheet

Year Ending December 20XX

	Beginning Balance	1	2	3	4
Current Assets					
Cash	205,000	230,359	265,490	352,267	392,968
Accounts Receivable	200,000	200,000	205,200	215,600	200,000
Inventory					
Raw Material	9,672	11,904	13,764	9,672	9,672
Work-in-process	2,922	3,895	2,435	2,922	2,922
Finished Goods	24,000	29,216	38,954	24,346	29,216
Total Current Assets	441,594	475,374	525,843	604,807	634,777
Long-term Assets					
PP&E	500,000	500,000	500,000	500,000	500,000
Accumulated Depreciation	(200,000)	(206,000)	(212,000)	(218,000)	(224,000)
Total Long-term Assets	300,000	294,000	288,000	282,000	276,000
Total Assets	741,594	769,374	813,843	886,807	910,777
Current Liabilities					
Accounts Payable	200,000	200,171	201,622	202,267	199,948
Total Liabilities	200,000	200,171	201,622	202,267	199,948
Owners' Equity	541,594	569,203	612,221	684,540	710,829
Total Liabilities and Equity	741,594	769,374	813,843	886,807	910,777

Figure 9.32 Budgeted balance sheet.

LEARNING ACTIVITY 9.19

Prepare a budgeted balance sheet for the month of January for Amor Artisan Hair Accessories. You will need the following information:

- The beginning balance sheet (given in this Learning Activity)
- The cash budget
- The sales and cash receipts budgets
- The inventory balance from the cost of goods sold budget
- The depreciation charges from the manufacturing overhead budget
- The raw material purchases budget and cash disbursements for raw material purchases
- The beginning equity balance (given below) and the net income from the budget income statement

Amor Artisan Hair Accessories

Budgeted Balance Sheet

Quarter Ending March 20XX

	Beginning Balance	January
Current Assets		
Cash	$6,150	
Accounts Receivable	—	
Inventory		
Raw Material	1,850	
Work-in-process	—	
Finished Goods	—	
Total Current Assets	8,000	
Long-term Assets		
PP&E	2,000	
Accumulated Depreciation	—	
Total Long-term Assets	2,000	
Total Assets	10,000	
Current Liabilities		
Accounts Payable	500	
Total Liabilities	500	
Equity	9,500	
Total Liabilities and Equity	$10,000	

Ending cash balance from the January cash budget.

Beginning balance ($0) + Net sales ($19,600) – Cash receipts ($10,000) = $9,600

Ending raw material ($900), work-in-process ($209), and finished goods ($2,090) balances from the cost of goods sold budget.

January depreciation from the overhead budget

Beginning balance ($500) + Raw material purchases ($6,525) – Cash disbursements for raw material ($3,589) = $3,436

Beginning equity ($9,500) + Net income ($10,709) = $20,209

TECHNOLOGY, ANALYTICS, AND ARTIFICIAL INTELLIGENCE

Both existing and emerging technologies can help businesses budget efficiently and effectively. Let's look at the use of spreadsheets to prepare budgets and test if generative AI can assist with budget preparation.

Budgeting with Spreadsheets

Many organizations use spreadsheet programs like Microsoft Excel to prepare operating budgets due to their flexibility, user friendliness, and ability to handle complex calculations. Spreadsheets are easy to use, intuitive, and require little to no specialized training. Spreadsheets are also more economical than specialized budgeting software, which makes them ideal for small to mid-sized organizations. Spreadsheets are customizable, allowing users to tailor layouts, formulas, and formats to meet the specific needs of their organization without the constraints of a predesigned format. They are also easy to update. Spreadsheets like Excel have built-in features for making calculations, performing scenario analysis, and preparing data visualization through charts and graphs. Additionally, spreadsheets allow for linking sheets, and as a result, data in one sheet are automatically reflected in others, allowing for dynamic, real-time budget adjustments. Spreadsheets are ideally suited for preparing budgets and are an indispensable tool for many businesses. We explore the use of spreadsheets for budgeting in Appendix B, where we prepare the Bob Willis Custom Wheel Company budget using Microsoft Excel.

Budgeting with AI

OpenAI's ChatGPT can take instructions from a user and perform intelligent operations, including preparing elements of an operating budget. Consider the following assumptions, which were used to prepare the operating budget for Bob Willis' Custom Wheel Company presented throughout this chapter. Can you use ChatGPT to prepare the budget and reduce your time manually computing the data?

Sales Assumptions

Sales Budget	Units	Dollars
Quarter 1	1,000	$200,000
Quarter 2	1,200	$240,000
Quarter 3	1,600	$320,000
Quarter 4	1,000	$200,000
Sales Price	$200.00	

Finished Goods Inventory Assumptions

Target ending finished goods inventory (% next quarter's sales)	20%
Beginning finished goods inventory (Units)	200

Work in Process Inventory Assumptions

Target ending work in process (% of next quarter's ending finished goods)	10%
Beginning work in process	0
Ending work in process	0

Raw Material Inventory Assumptions

Raw material requirements:	Spoke Wire	Stainless Rim Steel
Raw material items per finished goods unit (Linear feet)	27.00	5.00
Cost per unit	$1.00	$7.00
Target ending inventory (% next quarter's production needs)	15%	15%
Beginning raw material inventory (Linear feet)	5,400.00	950.00

Direct Labor Assumptions

Direct labor required per unit (Hours)	0.75
Direct labor cost per hour	$25.00

Overhead Assumptions

Gas and electricity Per Unit	$ 0.75
Maintenance cost per unit	$ 4.00
Indirect material cost per unit	$ 1.50
Inspection cost per batch	$25.00
Number of units produced per batch	10

Selling General and Administrative Assumptions

Sales commission rate	5.0%
Freight out cost per unit	$12.00

Cash Flow Assumptions

Current quarter cash receipt rate	85%
Prior quarter cash receipt rate	13%
Uncollectable accounts percentage	2%
Current quarter cash payment rate	90%
Prior quarter cash payment rate	10%

ANALYSIS USING CHATGPT

Professor

Please use the following assumptions and build a sales budget by quarter. Place the budget in a table with a vertical column for each quarter and a vertical column with an annual total.

Sales Assumptions

	Units	Dollars
Quarter 1	1,000	$200,000
Quarter 2	1,200	$240,000
Quarter 3	1,600	$320,000
Quarter 4	1,000	$200,000
Sales Price	$200.00	

ChatGPT

Certainly! Here's the sales budget by quarter in a table format with a vertical column for each quarter and a vertical column with the annual total:

	Quarter 1	Quarter 2	Quarter 3	Quarter 4	Annual Total
Units Sold	1,000	1,200	1,600	1,000	
Sales Price	$ 200.00	$ 200.00	$ 200.00	$ 200.00	
Sales Revenue	$200,000	$240,000	$320,000	$200,000	$960,000

Professor

Use this sales budget units to create a production budget for the four quarters. Assume the beginning inventory units for the first quarter is 200 units. Compute the desired ending inventory units for each quarter. Assume the desired ending inventory units is 20% of the next quarter's sales in units. Assume the ending inventory for the first quarter becomes the beginning inventory for the second quarter and repeat that pattern for subsequent quarters. Also assume sales for the first quarter in the next year are 1,200 units.

ChatGPT

Based on the provided sales budget units, assumptions, and inventory flow, I'll create a production budget for the four quarters. I'll calculate the desired ending inventory units for each quarter, assuming it's 20% of the next quarter's sales in units. The ending inventory of each quarter will become the beginning inventory of the subsequent quarter.

Given: Beginning Inventory (Q1): 200 units Sales for Q1 next year: 1,200 units

Here's the production budget:

	Q1	Q2	Q3	Q4
Sales (Units)	1,000	1,200	1,600	1,000
Beginning Inventory	200	?	?	?
Ending Inventory	?	?	?	?
Production	?	?	?	?

To calculate the desired ending inventory for each quarter, we'll use the formula:

Desired Ending Inventory = Sales of the following quarter * 20%

Now let's calculate the desired ending inventory for each quarter and complete the production budget:

Q1 Desired Ending Inventory = Q2 Sales * 20% = 1,200 * 0.20 = 240 units Q2 Desired Ending Inventory = Q3 Sales * 20% = 1,600 * 0.20 = 320 units Q3 Desired Ending Inventory = Q4 Sales * 20% = 1,000 * 0.20 = 200 units Q4 Desired Ending Inventory = Q1 (next year) Sales * 20% = 1,200 * 0.20 = 240 units

Now, let's calculate the production for each quarter using the beginning inventory, desired ending inventory, and sales:

Q1 Production = Q1 Sales + Desired Ending Inventory (Q1) – Beginning Inventory (Q1) = 1,000 + 240 – 200 = 1,040 units Q2 Production = Q2 Sales + Desired Ending Inventory (Q2) – Beginning Inventory (Q2) = 1,200 + 320 – 240 = 1,280 units Q3 Production = Q3 Sales + Desired Ending Inventory (Q3) – Beginning Inventory (Q3) = 1,600 + 200 – 320 = 1,480 units Q4 Production = Q4 Sales + Desired Ending Inventory (Q4) – Beginning Inventory (Q4) = 1,000 + 240 – 200 = 1,040 units

Completing the production budget table:

	Q1	Q2	Q3	Q4
Sales (Units)	1,000	1,200	1,600	1,000
Beginning Inventory	200	240	320	200
Ending Inventory	240	320	200	240
Production	1,040	1,280	1,480	1,040

Please note that the sales for the first quarter in the next year are assumed to be 1,200 units.

The ChatGPT results match the results presented in Figures 9.2 and 9.4, illustrating that ChatGPT can formulate an accurate budget with adequate instructions. However, initial attempts to produce a production budget resulted in inaccuracies as the instructions need to be precise and devoid of ambiguity. So how do you know when AI is inaccurate? The answer lies in your knowledge and ability to recognize its faults and limitations.

LEARNING ACTIVITY 9.20

Prepare the total production in units for the first quarter for Amor Artisan Hair Accessories using ChatGPT and the following assumptions:

Sales Assumptions

Sales Budget	Units	$ Dollars
January	2,000	$20,000
February	2,000	$20,000
March	2,000	$20,000
Sales Price	$10.00	

Other Assumptions

Target ending finished goods inventory (% next month's sales)	25%
Beginning finished goods inventory (in units)	0
April Sales in Units	2,000

Key Terms

operating budget A detailed projection of activities, revenues, and expenses over an operating cycle, typically a year.
benchmark A standard to compare with actual results.
master budget A combination of the functional level budgets that incorporates a cash forecast and projected financial statements.
full absorption costing The concept of spreading all production costs across all of the units produced.

cost of goods manufactured Total manufacturing costs net of any change in manufacturing work-in-process during the period.
work-in-process Any product that is partially complete during the period.
total manufacturing cost The raw material used, direct labor consumed, and manufacturing overhead costs incurred during a given period.
raw material used The difference between raw material purchases and the change in raw material inventory.
gross sales The total revenue a business generates from selling its products or services, without accounting for deductions for returns, discounts, allowances, or bad debts.
bad debts Money from sales that is not likely to be collected.
net sales Sales a business generates after accounting for any deductions for returns, allowances, discounts, and bad debts.

LEARNING ACTIVITY SOLUTIONS

Learning Activity 9.1

1. *Compute the net present value for each investment assuming a hurdle rate of 15%.*

Pizza Oven		*Braising Oven*	
Annual Cash Flow	*$ 4,000*	*Annual Cash Flow*	*$ 2,400*
Present Value of an Annuity Multiplier	*x 3.353*	*Present Value of an Annuity Multiplier*	*x 3.353*
	$ 13,412		*$ 8,047*
Initial Investment	*($12,000)*	*Initial Investment*	*($9,000)*
Net Present Value	*$ 1,412*	*Net Present Value*	*($ 953)*

2. *Compute the internal rate of return for each investment.*

Pizza Oven		*Braising Oven*	
Annual Cash Flow	*$12,000*	*Annual Cash Flow*	*$ 9,000*
Initial Investment	*÷ 4,000*	*Initial Investment*	*÷ 2,400*
Present Value of an Annuity Multiplier	*3.00*	*Present Value of an Annuity Multiplier*	*3.75*
Rate of Return for 5 Years Closest to Present Value of an Annuity Multiplier	*20%*	*Rate of Return for 5 Years Closest to Present Value of an Annuity Multiplier*	*10%*

3. *Which investment should Tru choose and why?*
   Tru should choose the pizza oven because it yields a positive net present value and the larger internal rate of return.

Learning Activity 9.2

Which budget is the most difficult to compute but is most essential for accuracy?

b. The sales budget. *The sales budget relies heavily on professional judgment and knowledge of a customer base. The subsequent budgets are based on calculations stemming from the sales budget. As a result, accuracy of the sales budget has a significant impact on the accuracy of the entire budget.*

Learning Activity 9.3

Amor Artisan Hair Accessories

Production Budget

Quarter Ending March 20XX

Production Budget	January	February	March	Quarter
Sales, units	*2,000*	*2,000*	*2,000*	*6,000*
Plus target ending inventory, units	*500*	*500*	*500*	*500*
Units required to meet sales and inventory needs	*2,500*	*2,500*	*2,500*	*6,500*
Less beginning inventory, units	-	*500*	*500*	-
Production needed	*2,500*	*2,000*	*2,000*	*6,500*

Learning Activity 9.4

	Leather Banding			
	January	February	March	Quarter
Finished hairbands to be produced	*2,500*	*2,000*	*2,000*	*6,500*
Linear feet of leather	*4*	*4*	*4*	*4*
Leather required to meet production	*10,000*	*8,000*	*8,000*	*26,000*
Add: Target ending inventory in linear feet	*2,000*	*2,000*	*2,500*	*2,500*
Total linear feet of leather needed	*12,000*	*10,000*	*10,500*	*28,500*
Less: Beginning inventory in linear feet	*2,500*	*2,000*	*2,000*	*2,500*
Purchases needed (in linear feet)	*9,500*	*8,000*	*8,500*	*26,000*
Cost per linear foot	*$ 0.25*	*$ 0.25*	*$ 0.25*	*$ 0.25*
Total cost of leather purchases	*$ 2,375*	*$ 2,000*	*$ 2,125*	*$ 6,500*

	Beads			
	January	February	March	Quarter
Units to be produced	*2,500*	*2,000*	*2,000*	*6,500*
Beads per finished hairband	*50*	*50*	*50*	*50*
Beads required to meet production	*125,000*	*100,000*	*100,000*	*325,000*

Add: Target ending inventory in beads	10,000	10,000	10,000	10,000
Total beads needed	135,000	110,000	110,000	335,000
Less: Beginning inventory in beads	31,250	10,000	10,000	31,250
Purchases needed (in beads)	103,750	100,000	100,000	303,750
Cost per bead	$ 0.04	$ 0.04	$ 0.04	$ 0.04
Total cost of bead purchases	$ 4,150	$ 4,000	$ 4,000	$ 12,150
Total cost of leather purchases	2,375	2,000	2,125	6,500
Total cost of bead purchases	4,150	4,000	4,000	12,150
Total raw material purchases	$ 6,525	$ 6,000	$ 6,175	$ 18,650

Learning Activity 9.5

	January	February	March	Quarter
Units to be produced (from production budget)	2,500	2,000	2,000	6,500
Direct labor hours per unit	0.25	0.25	0.25	0.25
Direct labor hours required	625	500	500	1,625
Cost per direct labor hour	$ 3.00	$ 3.00	$ 3.00	$ 3.00
Total direct labor cost	$ 1,875	$ 1,500	$ 1,500	$ 4,875

Learning Activity 9.6

Armor Artisan Hair Accessories

Manufacturing Overhead Budget

Quarter Ending March 20XX

	January	*February*	*March*	*Quarter*
Fixed Costs				
Storage rent	350	350	350	1,050
Production manager salary	400	400	400	1,200
Depreciation	25	25	25	75
Total Fixed Costs	775	775	775	2,325
Variable Costs				
Indirect material	125	100	100	325
Inspection	50	40	40	130
Total Variable Costs	175	140	140	455
Total Overhead Costs	$ 950	$ 915	$ 915	$ 2,780

Learning Activity 9.7

Step 1

Amor Artisan Hair Accessories
Per Unit Cost Schedule
Quarter Ending March 20XX

Fixed and variable overhead costs from Learning Activity 9.6

	Total Cost	Units	Cost Per Unit
Fixed Costs	2,325		
Variable Costs	455		
Total Overhead	$ 2,780		
Direct Material			
Direct Labor			
Estimated Total Cost Per Finished Band			

Step 2

Amor Artisan Hair Accessories
Per Unit Cost Schedule
Quarter Ending March 20XX

Quarterly production from Learning Activity 9.3

	Total Cost	Units	Cost Per Unit
Fixed Costs	2,325	÷ 6,500	
Variable Costs	455	÷ 6,500	
Total Overhead	$ 2,780	÷ 6,500	
Direct Material			
Direct Labor			
Estimated Total Cost Per Finished Band			

Step 3

Amor Artisan Hair Accessories

Per Unit Cost Schedule

Quarter Ending March 20XX

	Total Cost	Units	Cost Per Unit
Fixed Costs	2,325	÷ 6,500	= 0.36
Variable Costs	455	÷ 6,500	= 0.07
Total Overhead	$ 2,780	÷ 6,500	= 0.43
Direct Material			
Direct Labor			
Estimated Total Cost Per Finished Band			

Divide overhead costs by the units produced to get the overhead cost per unit

Step 4

Amor Artisan Hair Accessories

Per Unit Cost Schedule

Quarter Ending March 20XX

	Total Cost	Units	Cost Per Unit
Fixed Costs	2,325	÷ 6,500	= 0.36
Variable Costs	455	÷ 6,500	= 0.07
Total Overhead	$ 2,780	÷ 6,500	= 0.43
Direct Material			3.00
Direct Labor			
Estimated Total Cost Per Finished Band			

Data from Learning Activity 9.4 assumptions:

(4 linear ft. of band × $0.25 per ft.) + (50 beads × $0.04 per bead)

Step 5

Amor Artisan Hair Accessories

Per Unit Cost Schedule

Quarter Ending March 20XX

	Total Cost	Units	Cost Per Unit
Fixed Costs	2,325	÷ 6,500	= 0.36
Variable Costs	455	÷ 6,500	= 0.07
Total Overhead	$ 2,780	÷ 6,500	= 0.43
Direct Material			3.00
Direct Labor			0.75
Estimated Total Cost Per Finished Band			

Data from Learning Activity 9.5 assumptions:

(0.25 direct labor hours per unit × $3.00 per unit)

Step 6

Amor Artisan Hair Accessories

Per Unit Cost Schedule

Quarter Ending March 20XX

	Total Cost	Units		Cost Per Unit
Fixed Costs	*2,325*	÷ *6,500*	=	*0.36*
Variable Costs	*455*	÷ *6,500*	=	*0.07*
Total Overhead	$ *2,780*	÷ *6,500*	=	*0.43*
Direct Material				*3.00*
Direct Labor				*0.75*
Estimated Total Cost Per Finished Band				$ *4.18*

Total Overhead + Direct Material + Direct Labor

Learning Activity 9.8

	January	February	March	Quarter
Desired ending units (from Learning Activity 9.3)	*500*	*500*	*500*	*500*
Cost per finished Hair Band (from Learning Activity 9.7)	*4.18*	*4.18*	*4.18*	*4.18*
*Ending finished goods value (in dollars)**	*$2,090*	*$2,090*	*$2,090*	*$2,090*

Learning Activity 9.9

Direct Material	January	February	March	Quarter
Raw Material Purchases	*6,525*	*6,000*	*6,375*	*19,500*
Add: Beginning Raw Material Inventory	*1,850*	*900*	*900*	*1,850*
Less: Ending Raw Material Inventory	*900*	*900*	*1,025*	*1,025*
Raw Material Used	*7,475*	*6,000*	*6,000*	*19,475*

Learning Activity 9.10

	January	February	March	Quarter
Raw Material Used	*7,475*	*6,000*	*6,000*	*19,475*
Direct Labor	*1,875*	*1,500*	*1,500*	*4,875*
Manufacturing Overhead	*950*	*915*	*915*	*2,780*
Total Manufacturing Cost	*$10,300*	*$8,415*	*$8,415*	*$27,130*

Learning Activity 9.11

	January	February	March	Quarter
Ending Finished Goods in Units	*500*	*500*	*500*	*500*
Cost per Finished Goods Unit	*4.18*	*4.18*	*4.18*	*4.18*
Ending Finished Goods in Dollars	*2,090*	*2,090*	*2,090*	*2,090*

	January	February	March	Quarter
Total Manufacturing Cost	*10,300*	*8,415*	*8,415*	*27,130*
Add: Beginning Work-in-Process Inventory	—	*209*	*209*	—
Less: Ending Work-in-Process Inventory	*209*	*209*	*209*	*209*
Cost of Goods Manufactured	*10,091*	*8,415*	*8,415*	*26,921*

Learning Activity 9.12

Cost of Goods Manufactured	*10,091*	*8,415*	*8,415*	*26,921*
Add: Beginning Finished Goods Inventory	—	*2,090*	*2,090*	*2,090*
Less: Ending Finished Goods	*2,090*	*2,090*	*2,090*	*2,090*
Cost of Goods Sold	*$ 8,001*	*$ 8,415*	*$ 8,415*	*$ 26,921*

Learning Activity 9.13

	January	February	March	Quarter
Freight Out	*40*	*40*	*40*	*120*
Office Salary	*500*	*500*	*500*	*1,500*
Advertising	*300*	*300*	*300*	*900*
Insurance	*50*	*50*	*50*	*150*
Total Selling and Administrative Expenses	*$ 890*	*$ 890*	*$ 890*	*$ 2,670*

Learning Activity 9.14

Cash Receipts Budget	January	February	March	Quarter
Total Sales	*$ 20,000*	*$ 20,000*	*$ 20,000*	*$ 60,000*
Receipts from Current Month Sales	*10,000*	*10,000*	*10,000*	*30,000*
Receipts from Prior Month Sales	*0*	*9,600*	*9,600*	*19,200*
Cash Receipts	*$ 10,000*	*$ 19,600*	*$ 19,600*	*$ 49,200*

Learning Activity 9.15

Cash Disbursements for Material Purchases	January	February	March	Quarter
Material Purchases	*7,125*	*6,000*	*6,375*	*19,500*
Payments for Current Purchases	*3,919*	*3,300*	*3,506*	*10,725*
Payments for Prior Month Purchases	*0*	*3,206*	*2,700*	*5,906*
Cash Disbursements for Material Purchases	*$ 3,919*	*$ 6,506*	*$ 6,206*	*$ 16,631*

Learning Activity 9.16

Other Cash Disbursements	January	February	March	Quarter
Direct Labor	*1,875*	*1,500*	*1,500*	*4,875*
Overhead	*950*	*915*	*915*	*2,780*
Less Overhead Depreciation	*(25)*	*(25)*	*(25)*	*(75)*
Selling and Administrative	*890*	*890*	*890*	*2,670*
Total Cash Disbursements	*$ 3,690*	*$ 3,280*	*$ 3,280*	*$ 10,250*

Learning Activity 9.17

Cash Budget Summary	January	February	March	Quarter
Cash Receipts	*10,000*	*19,600*	*19,600*	*49,200*
Cash Disbursements for Material Purchases	*(3,589)*	*(6,236)*	*(6,069)*	*(16,361)*
Other Cash Disbursements	*(3,690)*	*(3,280)*	*(3,280)*	*(10,250)*
Change in Cash Balance	*2,391*	*10,084*	*10,251*	*22,589*
Beginning Cash Balance	*6,150*	*8,871*	*18,955*	*6,150*
Ending Cash Balance	*$ 8,871*	*$ 18,955*	*$ 29,206*	*$ 28,739*

Learning Activity 9.18

	January	February	March	Quarter
Sales Revenue	*20,000*	*20,000*	*20,000*	*60,000*
Bad Debts	*(400)*	*(400)*	*(400)*	*(1,200)*
Net Sales	*19,600*	*19,600*	*19,600*	*58,800*
Less: Cost of Goods Sold	*(8,001)*	*(8,415)*	*(8,415)*	*(24,831)*
Gross Margin	*11,599*	*11,185*	*11,185*	*33,969*
Selling and Administrative Expenses	*(890)*	*(890)*	*(890)*	*(2,670)*
Net Income	*$ 10,709*	*$ 10,295*	*$ 10,295*	*$ 31,299*

Learning Activity 9.19

Amor Artisan Hair Accessories

Budgeted Balance Sheet

Quarter Ending March 20XX

	Beginning Balance	January
Current Assets		
Cash	6,150	8,541
Accounts Receivable	—	9,600
Inventory		
Raw Material	1,850	1,500
Work-in-process	—	209
Finished Goods	—	2,090
Total Current Assets	8,000	21,940
Long-term Assets		
PP&E	2,000	2,000
Accumulated Depreciation	—	(25)
Total Long-term Assets	2,000	1,975
Total Assets	10,000	23,915
Current Liabilities		
Accounts Payable	500	3,706
Total Liabilities	500	3,706
Equity	9,500	20,209
Total Liabilities and Equity	10,000	23,915

Learning Activity 9.20

Here is the calculated production budget for the first quarter based on these assumptions:

Total Production for Q1: Amor Artisan Hair Accessories

Sales Assumptions

Sales Budget (Units and $):

January: 2,000 units, $20,000

February: 2,000 units, $20,000

March: 2,000 units, $20,000

Sales Price: $10.00 per unit

Other Assumptions
Target ending finished goods inventory: 25% of next month's sales
Beginning finished goods inventory: 0 units
April Sales: 2,000 units
Production Calculations
January:
Units Sold: 2,000
Target Ending Inventory: 25% of February Sales = 500 units
Beginning Inventory: 0 units
Required Production: 2,000 + 500 − 0 = 2,500 units
February:
Units Sold: 2,000
Target Ending Inventory: 25% of March Sales = 500 units
Beginning Inventory: 500 units
Required Production: 2,000 + 500 − 500 = 2,000 units
March:
Units Sold: 2,000
Target Ending Inventory: 25% of April Sales = 500 units
Beginning Inventory: 500 units
Required Production: 2,000 + 500 − 500 = 2,000 units
Total Production for Q1
Total Production = 2,500 (January) + 2,000 (February) + 2,000 (March) = 6,500 units

Review Questions

1. Which of the following is *not* a reason for preparing an operating budget? **(Learning Objective 1)**
   a. Facilitating planning for resource needs
   b. Providing a benchmark for comparison
   c. Minimizing employee involvement in goal setting
   d. Assigning responsibility and accountability
2. Which of the following is true about the budgeting process? **(Learning Objective 2)**
   a. Budgets are typically prepared without coordination between different departments.
   b. Managers only focus on cash flow during the budgeting process.
   c. The master budget combines multiple functional-level budgets to project financial outcomes.
   d. Sales and production schedules are independent and do not affect other budget schedules.
3. Which of the following best describes the purpose of a master budget? **(Learning Objective 2)**
   a. To outline specific departmental objectives for individual teams
   b. To combine all functional-level budgets into a comprehensive financial plan
   c. To focus solely on cash flow projections without considering other financial aspects
   d. To schedule employee training and development programs
4. How do businesses typically use technology when preparing budgets? **(Learning Objective 3)**
   a. By relying solely on manual calculations without any software assistance
   b. By using specialized budgeting software that is expensive and complex
   c. By utilizing spreadsheet applications like Microsoft Excel or Google Sheets for their flexibility, built-in functions, and ease of integration
   d. By exclusively using accounting software designed for large-scale financial audits
5. What is the primary purpose of the sales budget in the budgeting process? **(Learning Objective 4)**
   a. To calculate the cost of production and inventory requirements
   b. To estimate the quantity of goods or services a company expects to sell and project the sales revenue
   c. To determine the company's cash flow needs and capital expenditures
   d. To outline the schedule for employee training and development programs
6. How is the production budget typically determined based on the sales budget and inventory goals? **(Learning Objective 4)**
   a. By forecasting sales revenue and allocating resources based on past expenses
   b. By calculating the desired ending inventory as a percentage of the next quarter's expected sales and adjusting for beginning inventory
   c. By estimating the total number of units to be sold across all quarters and distributing production evenly
   d. By adjusting the sales price per unit to meet the desired profit margins and calculating the production accordingly

7. How is the amount of raw material purchases determined for a given quarter? **(Learning Objective 4)**
   a. By adding the required material for production to the target ending inventory and then deducting the beginning inventory
   b. By calculating the total production needs and multiplying by the cost per unit of raw material
   c. By forecasting future production needs and adjusting for seasonal demand fluctuations
   d. By estimating the total cost of raw materials needed and then dividing by the number of units produced
8. What costs are included in the full absorption costing method for developing the cost of goods sold (COGS) budget? **(Learning Objective 4)**
   a. Only direct materials
   b. Direct labor and manufacturing overhead
   c. Direct materials, direct labor, and manufacturing overhead
   d. Only manufacturing overhead
9. Which of the following costs would *not* be included in the selling and administrative expense budget? **(Learning Objective 4)**
   a. Sales commissions paid to sales personnel
   b. Depreciation of office equipment
   c. Executive and office salaries
   d. Direct labor used in the production process
10. Which of the following statements about the cash budget is true? **(Learning Objective 4)**
    a. The cash budget is prepared before sales and expense budgets.
    b. The cash budget does not include collections from prior sales.
    c. The cash budget helps to determine the future cash balance by summing cash receipts and cash disbursements.
    d. Depreciation is always included in the cash budget as it affects cash flow.
11. Which of the following best describes how cash receipts are handled in the cash budget? **(Learning Objective 4)**
    a. All sales are collected in the same month they occur.
    b. Sales made on account are ignored in the cash budget.
    c. Cash receipts include a portion of sales collected in the current period and some from prior periods.
    d. Cash receipts do not account for uncollected sales.
12. In the cash budget for Bob Willis' Custom Wheel Company, if 85% of sales are collected in the current quarter, 13% in the next quarter, and 2% go uncollected, how much will be collected from $240,000 in sales made during the second quarter? **(Learning Objective 4)**
    a. $204,000 in the second quarter and $31,200 in the third quarter
    b. $204,000 in the second quarter and $26,000 in the third quarter
    c. $240,000 in the second quarter and $31,200 in the third quarter
    d. $240,000 in the second quarter and $26,000 in the third quarter

13. Which of the following statements about cash disbursements for raw material purchases is true? **(Learning Objective 4)**
    a. Cash disbursements always occur in the same month as the purchases.
    b. Cash disbursements for raw materials are split between current and prior period purchases.
    c. Cash disbursements only include payments for current month purchases.
    d. Depreciation is included in cash disbursements for raw materials.
14. If Amor Artisan Hair Accessories pays 55% of material purchases in the current month and 45% in the next month, how much will be paid in February if material purchases were $10,000 in January and $12,000 in February? **(Learning Objective 4)**
    a. $5,500
    b. $12,000
    c. $10,500
    d. $11,100
15. Which of the following is the correct formula to calculate Gross Margin on a budgeted income statement? **(Learning Objective 4)**
    a. Net Sales – Bad Debts
    b. Sales Revenue – Cost of Goods Sold
    c. Net Sales – Cost of Goods Sold
    d. Sales Revenue – Selling and Administrative Expenses
16. In preparing a budgeted income statement, where do you find the projected figures for Selling and Administrative Expenses? **(Learning Objective 4)**
    a. From the sales budget
    b. From the cash receipts budget
    c. From the cost of goods sold budget
    d. From the selling and administrative expense budget
17. What adjustment is needed when updating the cash balance in a projected balance sheet? **(Learning Objective 4)**
    a. Add cash collections from sales and subtract cash disbursements.
    b. Subtract the beginning cash balance from the ending cash balance.
    c. Add raw material purchases to the beginning cash balance.
    d. Subtract depreciation charges from the beginning cash balance.
18. How should Accumulated Depreciation be treated on a projected balance sheet? **(Learning Objective 4)**
    a. It should be added to the PP&E value to calculate the Total Long-term Assets.
    b. It should be subtracted from the PP&E value to reflect the net book value.
    c. It should be included in Current Liabilities.
    d. It should be added to Total Current Assets.
19. When calculating the projected equity balance at the end of the period, which of the following should be included? **(Learning Objective 4)**
    a. Only the beginning equity balance.
    b. The beginning equity balance plus net income for the period.
    c. The ending cash balance minus the total liabilities.
    d. The net income plus the total liabilities.

Short Exercises

S:9-1 (Learning Objective 1)

Explain how an operating budget can help a company like Blackhawk Custom Cycles improve efficiency and control production costs.

S:9-2 (Learning Objective 2)

Briefly describe the role of strategic planning in the budgeting process and explain how it influences the preparation of a budget.

S:9-3 (Learning Objective 4)

Briefly explain how the inventory levels and the cost of purchases are impacted by changes in production forecasts and desired ending inventory levels.

S:9-4 (Learning Objective 4)

In preparing the Cost of Goods Sold (COGS) budget, why is it important to calculate the per unit production cost using full absorption costing, and how does this method affect the estimated ending inventory in dollars?

a. Full absorption costing only considers variable costs, making the cost per unit lower and more accurate for ending inventory calculations.
b. Full absorption costing spreads all production costs, including fixed and variable overhead, across all units produced, ensuring that the estimated ending inventory reflects the true cost of production by multiplying the number of ending inventory units by the per unit cost.
c. Full absorption costing excludes fixed overhead costs, focusing only on direct labor and materials, which simplifies the COGS calculation but leads to understated inventory values.
d. Full absorption costing allocates only direct material costs to each unit, which inflates the cost of ending inventory.

S:9-5 (Learning Objective 4)

Calculate the total variable selling and administrative costs for quarter 2 if the company expects to sell 2,400 units for $100 each in that quarter.
Variable Costs:

- Sales commissions: 5% of the sales price for each unit
- Freight out: $12 per unit

S:9-6 (Learning Objective 4)

Amor Artisan Hair Accessories has budgeted sales of $20,000 in January and $20,000 in February. Based on their collection pattern (50% in the current month, 48% in the next month, and 2% uncollected), compute the cash receipts for February.
Assumptions:

- 50% of February sales are collected in February
- 48% of January sales are collected in February

Exercises

E:9-7 (Learning Objective 1)

Assume Blackhawk Custom Cycles anticipates a 25% increase in motorcycle demand for the upcoming year. If the company does not adequately plan for this demand, explain at least three negative outcomes that could arise from a lack of planning. How would a well-prepared operating budget help prevent these issues?

E:9-8 (Learning Objective 2)

Assume a company is in the early stages of preparing its master budget. Identify the sequence in which budget schedules should be completed. Why is it important for these schedules to be completed in this order?

E:9-9 (Learning Objective 3)

Discuss the advantages of using spreadsheet applications like Microsoft Excel or Google Sheets in the budgeting process for businesses. How do these tools enhance the budgeting process, and what specific features make them particularly useful?

E:9-10 (Learning Objective 4)

How does full absorption costing affect the calculation of the cost of goods sold (COGS) budget, and why is it critical to include direct materials, direct labor, and manufacturing overhead in the per unit production cost when developing the COGS budget?

E:9-11 (Learning Objective 4)

Develop a cash receipts budget for Amor Artisan Hair Accessories for their first quarter of operations (January through March) based on the following sales projections:

Month	Projected Sales ($)
January	20,000
February	20,000
March	20,000

The collection pattern is as follows:

- 50% of current month sales are collected during the current month.
- 48% are collected in the next month.
- 2% are uncollected.

Since this is the first year of operations, there are no preexisting sales to collect from.

E:9-12 (Learning Objective 4)

Amor Artisan Hair Accessories has the following pattern for raw material payments:

- 60% of the purchases are paid in the current month.
- 40% of the purchases are paid in the following month.

The company makes the following material purchases during the first quarter of the year:

- January: $15,000
- February: $18,000
- March: $20,000

Required

Prepare a cash disbursements budget for January, February, and March, calculating the total cash disbursements for each month and the quarter.

Problems

P:9-13 (Learning Objective 1)

Assume Blackhawk Custom Cycles prepares its annual operating budget and forecasts a 30% increase in demand for the upcoming year. The company plans to increase production by hiring 10 more workers and purchasing an additional production machine. The cost of each new worker is $60,000 annually (including wages and benefits), and the production machine costs $300,000.

Blackhawk's current workforce of 50 employees and 5 machines can handle the demand, but only by requiring significant overtime (which costs 1.5 times regular wages). Current employees earn $50,000 annually. Overtime is expected to account for 20% of their work hours if no new workers or machines are added.

Required

1. Calculate the total labor cost for the year if no new workers are hired and overtime is used.
2. Calculate the total labor cost for the year if 10 new workers are hired and no overtime is needed.
3. Determine the total cost difference between hiring new workers and using overtime.
4. Explain why, beyond cost, hiring additional workers might be a better long-term strategy for Blackhawk.

P:9-14 (Learning Objective 2)

Imagine your company, Green World Manufacturing Co., is preparing its budget for the upcoming year. The sales manager projects $5 million in sales, requiring the production of 100,000 units of product. To meet this demand, the production manager needs to budget for direct materials, direct labor, and manufacturing overhead. Here's what the company needs to budget:

- Direct materials: Each unit requires $15 of raw materials.
- Direct labor: Labor costs $20 per unit.
- Manufacturing overhead: Overhead is calculated at 50% of direct labor costs.

In addition to production, Green World must budget for selling and administrative expenses, which total $200,000 annually, and capital expenditures of $300,000 for new machinery.

Required

1. Prepare the direct materials, direct labor, and manufacturing overhead budgets.
2. Calculate the total production cost for 100,000 units.
3. Discuss why this sequential approach to budgeting is critical for ensuring accurate financial projections.

P:9-15 (Learning Objective 4)

MC Aviation Components manufactures aircraft parts and needs to prepare its raw material budget for two components: titanium alloy and aluminum sheet metal. The company uses the following information:

- Each aircraft part requires 50 linear feet of titanium alloy and 10 linear feet of aluminum sheet metal.
- Desired ending inventory for titanium alloy is 20% of the next quarter's production needs. For aluminum sheet metal, the target ending inventory is also set at 15% of the next quarter's production needs.
- The production forecast for the current quarter is 1,800 and 2,000 next quarter.
- Current inventory is 12,000 linear feet of titanium alloy and 2,500 linear feet of aluminum sheet metal.

Required

1. Calculate the total linear feet of titanium alloy and aluminum sheet metal required to be purchased during the current quarter to meet production and inventory needs.

P:9-16 (Learning Objective 4)

MC Aviation Components, a manufacturer of aircraft parts, is preparing a direct labor budget for one quarter. The company manufactures specific parts for aircraft, and the key information regarding direct labor is as follows:

- Each aircraft part requires 0.75 hours (or 45 minutes) of direct labor to produce.
- The company pays an average of $25 per hour for direct labor (which includes wages, taxes, and insurance costs).
- For the quarter, the company plans to produce 1,040 units.

Required

Compute the direct labor budget for MC Aviation for the quarter.

P:9-17 (Learning Activity 4)

MC Aviation Components, a manufacturer of aircraft parts, is preparing a manufacturing overhead budget for one quarter. The company's overhead expenditures include both fixed and variable costs, which are triggered by production activity. Following are the key details regarding the fixed and variable overhead costs for the upcoming quarter:

Fixed Costs

- Gas and electricity (fixed charge): $3,000 per quarter
- Facility rent: $9,000 per quarter
- Production manager salary: $22,500 per quarter
- Depreciation: $4,500 per quarter

Variable Costs

- Gas and electricity (variable charge): $0.75 per unit produced
- Maintenance and upkeep: $4 per unit produced
- Indirect material: $1.50 per unit produced
- Inspection: $25 for every tenth unit produced

For the upcoming quarter, MC Aviation Components plans to produce **1,040 units**.

Required

Calculate the total fixed costs, total variable costs, and total overhead costs for the quarter.

P:9-18 (Learning Objective 4)

Prepare a selling and administrative expense budget for quarter 3, assuming the company plans to sell 3,200 units and the sales price per unit is $100. Also, assume that fixed costs remain unchanged. Selling and Administrative costs are as follows:

Variable Costs

- Sales commissions: 5% of the sales price for each unit
- Freight out: $12 per unit sold

Fixed Costs

- Executive salary: $10,000
- Office salary: $5,000
- Advertising: $2,500
- Insurance: $1,500
- Depreciation: $1,500

P:9-19 (Learning Objective 4)

Amor Artisan Hair Accessories is preparing a cash budget for the first quarter of the first year of business. The company has the following information:

Beginning Cash Balance

- January 1: $10,000

Sales and Collections

Sales for the quarter are as follows:

- January: $25,000
- February: $30,000
- March: $35,000

Amor Artisan collects 50% of sales in the month of sale, 48% in the following month, and 2% is uncollected.

Material Purchases and Payments

Material purchases for the quarter are:

- January: $10,000
- February: $12,000
- March: $15,000

Sixty percent of the purchases are paid in the month of purchase, and 40% are paid in the following month.

Other Expenses

Monthly fixed expenses include:

- Wages: $5,000
- Rent: $2,500
- Utilities: $1,000
- Depreciation: $500 per month

Required

Prepare a cash budget for January, February, and March, showing the beginning cash balance, cash receipts, cash disbursements, and ending cash balance. If the company needs to borrow cash, include the borrowing in the budget.

CHAPTER 10

Flexible Budgeting and Variance Analysis

Learning Objectives

10.1 Identify cost variances and explain why they are favorable or unfavorable.
10.2 Prepare a flexible budget and compare its usefulness to that of a static budget.
10.3 Describe the concept of standard costing and its advantages and disadvantages.
10.4 Summarize how standard costs are developed and computed.
10.5 Compute and explain material and labor variances.
10.6 Compute and explain manufacturing overhead variances.

Accounting in Life

Andrea Piacquadio / Pexels / Public Domain

What kind of fuel do you put in your car? If you have a new automobile, you may have the option of using regular gasoline, which usually has between 0% and 10% ethanol content, and E85, which contains 85% ethanol. E85 is generally cheaper than regular gasoline, but between 20% and 30% less efficient. Let us assume you drive a new sedan that gets 34 miles per gallon on the highway using regular gasoline. Would you be better off financially using E85 if it costs $1.80 per gallon and regular gasoline cost $2.30? Assume your gas mileage is 30% better using gasoline.

The solution is as follows. At 70% fuel efficiency, the sedan would get 23.8 miles per gallon. A 500-mile trip would cost approximately $37.82 using E85 (500 miles ÷ 23.8 miles per gallon) × $1.80 per gallon. A 500-mile trip would cost approximately $33.82 using gasoline (500 ÷ 34.0 miles per gallon) × $2.30 per gallon. This indicates that using E85 would cost approximately $4.00 more than using gasoline.

Under this scenario, E85 initially looks like a cost savings, but it is actually more expensive than regular gasoline when you consider fuel efficiency. Businesses must also consider all related costs to an operation to make the most cost-efficient decision.

Let's Review

Superior performance analysis starts with a baseline, which is a budget. We learned in the last chapter how businesses prepare an operating budget systematically. The preparation of an operating budget requires both a systematic approach and the use of professional judgment and assumptions. The operating budget is a starting point for operational planning and control.

LEARNING ACTIVITY 10.1

The following items represent a facet of the budgeting process. Rearrange the items into the proper sequence to prepare an operating budget.

A. Production	______
B. Income Statement	______
C. Cost of Goods Sold	______
D. Sales	______
E. Balance Sheet	______
F. Direct Labor	______

How Do Businesses Evaluate Deviations from Budgeted Expectations?

Learning Objective 10.1
Identify cost variances and explain why they are favorable or unfavorable.

Preparing a budget requires estimations and assumptions. Inevitably, actual business results will vary from budgeted expectations. We call the differences between budgeted cost expectations and actual results **cost variances**:

- When actual results end in a higher profit for the company relative to budget expectations, there is a **favorable variance**.
- When actual results end in lower profit for the company compared to budget expectations, there is an **unfavorable variance**.

Favorable and unfavorable cost variances are driven by many factors. However, prices and quantities are the primary drivers of cost variances. Price variances happen when a company pays more or less for materials, supplies, or employee salaries, for example. Quantity variances are related to the consumption of resources like raw materials or people's time. Thus, favorable cost variances might be a function of reduced raw material usage, increased efficiency resulting in lower labor costs, or lower raw material costs due to better bargaining and lower raw material prices. Unfavorable cost variances are typically the result of higher prices or low efficiency.

Variance results can be hard to decipher, and their cause might not always be so evident. For example, a firm may contract with a new supplier to buy raw material at a reduced price. The reduced price may cause a materials price variance. However, the cheaper material may be inferior and difficult to manipulate and transform in the manufacturing process, resulting in the need for more time and effort to produce the desired part. More time and labor costs result in an unfavorable labor variance. If the increase in labor cost outweighs the cost savings generated by using the inferior raw material, the change in supplier would have been a bad choice.

Ultimately, the calculation of variances offers managers a tool for looking at organizational performance. Managers must analyze the variances. **Variance analysis** is a process managers use to examine variances and identify the root cause. The remainder of this chapter is dedicated to variance analysis.

LEARNING ACTIVITY 10.2

Match the following scenarios with the correct type of variance:

Scenario	Type of Variance
1. Actual labor costs were lower than budgeted expectations.	A. Unfavorable price variance
2. A company paid more than expected for raw materials.	B. Favorable labor variance

LEARNING ACTIVITY 10.2

Scenario	Type of Variance
3. Less raw material was used than planned.	C. Unfavorable quantity variance
4. More hours were needed to complete production than anticipated.	D. Favorable quantity variance
5. A supplier offered a discount, reducing the cost of materials below the budget.	E. Unfavorable labor variance
	F. Favorable price variance

How Do Budgets Deal with Changes in Assumptions?

Learning Objective 10.2

Prepare a flexible budget and compare its usefulness to that of a static budget.

The one constant in business is *change*. The business environment, customers' desires and demands, and internal processes all change over time. Sometimes, change occurs gradually, and sometimes businesses are shocked, bringing change relatively quickly. Think about what happened during the COVID-19 crisis. In the spring of 2020, many state governments implemented mandatory lockdowns, which prevented people from going about their normal daily routines. The impact on business was equally significant. Service businesses like restaurants saw an immediate reduction in customers eating in, while the demand for delivery skyrocketed. Businesses that were able to adjust and manage the sudden business shock were able to stay in business. Many others were not so lucky.

We learned to prepare budgets in the last chapter. We use budgets to compare our expected or budgeted results to actual results. We built a static master budget in the last chapter. A **static budget** is a budget prepared using a single level of business activity. For instance, we might budget for costs and expenditures, assuming a certain level of sales or production. A static budget does not adjust to changes in sales or production activity. Suppose we use the static budget for comparative purposes. In that case, the business compares actual results with the budget data at the estimated activity level used when developing the static master budget. However, the chance that we can correctly predict a level of business activity is slim. Budgets are built on a foundation of assumptions and expectations. It is nearly impossible for a business to predict precisely what will happen in the business environment. So, what happens if the assumptions that went into the budget do not come to fruition? What happens if, for example, a budget is based on a level of expected sales or production that differs from the actual results?

In cases where the actual activity level differs from the assumed level of activity used to compute the static master budget, the business must adjust its budget to be at the same level of activity as the actual results. It can then compare budget results and actual results based on the

Bob Willis Custom Wheels
Manufacturing Overhead Budget Variance Analysis
First Quarter 20XX

	Budget	Actual	Variance
Units produced	1,040 Units	1,100 Units	60 Units
Fixed Costs			
Gas and electricity	3,000	3,200	200U
Facility rent	9,000	9,000	-
Production manager salary	22,500	22,500	-
Depreciation	4,500	4,000	(500)F
Total Fixed Costs	$ 39,000	$ 38,700	$ (300)F
Variable Costs			
Gas and electricity	780	800	20U
Maintenance	4,160	4,300	140U
Indirect material	1,560	1,400	(160)F
Inspection	2,600	3,000	400U
Total Variable Costs	$ 9,100	$ 9,500	$ 400U
Total Overhead Costs	$ 48,100	$ 48,200	$ 100U

The difference between budgeted and actual units produced is a 60 Units. The difference is a "Variance"

The company had $300 less total actual fixed costs than budget. The lower costs is called "Favorable" (F).

Higher actual costs compared to budgeted are "Unfavorable" (F) variances. There were $100 more total overhead costs than budgeted.

Figure 10.1 Overhead budget variance analysis.

same underlying activity level. We call this adjusted budget a flexible budget. A **flexible budget** is a budget that is adjusted to the actual level of business activity. The flexible budget is useful because it is adaptable to changes in operating conditions, and it allows for a relevant comparison of actual and budgeted results. Let us look at an example. Bob Willis Custom Wheels conducted an analysis of manufacturing overhead costs during the first quarter of the current year, which appears in Figure 10.1.

Variance Analysis

The data from Bob Willis Custom Wheels manufacturing overhead cost variance analysis in Figure 10.1 shows that the company produced 1,100 units compared to an estimated 1,040 units during the first quarter. Willis also spent a total of $48,200 on overhead costs during the period. The company budgeted $48,100 in overhead costs. Looking at the difference between budget and actual costs, we see $100 more in actual overhead costs. Higher actual costs are generally considered an "unfavorable" variance because the extra costs would ultimately reduce net profits. Lower actual costs are generally considered "favorable" variances because the reduced costs would ultimately result in higher net profits. Bob Willis has spent $100 more than budgeted in this situation, which would appear to be an unfavorable variance.

Favorable Versus Unfavorable Variance Analysis

We compute Bob Willis' unfavorable variance by making a comparison between budgeted overhead costs based on a budget of 1,040 units produced and the actual overhead costs based on the actual production quantity of 1,100 units. To make a useful comparison, we must compute Bob Willis' *flexible budget*, the budget at the actual production quantity of 1,100 units. Preparing the flexible budget first requires calculating the variable costs using the expected variable costs per unit produced. An adjustment to fixed costs is not necessary because they are not affected by changes in production volume. Bob Willis' variable costs per unit are shown in Figure 10.2.

Bob Willis can use the revised variable costs to compute a flexible budget for comparing with actual activity, as illustrated in Figure 10.3.

Recomputing the budgeted variable costs using the actual production volume of 1,100 units results in a flexible budget that has a favorable overhead cost variance of $425, whereas the original budget showed a $100 unfavorable cost variance. The $100 unfavorable overhead cost variance is misleading; in fact, Bob Willis is controlling costs favorably to the tune of $425 for the quarter.

Variable Costs	Original Budget		Budgeted Production		Cost per Unit		Actual Production		Flexible Budget
Gas and electricity	$ 780	×	1,040	=	$ .75	×	1,100	=	$ 825
Maintenance	$ 4,160	×	1,040	=	$4.00	×	1,100	=	$ 4,400
Indirect material	$ 1,560	×	1,040	=	$1.50	×	1,100	=	$ 1,650
Inspection	$ 2,600	×	1,040	=	$2.50	×	1,100	=	$ 2,750
Total Variable Costs	$ 9,100								$ 9,625

Figure 10.2 Flexible variable cost calculations.

Bob Willis Custom Wheels
Manufacturing Overhead Budget Variance Analysis
First Quarter 20XX

	Flexible Budget	Actual	Variance
Units produced	1,100 Units	1,100 Units	60 Units
Fixed Costs			
Gas and electricity	3,000	3,200	200U
Facility rent	9,000	9,000	-
Production manager salary	22,500	22,500	-
Depreciation	4,500	4,000	(500)F
Total Fixed Costs	$ 39,000	$ 38,700	$ (300)F
Variable Costs			
Gas and electricity	825	800	(25)F
Maintenance	4,400	4,300	(100)F
Indirect material	1,650	1,400	(250)F
Inspection	2,750	3,000	250U
Total Variable Costs	$ 9,625	$ 9,500	$ (125)F
Total Overhead Costs	$ 48,625	$ 48,200	$ (425)F

The flexible budget shows a favorable variance of $425 whereas the original analysis showed unfavorable variance of $100

Figure 10.3 Overhead flexible budget variance analysis.

LEARNING ACTIVITY 10.3

We introduced Amor Artisan Hair Accessories in Chapter 9. Amor produces hairbands. Consider Amor's following expected production volume and overhead cost assumptions.

	January	February	March	Quarter
Finished Hairbands to be produced (in units)	2,500	2,000	2,000	6,500

Overhead Assumptions	
Storage costs per month	$ 350.00
Production supervisor wage	$ 400.00
Depreciation	$ 25.00
Indirect material cost per unit	$ 0.05
Inspection cost per batch	$ 10.00
Number of units produced per batch	500

Using the provided estimated production and the manufacturing overhead assumptions, compute the manufacturing overhead budget for the first quarter:

Amor Artisan Hair Accessories
Manufacturing Overhead Budget
Quarter Ending December 20XX

	January	February	March	Quarter
Fixed Costs				
Storage Rent				
Production Manager Salary				
Depreciation				
Total Fixed Costs				
Variable Costs				
Indirect Material				
Inspection				
Total Variable Costs				
Total Overhead Costs				

How Do Businesses Know if They Are Producing Individual Products or Providing Individual Services Efficiently?

Learning Objective 10.3
Describe the concept of standard costing and its advantages and disadvantages.

Standard cost is the expected cost of a single unit of a product or service. In theory, a standard cost is a unit-level budget. Standard costs are computed for each cost element, including direct materials, direct labor, and manufacturing overhead. Standard costs are a function of cost and quantity. We determine the standard cost for each element by multiplying the standard price expected to be paid for a unit of material, labor, or overhead by the standard quantity of units to be consumed.

Expected Price × Expected Quantity = Standard Cost

Standard costs are useful to organizations because they offer a basis for performing variance analysis. **Variance analysis** is the process of comparing actual costs and standard costs and the reasons for any difference. Variance analysis is a form of managerial control that can make managers more efficient by practicing management by exception, the process of investigating variances that are exceptions from tolerable deviations. The use of standard costing is also useful because employees become more cognizant of costs as they participate in the development of standards and the review of variances. Finally, standard costing simplifies cost accounting and inventory costing. Figure 10.4 sums up the benefits of standard costing.

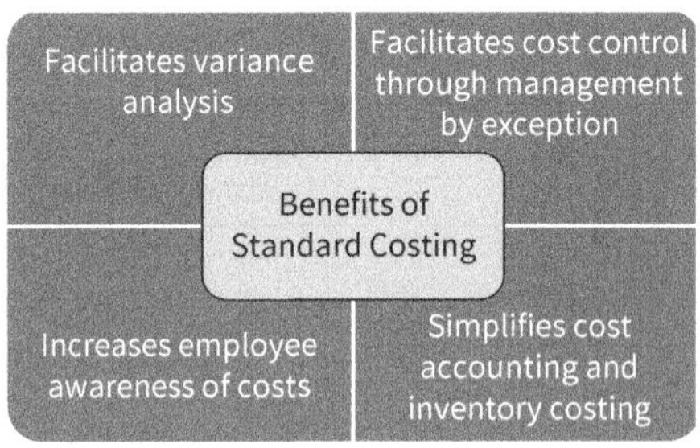

Figure 10.4 Benefits of standard costing.

How Are Standard Costs Established?

Learning Objective 10.4
Summarize how standard costs are developed and computed.

Establishing standard costs requires input from a wide range of people in an organization, particularly those responsible for controlling costs and the consumption of resources. For example, establishing material cost expectations may be the purchasing department's responsibility, and the direct labor rate might require input from human resources.

Expected material consumption and labor usage would presumably require information from production operations.

It is also important to set standards at the appropriate level of operating efficiency. Firms may elect to set standards assuming the ideal operating efficiency levels or set standards at normal efficiency levels. Standards set at ideal efficiency may not be attainable and irrelevant for comparative purposes. Standards set at normal levels that are attainable under efficient conditions are more practical for later comparisons of actual costs to standards.

Standard Direct Material Costs

Standard direct material costs are the standard direct material price per unit of material multiplied by the standard quantity of direct material per finished goods produced. The standard direct materials price is the expected cost per unit of direct materials per unit of finished goods. The standard price per unit of direct material is based on the purchasing department's best estimate developed through its interactions and negotiations with suppliers. The standard direct material quantity is the quantity of direct materials expected to be used in each unit of finished goods. The standard direct material quantity is conveyed as a physical measure such as gallons, pounds, inches, etc. Note, the standard direct material quantity should include allowances for *normal* scrap or waste and normal inventory storage and delivery costs.

$$\begin{array}{c}\textbf{Standard Direct Material Price}\\ \times\\ \textbf{Standard Direct Material Quantity}\end{array} = \textbf{Standard Direct Material Cost}$$

Standard Direct Labor Costs

Standard direct labor costs are based on the standard labor rate per hour multiplied by the standard number of labor hours per finished good unit produced. The standard direct labor rate is the expected cost per direct labor hour when producing a unit of finished goods. The standard direct labor rate is based on the human resource department's best estimate of labor costs and usually includes anticipated pay raises, contracts, and adjustments. The standard direct labor quantity is the expected amount of direct labor needed to produce each unit of finished goods. The standard direct labor quantity is generally conveyed in hours or fractions thereof and should include allowances for normal cleanup, break periods, and rest.

$$\begin{array}{c}\textbf{Standard Direct Labor Rate}\\ \times\\ \textbf{Standard Direct Labor Quantity}\end{array} = \textbf{Standard Direct Labor Cost}$$

Standard Overhead Costs

Standard overhead costs consist of both fixed and variable overhead cost components, which are commonly computed independently of one another. **Standard fixed overhead costs** are costs, other than direct material and direct labor, which are related to production, but do not change with production quantities. Standard fixed overhead costs consist of things like the salaries of production supervisory and support staff, the depreciation cost of buildings, fixtures, and equipment, or the cost of rent. **Standard variable overhead costs** are costs, other than direct material and direct labor, which are related to production and vary directly with production quantities. Items that commonly make up standard variable overhead costs include the cost of repairs and maintenance, the use of indirect materials, the cost of inspecting finished goods, and gas and electricity costs that arise from operating machinery and equipment. Establishing the standard variable overhead cost is difficult because there is such a wide variety of variable overhead costs.

Selecting an appropriate cost driver for overhead is more complex than for material and labor, where we use material quantities or labor hours. We are required to use a *proxy* to measure activity and compute a variable overhead rate. The proxy should have a cause-and-effect relationship with all variable overhead costs, but finding such a measure can be challenging. Common proxies include *units produced, direct labor hours, machine run time*, or even a percentage of *direct labor dollars*.

The development of standard costs commonly takes place during the budgeting process. Let us examine the standard costs for Bob Willis Custom Wheel Company. Recall that in Chapter 9 we calculated the material, labor, and overhead costs per unit. The estimated cost per finished wheel is based on the data and assumptions in Figure 10.5.

Bob Willis Custom Wheels' actual cost and production data are shown in Figure 10.6.

	Unit of Measure	Cost Per Unit of Measure	Total Cost Per Unit of Finished Good
Direct Material – Rim Steel	5 Ln. Ft.	$7.00	$35.00
Direct Material – Wire Spokes	27 Ln. Ft	$1.00	$27.00
Direct Labor	.75 Hrs	$25.00	$18.75
Variable Overhead	.75 Hrs	$11.667	$8.75
Total Variable Costs Per Finished Good Unit			$89.50
Budgeted Fixed Overhead		$156,000	
Budgeted Wheel Production		÷ 4,840 Wheels	
			$32.23
Budgeted Costs Per Wheel			$121.73

Figure 10.5 Standard cost per wheel for Bob Willis Custom Wheel Company.

	Unit of Measure	Cost Per Unit of Measure	Total Cost Per Unit of Finished Good
Direct Material – Rim Steel	5.5 Ln. Ft.	$6.00	$33.00
Direct Material – Wire Spokes	30 Ln. Ft	$.85	$25.50
Direct Labor	.8 Hrs	$23.75	$19.00
Variable Overhead	.8 Hrs	$11.25	$9.00
Total Variable Costs Per Finished Good Unit			$86.50
Actual Fixed Overhead		$162,000	
Actual Wheel Production		÷5,000 Wheels	
			$32.40
Actual Costs Per Wheel			$118.90

Figure 10.6 Actual cost per wheel for Bob Willis Custom Wheel Company.

How Do Companies Assess the Difference Between Budgeted and Actual Results for Material and Labor Costs?

Learning Objective 10.5
Compute and explain material and labor variances.

In business, every penny counts; management of material and labor costs is crucial to maintaining profitability. Material and labor variances—the differences between expected and actual material costs or expected and actual labor costs are key indicators of how well a company controls resources. These variances can arise from fluctuating raw material and labor prices, supplier performance issues, or inefficiencies in the production process. By closely monitoring and analyzing material and labor variances, businesses can identify areas where costs are spiraling out of control, enabling timely corrective actions that safeguard margins. This section explores the intricacies of both material and labor variances, guiding you through their calculation, interpretation, and strategic implications.

Cọ Sơn Thanh Bình / Pexels / Public Domain

Direct Materials Variance

The **direct materials variance** is the difference between standard material costs and actual material costs. That variance is the result of a disparity in the price and quantity of direct materials purchased and used compared to expectations during the budgeting process. The formula for the direct material variance is displayed here. You can see it compares actual to standard and is a function of both price and quantity.

$$\begin{array}{c} \textbf{Actual Direct Material Quantity} \\ \times \\ \textbf{Actual Direct Material Price} \end{array} - \begin{array}{c} \textbf{Standard Direct Material Quantity} \\ \times \\ \textbf{Standard Direct Material Price} \end{array} = \begin{array}{c} \textbf{Total} \\ \textbf{Direct Material} \\ \textbf{Variance} \end{array}$$

How do you interpret the direct materials variance?

- An unfavorable direct material variance suggests that higher prices were paid for direct materials, or more direct materials were used compared to expectations, indicating inefficiency.
- A favorable variance indicates lower purchase prices for raw materials or greater efficiency when using direct materials. The overall cost of direct materials is less than expected and driven by the standard price or the amount of direct materials used in production is less than expected.

Let us look at an example. Figure 10.7 displays the standard direct material expected to be used and the actual material used to produce a batch of custom wheels at Bob Willis Custom Wheel Company.

Direct Material Price Variance

The **direct material price variance** is driven by the difference between the standard (or expected) price per unit of direct material and the dollar amount actually paid for a unit of direct material. The formula for the direct material price variance follows. You can see that the formula isolates the difference between actual and standard price by holding the material quantity constant.

$$\begin{array}{c} \textit{Actual Direct Material Quantity} \\ \times \\ \underline{\textbf{Actual}}\ \textbf{Direct Material Price} \end{array} - \begin{array}{c} \textit{Actual Direct Material Quantity} \\ \times \\ \underline{\textbf{Standard}}\ \textbf{Direct Material Price} \end{array} = \begin{array}{c} \textbf{Direct Material} \\ \textbf{Price} \\ \textbf{Variance} \end{array}$$

	Unit of Measure	Cost Per Unit of Measure	Total Cost Per Unit of Finished Good
Standard Costs Per Wheel			
Direct Material - Rim Steel	5 Ln. Ft.	$7.00	$35.00
Direct Material – Wire Spokes	27 Ln. Ft	$1.00	$27.00
Actual Costs Per Wheel			
Direct Material - Rim Steel	5.5 Ln. Ft.	$6.00	$33.00
Direct Material – Wire Spokes	30 Ln. Ft	$.85	$25.50
Budgeted Wheel Production	4,840 Wheels		
Actual Wheel Production	5,000 Wheels		

Figure 10.7 Standard and actual direct material costs at Bob Willis Custom Wheels.

Let us illustrate the direct material price variance for rim steel using the figures from Figure 10.6 into our direct material price variance formula. Recall the actual direct material quantity is a function of both the actual amount of steel used per wheel (5.5 linear feet) and the actual number of wheels produced (5,000 wheels). As a result, the actual amount of steel used amounted to 27,500 linear feet. The actual direct material price per linear foot of steel was \$6 whereas the standard price was \$7. The difference of \$1 per linear foot multiplied by the 27,500 linear feet of steel used resulted in a \$27,500 favorable direct material price variance. It is *favorable* because the actual price paid for the rim steel is less than expected, resulting in cost savings.

(5.5 ln. ft. × 5,000 Wheels)		**(5.5 ln. ft. × 5,000 Wheels)**		**Direct Material**
×	−	×	=	**Price**
\$6		\$7		**Variance**
\$165,000	−	**\$192,500**	=	**\$27,500 Favorable**

Direct Material Quantity Variance

The **direct material quantity variance** represents the difference between the actual and expected amount of direct materials used in production (the standard direct material quantity). The formula for the direct material quantity variance follows. Notice that the formula isolates the difference between actual and standard direct material quantity by holding the direct material price constant.

<u>Actual</u> Direct Material Quantity		**<u>Standard</u> Direct Material Quantity**		**Direct Material**
×	−	×	=	**Quantity**
Standard Direct Material Price		***Standard Direct Material Price***		**Variance**

Let us illustrate the direct material quantity variance for rim steel by inserting the figures from Figure 10.6 into the direct material quantity variance formula. The actual amount of rim steel used amounted to 27,500 linear feet. That is a function of the 5.5 linear feet of rim steel used per wheel and the actual number of wheels produced (5,000 wheels). The standard amount of steel is composed of 5.0 linear feet of steel expected to be used per wheel times the actual number of wheels produced (5,000 wheels) or 25,000 linear feet. We multiply those values by the standard direct material price, which is held constant at \$7 per linear foot, to arrive at values of \$192,500 and \$175,000 for a direct material quantity variance of \$17,500. The variance is *unfavorable* because the actual amount of steel per wheel, 5.5 linear feet, is more than the expected amount of 5.0 linear feet.

(5.5 ln. ft. × 5,000 Wheels)		**(5.0 ln. ft. × 5,000 Wheels)**		**Direct Material**
×	−	×	=	**Quantity**
\$7.00		\$7.00		**Variance**
\$192,500	−	\$175,000	=	**\$17,500 Unfavorable**

Combining Price and Quantity Variance

A two-column visualization is a useful way to analyze material cost variances. The two-column approach combines both the price and quantity variance calculations into a display. A two-column approach follows. Notice that you can see that the favorable direct materials price variance of $27,500 and the unfavorable direct material quantity variance of $17,500 combine to make a total direct material cost variance of $10,000, which is favorable.

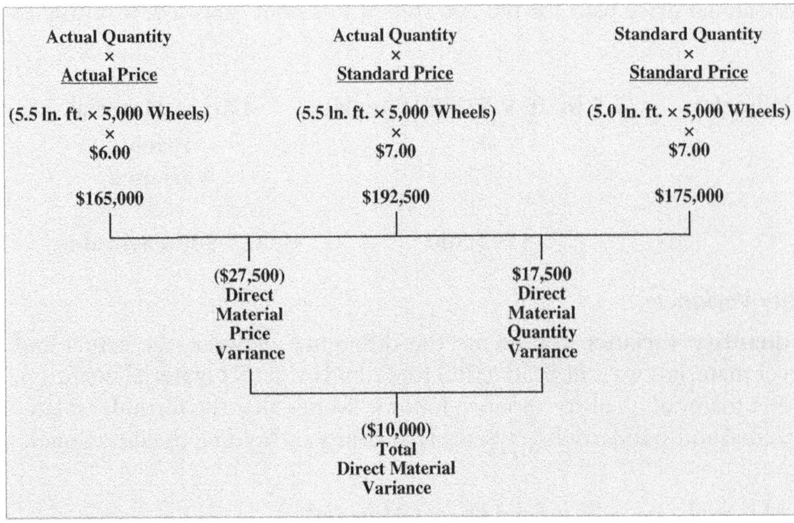

Root Cause Analysis

When evaluating variances, it is useful to narrow in on the root cause of the variance and identify responsible parties. The **root cause** is the underlying reason for the occurrence of the variance. Material price variances are usually the responsibility of the purchasing department because the purchasing department negotiates pricing with suppliers. Material quantity variances are usually the responsibility of the production department, which transforms the raw material into a finished product. However, there can be interaction between the two facets of a material variance. For example, the purchasing department could conceivably create favorable direct materials price variances by purchasing from a lower-quality supplier with lower prices. However, lower-quality material may be consumed at a higher rate because of its inferiority, which drives a direct material quantity variance. For that reason, businesses must consider variances together and identify the root cause.

We use the two-column approach illustrated to evaluate the cost of the spokes produced by Bob Willis Custom Wheels. Notice that the unfavorable direct material price variance of $20,250 and the favorable direct materials quantity variance of $12,750 combine to make a total direct material cost variance of $7,500, which is unfavorable.

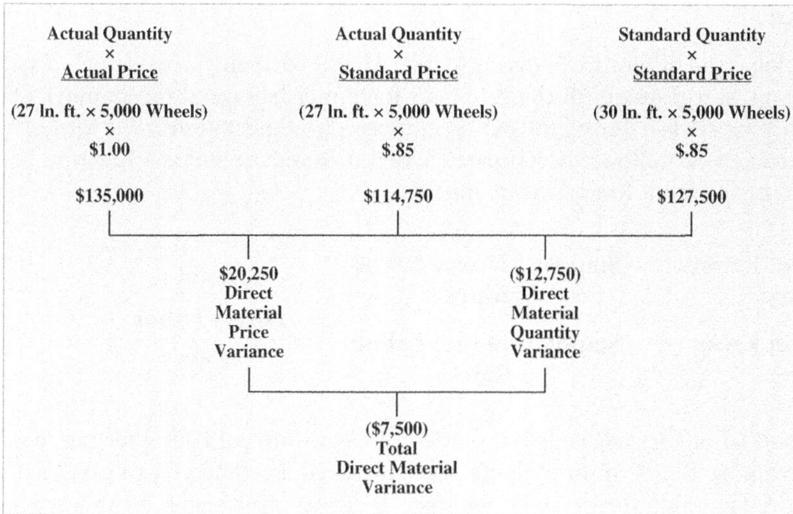

LEARNING ACTIVITY 10.4

Amor Artisan Hair Accessories is expected to produce 2,500 hairbands in the first quarter of this year. The actual production amounted to 2,400 hairbands. Actual and standard costs for the hairbands' direct material components, thread, and beads are as follows:

	Unit of Measure	Cost per Unit of Measure	Total Cost per Unit of Finished Good
<u>Standard Costs per Hairband</u>			
Direct Material—Thread	4 Ln. Ft.	$0.25	$1.00
Direct Material—Beads	50 Beads	$0.04	$2.00
<u>Actual Costs per Hairband</u>			
Direct Material—Thread	4.25 Ln. Ft.	$0.20	$0.85
Direct Material—Beads	52 Ln. Ft	$0.05	$2.60
Budgeted Hairband Production	2,500 Hairbands		
Actual Hairband Production	2,400 Hairbands		

Use a two-column approach to compute the materials price variance, the materials usage variance, and the total materials variance for thread used in Amor Artisan Hairbands for the first quarter. Indicate whether the variances are favorable or unfavorable.

Direct Labor Variance

The **direct labor variance** is the difference between standard labor costs and actual labor costs. That variance is the result of a disparity in the rate paid for direct labor and the number of direct labor hours employees worked during the period compared to expectations. The formula for the direct labor variance is as follows. It compares actual to standard and is a function of both labor rates (the price) and labor hours (the quantity).

$$\left(\begin{array}{c}\textbf{Actual Direct Labor Hours}\\ \times\\ \textbf{Actual Direct Labor Rate}\end{array}\right) - \left(\begin{array}{c}\textbf{Standard Direct Labor Hours}\\ \times\\ \textbf{Standard Direct Labor Rate}\end{array}\right) = \textbf{Total Direct Labor Variance}$$

An unfavorable direct labor variance suggests that employees were paid a higher rate per hour for direct labor, or more hours of direct labor were incurred as compared to expected, indicating inefficiency. A favorable direct labor variance indicates efficiencies in incurring direct labor costs and in production efficiency as the rate employees are paid per labor hour is less than the standard rate or the number of direct labor hours worked in production is less than expected. Let us look at examples related to direct labor hours. Figure 10.8 displays the standard and actual direct labor hours used in the production of a batch of custom wheels at Bob Willis Custom Wheel Company and the labor rates.

Direct Labor Rate Variance

The **direct labor rate variance** is driven by the difference between the standard (or expected) direct labor cost and the actual amount paid for time worked. The formula for the direct labor rate variance is as follows. You can see the formula isolates the difference between the actual and standard rates by holding the direct labor hours constant.

	Unit of Measure	Cost Per Unit of Measure	Total Cost Per Unit of Finished Good
Standard Costs Per Wheel			
Direct Labor	.75 Hrs	$25.00	$18.75
Actual Costs Per Wheel			
Direct Labor	.8 Hrs	$23.75	$19.00
Budgeted Wheel Production	4,840 Wheels		
Actual Wheel Production	5,000 Wheels		

Figure 10.8 Standard and actual direct labor costs at Bob Willis Custom Wheels.

Actual Direct Labor Hours		*Actual Direct Labor Hours*		**Direct Labor**
×	−	×	=	**Rate**
Actual Direct Labor Rate		**Standard Direct Labor Rate**		**Variance**

Let us illustrate the direct labor rate variance for wheel production by inserting the figures from Figure 10.8 into the direct labor rate variance formula. Recall actual direct labor hours are a function of both the actual number of hours it takes to produce a wheel (0.8 hours), and the actual number of wheels produced (5,000 wheels). As a result, it took 4,000 actual hours to build the 5,000 wheels. The actual direct labor rate per hour was \$23.75 on average. The standard direct labor rate was \$25.00. The difference of \$1.25 per hour multiplied by the 4,000 hours it took to build the 5,000 wheels results in a direct labor rate variance of \$5,000. This is a *favorable* variance because the actual rate paid to employees was lower than expected, resulting in cost savings.

(0.8 hours × 5,000 Wheels)		**(0.8 hours × 5,000 Wheels)**		**Direct Labor**
×	−	×	=	**Rate**
\$23.75 per hour		**\$25.00 per hour**		**Variance**
\$95,000	−	**\$100,000**	=	**\$5,000 Favorable**

Direct Labor Efficiency Variance

The **direct labor efficiency variance** is driven by the difference between the actual and expected amount of direct labor hours worked in the production process. The formula for the direct labor efficiency variance follows. The formula isolates the difference between actual and standard direct labor hours by holding the direct labor rate constant.

Actual Direct Labor Hours		**Standard Direct Labor Hours**		**Direct Labor**
×	−	×	=	**Efficiency**
Standard Direct Labor Rate		*Standard Direct Labor Rate*		**Variance**

Let us illustrate the direct material quantity variance for rim steel using the figures from Figure 10.8 in our direct labor efficiency variance formula. The actual amount of direct labor hours consumed amounted to 4,000 hours. That is a function of the 0.8 hours per wheel and the actual number of wheels produced, 5,000. The standard number of hours expected is composed of 0.75 expected hours per wheel times 5,000 wheels, or 3,750 hours. The actual number of hours (4,000) and the standard number of hours (3,750) are multiplied by the standard direct rate, which is held constant at \$25 per hour, to arrive at values of \$100,000 and

$93,750, respectively, for a direct labor efficiency variance of $6,250. The variance is *unfavorable* because the actual number of labor hours of 4,000 exceeded the expected hours of 3,750, meaning Bob Willis Wheels was less efficient than expected.

(0.8 hours × 5,000 Wheels) × **$25.00**	−	**(0.75 hours × 5,000 Wheels)** × **$25.00**	=	**Direct Labor Efficiency Variance**
$100,000	−	**$93,750**	=	**$6,250 Unfavorable**

A two-column visualization is a useful way to analyze labor cost variances. The two-column approach combines both the rate and efficiency variance calculations into a display. The two-column approach shows that the favorable direct labor rate variance of $5,000 and the unfavorable direct labor efficiency variance of $6,250 combine to make a total labor cost variance of $1,250, which is unfavorable.

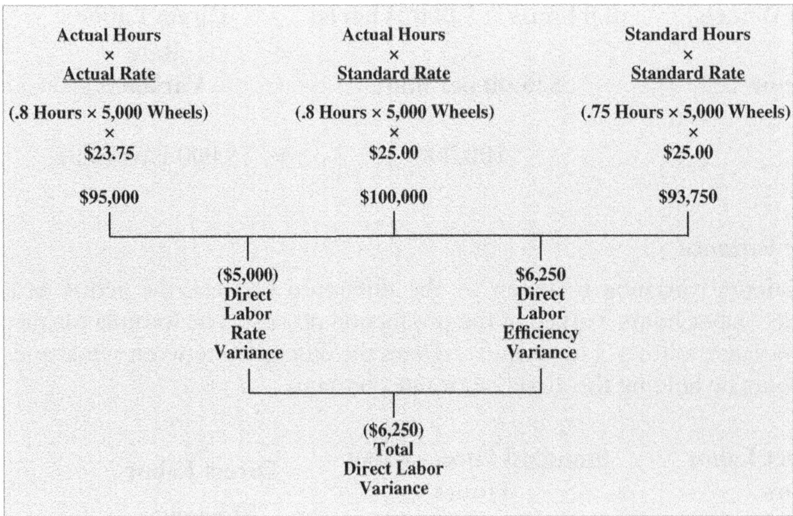

Root Cause Analysis

Labor rate variances are usually the responsibility of the human resources department and labor negotiations, but they can also be influenced by changes in the workforce, retirements, and economic conditions. Labor efficiency variances are usually the responsibility of the production department, which transforms the raw material into a finished product. However, there can be interaction between the two facets of labor variances and even trickle-down effects from material purchasing. For example, a firm could conceivably reduce labor rates by inducing more experienced and higher-paid employees to retire and replacing them with new lower-paid employees. However, those lower-paid new employees may be less efficient than the experienced staff. As a result, an action that caused a favorable rate variance may result in an unfavorable efficiency variance. It is possible that this might be the cause of the favorable rate variance and unfavorable efficiency variance in our example.

The purchasing department could conceivably create favorable direct materials price variances by purchasing from a lower quality supplier with lower prices. However, lower-quality material may be more difficult to manufacture and require more hours to convert to a finished product. Thus, a seemingly positive decision in purchasing could have detrimental effects on production. Business decisions can have wide-ranging effects and experienced cost accountants are skilled at narrowing variances down to the root cause, even when it is not obvious.

LEARNING ACTIVITY 10.5

Consistent with Learning Activity 10.3, Amor Artisan Hair Accessories expected to produce 2,500 hairbands in the first quarter of this year. The actual production amounted to 2,400 hairbands. Actual and standard costs for the direct labor associated with hairbands are as follows:

	Unit of Measure	Cost Per Unit of Measure	Total Cost Per Unit of Finished Good
<u>Standard Costs per Hairband</u>			
Direct Labor	0.25 hours	$ 3.00	$ 0.75
<u>Actual Costs per Hairband</u>			
Direct Labor	0.30 hours	$ 2.80	$0.84
Budgeted Hairband Production	2,500 Hairbands		
Actual Hairband Production	2,400 Hairbands		

Use a two-column approach to compute the labor rate variance, the labor efficiency variance, and the total labor variance for Amor Artisan Hair Accessories' hairbands for the first quarter. Indicate whether the variances are favorable or unfavorable.

How Do Companies Assess the Difference Between Budgeted and Actual Results for Production Support Costs for Equipment, Supplies, or Indirect Labor?

Learning Objective 10.6
Compute and explain manufacturing overhead variances.

The **manufacturing overhead variance** is the difference between standard overhead costs and actual overhead costs. As such, it is conceptually similar to the material and labor variances. The manufacturing overhead variance, however, is commonly split into two components: the *variable* overhead variance and the *fixed* overhead variance. The two sides of the overhead equation are affected differently by production volumes and purchases of assets and other resources. As a result, we will look at variable and fixed aspects separately.

Variable Manufacturing Overhead Variance

Much like the direct labor variance, the variable manufacturing overhead variance is usually computed using hours of production time and a variable overhead rate per hour. Hours of production are commonly measured in machine hours or labor hours. For ease of illustration, we use direct labor hours as our overhead cost driver, our basis for computing overhead rates and allocating overhead costs discussed in Chapter 9. The formula for the variable manufacturing overhead variance compares actual to standard and is a function of both direct labor hours, the cost driver, and the variable overhead rate:

$$\left(\begin{array}{c}\textbf{Actual Direct Labor}\\\textbf{Hours}\\\times\\\textbf{Actual Variable Overhead}\\\textbf{Rate}\end{array}\right) - \left(\begin{array}{c}\textbf{Standard Direct Labor}\\\textbf{Hours}\\\times\\\textbf{Standard Variable Overhead}\\\textbf{Rate}\end{array}\right) = \begin{array}{c}\textbf{Total}\\\textbf{Variable Overhead}\\\textbf{Variance}\end{array}$$

How do you interpret the variable overhead variance?

- An unfavorable variable overhead variance suggests that a higher amount was paid for variable overhead items or more direct labor hours were incurred than expected.
- A favorable variance indicates a lower amount was paid for variable overhead items or fewer direct labor hours were incurred than expected.

Let us look at an example. Figure 10.9 displays the standard and actual variable overhead costs when producing a batch of custom wheels at Bob Willis Custom Wheel Company.

Let us illustrate the variable manufacturing overhead variance using the figures from Figure 10.9 in our computations. The actual direct labor hours are a function of the actual number of wheels produced (5,000 wheels) multiplied by the actual number of direct labor hours per wheel (0.8 hours), resulting in 4,000 direct labor hours. We multiply the 4,000 direct

	Direct Labor Hours per Finished Good Unit	Variable Overhead per Direct Labor Hour	Total Cost Per Finished Good Unit
Standard Cost Per Wheel	.75 Hrs	$11.667	$8.75
Actual Cost Per Wheel	.80 Hrs	$11.25	$9.00
Budgeted Wheel Production	4,840 Wheels		
Actual Wheel Production	5,000 Wheels		

Figure 10.9 Standard and actual direct variable overhead costs.

labor hours by the actual variable overhead rate of $11.25, to calculate actual variable overhead costs of $45,000. The standard direct labor hours are a function of the actual number of wheels produced (5,000 wheels) multiplied by the standard number of direct labor hours per wheel (0.75 Hours), resulting in 3,750 direct labor hours. We multiply the 3,750 direct labor hours by the standard variable overhead rate of $11.667 to calculate actual variable overhead costs of $43,750. The difference between $45,000 in actual variable overhead costs and $43,750 of standard variable overhead costs results in a total variable overhead cost variance of $1,250. This is an *unfavorable* variance because the actual overhead costs are greater than the standard (or expected), resulting in a cost overage.

(0.80 Hours × 5,000 Wheels)		**(0.75 ln. ft. × 5,000 Wheels)**		**Total**
×	−	×	=	**Variable Overhead**
$11.25		**$11.667**		**Variance**
$45,000	−	**$43,750**	=	**$1,250 Unfavorable**

Variable Efficiency: Rate and Efficiency Variances

A two-column visualization is a useful way to analyze the variance further and explore the effect of differences in the amounts paid for overhead expenses or the **variable overhead rate variance**, as well as differences in the consumption of the cost driver or the **variable overhead efficiency variance**. The two-column approach combines both the rate and efficiency variance calculations into one illustration. The two-column approach follows; note that you can see the favorable variable overhead rate variance of $1,670 is due to the difference in the actual variable overhead rate of $11.25 per labor hour compared to the standard rate of $11.667. The unfavorable efficiency variance of $2,920 is due to the difference in the actual variable overhead rate of $11.25 per labor hour compared to the standard rate of $11.667. The favorable variable overhead rate variance of $1,670 and the unfavorable variable overhead efficiency variance of $2,920 are combined to make a total variable overhead variance of $1,250, which is unfavorable.

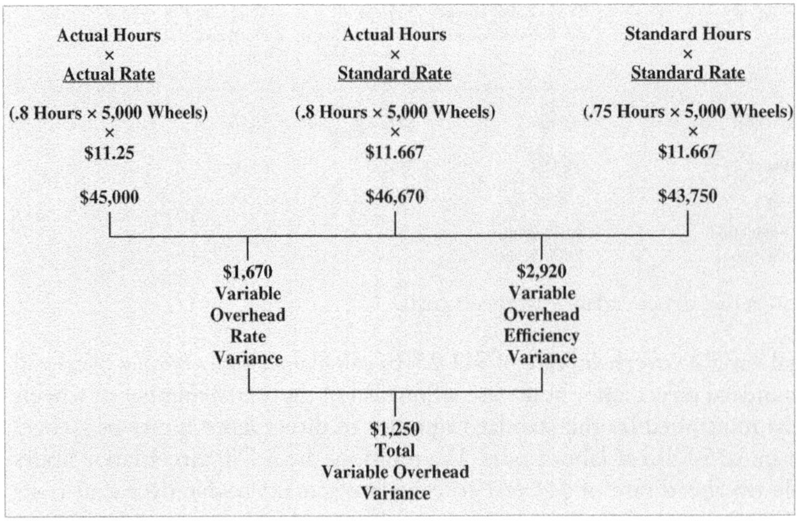

Root Cause Analysis

The root cause of variable overhead variances is due to several sources, including the costs of variable overhead items like supplies, gas, and electricity or efficiencies in production. The variable overhead rate variance is driven by differences between the actual variable overhead rate and the predetermined variable overhead rate developed during the budgeting and planning process (discussed in Chapter 9). The overhead rate is allocated by holding the level of activity, hours in our example, constant. The variable overhead efficiency variance is driven by differences between the actual level of activity and the standard level of activity used to apply variable overhead costs to products or services, in our example labor hours. By holding the variable overhead rate constant and the number of units (wheels) constant in our computations of actual hours and standard hours, we can determine the hours required to produce a single unit. As a result, the variable overhead efficiency variance is a function of differences in the actual number of hours required to produce a unit of the product and the expected or budgeted hours per unit.

Fixed Manufacturing Overhead Variance

The **fixed manufacturing overhead variance** is the difference between actual fixed overhead costs and standard fixed overhead costs. The fixed manufacturing overhead variance is driven by differences between actual and expected spending on fixed overhead items, such as facility rent or the cost of salaried production employees like a production manager. The formula for the fixed manufacturing overhead variance compares actual and standard fixed overhead expenditures is as follows:

$$\begin{array}{c}\textbf{Actual Fixed Overhead}\\\textbf{Expenditures}\end{array} - \begin{array}{c}\textbf{Standard Fixed Overhead}\\\textbf{Expenditures}\end{array} = \begin{array}{c}\textbf{Total}\\\textbf{Fixed Overhead}\\\textbf{Variance}\end{array}$$

LEARNING ACTIVITY 10.6

Actual and standard variable overhead costs, direct labor hours, and production associated with hairbands produced at Amor Artisan Hair Accessories are as follows:

	Direct Labor Hours per Finished Good Unit	Variable Overhead per Direct Labor Hour	Total Cost per Finished Good Unit
Standard Cost per Hairband	0.25 Hrs	$0.28	$0.07
Actual Cost per Hairband	0.30 Hrs	$0.30	$0.09
Budgeted Hairband Production	2,500 Hairbands		
Actual Hairband Production	2,400 Hairbands		

Use a two-column approach to compute the variable overhead rate variance, the variable overhead efficiency variance, and the total variable overhead variance for Amor Artisan Hairbands for the first quarter. Indicate whether the variances are favorable or unfavorable.

Fixed overhead costs are, by definition, unaffected by volume and production volume, but it is still useful to break down the fixed overhead costs in a manner similar to variable overhead. We can break fixed overhead down into the same basic elements that we use to compute variable overhead.

$$\begin{matrix}\textbf{Actual Direct Labor Hours} \\ \times \\ \textbf{Actual Fixed Overhead Rate}\end{matrix} - \begin{matrix}\textbf{Standard Direct Labor Hours} \\ \times \\ \textbf{Standard Fixed Overhead Rate}\end{matrix} = \begin{matrix}\textbf{Total} \\ \textbf{Fixed Overhead} \\ \textbf{Variance}\end{matrix}$$

Figure 10.10 displays the standard and actual variable overhead costs when producing a batch of custom wheels at Bob Willis Custom Wheel Company. We calculate the actual fixed overhead rate of $42 per labor hour by dividing actual fixed overhead costs ($168,000) by the actual labor hours (5,000 wheels × 0.8 hours per wheel = 4,000 hours) incurred during the period. The standard fixed overhead data comes from the budget discussed in Chapter 9.

	Total Fixed Overhead Costs	Direct Labor Hours per Finished Good Unit	Fixed Overhead per Direct Labor Hour	Total Cost Per Finished Good Unit
Standard Cost Per Wheel	$161,138	.75 Hrs	$42.97	$32.23
Actual Cost Per Wheel	$168,000	.80 Hrs	$42.00	$35.20
Budgeted Wheel Production		4,840 Wheels		
Actual Wheel Production		5,000 Wheels		

Figure 10.10 Standard and actual fixed overhead costs.

Let us illustrate the fixed manufacturing overhead variance using the figures from Figure 10.10 in our computations. The actual direct labor hours are a function of the actual number of wheels produced (5,000 wheels) multiplied by the actual number of direct labor hours per wheel (.8 Hours), resulting in 4,000 direct labor hours. That value is multiplied by the actual fixed overhead rate of $42.00, resulting in actual fixed overhead costs of $168,000. The standard direct labor hours are a function of the actual number of wheels produced (5,000 wheels) multiplied by the standard number of direct labor hours per wheel (0.75 hours), resulting in 3,750 direct labor hours. That value is multiplied by the standard variable overhead rate of $42.97, resulting in standard fixed overhead costs of $161,138. The difference between $168,000 in actual fixed overhead costs and $161,138 of standard fixed overhead costs results in a total fixed overhead cost variance of $6,862. This is an *unfavorable* variance because the actual fixed overhead costs are greater than the standard (or expected), resulting in a cost overage.

(0.80 Hours × 5,000 Wheels) × **\$42.00**	−	**(0.75 In. ft.× 5,000 Wheels)** × **\$42.97**	=	**Total Fixed Overhead Variance**
\$168,000	−	**\$161,138**	=	**\$6,862 Unfavorable**

A *three-column* visualization is a useful way to analyze the fixed overhead variance in order to evaluate the effect of differences in the amounts paid for fixed overhead expenses or the **fixed overhead spending variance**, differences in budget expectations related to production and efficiency, and actual results called the **fixed overhead efficiency variance**, and differences in budgeted and standard values that are driven by unit production volume, which we call the **fixed overhead volume variance**.

The favorable fixed overhead rate variance of $3,880 is due to the actual fixed overhead rate of $42.00 per labor hour being lower than the standard rate of $42.97. An unfavorable fixed overhead budget variance of $15,899 is due to differences in actual production volume, 5,000 units, and hours per unit of production, 0.8 hours, and the budgeted values of 4,840 units and 0.75 hours, respectively. The favorable fixed overhead volume variance of $5,157 is due to the difference between 5,000 units produced and 4,840 budgeted units of production. Greater usage of fixed costs, such as investments in buildings or equipment, are viewed favorably from a standard costing perspective. The fixed overhead spending and budget variances constitute a

controllable variance because factors such as spending rates and hours per unit of production are generally controlled by the production department. The fixed overhead volume variance is considered an **uncontrollable variance** because differences between budgeted production and standard production volume may be driven by other factors unrelated to production management, such as sales volume. The fixed overhead volume variance is commonly attributed to the sales department.

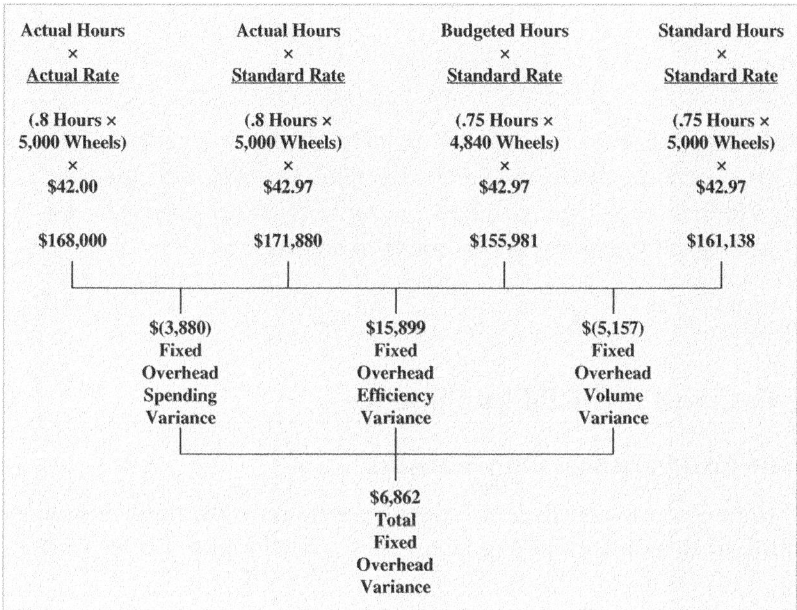

LEARNING ACTIVITY 10.7

Actual and standard fixed overhead costs, direct labor hours, and production associated with hairbands produced at Amor Artisan Hair Accessories are as follows:

	Total Fixed Overhead Costs	Direct Labor Hours per Finished Good Unit	Fixed Overhead per Direct Labor Hour	Total Cost Per Finished Good Unit
Standard Cost per Hairband	$2,325	0.25 Hrs	$3.875	$0.97 (rounded)

LEARNING ACTIVITY 10.7

Actual Cost per Hairband	$2,880	0.30 Hrs	$4.00	$1.20
Budgeted Hairband Production		2,500 Hairbands		
Actual Hairband Production		2,400 Hairbands		

Use a three-column approach to compute the fixed overhead rate variance, the fixed overhead efficiency variance, the fixed overhead volume variance, and the total fixed overhead variance for hairbands produced by Amor Artisan Hair Accessories for the first quarter. Indicate whether the variances are favorable or unfavorable.

Technology, Analytics, and Artificial Intelligence

Using Excel to Examine Cost Variances with Statistics

In this section, we will explore how to use Excel to apply a common data analysis technique to investigate cost control, in this case, employee labor rates and efficiency. Let us look at two examples.

Example 1: Comparing Labor Rates

In our first example, consider the hourly wages of employees at Nutrino Pet Products, a leading pet food producer. Nutrino Pet Products is evaluating whether the average hourly wage of its production employees has changed year-over-year. The company's leadership desires to reduce overall wage rates while remaining competitive and attracting top talent, yet not paying more than necessary to maximize corporate profits. To reduce wage rates, Nutrino implemented an early retirement incentive payment to encourage longer-term and more highly paid hourly employees to retire so the company can replace them with a lower-paid workforce and effectively reduce hourly labor costs. There are modest differences in the labor rates between the current and prior years' workforces, but Nutrino's management would like to know if that is due to normal turnover, or if the incentive plan is having its desired effects on labor rates. Data analytic techniques that apply statistics can help management be certain about the impact.

You may recall from your elementary statistics classes that you can use a t-test to assess the difference between two sample means. A **t-test** is a statistical method used to compare the means of two groups to determine if there is a statistically significant difference between the two samples or if the difference is likely due to random chance. The t-tests result in a **t-statistic,** which measures the size of the difference between the two samples relative to the variability within the

MART PRODUCTION / Pexels / Public Domain

two samples. A resultant **p-value** measures the probability that no actual difference exists. If the p-value is less than 0.05, the common benchmark for statistical significance, there is a less than 5% probability that the difference between the two means is due to chance. If the p-value is greater than 0.05, the difference between the two samples is likely to be due to random change.

To perform a t-test in Microsoft Excel, you must first click on the Data tab. Underneath the Data tab, you will find an option on the far right to perform Data Analysis. Click it. Figure 10.11 illustrates how to access the data analysis function in Microsoft Excel. If Data Analysis is not an option underneath your Data tab, you must turn on the Analysis ToolPak by clicking *File*, then *Options*, then *Add-Ins*, then *Go* (next to Manage Excel Add-Ins), then click the *Check Box* next to Analysis ToolPak, then click *OK*.

After selecting Data Analysis under the Data tab, you will have options to perform a number of statistical analyses. Scroll down until you find t-test, two-sample assuming equal variances. Highlight it and click *OK*. Figure 10.12 illustrates.

Then highlight the prior year Nutrino_Production_Employee_Wages (Prior Year) column in the Nutrino Wage Data Excel file, including the header ($B$1:$B$91), into the Variable 1 Range. Highlight the Nutrino_Production_Employee_Wages (Current Year) column into the Variable 2 Range, including the header ($A$1:$A$101). Enter "0" in the Hypothesized

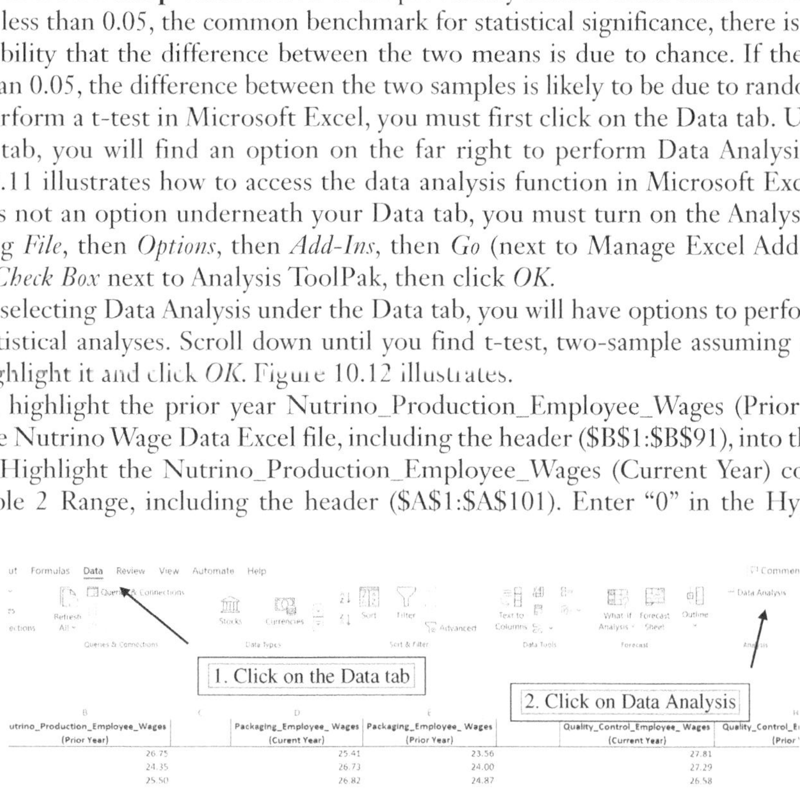

Figure 10.11 Data analysis function in Microsoft Excel.

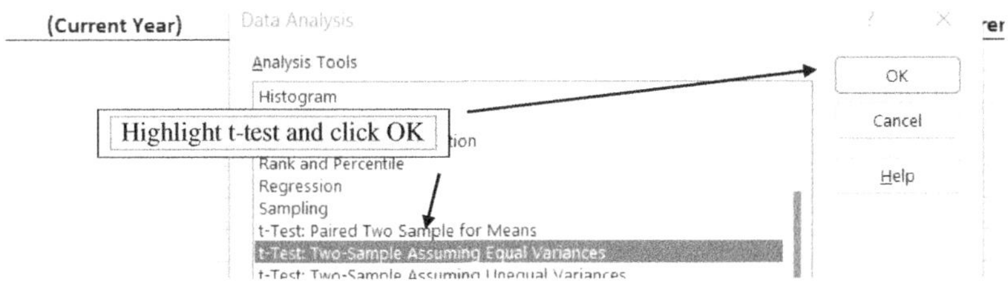

Figure 10.12 Statistical functions under the Data Analysis tool option.

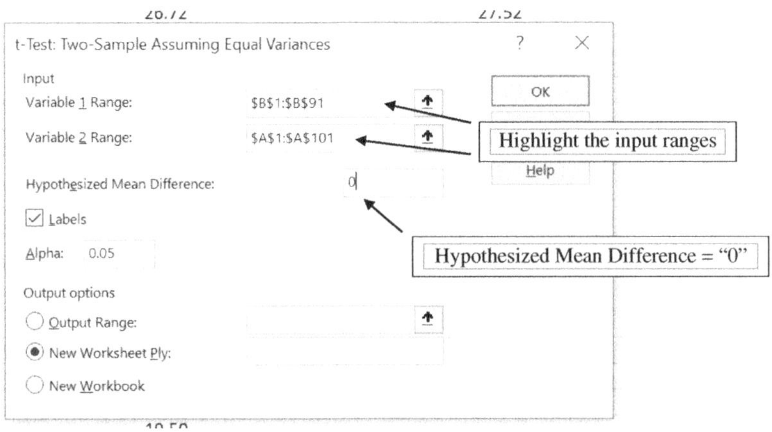

Figure 10.13 t-Test two-sample assuming equal variances input screen.

Mean Difference. Check the Labels Box since you highlighted the column labels. Leave the Alpha value at 0.05. Select the New Worksheet Ply: Output option. See Figure 10.13.

The output for the t-test computes the mean and variances for the two samples, the t-statistic, along with the critical values and p-values for both a one-tailed and two-tailed test. The difference between a one-tailed and two-tailed test is that the one-tailed test assumes a directional difference, either a positive or negative difference in wages between our two samples in this example. The two-tailed result tests for a difference, regardless of the sign. In this case, since we are concerned to find out if the wages have decreased from the prior year to the current year, we can look at the one-tailed test results.

The key output in Figure 10.14 illustrates a t-statistic of 3.839, a t-critical value for the 0.05 confidence level for a one-tailed test of 1.652, and a p-value of 0.0000084. To interpret the results, compare the t-statistic and the t-critical value. Since the t-statistic is larger than the critical value, we reject a hypothesis that the differences or variances between the two samples are equal, statistically speaking. But, to ease in interpreting the results, we might say we have found that the difference between the two samples is statistically significant, and the current year's wages are lower. The p-value indicates a 0.0000084 probability that the difference is due to random chance.

t-Test: Two-Sample Assuming Equal Variances

	Nutrino_Production_ Employee_Wages (Prior Year)	Nutrino_Production_ Employee_Wages (Current Year)
Mean	24.84811111	23.8088
Variance	2.223269426	4.592386424
Observations	90	100
Pooled Variance	3.470836356	
Hypothesized Mean Difference	0	
df	188	
t Stat	3.839484826	
P(T<=t) one-tail	8.41853E-05	
t Critical one-tail	1.652999113	
P(T<=t) two-tail	0.000168371	
t Critical two-tail	1.972662692	

Key Output

Figure 10.14 t-Test two-sample assuming equal variances output.

	A	B	C	D
1	Batch Number	Hours	Standard Hours	
2	1	2.784507123	2.65	
3	2	2.689260355	2.65	
4	3	2.807153281	2.65	
5	4	2.938454478	2.65	
6	5	2.674876994	2.65	
7	6	2.674879456	2.65	
8	7	2.213444	2.65	
9	8	2.825115209	2.65	
10	9	2.639578842	2.65	

Figure 10.15 Nutrino hours data.

Example 2: Comparing Labor Efficiency with Standard

As Nutrino's experienced employees retire and are replaced by a less experienced labor force, management is concerned if the change has resulted in a significantly different level of productivity and, as a result, inefficiency. Let's look at the data. Currently, the standard labor time to produce a batch of dog food is 2.65 hours per batch. Since the implementation of the early retirement incentive package, Nutrino has produced 893 batches of dog food with an average labor time of 2.71 hours per batch. There is an overall difference, but is that difference significant and can Nutrino's management conclude productivity was influenced by employee turnover? We can use another t-test to analyze the data. Start by opening the Nutrino Hours Data Excel file to access the data for each batch, including the labor hours and the standard labor hours, as shown in Figure 10.15.

Perform the t-test using the t-Test Paired Two Sample for Means in Excel (Figure 10.16). This option is used for data that is paired and has the same sample size. Since we are matching our batch observations with the expected standard hours for each batch, we can use this test, as

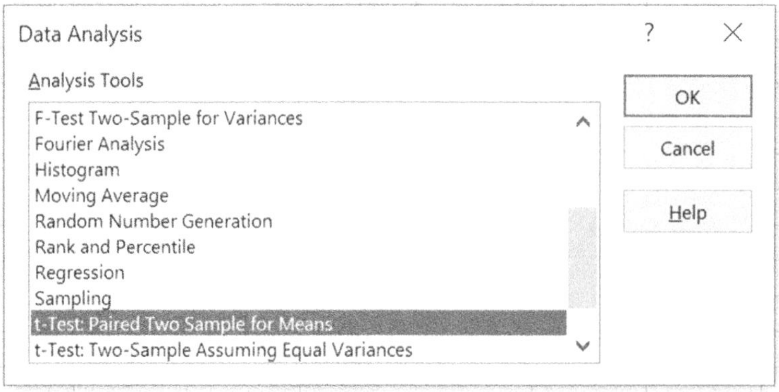

Figure 10.16 Statistical function selection.

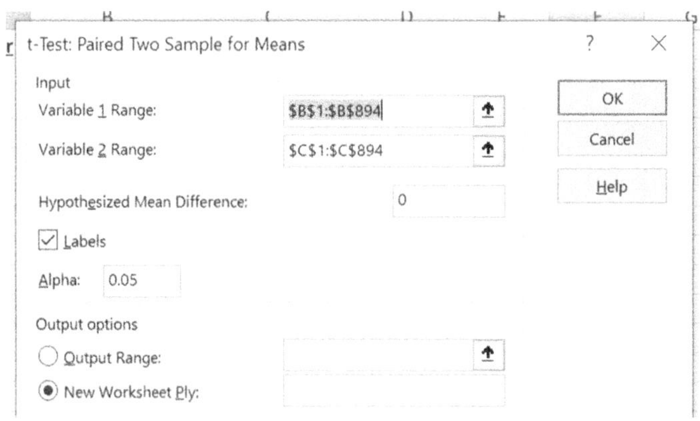

Figure 10.17 t-Test inputs.

opposed to the t-test two-sample assuming equal variances used previously, which accounts for unequal sample sizes.

The inputs are similar between the two t-test options. This example highlights the batch hours ($B$2:$B$894) and the standard for each batch ($C$2:$C$894), as shown in Figure 10.17.

The key output in Figure 10.18 illustrates a t-statistic of 12.079, a t-critical value for the 0.05 confidence level for a one-tailed test of 1.646, and a p-value of 1.6E–31 suggesting the labor hours have increased and the company is less efficient.

Insights into Nutrino

For Nutrino, applying a t-test to analyze the data helps management confirm that it is being successful in lowering overall average wages through the use of the retirement incentive for existing employees. Higher-paid employees are accepting the retirement package and are being replaced by lower-wage workers. However, the implementation of the program has resulted in hiring new employees who are less efficient, and overall labor hours per batch of dog food have increased. Our statistical analysis makes us confident in those two conclusions. The overall change in labor rates fell from \$24.85 to \$23.81, while hours per batch increased to 2.71 from a standard of 2.65. Over 893 batches resulted in labor costs of \$57,620. Expected labor costs for the 893 batches would be \$58,806 (\$24.85 per hour × 2.65 hours per batch over 893 batches). Nutrino's program is reducing overall costs modestly, but much of the labor rate savings are being offset by reduced efficiency.

t-Test: Paired Two Sample for Means

	Hours	*Standard Hours*
Mean	2.710028061	2.65
Variance	0.022053632	2.01405E-27
Observations	893	893
Pearson Correlation	5.35883E-15	
Hypothesized Mean Difference	0	
df	892	
t Stat	12.07925025	Key Output
P(T<=t) one-tail	1.60157E-31	
t Critical one-tail	1.646563675	
P(T<=t) two-tail	3.20313E-31	
t Critical two-tail	1.962627032	

Figure 10.18 t-Test paired two sample for means.

LEARNING ACTIVITY 10.8

Actual and standard fixed overhead costs, direct labor hours, and production associated with hairbands produced at Amor Artisan Hair Accessories are as follows:

	Direct Labor Hours per Finished Good Unit
Standard Hours per Hairband	0.295 Hrs
Actual Hours per Hairband	0.30 Hrs
Budgeted Hairband Production	2,500 Hairbands
Actual Hairband Production	2,400 Hairbands

LEARNING ACTIVITY 10.8

Amor purchased raw material from a new supplier that helped control raw material costs, but the labor hours per hair band seem to have increased relative to expectations. Use the Amor Labor Hours Excel file and a Paired t-Test in the Excel Data Analysis ToolPak to test if the labor hours per hairband have indeed increased above the standard. Run the analysis using data in the population tab, and rerun the analysis using the data in the sample_of_10 tab. What are your conclusions?

Key Terms

cost variance The difference between actual results and budgeted or planned results.
favorable variance The actual results from a business activity end in a higher profit than budgeted results.
unfavorable variance The actual results from a business activity end in a lower profit than budgeted results.
variance analysis The process in which managers examine variances and identify the root cause.
static budget A budget that is prepared using a single level of business activity.
flexible budget A budget that is adjusted to the actual level of business activity.
standard cost The expected cost of a single unit of a product or service.
variance analysis The process of comparing actual costs and standard costs and the reasons for any difference.
standard direct material cost The material price per unit of material multiplied by the standard quantity of direct material per finished goods produced.
standard direct labor cost The standard labor rate per hour multiplied by the standard number of labor hours per finished good unit produced.
standard fixed overhead costs Costs, other than direct material and direct labor, which are related to production, but do not change with production quantities.
standard variable overhead costs Cost, other than direct material and direct labor, which are related to production and vary directly with production quantities.
direct materials variance The difference between standard material costs and actual material costs.
direct material price variance The portion of the direct materials variance that is attributable to the difference between the standard price per unit of direct material and the dollar amount actually paid for a unit of direct material.
direct material quantity variance The portion of the direct materials variance that is attributable to the difference between the actual and expected amount of direct materials used in production.
root cause The underlying reason for the occurrence of a variance.
direct labor variance The difference between standard labor costs and actual labor costs.

direct labor rate variance The portion of the direct labor variance that is attributable to the difference between the standard direct labor rate and the actual amount paid for time worked.
direct labor efficiency variance The portion of the direct labor variance that is attributable to the difference between the actual and expected amount of direct labor hours worked in the production process.
manufacturing overhead variance The difference between standard overhead costs and actual overhead costs.
variable manufacturing overhead variance The difference between standard variable overhead costs and actual variable overhead costs.
standard fixed overhead costs Costs, other than direct material and direct labor, which are related to production but do not change with production quantities.
standard variable overhead costs Variable overhead costs, other than direct material and direct labor, which vary directly with production quantities.
variable overhead rate variance The difference between actual and standard variable overhead attributable to difference in the actual of standard variable overhead rate.
variable overhead efficiency variance The difference between actual and standard variable overhead attributable to difference in the actual of standard hours per unit produced.
fixed manufacturing overhead variance The difference between actual fixed overhead costs and standard fixed overhead costs applied to the cost of products.
fixed overhead spending variance The difference in the amount spent on actual fixed overhead costs and standard fixed overhead costs.
fixed overhead efficiency variance The difference in fixed overhead costs that is attributable to differences in actual production volume and budgeted production volume.
fixed overhead volume variance The difference in fixed overhead costs attributable to differences in budgeted production volume and standard production volume.
controllable variance The sum of the fixed overhead spending variance and the fixed overhead efficiency variance that are assumed to be under the control of production management.
uncontrollable variance The fixed overhead volume variance attributable to the difference between budgeted production volume and standard production volume that may be influenced by factors not controlled by production management such as sales volume.
t-test A statistical method used to compare the means of two groups to determine if there is a statistically significant difference between the two samples or if the difference is likely due to random chance.
t-statistic Measures the size of the difference between the two samples relative to the variability within the two samples.
p-value Measures the probability that no actual difference exists.

LEARNING ACTIVITY SOLUTIONS

Learning Activity 10.1

D, A, F, C, B, E

Learning Activity 10.2

1. *B. Favorable Labor Variance*
2. *A. Unfavorable Price Variance*
3. *D. Favorable Quantity Variance*
4. *E. Unfavorable Labor Variance*
5. *F. Favorable Price Variance*

Learning Activity 10.3

Amor Artisan Hair Accessories
Manufacturing Overhead Budget
Quarter Ending December 20XX

	January	February	March	Quarter
Fixed Costs				
Storage Rent	350	350	350	1,050
Production manager salary	400	400	400	1,200
Depreciation	25	25	25	75
Total Fixed Costs	775	775	775	2,325
Variable Costs				
Indirect material	125	100	100	325
Inspection	50	40	40	130
Total Variable Costs	175	140	140	455
Total Overhead Costs	$ 950	$ 915	$ 915	$ 2,780

Learning Activity 10.4

Actual Quantity × Actual Price	Actual Quantity × Standard Price	Standard Quantity × Standard Price
(4.25 ln. ft. × 2,400 hairbands) × \$.20	(4.25 ln. ft. × 2,400 hairbands) × \$.25	(4.00 ln. ft. × 2,400 Hairbands) × \$.25
\$2,040	\$2,550	\$2,400

\$510
Direct Material Price Variance (Favorable)

(\$150)
Direct Material Quantity Variance (Unfavorable)

\$360
Total Direct Material Variance (Favorable)

Learning Activity 10.5

Actual Hours × Actual Rate	Actual Hours × Standard Rate	Standard Hours × Standard Rate
(.30 hours × 2,400 hairbands) × \$2.80	(.30 hours × 2,400 hairbands) × \$3.00	(.25 hours × 2,400 Hairbands) × \$3.00
\$2,016	\$2,160	\$1,800

\$144
Direct Labor Rate Variance (Favorable)

(\$360)
Direct Labor Efficiency Variance (Unfavorable)

\$216
Total Direct Labor Variance (Unfavorable)

Learning Activity 10.6

Actual Hours × <u>Actual Rate</u>	Actual Hours × <u>Standard Rate</u>	Standard Hours × <u>Standard Rate</u>
(.3 Hours × 2,400 Hairbands) × $.30	(.3 Hours × 2,400 Hairbands) × $.28	(.25 Hours × 2,400 Hairbands) × $.28
$216.00	$201.60	$168.00

$(14.40)
Variable
Overhead
Rate
Variance
(Unfavorable)

$33.60
Variable
Overhead
Efficiency
Variance
(Unfavorable)

$48.00
Total
Variable Overhead
Variance
(Unfavorable)

Learning Activity 10.7

Actual Hours × <u>Actual Rate</u>	Actual Hours × <u>Standard Rate</u>	Budgeted Hours × <u>Standard Rate</u>	Standard Hours × <u>Standard Rate</u>
(.30 Hours × 2,400 Hairbands) × $4.00	(.30 Hours × 2,400 Hairbands) × $3.875	(.25 Hours × 2,500 Hairbands) × $3.875	(.25 Hours × 2,400 Wheels) × $3.875
$2,880	$2,790	$2,422 (Rounded)	$2,325

$(90)
Fixed
Overhead
Spending
Variance
(Unfavorable)

$(368)
Fixed
Overhead
Efficiency
Variance
(Unfavorable)

$(97)
Fixed
Overhead
Volume
Variance
(Unfavorable)

$(555)
Total
fixed
Overhead
Variance
(Unfavorable)

Learning Activity 10.8

Population Result

t-Test: Paired Two Sample for Means

	Hours	Standard Hours
Mean	0.308875014	0.295
Variance	0.018017969	5.7019E−29
Observations	2400	2400
Pearson Correlation	−1.4992E−14	
Hypothesized Mean Difference	0	
df	2399	
t Stat	5.063911649	
P(T<=t) one-tail	2.20984E−07	
t Critical one-tail	1.645489042	
P(T<=t) two-tail	4.41969E−07	
t Critical two-tail	1.960953334	

Sample of 10 Result

t-Test: Paired Two Sample for Means

	Hours	Standard Hours
Mean	0.367209167	0.295
Variance	0.011761674	0
Observations	10	10
Pearson Correlation	#DIV/0!	
Hypothesized Mean Difference	0	
df	9	
t Stat	2.105512245	
P(T<=t) one-tail	0.032269144	
t Critical one-tail	1.833112933	
P(T<=t) two-tail	0.064538287	
t Critical two-tail	2.262157163	

Review Questions

1. What are differences between the actual costs a business incurs compared to budgeted costs called? **(Learning Objective 1)**
   a. Cost variances
   b. Budgetary slack
2. Cost variances are usually because of two factors which are **(Learning Objective 1)**
   a. price and quantity.
   b. cost and quality.
3. The use of inferior raw material could cause a labor variance. **(Learning Objective 1)**
   a. True
   b. False
4. Comparing a static budget with actual results is a useful way to evaluate variable cost variances. **(Learning Objective 2)**
   a. True
   b. False
5. Which of the following is most useful for comparing budget and actual results? **(Learning Objective 2)**
   a. Static budget
   b. Flexible budget
6. What is the difference between a static budget and a flexible budget? **(Learning Objective 2)**
   a. The static budget adjusts sales data while keeping cost data constant.
   b. The flexible budget adjusts the budget based on the actual activity level.
7. What is the expected cost for a single unit of a product or service is called? **(Learning Objective 3)**
   a. The standard cost
   b. The stated unit cost
8. The standard quantity is calculated by multiplying the **(Learning Objective 3)**
   a. Standard quantity per unit × Actual unit volume.
   b. Standard quantity per unit × Budgeted unit volume.
9. The standard quantity for direct materials should include estimates for scrap or waste. **(Learning Objective 3)**
   a. True
   b. False
10. A cost driver for overhead should have a cause-and-effect relationship with variable overhead costs. **(Learning Objective 3)**
    a. True
    b. False
11. When computing the direct material price variance, which element of total direct material cost would be held constant in the calculation? **(Learning Objective 4)**
    a. Price
    b. Quantity

12. The direct material quantity variance is driven by the difference between the actual and expected amount of materials used in production. **(Learning Objective 4)**
    a. True
    b. False
13. A favorable material variance is always a result of using less material than expected. **(Learning Objective 5)**
    a. True
    b. False
14. An unfavorable labor variance can be caused by using more hours producing a product or performing a service than expected or higher labor rates than expected. **(Learning Objective 5)**
    a. True
    b. False
15. What would a favorable labor efficiency variance mean? **(Learning Objective 5)**
    a. Fewer hours were used than expected.
    b. More hours were used than expected.
16. The fixed overhead variance is unaffected by changes in production volume. **(Learning Objective 6)**
    a. True
    b. False

Review Questions

S:10-1 (Learning Objective 1)

Which of the following is not normally a cause of cost variances?

a. Operational efficiency
b. Price negotiations
c. Taxes
d. All of these can cause variances.

S:10-2 (Learning Objective 2)

Which of the following is not a limitation of using a static budget?

a. It is based on assumptions.
b. It does not change in response to changes in activity.
c. It offers a snapshot in time.
d. All of these are limitations.

S:10-3 (Learning Objective 2)

Which of the following statements about a flexible budget is not true?

a. It allows comparison of budget and actual results.
b. It adjusts the budget to the actual level of business activity.
c. It adjusts the actual results to the budgeted activity level.
d. All of these are true.

S:10-4 (Learning Objective 3)

Which of the following is not a benefit of standard costing?

a. Standard costing ensures accuracy of costs across products.
b. Standard costing facilitates variance analysis.
c. Standard costing facilitates employee awareness of costs.
d. Standard costing simplifies accounting and inventory costing.

S:10-5 (Learning Objective 4)

The Richardson Company expects to pay production employees \$25 per hour and expects them to take 4.5 hours per unit to produce 900 units of their product, based on Richardson's annual budget. During the first quarter, Richardson paid production employees \$24 per hour, and it took approximately 5 hours per unit while producing 1,000 units of their product. What is Richardson's standard cost for the product?

a. \$101,250
b. \$112,500 (4.5 hours × 1,000 units) × \$25.00
c. \$120,000
d. \$125,000

S:10-6 (Learning Objective 5)

Anton's Injection Molding Company is evaluating the variances for plastic wheelbarrow buckets it makes for a large garden equipment company. The actual direct material quantity used in the current month includes 2.4 pounds of plastic for 6,200 buckets. The plastic cost \$2.25 per pound. Anton budgeted to use 2.5 pounds of plastic at a price of \$2.20, and to build 6,500 buckets. What was Anton's material price variance?

a. \$524 Favorable
b. \$744 Unfavorable
c. \$1,000 Unfavorable
d. \$1,346 Favorable

S:10-7 (Learning Objective 5)

Anton's Injection Molding Company is evaluating the variances for plastic wheelbarrow buckets it makes for a large garden equipment company. The actual direct material quantity used in the current month includes 2.4 pounds of plastic for 6,200 buckets. The plastic cost $2.25 per pound. Anton budgeted to use 2.5 pounds of plastic at a price of $2.20, and to build 6,500 buckets. What was Anton's material quantity variance?

a. $524 Favorable
b. $744 Unfavorable
c. $1,000 Unfavorable
d. $1,364 Favorable

S:10-8 (Learning Objective 5)

Anton's Injection Molding Company is evaluating the labor variances for plastic wheelbarrow buckets it makes for a large garden equipment company. The actual labor incurred in the previous month producing the buckets was 0.3 hours per bucket for 6,200 buckets. The average labor rate was $28 per hour. Anton budgeted 0.25 hours per bucket at a labor rate of $30 per hour to build 6,500 buckets. What was Anton's direct labor rate variance?

a. $2,500 Favorable
b. $2,620 Unfavorable
c. $3,720 Favorable
d. $5,400 Unfavorable

S:10-9 (Learning Objective 5)

Anton's Injection Molding Company is evaluating the labor variances for plastic wheelbarrow buckets it makes for a large garden equipment company. The actual labor incurred in the previous month producing the buckets was 0.3 hours per bucket for 6,200 buckets. The average labor rate was $28 per hour. Anton budgeted 0.25 hours per bucket at a labor rate of $30 per hour to build 6,500 buckets. What was Anton's direct labor efficiency variance?

a. $4,800 Favorable
b. $5,400 Favorable
c. $7,750 Unfavorable
d. $9,300 Unfavorable

S:10-10 (Learning Objective 6)

Anton's Injection Molding Company is evaluating the overhead variances for plastic wheelbarrow buckets it makes for a large garden equipment company. Anton's allocates overhead using direct labor hours as the cost driver. The actual labor incurred in the previous month producing the buckets was 0.3 hours per bucket for 6,200 buckets. The actual variable overhead rate was \$26 per hour. Anton budgeted 0.25 hours per bucket and an overhead rate of \$25 per hour and expected to build 6,500 buckets. What was Anton's total variable overhead variance?

a. \$2,840 Favorable
b. \$5,660 Favorable
c. \$7,750 Unfavorable
d. \$9,610 Unfavorable

S:10-11 (Learning Objective 6)

Anton's Injection Molding Company is evaluating the overhead variances for plastic wheelbarrow buckets it makes for a large garden equipment company. Anton's allocates overhead using direct labor hours as the cost driver. The actual labor incurred in the previous month producing the buckets was 0.3 hours per bucket for 6,200 buckets. The actual variable overhead rate was \$26 per hour. Anton budgeted 0.25 hours per bucket and an overhead rate of \$25 per hour and expected to build 6,500 buckets. What was Anton's variable overhead rate variance?

a. \$1,860 Unfavorable
b. \$2,400 Unfavorable
c. \$3,660 Favorable
d. \$5,410 Unfavorable

S:10-12 (Learning Objective 6)

Anton's Injection Molding Company is evaluating the overhead variances for plastic wheelbarrow buckets it makes for a large garden equipment company. Anton's allocates overhead using direct labor hours as the cost driver. The actual labor incurred in the previous month producing the buckets was 0.3 hours per bucket for 6,200 buckets. The actual variable overhead rate was \$26 per hour. Anton budgeted 0.25 hours per bucket and an overhead rate of \$25 per hour and expected to build 6,500 buckets. What was Anton's variable overhead efficiency variance?

a. \$2,840 Favorable
b. \$5,660 Favorable
c. \$7,750 Unfavorable
d. \$9,610 Unfavorable

S:10-13 (Learning Objective 6)

Anton's Injection Molding Company is evaluating the overhead variances for plastic wheelbarrow buckets it makes for a large garden equipment company. Anton's allocates overhead using direct labor hours as the cost driver. The actual labor incurred in the previous month producing the buckets was 0.3 hours per bucket for 6,200 buckets. Fixed overhead costs amounted to

$65,100. Anton budgeted 0.25 hours per bucket, expected to build 6,500 buckets, and to spend $58,500 on fixed overhead. What was Anton's fixed overhead variance?

a. $3,300 Favorable
b. $6,290 Favorable
c. $7,840 Unfavorable
d. $9,300 Unfavorable

Exercises

E:10-14 (Learning Objective 1)

The Central Rivers Manufacturing Company had the following cost and budget data for the previous year.

Requirement

Mark if the variance associated with each set of data is most likely favorable or unfavorable by placing a F next to the favorable variances and U next to the unfavorable variances.

Account	Actual	Budget	(F)avorable or (U)nfavorable Variance
Sales	$2,400,000	$2,200,000	
Cost of Goods Sold	$1,200,000	$1,000,000	
Fixed Operating Expenses	$ 500,000	$ 520,000	
Variable Labor	$ 480,000	$ 520,000	

E:10-15 (Learning Objective 2)

The Spicholli Past Company had the following cost and budget data related to production of boxed dry spaghetti for the previous year.

Account	Actual	Budget
Boxes Produced	5,000,000	4,800,000
Sales	$2,600,000	$2,400,000
Variable Cost of Goods Sold	$1,200,000	$1,200,000
Fixed Operating Expenses	$ 600,000	$ 660,000

Requirement

Complete Spicholli's flexible budget column, compute and enter the variance between each flexible budget and actual columns, and mark if the variance associated with each set of data is favorable or unfavorable by placing a F next to the favorable variances and U next to the unfavorable variances.

Account	Actual	Flexible Budget	(F)avorable or (U)nfavorable Variance
Boxes Produced	5,000,000		
Sales	$2,600,000		
Variable Cost of Goods Sold	$1,200,000		
Fixed Operating Expenses	$ 600,000		

E:10-16 (Learning Objective 4)

Enzo Italian Footwear produces high-end ladies' sandals. Estimated Cost data for Enzo's Naples model sandals are listed here.

	Unit of Measure	Cost per Unit of Measure	Total Cost per Pair
Direct Material	2.0 sq. ft.	$ 12.00	$24.00
Direct Labor	1.20 hrs.	$ 15.00	$18.00
Variable Overhead	1.20 hrs.	$ 10.00	$12.00
Total Variable Costs per Pair			$54.00
Budgeted Direct Fixed Overhead		$60,000	
Budgeted Sandal Production		÷ 4,000 pairs	
Total Fixed Overhead per Pair			$15.00
Budgeted Costs per Pair			$69.00

Requirement

Assuming Enzo produced 4,500 pairs of sandals, compute the total standard direct material, direct labor, variable overhead, and fixed overhead costs by completing the following table:

Total Standard Direct Material Cost	
Total Standard Direct Labor Cost	
Total Standard Variable Overhead Cost	
Total Standard Fixed Overhead Cost	
Total Standard Costs	

E:10-17 (Learning Objective 5)

Enzo Italian Footwear produces high-end ladies' sandals. Estimated cost data for Enzo's Naples model sandals are listed here.

	Unit of Measure	Cost per Unit of Measure	Total Cost per Pair
Direct Material	2.0 sq. ft.	$ 12.00	$24.00
Direct Labor	1.20 hrs.	$ 15.00	$18.00
Variable Overhead	1.20 hrs.	$ 10.00	$12.00
Total Variable Costs per Pair			$54.00
Budgeted Direct Fixed Overhead		$60,000	
Budgeted Sandal Production		÷ 4,000 pairs	
Total Fixed Overhead per Pair			$15.00
Budgeted Costs per Pair			$69.00

Actual Cost data for Enzo's Naples model sandal are listed here.

	Unit of Measure	Cost per Unit of Measure	Total Cost per Pair
Direct Material	2.2 sq. ft.	$ 12.50	$27.50
Direct Labor	1.0 hrs.	$ 16.50	$16.50
Variable Overhead	1.0 hrs.	$ 11.00	$11.00
Total Variable Costs per Pair			$55.00
Actual Direct Fixed Overhead		$65,250	
Actual Sandal Production		÷ 4,500 pairs	
Total Fixed Overhead per Pair			$14.50
Actual Costs per Pair			$69.50

Requirement

Assuming Enzo produced 4,500 pairs of sandals, complete the following table and compute the total direct material and direct labor variances for Enzo and indicate if the variances are (F) avorable or (U)nfavorable:

Total Direct Material Variance	
Total Direct Material Price Variance	
Total Direct Material Quantity Variance	

Total Direct Labor Variance	
Total Direct Labor Rate Variance	
Total Direct Labor Efficiency Variance	

E:10-18 (Learning Objective 6)

Enzo Italian Footwear produces high-end ladies' sandals. Estimated cost data for Enzo's Naples model sandals are listed here.

	Unit of Measure	Cost per Unit of Measure	Total Cost per Pair
Direct Material	2.0 sq. ft.	$ 12.00	$24.00
Direct Labor	1.20 hrs.	$ 15.00	$18.00
Variable Overhead	1.20 hrs.	$ 10.00	$12.00
Total Variable Costs per Pair			$54.00
Budgeted Direct Fixed Overhead		$60,000	
Budgeted Sandal Production		÷ 4,000 pairs	
Total Fixed Overhead per Pair			$15.00
Budgeted Costs per Pair			$69.00

Actual Cost data for Enzo's Naples model sandal are listed here.

	Unit of Measure	Cost per Unit of Measure	Total Cost per Pair
Direct Material	2.2 sq. ft.	$ 12.50	$27.50
Direct Labor	1.0 hrs.	$ 16.50	$16.50
Variable Overhead	1.0 hrs.	$ 11.00	$11.00
Total Variable Costs per Pair			$55.00
Actual Direct Fixed Overhead		$65,250	
Actual Sandal Production		÷ 4,500 pairs	
Total Fixed Overhead per Pair			$14.50
Actual Costs per Pair			$69.50

Requirement

Assuming Enzo produced 4,500 pairs of sandals, complete the following table and compute the total manufacturing overhead variances for Enzo and indicate if the variances are (F)avorable or (U)nfavorable:

Total Variable Overhead Rate Variance	
Total Variable Overhead Efficiency Variance	
Total Variable Overhead Variance	

Total Fixed Overhead Spending Variance	
Total Fixed Overhead Efficiency Variance	
Total Fixed Overhead Volume Variance	
Total Fixed Overhead Variance	

Problems

P:10-19 (Learning Objective 2)

Panther Enterprises prepared the following budget cost analysis for the current year. The report compares current activity to the annual budget.

	Budget	**Actual**	**Variance**
Units Produced	(90,000 units)	(89,000 units)	
Variable Costs:			
Cleaning supplies	$ 72,000	$ 71,500	$ 500 (F)
Electricity	27,000	26,750	250 (F)
Maintenance	18,000	16,900	1,100 (F)
Fixed Costs:			
Supervisor salaries	90,000	89,500	500 (F)
Depreciation	60,000	61,500	1,500 (U)
Rent	80,000	80,000	-0-
Total Budgeted Costs	$ 347,000	$ 346,150	$ 850 (F)

Requirement

Prepare a flexible budget report to provide a more meaningful analysis of the difference between budget and actual costs.

P:10-20 (Learning Objective 4)

Wooldridge Pharmaceuticals uses a standard cost system to account for production costs and to facilitate analysis of cost performance. Wooldridge planned to produce 1.0 million vials but actually produced 1.2 million vials of its wonder drug, Beluxa. Consider the following data pertaining to the production of Beluxa

	Budget	Actual
Direct Material Cost	$ 400,000	$ 460,000
Direct Labor Cost	$ 200,000	$ 240,000
Variable Overhead Cost	$1,100,000	$1,400,000
Fixed Overhead Cost	$5,200,000	$5,400,000

Requirement

Use the supplied data to compute the standard direct material cost, the standard direct labor cost, the standard variable overhead cost, and the standard fixed overhead cost.

P:10-21 (Learning Objective 5)

Syntech Semiconductors expected to produce 2,500,000 C10 Microchips this year. The actual production amounted to 2,200,000 Microchips. Actual and Standard costs for the direct material and direct labor elements of the production costs are as follows:

	Unit of Measure	Cost per Unit of Measure	Total Cost per Microchip
Standard Costs Per Microchip			
Direct Material	0.4 nanometers	$100.00	$40.00
Direct Labor	0.10 hours	$ 60.00	$ 6.00
Actual Costs Per Microchip			
Direct Material—Thread	0.42 nanometers	$ 98.00	$41.16
Direct Material—Beads	0.11 hours	$ 52.00	$ 5.72

Requirements

a. Use a two-column approach and the following figure to compute the materials price variance, the materials quantity variance, and the total materials variance for Syntech Semiconductors. Indicate whether the variances are favorable or unfavorable.

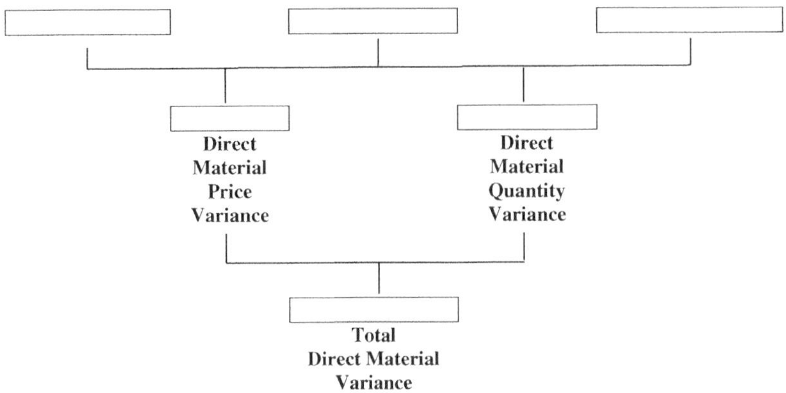

b. Use a two-column approach and the following figure to compute the labor rate variance, the labor efficiency variance, and the total labor variance for Syntech Semiconductors. Indicate whether the variances are favorable or unfavorable.

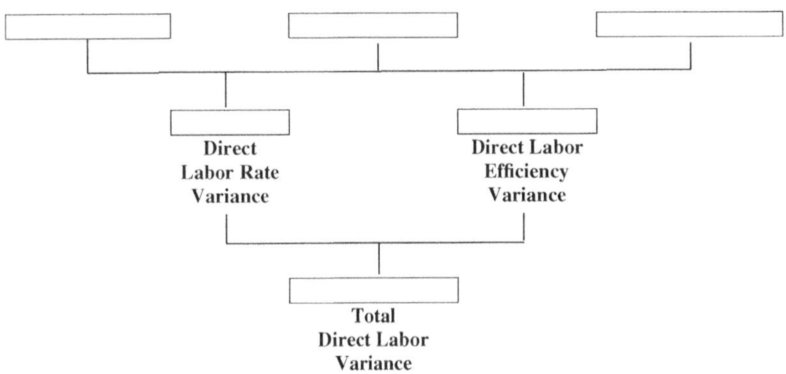

P:10-22 (Learning Objective 6)

Syntech Semiconductors expected to produce 2,500,000 C10 Microchips this year. The actual production amounted to 2,200,000 Microchips. Actual and standard costs for overhead are as follows

	Unit of Measure	Cost per Unit of Measure	Total Cost per Pair
Variable Overhead	0.20 machine hrs.	$ 50.00	$10.00
Budgeted Direct Fixed Overhead		$100,000,000	
Budgeted Chip Production (Chips)		÷ 2,500,000	
Total Fixed Overhead per Chip			$40.00
Budgeted Costs per Chip			$50.00

Actual cost data for Syntech Semiconductors follow.

	Unit of Measure	Cost per Unit of Measure	Total Cost per Pair
Variable Overhead	0.22 machine hrs.	$ 50.00	$11.00
Actual Direct Fixed Overhead		$90,200,000	
Actual Chip Production (Chips)		÷ 2,200,000	
Total Fixed Overhead per Chip			$41.00
Actual Costs per Chip			$69.50

Requirements

a. Use a two-column approach and the following figure to compute the variable overhead variance for Syntech Semiconductors. Indicate whether the variances are favorable or unfavorable.

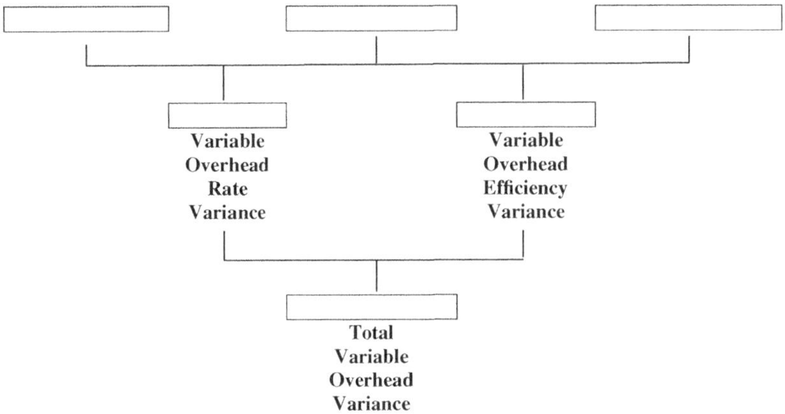

b. Use a three-column approach to compute the fixed overhead variances for Syntech Semiconductors. Indicate whether the variances are favorable or unfavorable.

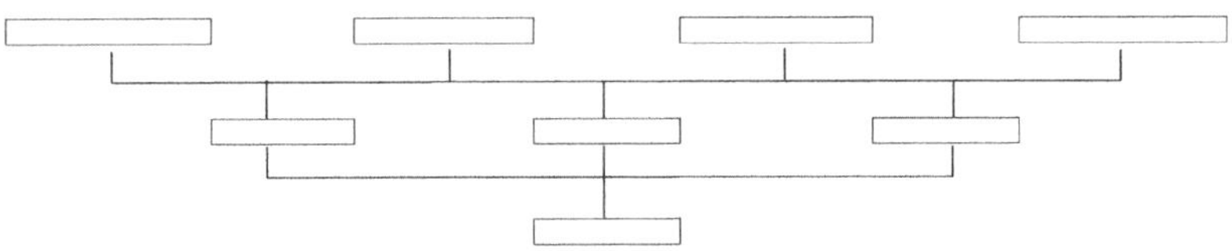

Technology, Analytics, and Artificial Intelligence

T:10-23 (Technology, Analytics, and Artificial Intelligence)

Using the Data Analysis ToolPak in Microsoft Excel, compute a t-test to compare Nutrino Corp's Quality Control Employees' pay in the current year versus the prior year. Use the Nutrino Wage Data Excel file included with your book material. Note, the sample sizes between the current year and prior year vary, suggesting a the two-sample assuming equal variances test should be used.

T:10-24 (Technology, Analytics, and Artificial Intelligence)

Using the Data Analysis ToolPak in Microsoft Excel, compute a t-test to compare Nutrino Corp's Packaging Employees' pay in the current year versus the prior year. Use the Nutrino Wage Data Excel file included with your book material. Note, the sample sizes between the current year and prior year vary, suggesting a the two-sample assuming equal variances test should be used.

CHAPTER 11

Performance Evaluation

Learning Objectives

11.1 Explain the concept of responsibility accounting in performance evaluation.
11.2 Describe how a business evaluates cost center, revenue center, and profit center performance.
11.3 Compare the return on investment and residual income methods for evaluating investment center performance.

Accounting in Life

Liliana Drew / Pexels / Public Domain

Investing in an exercise routine can yield significant benefits, but it requires a commitment of time and energy. Imagine waking up at 5:30 a.m., lacing your running shoes, and hitting the pavement. The initial stages are tough—your legs ache, and you crave more sleep. But a doctor's warning about rising cholesterol can be the wake-up call that drives you to make a change. The effort might feel overwhelming at first, but the rewards will soon appear. You may begin to lose weight, your energy levels might increase, and your mind could feel clearer. Add in better sleep and increased productivity at work, and you'll likely find yourself feeling happier overall.

The biggest return, though, could come at your next doctor's visit: lower cholesterol. As you run through the quiet morning streets, you might realize the true value of your investment—reclaimed health and vitality, worth every ounce of effort.

Let's Review

Controlling costs is one way to improve company profits. In Chapter 10 we learn to effectively evaluate how well a business controls manufacturing and production costs using flexible budgeting principles and variance analysis. The two concepts are useful ways to compare actual production cost differences with expected production costs. Performing a meaningful analysis requires setting a common basis from which to perform comparisons.

LEARNING ACTIVITY 11.1

Single Shot Coffee Company produces single-serve coffee cartridges that are compatible with most single-serve coffee makers. Consider Single Shot's expected production volume and overhead cost assumptions:

	January	February	March	Quarter
Single-serve coffee cartridges produced	250,000	200,000	200,000	650,000

Overhead Assumptions			
	Budget	Actual	Variance
Storage costs per month		$3,500.00	
Production supervisor wage		$8,000.00	
Equipment Depreciation		$5,500.00	
Indirect material cost per unit		$ 0.05	
Inspection cost per batch		$ 40.00	
Number of units produced per batch		5,000	

Using the estimated production and the manufacturing overhead assumptions, finish computing the January manufacturing overhead budget, assuming Single Shot uses flexible budgeting principles.

Single Shot Coffee Company Manufacturing Overhead Budget Quarter Ending December 20XX	
	January
Fixed Costs	
Storage Rent	$3,500
Production manager salary	
Depreciation	$5,500
Total Fixed Costs	
Variable Costs	
Indirect material	
Inspection	
Total Variable Costs	
Total Overhead Costs	

How Do Businesses Decide What Information Is Relevant When Evaluating Performance in a Decentralized Organization?

Learning Objective 11.1

Explain the concept of responsibility accounting in performance evaluation.

To evaluate an employee's performance, you need to select and analyze relevant information that falls within their responsibility and line of control. The concept of **responsibility accounting** involves gathering, analyzing, and reporting on costs and revenues that fall directly under a manager's purview. **Control** can be defined as having the capacity to make operational decisions that impact costs and revenues. Responsibility accounting differs from budgeting because it separates *controllable* and *noncontrollable* costs and revenues: managers are only evaluated on costs and revenues they control. This distinction is important because failure to isolate factors that managers control can result in misleading performance evaluation reports.

For example, an organization would not use profitability as a basis for evaluating a sales manager's performance since profitability is influenced by factors that are outside the sales manager's control, such as cost control. Thus, a more accurate way to evaluate the sales manager's performance would be to look specifically at sales generated by the manager and any direct costs associated with those sales.

Responsibility accounting is particularly important in a decentralized company. **Decentralization** means that control over operational decision-making is delegated to various managers throughout the company. Managers usually have distinct areas of responsibility that impact particular revenue and expense accounts. A **responsibility center** is a set of revenue and expense accounts that fall under a manager's line of authority and are commonly classified into four types: cost centers, revenue centers, profit centers, and investment centers.

We examine these four responsibility centers in the remainder of this chapter.

How Do Businesses Evaluate Their Performance at Controlling Costs or Generating Revenues and Profits?

Learning Objective 11.2
Explain how a business would evaluate cost center, revenue center, and profit center performance.

Businesses commonly segment their responsibility reports based on cost control, revenue generated, or both.

Cost Centers

A **cost center** is a part of the organization that incurs costs and expenses but does not generate revenue. A cost center manager's performance is based on the ability to keep controllable costs down or within budget. Two examples of cost centers would be an administrative or

LEARNING ACTIVITY 11.2

Match the term with the letter of the correct definition:

Term		Definition
Control	____	**a.** Control over operational decision-making is delegated to various managers throughout the company.
Decentralization	____	**b.** A set of revenue and expense accounts fall under a manager's line of authority.
Responsibility accounting	____	**c.** Manager has the capacity to make the operational decisions that impact particular costs and revenues.
Responsibility center	____	**d.** The process of gathering, analyzing, and reporting on costs and revenues fall directly under a manager's control.

production department. An administrative department focuses on providing internal administrative services to other areas of an organization to allow them to operate. A production department focuses on producing products and does not focus on the sales of products.

A **cost center performance report** compares actual costs incurred for a period with budget expectations developed using flexible budgeting principles. A cost center performance report includes both controllable and noncontrollable costs. Thus, the report includes direct and indirect fixed and variable costs. Recall, direct costs are costs that are traceable to a specific cost center and are incurred solely for the cost center. Indirect costs, or common costs, are for the benefit of more than one cost center.

Using noncontrollable costs to evaluate a cost center's manager would be unfair and inconclusive. The most appropriate way to evaluate cost center performance is to examine the controllable portion of variances using flexible budgeting principles. Businesses should use a **cost center responsibility report**, which compares controllable costs incurred for a period with budget expectations.

In Chapter 9 we developed a budget for Bob Willis Custom Wheel Company, including a budget for the selling and administrative department. The administrative department can be considered a cost center. The cost center performance report and responsibility report for the administrative department are presented in Figure 11.1.

Bob Willis Custom Wheel Company
Selling and Administrative Department ***Performance*** Report
First Quarter 20XX

	Flexible Budget	Actual	Variance	% Variance
Sales Commissions	$ 10,000	$ 11,000	$ 1,000 U	9.0% U
Freight Out	12,000	12,400	400 U	3.2% U
Manager Salary	10,000	10,000	- 0 -	- 0 -
Office Salary	5,000	5,500	500 U	9.0% U
Advertising	2,500	2,000	500 F	25.0% F
Insurance	1,500	1,350	150 F	11.1% F
Depreciation	1,500	1,750	250 U	14.2% U
Total Administrative Expenses	$ 42,500	$ 44,000	$ 1,500 U	3.4% U

F = Favorable Variance
U = Unfavorable Variance

Bob Willis Custom Wheel Company
Selling and Administrative Department ***Responsibility*** Report
First Quarter 20XX

	Flexible Budget	Actual	Variance	% Variance
Office Salary	5,000	5,500	500 U	9.0% U
Advertising	2,500	2,000	500 F	25.0% F
Insurance	1,500	1,350	150 F	11.1% F
Total Administrative Expenses	$ 9,000	$ 8,850	$ 150 F	1.7% F

The percent variance of 1.7% is calculated by dividing the variance by the actual results or: $150 ÷ $8,850 = 1.7%

Figure 11.1 Cost center performance and responsibility reports.

The performance report in Figure 11.1 shows a $1,500 or 3.4% unfavorable variance based on the difference between the flexible budget and actual columns. Notice that the performance report is based on all costs incurred by the department, including both the direct and indirect costs. Also notice that the responsibility report does not include sales commissions, freight out, manager salary, or depreciation. The sales commissions and freight expenses are direct variable expenses that are tied to unit sales and, as a result, are uncontrollable. The manager is the individual to whom this report applies, and managers typically do not have control over the size of their salary, so it is not included. Finally, depreciation on equipment or other investments is not included, as cost center managers typically do not have control over investment decisions.

The responsibility report is narrowed down to just the office salary, advertising, and insurance. Notice in Figure 11.1 that spending on office salaries is $500 above budget, while advertising and insurance are below budget by a total of $650. As a result, the total variance is favorable by $150 or 1.7%. This suggests that the manager is managing the administrative costs that fall under their control effectively.

Revenue Centers

A **revenue center** is a part of the organization that generates sales but does not set pricing or control costs other than those directly related to the sales-generating activities. Thus, a revenue center manager's performance is based on their ability to generate unit sales while keeping direct expenses within budget parameters. Let us use a company's sales department as an example of a revenue center. A sales department's performance is based on the sales variance that is calculated much like we calculated cost variances in Chapter 10 using flexible budgeting principles.

Sales Variance

The **sales variance** is the difference between the budgeted and actual sales revenue. The variance is the result of a disparity in the price or quantity of units sold relative to expectations. The formula for the sales variance compares actual to budget and is a function of both price and quantity:

$$\begin{array}{c}\textbf{actual sales quantity}\\ \times\\ \textbf{actual sales price}\end{array} - \begin{array}{c}\textbf{budgeted sales quantity}\\ \times\\ \textbf{budgeted sales price}\end{array} = \textbf{Sales variance}$$

How does a business interpret the sales variance?

- A favorable sales variance suggests that either more units were sold, or they were sold for a higher price.
- An unfavorable variance indicates fewer units were sold, or they were sold for lower prices.

Let us illustrate with the budget and actual sales for the first quarter at Bob Willis Custom Wheel Company:

Actual		Budget		
1,075 wheels × $190 per wheel	–	**1,000 wheels × $200 per wheel**	=	**Sales Variance**
$204,250	–	**$200,000**	=	**$4,250 favorable**

Bob Willis Custom Wheels had a favorable total sales variance of $4,250 in the first quarter as the actual sales were $204,250 compared to a budget of $200,000.

Sales Quantity Variance

The **sales quantity variance** is driven by the difference between the actual and budgeted sales quantities. The formula for the sales quantity variance isolates the difference between actual and budgeted quantities by holding the sales price constant at the budgeted sales price.

actual sales quantity × ***budgeted sales price***	–	**budgeted sales quantity** × ***budgeted sales price***	=	**Sales Quantity Variance**

Let us illustrate with the budgeted and actual sales figures we used above for Bob Willis Wheels, where 1,075 wheels were sold for $190 per wheel compared to a budget of 1,000 wheels at a price of $200 per wheel. The actual sales quantity of 1,075 wheels and the budgeted sales quantity of 1,000 wheels are multiplied times the budgeted price per wheel of $200, resulting in expected sales of $215,000 at the actual sales quantity of 1,075 wheels versus budgeted sales of $200,000 at the budgeted sales quantity of 1,000 wheels. The difference of $15,000 is favorable and is attributable to the 75 wheels that were sold above the budget.

1,075 wheels × $200 per wheel	–	**1,000 wheels × $200 per wheel**	=	**Sales Quantity Variance**
$215,000	–	**$200,000**	=	**$15,000 favorable**

Ignore the actual sales price and use the budgeted sales price for both elements of the sales quantity variance computation. This allows you to isolate the effect of the difference between actual and budgeted sales quantities without concern for differences in sales price.

Sales Price Variance

The **sales price variance** is driven by the difference between the actual and budgeted sales prices. The formula for the sales price isolates the difference between actual and budgeted sales prices by holding the sales quantity constant.

actual sales quantity		actual sales quantity		Sales
×	−	×	=	Price
actual sales price		*budgeted sales price*		Variance

Let us illustrate by inserting the budgeted and actual sales into the formula. The actual sales quantity of 1,075 wheels is multiplied by the actual sales price of $190 per wheel and the budgeted sales price of $200 per wheel, resulting in expected sales of $204,250 at the actual sales price of $190 per wheel versus sales of $215,000 at the budgeted sales price of $200 per wheel. The difference of $10,750 is unfavorable and is attributable to the sales price of $190 per wheel falling below the budgeted price of $200 per wheel.

1,075 wheels		1,075 wheels		Sales
×	−	×	=	Price
$190 per wheel		$200 per wheel		Variance
$204,250	−	$215,000	=	$10,750 unfavorable

Sales Variance Analysis

As shown in Figure 11.2, a two-column visualization is a useful way to analyze sales variances. The two-column approach combines the price and quantity variance calculations into one display. The left-hand column is based on actual sales; the right-hand column is based on budgeted sales; and the center column uses flexible budgeting principles based on a combination of the actual sales quantity times the budgeted sales price. You can see the favorable direct materials price variance of $27,500 and the unfavorable direct materials quantity variance of $17,500 combine to make a total direct materials cost variance of $10,000, which is favorable.

The two-column approach can be converted into a **revenue center responsibility report** that compares actual sales to flexible budget and budget sales, as illustrated in Figure 11.3.

Profit Centers

A **profit center** is a part of the organization responsible for generating revenue, setting prices, and controlling costs. A profit center manager's performance is based on sales, variable costs, and direct fixed costs. An example of a profit center would be a division of a larger corporation or an individual fast-food restaurant in a larger fast-food chain.

The profit center performance report for Bob Willis Custom Wheel Company's spoke wheel division in Figure 11.4 illustrates the division's profit relative to budgeted profit using flexible budgeting principles. The division's profit was $11,540 below the flexible budget expectations, resulting in a 15.3% unfavorable variance.

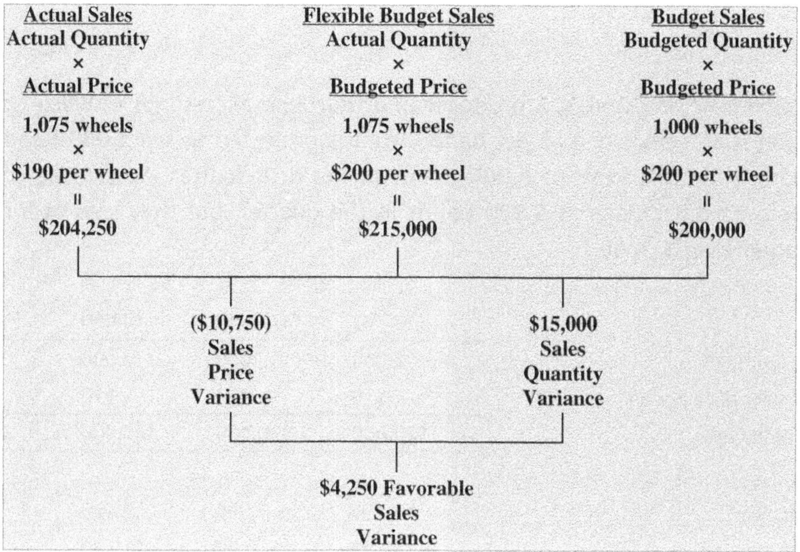

Figure 11.2 Two-column sales variance analysis.

Bob Willis Custom Wheel Company
Sales Department ***Responsibility*** Report
First Quarter 20XX

	Actual Sales	Sales Price Variance	Flexible Budget Sales	Sales Quantity Variance	Budget Sales
Custom Wheels	$204,250	$10,750U	$215,000	$15,000 U	$200,000

Figure 11.3 Revenue center responsibility report.

Bob Willis Custom Wheel Company
Spoke Wheel Division ***Performance*** Report
First Quarter 20XX

	Actual	Flexible Budget	Flexible Budget Variance	% Variance
Net Sales Revenue	$204,250	$215,000	$10,750	6.7% U
Variable Costs	$104,813	$103,523	$ 1,290	1.3% U
Contribution Margin	$ 99,437	$111,477	$12,040	10.8% U
Traceable Fixed Costs	$ 35,500	$ 36,000	$ 500	1.6% F
Division Profit	$ 63,937	$ 75,477	$11,540	15.3% U

Figure 11.4 Profit center performance report.

LEARNING ACTIVITY 11.3

Amor Artisan Hair Accessories, a producer of artisan hair accessories in Belize, plans to sell hair bands at a price of $10 per band. Amor is projected to sell 2,000 bands every month during the first year, or 6,000 bands in the first quarter. Actual sales came in slightly below expectations at 5,800 bands in the quarter, but they sold at a price of $10.99 rather than $10.00.

	January	February	March	Quarter
Budgeted unit sales	2,000	2,000	2,000	6,000
Budgeted sales price per unit	× $10	× $10	× $10	× $10
Total budgeted sales	$20,000	$20,000	$20,000	$60,000
Actual unit sales	1,900	1,900	2,000	5,800
Actual sales price per unit	× $10.99	× $10.99	× $10.99	× $10.99
Total sales	$20,881	$20,881	$21,980	$63,742

Complete the following exercise to compute the sales variance, the sales price variance, and the sales quantity variance:

Actual Sales for the Quarter	**Flexible Budget Sales for the Quarter**	**Budget Sales for the Quarter**
_______ **Bands**	_______ **Bands**	_______ **Bands**
×	×	×
$_______ **per Band**	$_______ **per Band**	$_______ **per Band**
=	=	=
$_______	$_______	$_______

$_______	$_______
sales price variance	**sales quantity variance**

$_______

sales variance

The **profit center performance report** includes sales, variable costs, and traceable fixed costs. Direct fixed costs include a portion of utilities, rent, supervisory salary, and depreciation for equipment used directly on spoke wheels. Indirect fixed costs are accounted for separately since they are shared across divisions or product lines. In this case, centralized administrative costs, depreciation on shared assets, business insurance, and marketing costs are shared costs. Those costs are either excluded or a portion is allocated as *traceable* fixed costs. In Figure 11.4, the traceable fixed costs include a portion of shared administrative expenses along with direct utilities, supervisory salaries, rent, and depreciation.

How Do Businesses Decide if They Made a Good Investment?

Learning Objective 11.3
Compare the return on investment and residual income methods for evaluating investment center performance.

An **investment center** is a part of the organization responsible for generating revenue, setting prices, controlling costs, and controlling funds invested. Investment centers are usually autonomous divisions within an organization where the manager is responsible for profit maximization and has control over both operational decisions and capital investment decisions. The evaluation of investment center performance is typically based on how effectively assets are utilized. Thus, an investment center's performance is a function of both operating income and asset investment. We will look at two formulas commonly used for evaluating investment center performance: return on investment and residual income.

Return on Investment

Return on investment (ROI) is a formula for measuring a business unit's operating income relative to its average operating assets. The formula for ROI is as follows:

$$\textbf{Return on Investment} = \frac{\textbf{Operating Income}}{\textbf{Average Operating Assets}}$$

Let's look at an example related to Icamna Shaved Ice, which originally operated a shaved ice business out of a modified Airstream trailer. Let us assume the owner elected to expand the business by opening a new store located in a local strip mall and near a busy shopping district. The owner invested \$250,000 to start the store, all of which went toward purchasing equipment and fixtures in the store, inventory, and cash reserves. The new store's first year of operations netted \$47,500 in operating income. Operating Assets at the end of the first year amounted to \$275,000. The ROI was, therefore 18.1%, computed as follows:

$$\frac{\$47{,}500}{(\$250{,}000 + \$275{,}000) \div 2} = 18.1\%$$

Note that the average operating assets are computed by adding the operating asset values at the beginning of the year ($250,000) and the end of the year ($275,000) and dividing that value by two.

Icamna can improve its ROI by either improving its operating income or by reducing its average operating assets. **Operating income** is a company's income after subtracting operating expenses from sales revenue. **Operating expenses** are expenses incurred in a firm's normal course of business, including things like costs for marketing, rent, insurance, inventory, equipment, payroll, or other selling or administrative expenses that occur in the normal course of business. Expenses like interest, taxes, or special nonrecurring items are usually treated as non-operating expenses. Operating income also does not include revenue generated from investments held for sale or special and nonrecurring forms of income. Improving sales or controlling operating expenses is one way a company can improve ROI.

The other way a company can improve ROI is to reduce average operating assets while continuing to generate the same operating income. **Operating assets** are assets used to generate revenue in the normal course of business operations. Examples of operating assets include cash, accounts receivable, inventory, buildings and equipment (less accumulated depreciation), and intangible assets such as patents. Keeping cash, receivable, and inventory balances low can reduce operating assets and increase ROI. Delaying costly upgrades to machinery and equipment can also reduce operating assets. However, businesses must carefully weigh the savings from delaying equipment upgrades with increased maintenance expenses to keep old equipment running.

LEARNING ACTIVITY 11.4

Epic Enterprises is a sports entertainment company that owns two baseball franchises in the Great River League, an independent semi-professional baseball league located in the upper Midwest. Epic owns the Rock Island Red Fins and the Duluth Ducks. Epic was required to make a bigger investment in the Rock Island franchise because the company owns the team and the stadium. The Ducks rent stadium usage from the local municipality. Use the following information to determine if Epic's investment in the Red Fins or the Ducks is greater:

	Rock Island Red Fins	Duluth Ducks
Operating Assets	$6,400,000	$3,100,000
Operating Income	$ 320,000	$ 180,500
Input the Return on Investment	______	______

ACCOUNTING IN LIFE

Do you maintain your ride? An automobile is one of the most expensive items a person can possess. According to a recent study by the American Automobile Association (AAA), a new car can cost you an average of $9,000 annually when factoring in the cost of tires, insurance, recommended maintenance, and most of all, the sticker price. Cars depreciate quickly, and the key to saving money on vehicle ownership is extending the life of your car and delaying a new purchase. The best way to keep your car on the road longer is to get it serviced. However, the AAA finds that one in three drivers skip recommended maintenance, which can result in your car failing prematurely, increased maintenance costs, and potentially the need for a new car. The AAA recommends that car owners set aside $50 per month to pay for adequate maintenance, which can nearly double the life of your ride.

Artem Podrez / Pexels / Public Domain

Residual Income

Residual income (RI) is the amount of income an investment created above the minimum required return. The formula for RI is as follows:

$$\textbf{Operating Income} - (\textbf{Average Operating Assets} \times \textbf{Desired Rate of Return}) = \textbf{Residual Income}$$

Let's revisit the example related to Icamna Shaved Ice. Recall that the owner invested \$250,000 to start a new store, and the store's first year of operations netted \$47,500 in operating income. Operating Assets at the end of the first year amounted to \$275,000. The owner desires a 15% rate of return. Residual income is \$8,125, computed as follows:

$$\$47{,}500 - ((\$250{,}000 + \$275{,}000) \div 2) \times 15\%$$
$$\$47{,}500 - \$262{,}500 \times 15\%$$
$$\$47{,}500 - \$39{,}375 = \$8{,}125$$

LEARNING ACTIVITY 11.5

Let's revisit Epic Enterprises, owner of two semi-professional baseball franchises in the Great River League, the Rock Island Red Fins and the Duluth Ducks. Epic Desires a 10% return on business investments. Compute Epic's RI on its investments in the Red Fins and the Ducks using the following information:

	Rock Island Red Fins	Duluth Ducks
Average Operating Assets	\$6,400,000	\$3,100,000
Operating Income	\$ 320,000	\$ 180,500
Input the Residual Income	______	______

Technology, Analytics, and Artificial Intelligence

Using Excel Functions to Calculate ROI and RI

In this section, we will use Microsoft Excel to calculate ROI and RI efficiently. Let us look at an example.

Beltron Products is analyzing the performance of two of its product lines. The first is the Beltron Air Purifier, a powerful air filtration system that allows users to control and monitor the quality of the air in their homes from anywhere via the internet. The Air Purifier is targeted toward health-conscious individuals and the medical industry. The second is the Beltron UltraCharge Power Bank, which is a portable power bank with fast charging and a built-in solar panel for emergency charging outdoors with a digital interface. The UltraCharge is targeted toward travelers and outdoors enthusiasts.

The financial performance for each product line and Beltron's investment in each product are listed next. Beltron requires a 12% rate of return on their products.

	Revenue	**Operating Expenses**	**Invested Capital**
Air Purifier	\$500,000	\$300,000	\$1,000,000
UltraCharge	\$800,000	\$500,000	\$1,200,000

Computing the ROI and RI can be performed quickly using Microsoft Excel. You might start by copying the data into Excel (see Figure 11.5).

Solving for ROI and RI in Excel requires building the formulas for each product. The ROI formula for the Air Purifier is ((B2-C2)/D2)*100 and for the UltraCharge ((B3-C3)/D3)*100. This returns a percentage of 20% for the Air Purifier and 25% for the UltraCharge, as shown in Figure 11.6.

The RI formula for the Air Purifier is (B2-C2)-(D2*12%) and for the UltraCharge (B3-C3)-(D3*12%), assuming the 12% required rate of return. This returns a value of $80,000 for the Air Purifier and $156,000 for the UltraCharge as shown in Figure 11.7.

	A	B	C	D	E
1	**Product**	**Revenue**	**Operating Expenses**	**Invested Capital**	
2	Air Purifier	500000	300000	1000000	
3	UltraCharge	800000	500000	1200000	
4					

Figure 11.5 Beltron data in Excel.

E2 fx =((B2-C2)/D2)*100

	A	B	C	D	E
1	**Product**	**Revenue**	**Operating Expenses**	**Invested Capital**	**ROI (%)**
2	Air Purifier	500000	300000	1000000	20
3	UltraCharge	800000	500000	1200000	25
4					

((B2-C2)/D2)*100

Figure 11.6 Beltron ROI formula.

F2 fx =(B2-C2)-(D2*12%)

A	B	C	D	E	F
Product	**Revenue**	**Operating Expenses**	**Invested Capital**	**ROI (%)**	**Residual Income**
Air Purifier	500000	300000	1000000	20	$ 80,000
UltraCharge	800000	500000	1200000	25	$ 156,000

((B2-C2)-(D2*12%))

Figure 11.7 Beltron RI formula.

We might consider building a dashboard with visuals for our product lines. Let's build bar charts that allow us to visually compare the ROI and the RI for our various products. To develop a bar chart that displays the ROI per product line, use the following steps:

1. **Select the Data:** Highlight the cells under the "Product" and "ROI (%)" columns as shown in Figure 11.8.
2. **Insert the Chart:** Go to the **Insert** tab on the ribbon, then in the **Charts** group, select the **Bar Chart** (Clustered Bar Chart) (see Figure 11.9).
3. **Format the Chart:** Add a title by clicking on the default title and typing "ROI Comparison." (See Figure 11.10.)
4. Then, click on the chart and the "+" on the top right. Click on "Axis Titles: and Legend." Label the axes: **Horizontal Axis**: "Products" **Vertical Axis**: "ROI (%)" (see Figure 11.11).
5. Finally, your visualization is complete (Figure 11.12), but you can format the bars with different colors or styles if you like or make any other modifications you would like for better visualization.

A	B	C	D	E	F
Product	**Revenue**	**Operating Expenses**	**Invested Capital**	**ROI (%)**	**Residual Income**
Air Purifier	500000	300000	1000000	20	$ 80,000
UltraCharge	800000	500000	1200000	25	$ 156,000

Figure 11.8 Data selection.

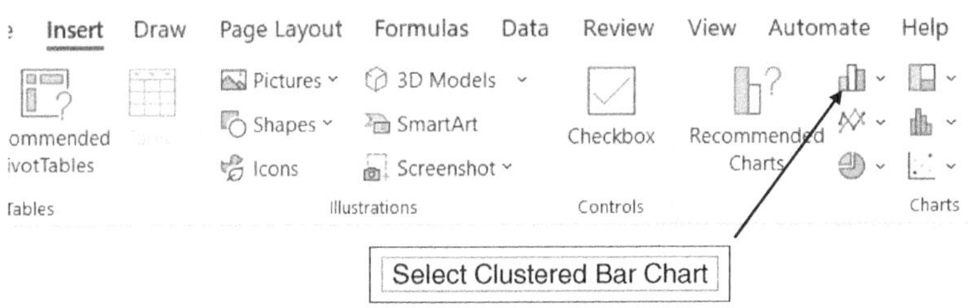

Figure 11.9 Insert bar chart.

Figure 11.10 Modify the chart title.

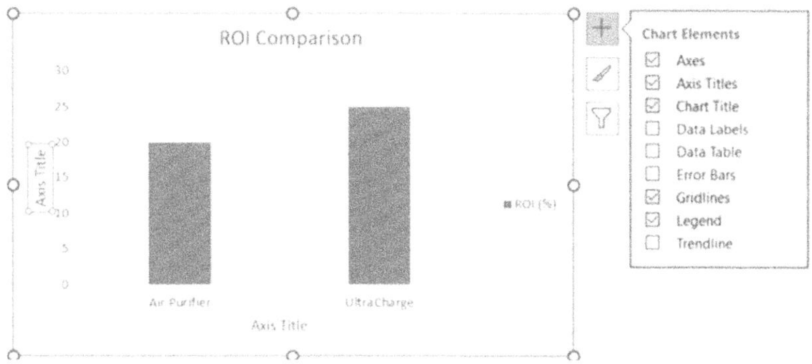

Figure 11.11 Add axis titles and a legend.

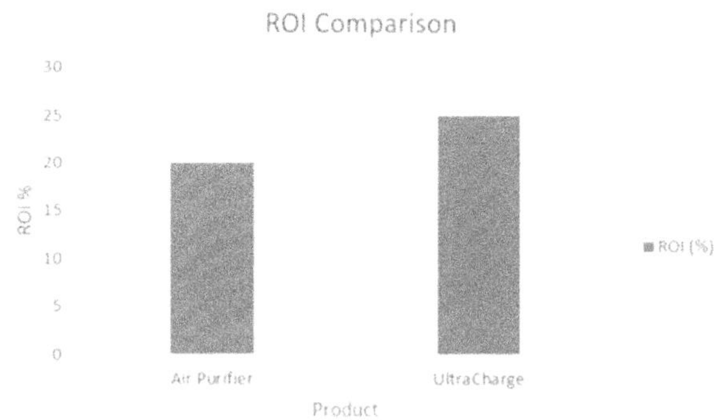

Figure 11.12 Finished chart.

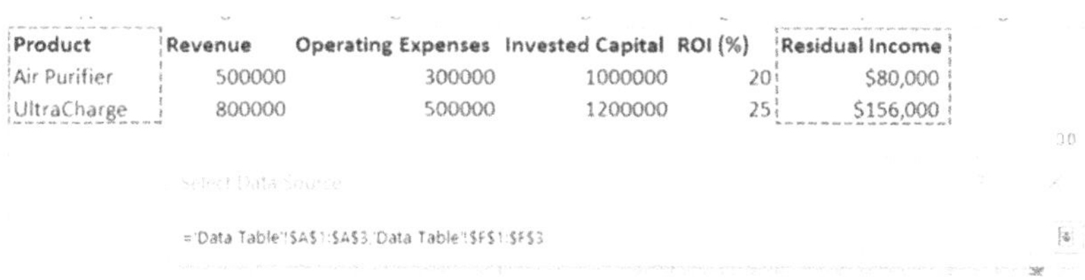

Product	Revenue	Operating Expenses	Invested Capital	ROI (%)	Residual Income
Air Purifier	500000	300000	1000000	20	$80,000
UltraCharge	800000	500000	1200000	25	$156,000

Figure 11.13 Select source data for RI chart.

You can develop a similar bar chart for RI using a number of different methods, but an easy way would be to **make a copy of the chart** by right-clicking on the chart, clicking copy, then paste a second chart. Then, right click on the new chart and click on **select data source**. From there, you can change source data to select the RI values instead of the ROI values, as shown in Figure 11.13.

You will need to update the **horizontal axis label** and the **chart title** by right-clicking on each and updating them manually, as shown in Figure 11.14.

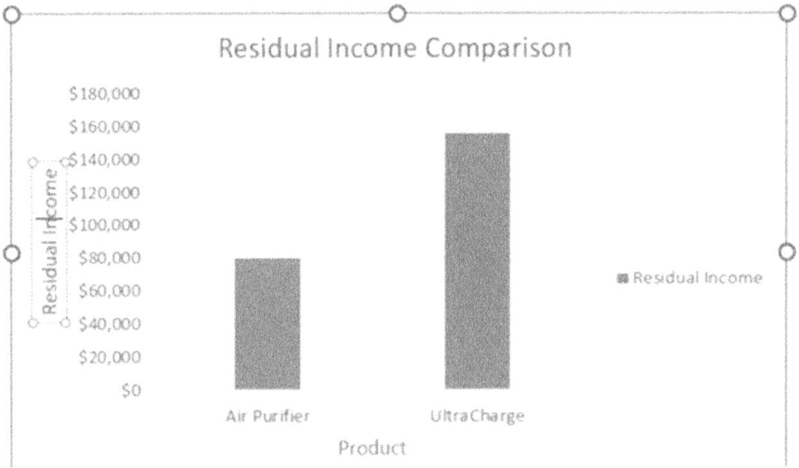

Figure 11.14 Update labels and finalize chart.

LEARNING ACTIVITY 11.6

EcoVolt Incorporated manufactures energy efficient products. The financial performance for each product line along with EcoVolt's investment in each product follow. EcoVolt requires an 18% rate of return on their products.

	Revenue	Operating Expenses	Invested Capital	ROI%	RI
Solar Max Panel	$600,000	$300,000	$1,600,000	____	____________
G-Charge Battery	$900,000	$450,000	$1,500,000	____	____________
Eco Lite Bulb	$300,000	$150,000	$ 600,000	____	____________

Required

1. Computing the ROI and RI for the three products using Microsoft Excel
2. Develop bar charts that allow for the comparison of the ROI and RI for the product lines

Key Terms

responsibility accounting The process of gathering, analyzing, and reporting on costs and revenues that fall directly under a manager's control.

control Having the capacity to make the operational decisions that impact particular costs and revenues.

decentralization Control over operational decision-making is delegated to various managers throughout the company.

responsibility center A set of revenue and expense accounts that fall under a manager's line of authority.

cost center A part of the organization that incurs costs and expenses but does not generate revenue.

cost center performance report A report that compares actual cost center costs incurred for a period with budget expectations.

cost center responsibility report A report that compares controllable cost center costs incurred for a period with budget expectations.

revenue center A part of the organization that generates revenue but does not set pricing or report on costs other than those directly related to the revenue-generating activities.

sales variance The difference between the budgeted and actual sales revenue.

sales quantity variance The difference between the actual and budgeted sales quantities.

sales price variance The difference between the actual and expected sales prices.

revenue center responsibility report A report that compares actual sales with flexible budget and budget sales.

profit center A part of the organization that is responsible for generating revenue as well as setting selling prices and controlling costs.

profit center performance report A report that compares sales, variable costs, and traceable fixed costs.

investment center A part of the organization that is responsible for generating revenue as well as setting selling prices and controlling costs.

return on investment (ROI) A formula for measuring a business unit's operating income relative to its average operating assets.

operating income A company's income after subtracting operating expenses from sales revenue.

operating expenses Expenses incurred in a firm's normal course of business.

operating assets Assets used to generate revenue in the normal course of business operations.

residual income (RI) The amount of income an investment created above the minimum required return.

LEARNING ACTIVITY SOLUTIONS

Learning Activity 11.1

Single Shot Coffee Company
Manufacturing Overhead Budget
Quarter Ending December 20XX

	January
Fixed Costs	
Storage Rent	$ 3,500
Production manager salary	$ 8,000
Depreciation	$ 5,500
Total Fixed Costs	$17,000
Variable Costs	
Indirect material	$12,500
Inspection	$ 2,000
Total Variable Costs	$14,500
Total Overhead Costs	$31,500

Learning Activity 11.2

Term		Definition
Control	c	**a.** Control over operational decision-making is delegated to various managers throughout the company.
Decentralization	a	**b.** A set of revenue and expense accounts fall under a manager's line of authority.
Responsibility accounting	d	**c.** Manager has the capacity to make the operational decisions that impact particular costs and revenues.
Responsibility center	b	**d.** The process of gathering, analyzing, and reporting on costs and revenues fall directly under a manager's control.

Learning Activity 11.3

Actual Sales for the Quarter	Flexible Budget Sales for the Quarter	Budget Sales for the Quarter
5,800 Bands × *$10.99* per Band	*5,800* Bands × *$10.00* per Band	*6,000* Bands × *$10.00* per Band
=	=	=
$63,742	*$58,000*	*$60,000*

$5,742
sales price variance

$(2,000)
sales quantity variance

$3,742
sales variance

Learning Activity 11.4

Input the Return on Investment *5%* *5.82%*

Learning Activity 11.5

Input the Residual Income *($320,000)* *($129,500)*

Learning Activity 11.6

1.

Product	*Revenue*	*Operating Expenses*	*Invested Capital*	*ROI (%)*	*RI*
Solar Max Panel	*$600,000*	*$300,000*	*$1,600,000*	*18.75*	*$ 12,000*
G-Charge Battery	*$900,000*	*$450,000*	*$1,500,000*	*30.00*	*$180,000*
Eco Lite Bulb	*$300,000*	*$150,000*	*$ 600,000*	*25.00*	*$ 42,000*

2\.

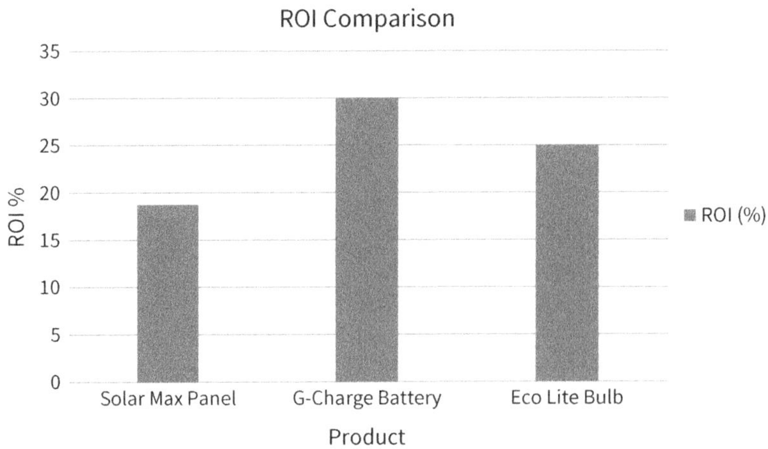

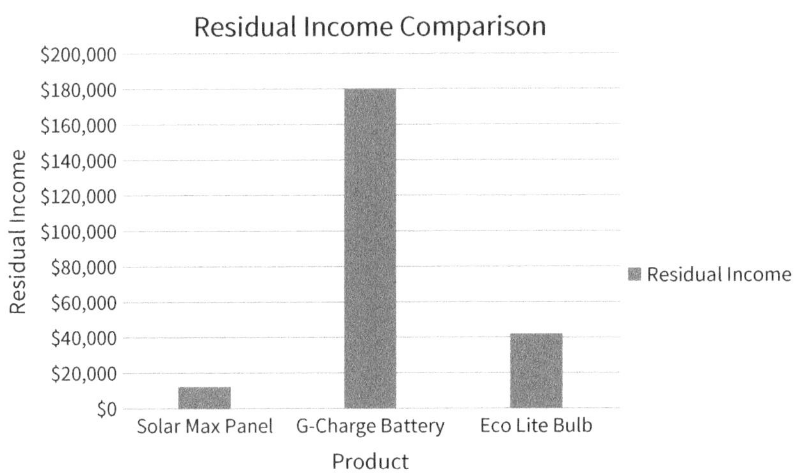

Review Questions

1. Gathering, analyzing, and reporting on costs and revenues that fall under a manager's review in what process? **(Learning Objective 1)**
   a. Responsibility accounting
   b. Managerial accounting
2. What is an important factor for determining a manager's responsibility? **(Learning Objective 1)**
   a. Control
   b. Magnitude

3. Control can be defined as having the capacity to make operational decisions that impact costs and revenues. **(Learning Objective 1)**
   a. True
   b. False
4. What is a set of revenue and expense accounts that fall under a manager's line of authority called? **(Learning Objective 1)**
   a. Accountability stream
   b. Responsibility center
5. In a decentralized company, operational control is delegated. **(Learning Objective 1)**
   a. True
   b. False
6. What is the difference between budgeted data and actual results called? **(Learning Objective 2)**
   a. A variance
   b. A deviation
7. What is part of the organization that generates sales but does not set pricing or have control over costs other than those directly related to the sales generating activities? **(Learning Objective 2)**
   a. Revenue center
   b. Cost center
8. What is a report that compares actual costs incurred for a period with budget expectations developed using flexible budgeting principles? **(Learning Objective 2)**
   a. Cost center performance report
   b. Variance report
9. A total variance is usually made up of both a price or cost component and a volume or quantity component. **(Learning Objective 2)**
   a. True
   b. False
10. The process of computing a sales quantity variance would involve holding **(Learning Objective 2)**
    a. the budgeted sales price constant.
    b. the actual sales price constant.
11. What is the part of the organization that is responsible for generating revenue, setting prices, controlling costs, and controlling funds invested? **(Learning Objective 3)**
    a. Profit center
    b. Investment center
12. What is metric that is useful for measuring operating income relative to the amount invested? **(Learning Objective 3)**
    a. Operating performance index
    b. Return on investment
13. What is the amount of income a company produces above a minimum rate of return called? **(Learning Objective 3)**
    a. Return on investment
    b. Residual income

14. The factor the distinguishes between operating assets and nonoperating assets is whether they **(Learning Objective 3)**
    a. are used in the normal course of business.
    b. generate revenue or expenses.

Short Exercises

S:11-1 (Learning Objective 1)

Responsibility accounting differs from budgeting because

a. controllable and noncontrollable costs and revenues are separated.
b. managers are only evaluated on costs and revenues they control.
c. evaluating budget results without considering control can result in misleading performance evaluations.
d. all of these are differences.

S:11-2 (Learning Objective 1)

Responsibility accounting is particularly important in a decentralized company because

a. control over decisions is delegated.
b. lines of authority are clear.
c. cost centers and revenue centers are affected by different data.
d. all of these are important reasons.

S:11-3 (Learning Objective 2)

Put an X in the correct column to indicate if the following would be reported on the cost center "performance" report or the cost center "responsibility" report.

	Performance Report	Responsibility Report
Manager salary		
Shop supplies		
Real estate taxes		
Depreciation		

S:11-4 (Learning Objective 2)

Consider the following data for Hendricks company:

Actual sales volume	400 units
Budgeted sales volume	500 units
Actual sales price	$10
Budgeted sales price	$9

What is the dollar value of the flexible budget for this item?

a. $360
b. $400
c. $450
d. $500

S:11-5 (Learning Objective 2)

Consider the following data for Hendricks company:

Actual sales volume	400 units
Budgeted sales volume	500 units
Actual sales price	$10
Budgeted sales price	$9

What is the dollar value of the sales price variance for this item?

a. $40
b. $50
c. $90
d. $100

S:11-6 (Learning Objective 2)

Consider the following data for Hendricks company:

Actual sales volume	400 units
Budgeted sales volume	500 units
Actual sales price	$10
Budgeted sales price	$9

What is the dollar value of the sales quantity variance for this item?

a. $40
b. $50
c. $90
d. $100

S:11-7 (Learning Objective 3)

Which of the following would be the least likely to be considered an operating expense?

a. Rent expense
b. Interest expense
c. Insurance expense
d. None of these would be an operating expense.

S:11-8 (Learning Objective 3)

Galliant Enterprises netted $1,200,000 in operating income last year. Galliant's operating assets at the beginning of the year were $10,500,000 and $13,500,000 at the end of the year.

Required

Compute Galliant's ROI amounts.

S:11-9 (Learning Objective 3)

Consider the data from S:11-8 regarding Galliant Enterprises. Galliant had $1,200,000 in operating income last year. Its operating assets at the beginning of the year were $10,500,000 and $13,500,000 at the end of the year. The company desires a 12% rate of ROIs.

Required

Compute Galliant's RI.

Exercises

E:11-10 (Learning Objective 1)

The general manager of Chisel Machining Inc. is evaluating data to evaluate the job performance of the production operations manager. The general manager is reviewing the following accounts for inclusion in the performance report.

Required

a. Place an X in the box next to the accounts that would most likely be included in the performance report.

Account	Included
Scrap and rework expense	
Training expense	
Advertising expense	
Direct labor expense	
Sales commissions	
Factory insurance expense	
Factory utilities expense	
Shop supplies expense	

b. Explain why some accounts were not chosen.

E:11-11 (Learning Objective 2)

Stanley Furnace Company builds electric furnaces for commercial and residential use. Stanley's management is developing a performance report for the residential furnace division. The report should select from the following data.

	Budget	Actual
Unit sales	10,000	9,000
Sales commissions	$ 35,000	$ 31,500
Freight out	$100,000	$ 99,000
Marketing expense	$150,000	$140,000
Direct production labor expense	$250,000	$270,000
Direct material expense	$100,000	$ 95,000
Shop supplies expense	$ 15,000	$ 18,000
Shop utilities expense	$ 20,000	$ 18,000
Misc. shop overhead	$ 24,000	$ 22,500

Required

Use the provided data to complete the cost center performance report for Stanley Furnace Company's residential furnace division.

Stanley Furnace Company

Residential Furnace Division Cost Performance Report

First Quarter 20XX

	Flexible Budget	Actual	Variance
Unit sales		9,000	
Sales commissions	$31,500	$ 31,500	-0-
Marketing expense		140,000	5,000 U
Freight out	90,000	99,000	9,000 U
Direct production labor expense		270,000	
Direct material expense		95,000	
Shop supplies expense		18,000	4,500 U
Shop utilities expense		18,000	
Misc shop overhead	21,600	22,500	
Total Expenses		$694,000	

E:11-12 (Learning Objective 2)

Stanley Furnace Company builds electric furnaces for commercial and residential use. Stanley's management is developing a performance report for the residential furnace division. The report should select from the following data.

	Budget	Actual
Unit sales	10,000	9,000
Sales commissions	$ 35,000	$ 31,500
Freight out	$100,000	$ 99,000
Marketing expense	$150,000	$140,000
Direct production labor expense	$250,000	$270,000
Direct material expense	$100,000	$ 95,000
Shop supplies expense	$ 15,000	$ 18,000
Shop utilities expense	$ 20,000	$ 18,000
Misc. shop overhead	$ 24,000	$ 22,500

Required

Use the supplied data to complete the following cost center responsibility report for Stanley Furnace Company's residential furnace division.

Stanley Furnace Company

Residential Furnace Division Cost Responsibility Report

First Quarter 20XX

	Flexible Budget	Actual	Variance
Unit sales		9,000	
Direct production labor expense		270,000	45,000 U
Direct material expense	90,000	95,000	
Shop supplies expense		18,000	4,500 U
Shop utilities expense		18,000	
Misc shop overhead	21,600	22,500	
Total Expenses		$432,500	

E:11-13 (Learning Objective 3)

Panther Construction is evaluating the profitability of its residential concrete construction division. The minimum rate of return Panther gives to various projects and lines of business is 20%. Selected data for the division is as follows:

Sales	$3,000,000
Net operating income (after tax)	$900,000
Operating assets at the beginning of the year	$4,500,000
Operating assets at the end of the year	$5,000,000

Required

a. Compute Panther's ROI.
b. Compute Panther's RI.
c. Would Panther make the investment?

Problems

P:11-14 (Learning Objective 2)

Gina Stevens, CEO Paradigm Pharma, a pharmaceutical manufacturing company, is working with Dave Dyerson, the company's human resource manager to develop performance reports for the divisional manager and the operations manager of the Paradigm's therapeutics division. Charles Kendrick is the divisional manager responsible for the division's sales, while Janet Sloan is responsible for production operations only. Selected data for the division are as follows:

	Budget	Actual
Unit sales	1,000,000	1,200,000
Sales	$4,000,000	$5,200,000
Sales representative incentives	$ 200,000	$ 240,000
Shipping costs	$ 40,000	$ 52,000
Fixed direct marketing expense	$ 420,000	$ 520,000
Fixed production equipment cost	$ 80,000	$ 80,000
Fixed R&D amortization cost	$ 800,000	$ 800,000
Direct production expenses	$1,200,000	$1,600,000
Indirect production expense	$ 200,000	$ 180,000

Required

a. Use the provided data to complete a profit center performance report for the therapeutics division of Paradigm Pharma managed by Charles Kendrick.
b. Use the provided data to complete a cost performance report for the operations of the therapeutics division of Paradigm Pharma managed by Janet Sloan.

P:11-15 (Learning Objective 3)

Use the data from P:11-14 related to Paradigm Pharma. Assume Paradigm's average operating assets in the Therapeutics Division are $16,800,000, which consists of capitalized R&D costs and production equipment. Also assume Paradigm expects investments to earn a 15% minimum rate of return.

Required

a. Compute Paradigm Pharma's ROI therapeutics division.
b. Compute Paradigm Pharma's RI for the therapeutics division.
c. Is Paradigm Pharma's therapeutics division meeting performance expectations based on these two metrics?

Technology, Analytics, and Artificial Intelligence

T:11-16 (Technology, Analytics, and Artificial Intelligence)

Versa Green Technologies specializes in manufacturing environmentally friendly products. Following is the financial performance for each product line and Versa GreenTech's in each product. Versa Green requires a 15% rate of return on their products.

Product	Revenue	Operating Expenses	Invested Capital	ROI%	Residual Income
Wind Stream Turbine	$750,000	$500,000	$2,500,000	____	________
Aqua Flow Filter	$1,200,000	$900,000	$3,000,000	____	________
Solar Shield Roof Tiles	$500,000	$300,000	$1,200,000	____	________

Required

1. Use Microsoft Excel to compute the ROI and RI for the three products.
2. Create bar charts to compare the ROI and RI for the product lines.

T:11-17 (Technology, Analytics, and Artificial Intelligence)

Glow Well Essentials manufactures premium health and beauty products. Following is the financial performance for each product line and Glow Well's investment in each product. Glow Well requires a 16% rate of return on its products.

Product	Revenue	Operating Expenses	Invested Capital	ROI%	Residual Income
Radiance Serum	$1,200,000	$800,000	$2,500,000	____	________
Hydrate+ Moisturizer	$ 900,000	$600,000	$2,000,000	____	________
Glow Lux Sunscreen	$ 700,000	$400,000	$1,800,000	____	________
Revive Night Cream	$ 500,000	$300,000	$1,000,000	____	________

Required

1. Use Excel to compute the ROI and RI for the four products.
2. Create bar charts to compare the ROI and RI for the product lines.

APPENDIX A: TECHNOLOGY OVERVIEW

Overview

Management accountants use various technologies to gather data, analyze it, and produce information that is valuable to the company's stakeholders. Analytics tools make the conversion of data to information faster, allowing accountants to provide more insight into the operations. Other tools such as artificial intelligence, generative artificial intelligence, and robotic process automation are helping accountants work more effectively and efficiently when analyzing financial data. With newer developments in software, accountants can now do advanced analytics and automate processes that previously could only be done by someone with programming experience. Figure A.1 is an AI-generated image using ChatGPT, one of the newer technologies used by accountants. This appendix summarizes some of the key technologies mentioned throughout the textbook.

Figure A.1 AI-generated image of an accountant working at a computer.
Source: Generated with AI using DALL-E from Open AI

Data Analytics

Data analytics is the process of taking raw data and producing useful information. The goal is to create new information and insights, leading to better decision-making. Data analytics is at the heart of what management accountants do daily. Before the recent surge in analytics and new tools, accountants provided management insight into financial information by analyzing existing data. What is new is the software tools that put advanced analytics in end-users' hands rather than only programmers'.

Data for management accountants comes from a variety of sources. Much of the data is from accounting information systems, which could be a stand-alone accounting system such as QuickBooks for small businesses or a financial module in an enterprise resource planning (ERP) system. But, management accountants may also download data from public sources, such as economic indicators or benchmark statistics for an industry. Using a variety of data sources in analytics provides greater insights for decision-making.

Accountants have long used Excel as an analytics tool but frequently face limitations regarding the number of records and the ability to merge data tables. Newer analytics tools, called **self-service business intelligence software**[1] (SSBI), put advanced analytics in the hands of accountants. SSBI tools typically have a graphical interface that supports users with a no-code or low-code experience.

Some of the SSBI software packages on the market include the following:

- **Tableau** specializes in interactive visualization and can analyze large amounts of data. The Tableau Prep Builder helps users clean the data before they start analysis.
- **Power BI** has many of the same functions as Tableau but integrates closely with Microsoft products and databases. The interface is similar to other Microsoft products, making it easy to use. However, it also provides many more advanced functions.
- **Alteryx** is best for data preparation and blending rather than in-depth analysis or visualization. Typically, Alteryx preps the data to integrate with other SSBI tools like Tableau or Power BI.

There are many other tools, but these three are some of the more common tools accounting professionals use. Also advancing the use of analytics in accounting is the increased volume of data available to provide insights. Companies can store larger amounts of data relatively cheaply, and faster computers with more processing capacity have fueled the increase in analytics in recent years.

Types of Analytics

There are four main types of analytics: descriptive, diagnostic, predictive, and prescriptive. Figure A.2 shows the types of analytics on a scale of time from the past to the future and complexity. The figure shows that descriptive and diagnostic look to the past, while predictive and prescriptive look forward to the future. Each type of analytics has a different

[1] Dzuranin, A., Geertz, G., and Leek, M (2023). *Data and Analytics in Accounting*. Hoboken, NJ: Wiley.

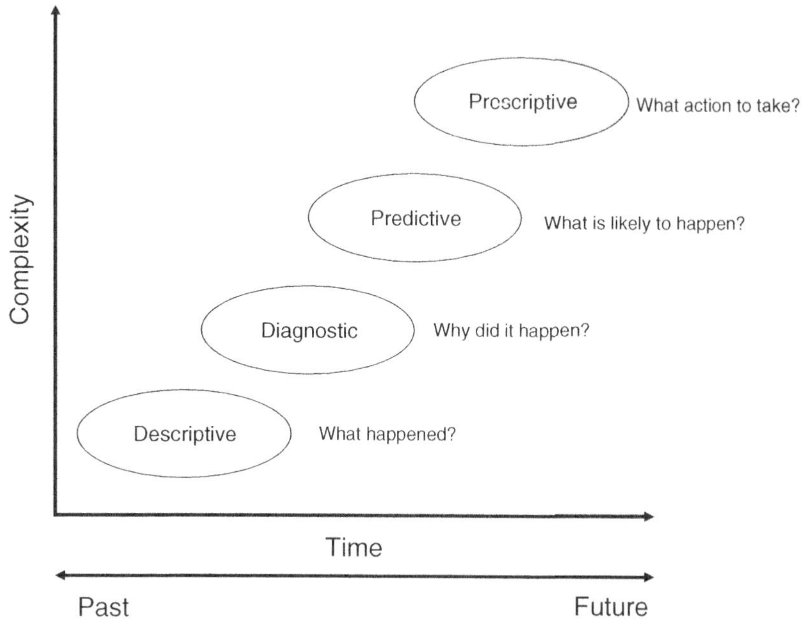

Figure A.2 Types of analytics.[2]
Source: Adapted from Vincent, N. and Igou, A. (2024).

function and type of information it provides. In addition, each type uses various techniques to help provide information.

Descriptive

Descriptive analytics look at the past and focus on answering what happened without further analysis into why. Descriptive analytics is usually the starting place for most analytics and the easiest as it provides an overview of the data before doing more complex analyses. Descriptive analytics would answer questions such as in what month were our sales the highest, did our costs increase over last year, who were our top customers last year, and what is our gross margin on a particular product?

Some typical techniques for descriptive analytics are shown in Table A.1.

Descriptive analytics can be done quickly using tools such as Excel, but Tableau or Power BI can also be used for more graphical visualizations or larger data sets. Most types of analysis require going beyond just descriptive techniques and other types of analytics to provide additional insights.

Diagnostic Analytics

Diagnostic analytics are also backward-looking, trying to determine why something happened. These techniques start with descriptive analytics findings and dig a bit further. For example, an

[2]Vincent, N., and Igou, A. (2024). *Emerging technologies for business professionals: A nontechnical guide to the governance and management of disruptive technologies*. Hoboken, NJ: Wiley.

accountant used diagnostic analytics to determine an unusual sales spike that occurred in June. The accountant would then use diagnostics analytics to determine why there was an unexpected spike in that month. Was there a promotion this year during June? Was there a higher demand for a specific product, or was there a location that had higher sales than average?

Some of the typical types of techniques for diagnostic analytics are shown in Table A.2

Data visualizations and dashboards are frequently used in conjunction with the previously described methods to help give a quick visual overview of the data. Most analytics tools can help users create visualizations that can quickly represent the data. See Figure A.3 of a dashboard created in Power BI.

Table A.1 Descriptive Analytics Techniques

Technique	Description	Sample Analysis
Data queries	Retrieve and organize data by using a query language, such as SQL or Access queries.	List the sales to Customer 100 in December 2025. What materials were purchased for Job #102?
Summary statistics	Calculations of standard statistics on a data set, such as mean, median, standard deviation, range, variance, maximum, range, or others.	What was the average sale of Product #431 by month during 2025? What was the highest sale made in November 2025?
Distributions	Summarizes the data by a subcategory.	Summarize the sales for 2025 by sales region. Summarize the cost of goods sold by product by month.
Filtering or data reductions	Extracting a subset of data for further analysis.	List the sales for the Midwest region by product.

Table A.2 Diagnostic Analytics Techniques

Technique	Description	Sample Analysis
Comparative descriptive analytics	Compare statistical analysis of company data to those of industry or historical benchmarks.	How does the increased cost of goods sold compare to others in the industry? How do our sales of Product #423 compare to last year?
Outliers	Review the data to see if particular data points differ significantly from the rest of the population. Visualizations can show outliers more easily.	Did we have any customer sales significantly larger than others?
Clustering	Find groups of objects that are more similar.	Which other customers are most similar to another?
Drill-down	List all the data records that are in a particular subset.	List the sales to Customer #421 in November 2025.

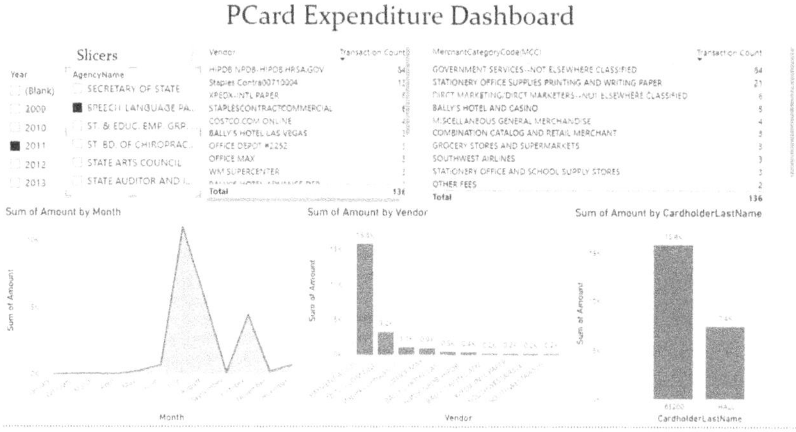

Figure A.3 Example of Power BI dashboard.

Predictive Analytics

As the name suggests, predictive analytics use past data to help determine what could happen in the future. These techniques use historical data from various sources to build a model. Then, the model will predict what may happen using current conditions and data. The model is built using mathematical methods to find connections between variables in the data. As more data are collected, the model "learns" and improves its predictions for future data.

For a more complex example of predictive analytics, a grocery store can use predictive analytics to forecast the grocery sales for the week leading up to a major holiday. The model learns from past historical sales data the things typically purchased before a holiday, such as baking supplies, wine, or ham. The grocery stores could add past weather data and other economic indicators to round out the model. Once the model is built with past data, the current conditions, such as the current prices and weather predictions, are updated. The model will use the information to predict the inventory items needed to meet the demand of a holiday rush. Predictive analytics models frequently use machine learning for forecasting. More details on how predictive analytics works will be in the next section.

Prescriptive Analytics

The final type of data analytics is prescriptive. It goes a step further than predictive analytics by predicting action to take. For example, after analyzing repair and usage data for equipment, a prescriptive model could recommend which preventive maintenance should be done on factory equipment first. These recommendations can help companies speed up decision-making by reviewing the recommended actions and integrating judgment to ensure the recommended action is the best option.

Prescriptive analytics can use a tool as simple as Goal-Seek in Excel to find the optimal value based on other parameters. For example, it could determine the product mix that provides the highest profit based on specified limitations. More complicated prescriptive analytics use artificial intelligence techniques to make recommendations.

Accountants use these types to find insights into existing data to give business leaders and managers more insight into planning, facilitating, and controlling the company's operations.

Artificial Intelligence—Machine Learning

Artificial intelligence (AI) is the ability of a computer to perform actions that would typically require human intelligence. There are examples of AI in many of the products and services we use daily. Some common examples include the following:

- Virtual assistants like Alexa or Siri use voice recognition and natural language processing (NLP) to understand requests and formulate answers in human language.
- Automobiles use computer vision and other AI techniques to warn you if you need to brake quickly due to an object ahead.
- Streaming services provide recommendations of movies to watch or playlists to listen to based on your past preferences.
- When you contact customer service for a retailer via web chat function, the retailer is likely using an AI-developed chatbot to answer standard questions.

As you can see, you are likely frequently using AI without considering how it works behind the scenes. Even though there are many types of AI systems, they are all built using a similar process. In short, every AI system uses existing data to train and build a model. Then, the model is used to make predictions, take action, or create content.

More specifically, building an AI application requires significant amounts of data. The more complex the model, the more data are needed for training and testing. The data can be in all forms, from structured data like databases to text data, such as emails, audio, images, or even video, depending on the model required. The data are split into training data and testing data.

First, the AI algorithm imports the training data. Depending on the statistical methods and other details the developer selects, the algorithm builds an initial model for prediction. Then, the testing data are used to determine the accuracy of the initial model. Making the model is often iterative until the developer finds the optimal model.

Machine Learning

Machine learning is the most commonly used type of AI. Machine learning uses computers to learn by finding patterns within the data to determine similarity and using mathematical models. The system will continue to adapt as it is trained on additional data; thus, it seems to "learn."

One of the things machine learning does well is prediction based on mathematical and statistical methods, making it a form of predictive analytics. Management accountants now use machine learning to aid with forecasting and other predictions. Consider this example: the accounting supervisor has asked to predict the factory maintenance costs for the next three years, and you want to try using machine learning.

First, you need to consider the types of data you should include in the model. Here is a sample list of things you would consider adding:

- Machine data—including the ID, machine age, type of machine, operating hours per month
- Maintenance records—dates and types of maintenance performed on each machine and the relevant costs
- Comparison of maintenance costs for similar machines—do the costs historically increase as this type of machine ages?
- Potential factors that increase maintenance—temperature, increased use, speed of operation
- Predicted production load—how many hours do we expect to use the machine?

The model would predict the approximate amount of machine maintenance over the next year. The model would predict the number of times and types of service each machine would likely need over the next 12 months by examining the past service of that machine and comparing it to other similar machines.

Supervised Learning

There are two main types of machine learning: supervised and unsupervised. With supervised machine learning, the algorithm is trained on labeled data. In other words, each input data point is labeled with the correct output. The machine learning algorithm trains on the labeled data to find similarities between the input data. It predicts the output of the unseen data using what it "learned" from the labeled data. Figure A.4 depicts a simple example of supervised machine learning that is built to determine if a picture of an animal is a dog or not.

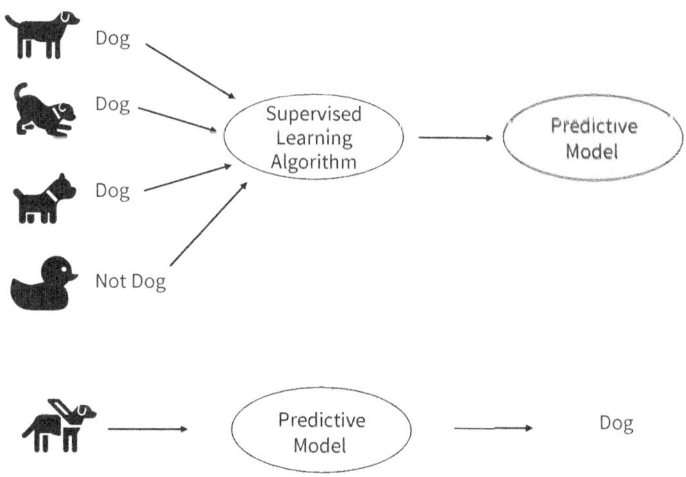

Figure A.4 Supervised machine learning.

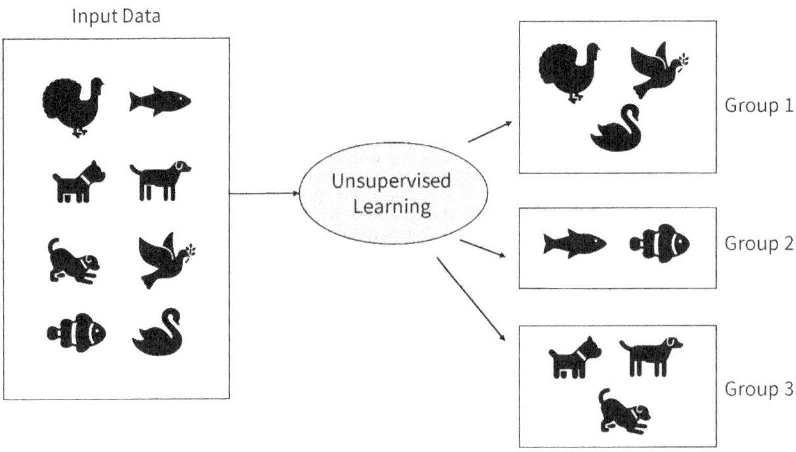

Figure A.5 Unsupervised learning.

The machine maintenance example describes supervised learning; the input data has the date, machine, and type of maintenance labeled for each service. The algorithm predicts the time and service needed in the next 12 months using this known information in the data. Another example of supervised learning is the spam filter on your email system. The model was trained using past emails labeled either spam or not. Based on the similarities in the spam emails, the model can predict whether new, unseen emails are spam.

Unsupervised Learning

Unsupervised learning algorithms train using unlabeled data. The goal is to find patterns in the data without knowing what the output should be. The goal is to find patterns and place the data into groups or clusters based only on relationships or similarities. The algorithm does not define these groups. Figure A.5 shows how unsupervised learning could cluster pictures of animals into groups based on their similarities. However, note that none of the resulting groups have a label, such as dogs, birds, or fish, only numbers.

One everyday use of unsupervised learning is customer segmentation. Any business with customer data can use this model but has not put them in defined groups. The model can cluster them in groups based on their similar characteristics. The characteristics can range from age, gender, purchasing habits, spending amounts, or frequency of visits. This output can give the marketing team insight into the habits of particular individuals that they can use for personalization.

Artificial Intelligence—Generative AI

Another form of artificial intelligence that has emerged is generative artificial intelligence, also known as GenAI. The most common GenAI tool is OpenAI's ChatGPT. **Generative AI** is the ability to create original artifacts, such as text, images, video, and voice, by learning from existing sources. Two users could enter the same prompt, and each would receive a unique output.

GenAI works similarly to a student learning to write better essays by reading examples. GenAI learns by training on large amounts of written texts of all varieties and images or music. From this, GenAI builds a model by examining patterns in the data. In some ways, we do the same thing. For example, if someone says, have a nice <blank>. You probably automatically fill in the blank with the word day. GenAI works in much the same manner. It does not memorize everything it sees but understands what goes together and predicts what makes sense.

When GenAI responds, it generates content by making educated guesses. It continues to predict one word at a time until it has completed the task. It gets feedback when the user clarifies a prompt or enters a rating at the end. GenAI seems to think and act human because of how quickly it works and some of the creative results it produces. However, it is only generating things based on probabilities. For example, most stories about heroes likely mention bravery; therefore, GenAI will include bravery in a story. Also, GenAI seems human because it has a conversational style. The model was trained and provided data to make it speak like a human. The model will continue to learn as it receives feedback and learns from additional data.

Figure A.6 is a fun example of Generative AI at work.

Besides using ChatGPT for fun, there are also ways that GenAI can make accountants' work easier. Here are some examples of tasks that GenAI can help accountants.

1. Draft financial reports. GenAI can summarize data and create financial summaries and analyses.
2. Create an initial budget based on historical data and economic indicators.
3. Create training documentation to explain complex accounting concepts to nonfinancial coworkers.
4. Find anomalies in financial transactions that could indicate fraud or errors.
5. Analyze contracts for terms by reading the text and answering questions regarding the contract.

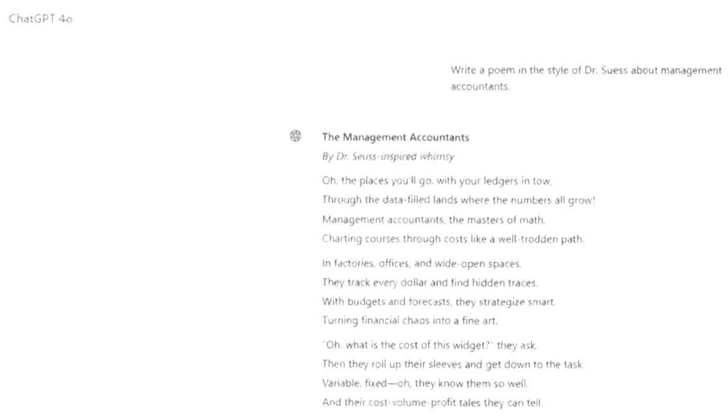

Figure A.6 Example of GenAI using ChatGPT.

As you can see, the possibilities for using GenAI are endless. One word of caution. Since many models use any data input by the user to train the model, check your company policy before loading sensitive data into one of the GenAI models. Depending on which GenAI tool you use, you can change settings to prevent your data from being used for training. Many companies also have private versions of secure GenAI models that can be used for sensitive data.

There are several different GenAI sites that you can use to write prompts and start your work. Each of them has distinct features and strengths that are constantly changing. All these models offer a free version and an upgraded paid version.

- ChatGPT (OpenAI) is the original large language model. It is excellent for various tasks, from drafting emails, analyzing data, and generating images and videos with the paid version.
- CoPilot (Microsoft) is based on ChatGPT's underlying language model. Its strength is its integration with other Microsoft products, allowing many users to be power users.
- Gemini (Google) combines AI with live web searches and quickly summarizes the results. Images are only with the paid version.
- Perplexity (privately held) is a newer model, and its strength is its research and accurate citations.
- Claude (Anthropic) promotes itself as the leader in GenAI for data security and ethical use of AI. However, it can perform most of the same tasks as the other models.

All these models interact with humans using prompts. Writing an effective prompt is much different than using a search engine like Google. To get more accurate information, it is important to write good prompts. If you use GenAI in the same way as a search engine you will likely not get the results you want.

Here are some tips for generating good prompts:

- Be clear and specific by precisely stating what you want and avoiding vague language. Rather than writing "Tell me about accounting," use a more specific prompt: "Explain the differences between financial and managerial accounting."
- Provide the context. This could include explaining your knowledge level as the user or the role you wish GenAI to take. For example, "explain accrual accounting concepts to someone without prior accounting knowledge."
- Use step-by-step instructions to help break down a long task into steps. You can also ask GenAI to break down a process to ensure each part is completed correctly. For example, you can ask, "List the steps for preparing a cash flow statement using the indirect method."
- Set the tone and style of the format you need, and GenAI will adapt its responses. For example, "Write a professional email to a client requesting additional information."

These are just a few ways to generate better prompts to get the information you want. Keep in mind that these models are continuously learning and changing. If you find something that GenAI does not do well today, it will likely be able to soon.

Robotic Process Automation

Robotic process automation (RPA) uses software to automate processes with little or no coding required. Unlike other automation techniques that need coding, RPA software has a graphical interface where end users can design a process that can run on demand, at a scheduled time, or upon a trigger, such as a new file. This new classification of software can change accountants' work by reducing repetitive and mundane tasks and replacing them with more value-added tasks. RPA differs from AI in that it does not learn from past actions or data; it just follows the steps designated by the designer. In short, RPA "takes the robot out of the human."[3]

RPA works best for well-defined processes without requiring significant human intervention or thought. In general, if you cannot create a flow chart to show the steps in the process, it is likely not a good match for RPA. Management accountants can use RPA to speed up many of the routine and otherwise tedious tasks performed day to day. Since nonprogrammers can now automate processes relatively quickly, it is an excellent option for accounting functions.

RPA will likely change how accountants work in the future by automating some of the more tedious tasks that accountants do and allowing them to work on tasks that require judgment. The following are some of the functions that RPA can assist accountants with:

- Processing email attachments
- Entering information into an ERP from a spreadsheet
- Reformatting data and creating reports
- Filling in forms
- Creating standard journal entries
- Completing bank reconciliations

As a result, accountants can be valued team members throughout the bot development process[4], even if they do not create the bot themselves. Therefore, accountants need a basic understanding of RPA, how it works, and the tasks it can automate.

Since most RPA software feels like a flowchart, the first step before creating a bot is to draw the flowchart. Figure A.7 shows a simple flowchart for an invoice process. Creating the flowchart will help you or the developer build the bot more easily.

How RPA works

RPA works the same as creating a macro in Microsoft Excel, except it can be used across multiple software packages. For example, RPA can create a script following the flowchart in Figure A.7. In this case, RPA can monitor an email account to which suppliers send copies of invoices in a standard format. The RPA script can download and save the PDF attachments to a specific file location. The script can then open each file, login to an ERP system, and enter details from

[3] Lhuer, X. (2016). *The next acronym you need to know about: RPA (robotic process automation)* [online]. McKinsey Digital. Available from: https://www.mckinsey.com/capabilities/mckinsey-digital/our-insights/the-next-acronym-you-need-to-know-about-rpa
[4] Coe, M., Igou, A., and Schwartz, N. (2021). Robotic process automation in accounting education. *CPA Journal*. Available from https://www.cpajournal.com/2021/12/01/icymi-robotic-process-automation-in-accounting-education/

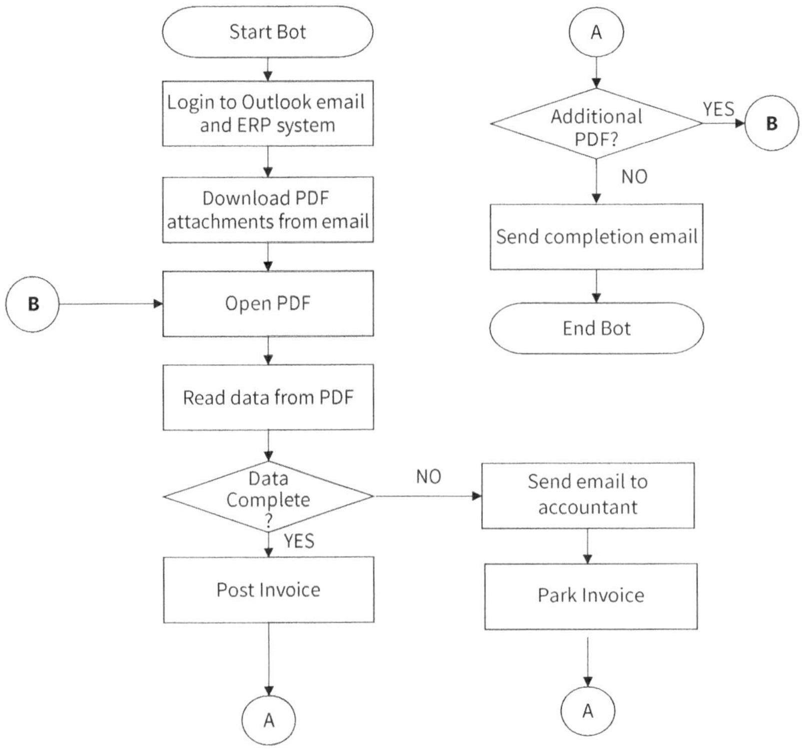

Figure A.7 Flowchart of the invoice process.

the PDF invoice into the ERP system. Once the script posts the invoice, it can email the appropriate person stating that the invoice posting is complete. The user can design the RPA script to handle exceptions. For example, if the invoice tax is incorrect, the bot will send an email to an accountant to resolve the issue.

There are three main components of RPA software:

1. The end user uses the studio or bot designer interface to design the RPA script or bot. The user can use a GUI (graphical user interface) to add the steps and create the process. An example of the studio from UIPath is shown in Figure A.8.
2. The bot orchestrator is the control hub for the RPA scripts. It will deploy, schedule, and monitor the execution of the bots. Bots may be triggered to run at a particular time, upon an action, or when a user executes the bot.
3. Bots are the executable RPA script that performs the tasks as designed in the studio.

To create the RPA script or bot, a user would use software such as UIPath, Power Automate, BluePrism, or Automation Anywhere. Most RPA software packages allow users to record and modify the steps or use the GUI to enter each process step. Before beginning to

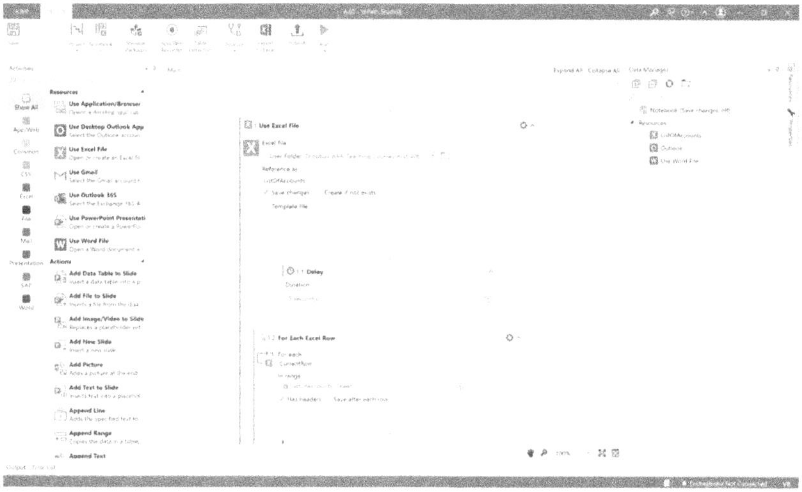

Figure A.8 UIPath's Studio X.

enter the process in the software, a user should flowchart the steps in the process, remembering to include each step a human would perform, including simple things like logging into a system or clicking on a field to select it. An RPA process can also include decision points and alternate paths. For example, suppose the invoice in the previous example has a blank tax field. In that case, the script can denote what should happen in that exception and follow the appropriate steps. Once the process is designed, the RPA software creates executable code in the background for the computer to execute.

Key Terms

self-service business intelligence software Software that enables users to independently analyze and visualize data through intuitive, no-code tools.
data analytics The process of taking raw data and producing useful information.
generative AI A form of artifical intelligence that generates new artifacts, such as language, audio, images, or video by learning from existing sources.

Obtaining Software

ChatGPT

ChatGPT, developed by OpenAI is not a separate software package but available at https://chatgpt.com/. For some of the functions, you need to have a login and password, but a paid account is not needed for the exercises in the book.

PowerAutomate—Microsoft's RPA software.

PowerAutomate ships free with Windows 11 or it can be downloaded at: https://apps.microsoft.com/detail/9nftch6j7fhv

Available for Windows only.

Power BI—Microsoft's data analysis and visualization software.

PowerBI is available with Office 365 license. You may download at: https://www.microsoft.com/en-us/download/details.aspx?id=58494

Available for Windows only.

Tableau—Data visualization software.

Free licenses are available for students and academics. Teaching materials are also available.

You may download at: https://www.tableau.com/academic/teaching

Available for Windows and macOS

WEKA (Waikato Environment for Knowledge Analysis)

A free tool developed by a Waikato University in New Zealand to practice machine learning. You may download at: https://sourceforge.net/projects/weka/

Available for Windows only

APPENDIX B: PLANNING AND BUDGETING FOR BUSINESS OPERATIONS USING SPREADSHEETS

Budgeting with Spreadsheets

Many organizations use spreadsheet packages like Microsoft Excel as a tool to prepare their operating budgets. Spreadsheets offer flexibility, user-friendliness, and ability to handle complex calculations. Spreadsheets, such as Microsoft Excel, are both easy to use and provide an easy to understand and intuitive interface for users to input, edit, and analyze data without requiring additional training or skills. Spreadsheets are also cost-effective compared to specialized budgeting software, making them extremely common for use at small to mid-sized organizations. In addition, spreadsheets offer easy customization, which allows organizations to tailor layouts, formulas, and formats to meet their specific needs. The flexibility of spreadsheets makes it easy to update budgets as new information becomes available, and they use built-in tools like charts and graphs to help visualize financial data for better analysis.

Organizations typically use spreadsheets for budgeting by creating separate sheets for different departments or expense categories where data such as sales, payroll, production, and other information are entered. Built-in functions like SUM, AVERAGE, and IF enable quick calculations and scenario analysis. Spreadsheets allow for sensitivity analyses and modeling various scenarios to allow managers to test different financial outcomes by adjusting assumptions or inputs.

Another important feature of spreadsheets is the ability to link sheets. Linking connects data between sheets so that changes in one location automatically update in other locations. For example, a formula from one sheet can pull data or even formulas from other sheets using cell references. This allows budgets to become dynamic tools for planning and forecasting and particularly useful when consolidating multiple departmental budgets into the master budget. Linking sheets together also reduces redundant data entry, enhances accuracy by minimizing errors, and supports collaboration by allowing departments to work on their own sheets that are ultimately rolled up into an organization-wide master budget. The flexibility of rolling up interconnected sheets allows for real-time analysis and for budgets to be updated on the fly.

Let's look at the Bob Willis Custom Wheel Company budget from Chapter 9 using the standard spreadsheet package, Microsoft Excel. Much like the budget we prepared by hand, the Excel-based budget starts with the assumptions and the beginning balance sheet, which we like to put on separate tabs. The beginning balance sheet gives us a starting point for many of our formulas, and the assumptions are the details for the current year. It is efficient to put all of the assumptions in one centralized location where we document and manage key variables, parameters, and estimates that drive the budget's calculations. The assumptions typically include essential data such as projected sales, fixed costs and variable cost rates, inventory estimates, cash collections and payment information, and more. When designed in this manner, the assumptions tab allows users to easily update estimates and parameters, automatically updating linked formulas and tabs throughout the spreadsheet. The budget assumptions tab enhances accuracy by providing a single source for data input. It simplifies adjustments, making it an important element of a good budget. The assumptions for the Bob Willis Custom Wheel Company are shown in Figure B.1.

	A	B	C	D
3	Sales Budget		Units	$ Dollars
4	Quarter 1		1,000	$200,000
5	Quarter 2		1,200	$240,000
6	Quarter 3		1,600	$320,000
7	Quarter 4		1,000	$200,000
8				
9	Sales Price		$200.00	
10				
11	Finished Goods Inventory Assumptions			
12	Target ending finished goods inventory (% next quarter's sales)		20%	
13	Beginning finished goods inventory (Units)		200	
14	Next year's first quarter estimated production		1,200	
15				
16	Work in Process Inventory Assumptions			
17	Target ending work in process (% of next quarter's ending finished ç		10%	
18	Beginning work in process			
19	Ending work in process			
20				
21	Raw Material Inventory Assumptions			
22	Raw material requirements:		Spoke Wire	Stainless Rim Steel
23	Raw material items per finished goods unit (Linear feet)		27.00	5.00
24	Cost per unit		$1.00	$7.00
25	Target ending inventory (% next quarter's production needs)		15%	15%
26	Beginning raw material inventory (Linear feet)		4,212.00	780.00
27	Raw material needed to meet production for next year first quarter (L		4,212.00	780.00
28				
29	Direct Labor Assumptions			
30	Direct labor required per unit (Hours)		0.75	
31	Direct labor cost per hour		$25.00	
32				
33	Overhead Assumptions			
34	Gas and electricity Per Unit		$0.75	
35	Maintenance cost per unit		$4.00	
36	Indirect matrial cost per unit		$1.50	
37	Inspection cost per batch		$25.00	
38	Number of units produced per batch		10	
39				
40	Selling General and Administrative Assumptions			
41	Sales commission rate		5.0%	
42	Frieght out cost per unit		$12.00	
43				
44	Cash Flow Assumptions			
45	Current quarter cash receipt rate		85%	
46	Prior quarter cash receipt rate		13%	
47	Uncollectable accounts percentage		2%	
48				
49	Current quarter cash payment rate		90%	
50	Prior quarter cash payment rate		10%	
51				
52	Sales 4th quarter last year		$200,000	
53	Purchases 4th quarter last year		$65,000	

Figure B.1 Budget assumptions.

The **sales budget** links to both the unit sales and sales price per unit in the budget assumptions. These formulas ensure that any updates to the assumptions, such as changes in sales volume or pricing, are automatically reflected in the sales budget calculations. Figure B.2 illustrates the sales budget formulas followed by the results.

The **production budget** stems from the unit sales in the sales budget. Notice that the production budget pulls in the unit sales values and multiplies those times the assumptions related to inventory target percentages. Beginning inventory is given, and ending inventory is a function of the proceeding period's ending inventory. This structure ensures that production levels are aligned with both current sales and future inventory needs and can be useful for managing production operations. Figure B.3 illustrates the production budget formulas followed by the results.

	A	B	C	D	E	F
1			Bob Wills' Custom Wheel Company			
2			Sales Budget			
3			Year Ending December 20XX			
4						
5			Quarter			
6		1	2	3	4	Year
7	Projected unit sales	=+Assumptions!C4	=+Assumptions!C5	=+Assumptions!C6	=+Assumptions!C7	=SUM(B7:E7)
8	Sales price per unit	=+Assumptions!$C$9	=+Assumptions!$C$9	=+Assumptions!$C$9	=+Assumptions!$C$9	=+Assumptions!$C$9
9	Total projected sales	=+B7*B8	=+C7*C8	=+D7*D8	=+E7*E8	=+F7*F8

	A	B	C	D	E	F
1		Bob Wills' Custom Wheel Company				
2		Sales Budget				
3		Year Ending December 20XX				
4						
5			Quarter			
6		1	2	3	4	Year
7	Projected unit sales	1,000	1,200	1,600	1,000	4,800
8	Sales price per unit	$ 200	$ 200	$ 200	$ 200	$ 200
9	Total projected sales	200,000	240,000	320,000	200,000	960,000

Figure B.2 Sales budget.

	A	B	C	D	E	F
1			Bob Wills' Custom Wheel Company			
2			Production Budget			
3			Year Ending December 20XX			
4						
5		1	2	3	4	Year
6	Sales, units	=+Sales!B7	=+Sales!C7	=+Sales!D7	=+Sales!E7	
7	Target ending inventory, units	=+C6*Assumptions!$C$12	=+D6*Assumptions!$C$12	=+E6*Assumptions!$C$12	=+Assumptions!C14*Assumptions!$C$12	
8	Units required	=SUM(B6:B7)	=SUM(C6:C7)	=SUM(D6:D7)	=SUM(E6:E7)	
9	Less beginning inventory, units	=+Assumptions!C13	=+B7	=+C7	=+D7	
10	Production needed	=B8-B9	=C8-C9	=D8-D9	=E8-E9	=SUM(B10:E10)

	A	B	C	D	E	F
1		Bob Wills' Custom Wheel Company				
2		Production Budget				
3		Year Ending December 20XX				
4						
5		1	2	3	4	Year
6	Sales, units	1,000	1,200	1,600	1,000	
7	Target ending inventory, units	240	320	200	240	
8	Units required	1,240	1,520	1,800	1,240	
9	Less beginning inventory, units	200	240	320	200	
10	Production needed	1,040	1,280	1,480	1,040	4,840

Figure B.3 Production budget.

The **direct material budget** stems from the production budget and outlines the materials required to meet production needs. Notice that the direct material budget pulls in the production quantities and multiplies those by assumptions related to material usage per unit. Beginning direct material inventory is given, and ending inventory is calculated based on target inventory percentages to ensure sufficient materials are available for future production. This format ensures that direct material purchases align closely with production demands while avoiding overstocking or shortages. Additionally, the direct material budget dynamically adjusts to changes in production levels, providing a flexible tool for managing material purchases. Figure B.4 illustrates the direct materials budget results followed by the formulas.

16			Wheel Spokes			
17			Quarter			
18		1	2	3	4	Year
19	Units to be produced	1,040	1,280	1,480	1,040	
20	Linear feet of spoke wire per finished wheel	27	27	27	27	
21	Spoke wire required to meet production	28,080	34,560	39,960	28,080	
22	Add: Target ending inventory in linear feet	5,184	5,994	4,212	4,212	
23	Total linear feet of spoke wire needed	33,264	40,554	44,172	32,292	
24	Less: Beginning inventory in linear feet	4,212	5,184	5,994	4,212	
25	Purchases needed (in linear feet)	29,052	35,370	38,178	28,080	130,680
26	Cost per linear foot	$ 1.00	$ 1.00	$ 1.00	$ 1.00	$ 1.00
27	Total cost of purchases	$ 29,052	$ 35,370	$ 38,178	$ 28,080	$ 130,680
28						
29			Wheel Rims			
30			Quarter			
31		1	2	3	4	Year
32	Units to be produced	1,040	1,280	1,480	1,040	
33	Linear feet of rim steel per finished wheel	5.00	5.00	5.00	5.00	
34	Rim steel required to meet production	5,200	6,400	7,400	5,200	
35	Add: Target ending inventory in linear feet	960	1,110	780	780	
36	Total linear feet of rim steel needed	6,160	7,510	8,180	5,980	
37	Less: Beginning inventory in linear feet	780	960	1,110	780	
38	Purchases needed (in linear feet)	5,380	6,550	7,070	5,200	24,200
39	Cost per linear foot	$ 7.00	$ 7.00	$ 7.00	$ 7.00	$ 7.00
40	Total cost of purchases	$ 37,660	$ 45,850	$ 49,490	$ 36,400	$ 169,400
41						
42	Total cost of spoke wire purchases	29,052	35,370	38,178	28,080	130,680
43	Total cost or wheel rim purchases	37,660	45,850	49,490	36,400	169,400
44	Total raw material purchases	66,712	81,220	87,668	64,480	300,080

16				Wheel Spokes		
17				Quarter		
18		1	2	3	4	Year
19	Units to be produced	=+B10	=+C10	=+D10	=+E10	
20	Linear feet of spoke wire per finished wheel	=+Assumptions!$C$23	=+Assumptions!$C$23	=+Assumptions!$C$23	=+Assumptions!$C$23	
21	Spoke wire required to meet production	=+B19*B20	=+C19*C20	=+D19*D20	=+E19*E20	
22	Add: Target ending inventory in linear feet	=+C21*Assumptions!$C$25	=+D21*Assumptions!$C$25	=+E21*Assumptions!$C$25	=+Assumptions!C27	
23	Total linear feet of spoke wire needed	=SUM(B21:B22)	=SUM(C21:C22)	=SUM(D21:D22)	=SUM(E21:E22)	
24	Less: Beginning inventory in linear feet	=+Assumptions!C26	=+B22	=+C22	=+D22	
25	Purchases needed (in linear feet)	=B23-B24	=C23-C24	=D23-D24	=E23-E24	=SUM(B25:E25)
26	Cost per linear foot	=+Assumptions!$C$24	=+Assumptions!$C$24	=+Assumptions!$C$24	=+Assumptions!$C$24	=+Assumptions!$C$24
27	Total cost of purchases	=B25*B26	=C25*C26	=D25*D26	=E25*E26	=SUM(B27:E27)
28						
29				Wheel Rims		
30				Quarter		
31		1	2	3	4	Year
32	Units to be produced	=+B10	=+C10	=+D10	=+E10	
33	Linear feet of rim steel per finished wheel	=+Assumptions!$D$23	=+Assumptions!$D$23	=+Assumptions!$D$23	=+Assumptions!$D$23	
34	Rim steel required to meet production	=+B32*B33	=+C32*C33	=+D32*D33	=+E32*E33	
35	Add: Target ending inventory in linear feet	=+C34*Assumptions!$D$25	=+D34*Assumptions!$D$25	=+E34*Assumptions!$D$25	=+Assumptions!D27	
36	Total linear feet of rim steel needed	=SUM(B34:B35)	=SUM(C34:C35)	=SUM(D34:D35)	=SUM(E34:E35)	
37	Less: Beginning inventory in linear feet	=+Assumptions!D26	=+B35	=+C35	=+D35	
38	Purchases needed (in linear feet)	=B36-B37	=C36-C37	=D36-D37	=E36-E37	=SUM(B38:E38)
39	Cost per linear foot	=+Assumptions!$D$24	=+Assumptions!$D$24	=+Assumptions!$D$24	=+Assumptions!$D$24	=+Assumptions!$D$24
40	Total cost of purchases	=B38*B39	=C38*C39	=D38*D39	=E38*E39	=SUM(B40:E40)
41						
42	Total cost of spoke wire purchases	=+B27	=+C27	=+D27	=+E27	=+F27
43	Total cost or wheel rim purchases	=+B40	=+C40	=+D40	=+E40	=+F40
44	Total raw material purchases	=+B42+B43	=+C42+C43	=+D42+D43	=+E42+E43	=+F42+F43

Figure B.4 Direct material budget.

	A	B	C	D	E	F
1			Bob Wills' Custom Wheel Company			
2			Direct Labor Budget			
3			Year Ending December 20XX			
4						
5		1	2	3	4	Year
6	Units to be produced (from production budget)	1,040	1,280	1,480	1,040	4,840
7	Direct labor hours per unit	0.75	0.75	0.75	0.75	0.75
8	Direct labor hours required	780	960	1,110	780	3,630
9	Cost per direct labor hour	$ 25.00	$ 25.00	$ 25.00	$ 25.00	$ 25.00
10	Total direct labor cost	$ 19,500	$ 24,000	$ 27,750	$ 19,500	$ 90,750

	A	B	C	D	E	F
1			Bob Wills' Custom Wheel Company			
2			Direct Labor Budget			
3			Year Ending December 20XX			
4						
5		1	2	3	4	Year
6	Units to be produced (from production budget)	=Production_Purchasing!B10	=Production_Purchasing!C10	=Production_Purchasing!D10	=Production_Purchasing!E10	=SUM(B6:E6)
7	Direct labor hours per unit	=Assumptions!$C$30	=Assumptions!$C$30	=Assumptions!$C$30	=Assumptions!$C$30	=Assumptions!$C$30
8	Direct labor hours required	=B6*B7	=C6*C7	=D6*D7	=E6*E7	=F6*F7
9	Cost per direct labor hour	=Assumptions!$C$31	=Assumptions!$C$31	=Assumptions!$C$31	=Assumptions!$C$31	=Assumptions!$C$31
10	Total direct labor cost	=B8*B9	=C8*C9	=D8*D9	=E8*E9	=F8*F9

Figure B.5 Direct labor budget.

The **labor budget** stems from the production budget and calculates the labor hours and costs required to meet production needs. Notice the labor budget pulls in the production unit quantities and multiplies those by assumptions related to labor hours per unit and hourly wage rates. The direct labor budget automatically reflects any adjustments to production levels, hours per unit assumptions, or labor rates. This approach provides a dynamic labor budget with current information for monitoring labor costs, planning workforce needs, and supporting labor management. Figure B.5 illustrates the labor budget results followed by the formulas.

The **manufacturing overhead budget** stems from the production budget and relies on key assumptions to estimate the costs associated with supporting production activities. Notice the manufacturing overhead budget pulls in the production quantities and applies assumptions related to variable overhead costs per unit, as well as fixed overhead costs. Variable costs, such as gas and electricity or maintenance, fluctuate with production levels. In contrast, fixed costs, such as depreciation or rent, remain constant regardless of output. The overhead budget dynamically adjusts to changes in production levels, ensuring overhead costs are aligned with actual production. Figure B.6 illustrates the manufacturing overhead budget results followed by the formulas.

The **cost of goods sold budget** is an important component in matching the expenses associated with producing and selling goods during the budget period with sales. It consists of two primary parts: calculating the total per-unit cost for the entire budget period and using this per-unit cost to determine the actual cost of goods sold and ending finished goods balances. The total per-unit cost is calculated by summing up the per unit costs of direct materials, direct labor, and manufacturing overhead from their respective budgets.

The cost of goods sold budget then utilized the per unit costs when calculating finished goods values. The cost of goods sold budget begins with direct materials and direct material purchases are adjusted by adding the beginning direct material inventory and subtracting the ending direct material inventory to calculate the direct material used during the period. Then, direct labor and manufacturing overhead costs are pulled from their respective budgets and added. These components are summed to calculate the total manufacturing cost.

	A	B	C	D	E	F
1			Bob Wills' Custom Wheel Company			
2			Manufacturing Overhead Budget			
3			Year Ending December 20XX			
4						
5		1	2	3	4	Year
6	Units produced	1,040	1,280	1,480	1,040	4,840
7						
8	Fixed Costs					
9	Gas and electricity	3,000	3,000	3,000	3,000	12,000
10	Facility rent	9,000	9,000	9,000	9,000	36,000
11	Production manager salary	22,500	22,500	22,500	22,500	90,000
12	Depreciation	4,500	4,500	4,500	4,500	18,000
13	Total Fixed Costs	39,000	39,000	39,000	39,000	156,000
14						
15	Variable Costs					
16	Gas and electricity	780	960	1,110	780	3,630
17	Maintenance	4,160	5,120	5,920	4,160	19,360
18	Indirect material	1,560	1,920	2,220	1,560	7,260
19	Inspection	2,600	3,200	3,700	2,600	12,100
20	Total Variable Costs	9,100	11,200	12,950	9,100	42,350
21						
22	Total Overhead Costs	$48,100	$50,200	$51,950	$48,100	$198,350

	A	B	C	D	E	F
1			Bob Wills' Custom Wheel Company			
2			Manufacturing Overhead Budget			
3			Year Ending December 20XX			
4						
5		1	2	3	4	Year
6	Units produced	1040	1280	1450	1040	4840
7						
8	Fixed Costs					
9	Gas and electricity	3000	3000	3000	3000	=SUM(B9:E9)
10	Facility rent	9000	9000	9000	9000	=SUM(B10:E10)
11	Production manager salary	22500	22500	22500	22500	=SUM(B11:E11)
12	Depreciation	4500	4500	4500	4500	=SUM(B12:E12)
13	Total Fixed Costs	=SUM(B9:B12)	=SUM(C9:C12)	=SUM(D9:D12)	=SUM(E9:E12)	=SUM(B13:E13)
14						
15	Variable Costs					
16	Gas and electricity	=+B6*Assumptions!$C$34	=+C6*Assumptions!$C$34	=+D6*Assumptions!$C$34	=+E6*Assumptions!$C$34	=SUM(B16:E16)
17	Maintenance	=+B6*Assumptions!$C$35	=+C6*Assumptions!$C$35	=+D6*Assumptions!$C$35	=+E6*Assumptions!$C$35	=SUM(B17:E17)
18	Indirect material	=+B6*Assumptions!$C$36	=+C6*Assumptions!$C$36	=+D6*Assumptions!$C$36	=+E6*Assumptions!$C$36	=SUM(B18:E18)
19	Inspection	=+B6*Assumptions!$C$37*Assumptions!$C$38	=+C6*Assumptions!$C$37*Assumptions!$C$38	=+D6*Assumptions!$C$37*Assumptions!$C$38	=+E6*Assumptions!$C$37*Assumptions!$C$38	=SUM(B19:E19)
20	Total Variable Costs	=SUM(B16:B19)	=SUM(C16:C19)	=SUM(D16:D19)	=SUM(E16:E19)	=SUM(B20:F20)
21						
22	Total Overhead Costs	=+B13+B20	=+C13+C20	=+D13+D20	=+E13+E20	=+F13+F20

Figure B.6 Manufacturing overhead budget.

To account for changes in work-in-process inventory, the beginning work-in-process inventory is added to the total manufacturing cost, and the ending work-in-process inventory is subtracted, resulting in the cost of goods manufactured, This figure is then adjusted by adding the beginning finished goods inventory (initially pulled from the balance sheet in the first quarter, then from the prior period ending inventory in subsequent quarters) and subtracting the ending finished goods inventory to compute the cost of goods sold. The ending finished goods inventory is calculated by multiplying the total per unit cost times the ending finished goods inventory for the respective period on the production budget. Figure B.7 illustrates the cost of goods sold budget results followed by the formulas.

The **selling and administrative budget** focuses on estimating the costs associated with operating the business outside of production and includes sales and marketing and other general administrative expenses. This budget can have both variable and fixed costs, but the majority of the expenses are usually fixed. Fixed costs include items such as salaries for office staff, insurance, depreciation, and much more. The variable components of the selling and administrative

Panel A: Per Unit Cost Schedule

	A	B	C	D
1			Bob Wills' Custom Wheel Company	
2			Per Unit Cost Schedule	
3			Year Ending December 20XX	
4				
5	Per Unit Costs	Cost	Units	Cost Per Unit
6	Fixed Costs	=+Overhead!F13	=+Production_Purchasing!F10	=+B6/C6
7	Variable Costs	=+Overhead!F20	=+C6	=+B7/C7
8	Total Overhead Per Unit	=+B7+B6	=+C7	=+D6+D7
9	Direct Material			=+Assumptions!C23*Assumptions!C24+Assumptions!D23*Assumptions!D24
10	Direct Labor			=+Assumptions!C31*Assumptions!C30
11	Estimated Total Cost Per Finished Wheel			=+D8+D9+D10

Bob Wills' Custom Wheel Company
Per Unit Cost Schedule
Year Ending December 20XX

Per Unit Costs	Cost	Units	Cost Per Unit
Fixed Costs	156,000	4,840	$ 32.23
Variable Costs	42,350	4,840	$ 8.75
Total Overhead Per Unit	$ 198,350	4,840	$ 40.98
Direct Material			$ 62.00
Direct Labor			$ 18.75
Estimated Total Cost Per Finished Wheel			$ 121.73

Panel B: Cost of Goods Sold

Bob Wills' Custom Wheel Comp
Cost of Good Sold Budget
Year Ending December 20XX

13				
14				
15				
16				
17	Direct Material	1	2	3
18	Raw Material Purchases	=+Production_Purchasing!B44	=+Production_Purchasing!C44	=+P
19	Add: Beginning Raw Material Inve	=+Balance_Sheet!B10	=+C20	=+D
20	Less: Ending Raw Material Invento	=+Production_Purchasing!B22*Production_Purchasing!B26+Production_Purchasing!B35*Production_Purc	=+Production_Purchasing!C22*Production_Purchasing!C26+Production_Purchasing!C35*Production_Purc	=+P
21	Raw Material Used	=+C18+C19-C20	=+D18+D19-D20	=+E
22	Direct Labor	=+Direct_Labor!B10	=+Direct_Labor!C10	=+D
23	Manufacturing Overhead	=+Overhead!B22	=+Overhead!C22	=+O
24	Total Manufacturing Cost	=+C21+C22+C23	=+D21+D22+D23	=+E
25	Add: Beginning Work In Process In	=+Balance_Sheet!B11	=+C26	=+D
26	Less: Ending Work In Process Inve	3895.40495867769	2434.62809917355	292
27	Cost of Goods Manufactured	=+C24+C25-C26	=+D24+D25-D26	=+E
28	Add: Beginning Finished Goods In	=+Balance_Sheet!B12	=+C28	=+D
29	Less: Ending Finished Goods	=+Production_Purchasing!B7*CGS!$D$11	=+Production_Purchasing!C7*CGS!$D$11	=+P
30	Cost of Goods Sold	=+C27+C28-C29	=+D27+D28-D29	=+E
31				

Bob Wills' Custom Wheel Company
Cost of Good Sold Budget
Year Ending December 20XX

Direct Material	1	2	3	4	Year
Raw Material Purchases	66,712	81,220	87,668	64,480	300,080
Add Beginning Raw Material Inventory	9,672	11,904	13,764	9,672	9,672
Less Ending Raw Material Inventory	11,904	13,764	9,672	9,672	9,672
Raw Material Used	64,480	79,360	91,760	64,480	300,080
Direct Labor	19,500	24,000	27,750	19,500	90,750
Manufacturing Overhead	48,100	50,200	51,950	48,100	198,350
Total Manufacturing Cost	132,080	153,560	171,460	132,080	589,180
Add Beginning Work In Process Inventory	2,922	3,895	2,435	2,922	2,922
Less Ending Work In Process Inventory	3,895	2,435	2,922	2,922	2,922
Cost of Goods Manufactured	131,107	155,021	170,973	132,080	589,180
Add Beginning Finished Goods Inventory	24,000	29,216	38,954	24,346	24,000
Less Ending Finished Goods	29,216	38,954	24,346	29,216	29,216
Cost of Goods Sold	$ 125,891	$ 145,282	$ 185,581	$ 127,211	$ 583,965

Figure B.7 Cost of goods sold budget.

budget in our example are sales commissions and freight costs, which are directly linked back to the assumptions. Sales commissions are calculated as a percentage of sales revenue, while freight costs are based on the number of units sold and the shipping cost per unit. Figure B.8 illustrates the selling and administrative budget results followed by the formulas.

The **cash budget** is a critical component of business financial planning and should provide a detailed estimate of cash inflows and outflows. The cash budget ensures the organization maintains sufficient liquidity to meet its obligations. We format our cash budget into four main parts: the cash receipts budget, cash disbursements for material purchases, other cash disbursements, and the cash budget summary. Each part pulls data from various related budgets and the assumptions.

The cash receipts section estimates the cash inflows generated primarily from sales. It pulls its data from the sales budget by separating total sales into current month cash receipts and collections from prior month sales. This breakdown ensures that cash flows reflect the timing of customer payments and any assumptions about the percentage of sales collected in each period.

	A	B	C	D	E	F
2		Selling and Administrative Budget				
3		Year Ending December 20XX				
4						
5		1	2	3	4	Year
6	Sales Commissions	10,000	12,000	16,000	10,000	48,000
7	Frieght Out	12,000	14,400	19,200	12,000	57,600
8	Executive Salary	10,000	10,000	10,000	10,000	40,000
9	Office Salary	5,000	5,000	5,000	5,000	20,000
10	Advertising	2,500	2,500	2,500	2,500	10,000
11	Insurance	1,500	1,500	1,500	1,500	6,000
12	Depreciation	1,500	1,500	1,500	1,500	6,000
13	Total Selling and Administrative Expenses	$ 42,500	$ 46,900	$ 55,700	$ 42,500	$ 187,600

	A	B	C	D	E	F
2			Selling and Administrative Budget			
3			Year Ending December 20XX			
4						
5		1	2	3	4	Year
6	Sales Commissions	=+Sales!B9*Assumptions!$C$41	=+Sales!C9*Assumptions!$C$41	=+Sales!D9*Assumptions!$C$41	=+Sales!E9*Assumptions!$C$41	=SUM(B6:E6)
7	Frieght Out	=+Sales!B7*Assumptions!$C$42	=+Sales!C7*Assumptions!$C$42	=+Sales!D7*Assumptions!$C$42	=+Sales!E7*Assumptions!$C$42	=SUM(B7:E7)
8	Executive Salary	10000	10000	10000	10000	=SUM(B8:E8)
9	Office Salary	5000	5000	5000	5000	=SUM(B9:E9)
10	Advertising	2500	2500	2500	2500	=SUM(B10:E10)
11	Insurance	1500	1500	1500	1500	=SUM(B11:E11)
12	Depreciation	1500	1500	1500	1500	=SUM(B12:E12)
13	Total Selling and Administrative Expenses	=+SUM(B6:B12)	=+SUM(C6:C12)	=+SUM(D6:D12)	=+SUM(E6:E12)	=SUM(B13:E13)
14						

Figure B.8 Selling and administrative budget.

This section focuses on cash outflows related to purchasing direct materials. It pulls data from the direct material purchases budget, breaking down payments into two categories: payments for current purchases and payments for prior month purchases. It also uses assumptions about collection patterns to estimate cash outflows.

This section includes other cash outflows related to production and administrative activities. It pulls data directly from the direct labor budget, manufacturing overhead budget, and selling and administrative budget. Depreciation, a noncash expense, is deducted from both overhead and selling and administrative costs to reflect only cash outflows. The result is the total cash disbursements, representing all cash payments outside of material purchases.

Finally, the cash inflow from the cash receipts budget, less the cash outflows from the cash disbursements for material purchases and other cash disbursements, are summarized to arrive at the cash balance for each period. Figure B.9 illustrates the cash budget results followed by the formulas.

The **budgeted income statement** consolidates data from the various budgets to project profitability over a specific period. It begins with sales revenue, taken from the sales budget, and deducts bad debts to account for uncollectible accounts. The result is net sales, the total revenue expected collected or realized. The cost of goods sold (COGS) is subtracted from net sales, which is taken directly from the COGS budget. In our example, we calculate gross margin, which is an indicator of operational efficiency. Next, selling and administrative expenses are deducted. They are pulled from the selling and administrative budget. The final figure is net income, which represents the organization's projected profit after deducting all operating expenses. Figure B.10 illustrates the budgeted income statement results followed by the formulas.

The budget is finalized with the **budgeted balance sheet**, which provides a comprehensive projection of the organization's financial position. The budgeted balance sheet integrates data from multiple budgets, including cash, sales, cost of goods sold, and the income statement, to forecast the balances of assets, liabilities, and equity.

	A	B	C	D	E	F
1			Bob Wills' Custom Wheel Company			
2			Cash Budget			
3			Year Ending December 20XX			
4						
5	Cash Receipts Budget	1	2	3	4	Year
6	Total Sales	200,000	240,000	320,000	200,000	960,000
7	Receipts from Current Month Sales	170,000	204,000	272,000	170,000	816,000
8	Receipts from Prior Month Sales	26,000	26,000	31,200	41,600	124,800
9	Cash Receipts	196,000	230,000	303,200	211,600	940,800
10						
11	Cash Disbursements For Material Purchases	1	2	3	4	Year
12	Material Purchases	66,712	81,220	87,668	64,480	300,080
13	Payments for Current Purchases	60,041	73,098	78,901	58,032	270,072
14	Payments for Prior Month Purchases	6,500	6,671	8,122	8,767	30,060
15	Cash Disbursements For Material Purchases	66,541	79,769	87,023	66,799	300,132
16						
17	Other Cash Disbursements	1	2	3	4	Year
18	Direct Labor	19,500	24,000	27,750	19,500	90,750
19	Overhead	48,100	50,200	51,950	48,100	198,350
20	Less Overhead Depreciation	(4,500)	(4,500)	(4,500)	(4,500)	(18,000)
21	Selling and Administrative	42,500	46,900	55,700	42,500	187,600
22	Less Selling and Administrative Depreciation	(1,500)	(1,500)	(1,500)	(1,500)	(6,000)
23	Total Cash Disbursements	104,100	115,100	129,400	104,100	452,700
24						
25	Cash Budget Summary	1	2	3	4	Year
26	Cash Receipts	196,000	230,000	303,200	211,600	940,800
27	Cash Disbursements For Material Purchases	(66,541)	(79,769)	(87,023)	(66,799)	(300,132)
28	Other Cash Disbursements	(104,100)	(115,100)	(129,400)	(104,100)	(452,700)
29	Change in Cash Balance	25,359	35,131	86,777	40,701	187,968
30	Beginning Cash Balance	205,000	230,359	265,490	352,267	205,000
31	Ending Cash Balance	230,359	265,490	352,267	392,968	392,968

	A	B	C	D	E	F
1			Bob Wills' Custom Wheel Company			
2			Cash Budget			
3			Year Ending December 20XX			
4						
5	Cash Receipts Budget	1	2	3	4	Year
6	Total Sales	=+Sales'B9	=+Sales'C9	=+Sales'D9	=+Sales'E9	=SUM(B6:E6)
7	Receipts from Current Month Sales	=+B6*Assumptions'$C$45	=+C6*Assumptions'$C$45	=+D6*Assumptions'$C$45	=+E6*Assumptions'$C$45	=SUM(B7:E7)
8	Receipts from Prior Month Sales	=+Assumptions'C52*Assumptions'C46	=+B6*Assumptions'$C$46	=+C6*Assumptions'$C$46	=+D6*Assumptions'$C$46	=SUM(B8:E8)
9	Cash Receipts	=+B7+B8	=+C7+C8	=+D7+D8	=+E7+E8	=SUM(B9:E9)
10						
11	Cash Disbursements For Material Purchases	1	2	3	4	Year
12	Material Purchases	=+Production_Purchasing'B44	=+Production_Purchasing'C44	=+Production_Purchasing'D44	=+Production_Purchasing'E44	=SUM(B12:E12)
13	Payments for Current Purchases	=+B12*Assumptions'C49	=+C12*Assumptions'$C$49	=+D12*Assumptions'$C$49	=+E12*Assumptions'$C$49	=SUM(B13:E13)
14	Payments for Prior Month Purchases	=+Assumptions'C53*Assumptions'$C$50	=+B12*Assumptions'$C$50	=+C12*Assumptions'$C$50	=+D12*Assumptions'$C$50	=SUM(B14:E14)
15	Cash Disbursements For Material Purchases	=+B13+B14	=+C13+C14	=+D13+D14	=+E13+E14	=+F13+F14
16						
17	Other Cash Disbursements	1	2	3	4	Year
18	Direct Labor	=+Direct_Labor'B10	=+Direct_Labor'C10	=+Direct_Labor'D10	=+Direct_Labor'E10	=SUM(B18:E18)
19	Overhead	=+Overhead'B22	=+Overhead'C22	=+Overhead'D22	=+Overhead'E22	=SUM(B19:E19)
20	Less Overhead Depreciation	=-Overhead'B12	=-Overhead'C12	=-Overhead'D12	=-Overhead'E12	=SUM(B20:E20)
21	Selling and Administrative	=+SGA'B13	=+SGA'C13	=+SGA'D13	=+SGA'E13	=SUM(B21:E21)
22	Less Selling and Administrative Depreciation	=-SGA'B12	=-SGA'C12	=-SGA'D12	=-SGA'E12	=SUM(B22:E22)
23	Total Cash Disbursements	=SUM(B18:B22)	=SUM(C18:C22)	=SUM(D18:D22)	=SUM(E18:E22)	=SUM(B23:E23)
24						
25	Cash Budget Summary	1	2	3	4	Year
26	Cash Receipts	=+B9	=+C9	=+D9	=+E9	=+F9
27	Cash Disbursements For Material Purchases	=-B15	=-C15	=-D15	=-E15	=-F15
28	Other Cash Disbursements	=-B23	=-C23	=-D23	=-E23	=-F23
29	Change in Cash Balance	=+B26+B27+B28	=+C26+C27+C28	=+D26+D27+D28	=+E26+E27+E28	=+F26+F27+F28
30	Beginning Cash Balance	=+Balance_Sheet'B7	=+B31	=+C31	=+D31	=+B30
31	Ending Cash Balance	=+B29+B30	=+C29+C30	=+D29+D30	=+E29+E30	=+E31

Figure B.9 Cash budget.

	A	B	C	D	E	F
1		Bob Wills' Custom Wheel Company				
2		Budgeted Income Statement				
3		Year Ending December 20XX				
4						
5		1	2	3	4	Year
6	Sales Revenue	200,000	240,000	320,000	200,000	960,000
7	Bad Debts	(4,000)	(4,800)	(6,400)	(4,000)	(19,200)
8	Net Sales	196,000	235,200	313,600	196,000	940,800
9	Less: Cost of Goods Sold	(125,891)	(145,282)	(185,581)	(127,211)	(583,965)
10	Gross Margin	70,109	89,918	128,019	68,789	356,835
11	Selling and Administrative Expenses	(42,500)	(46,900)	(55,700)	(42,500)	(187,600)
12	Net Income	27,609	43,018	72,319	26,289	169,235

	A	B	C	D	E	F
1		Bob Wills' Custom Wheel Company				
2		Budgeted Income Statement				
3		Year Ending December 20XX				
4						
5		1	2	3	4	Year
6	Sales Revenue	=+Sales!B9	=+Sales!C9	=+Sales!D9	=+Sales!E9	=SUM(B6:E6)
7	Bad Debts	=-B6*Assumptions!$C$47	=-C6*Assumptions!$C$47	=-D6*Assumptions!$C$47	=-E6*Assumptions!$C$47	=SUM(B7:E7)
8	Net Sales	=+B6+B7	=+C6+C7	=+D6+D7	=+E6+E7	=+F6+F7
9	Less: Cost of Goods Sold	=-CGS!C30	=-CGS!D30	=-CGS!E30	=-CGS!F30	=SUM(B9:E9)
10	Gross Margin	=+B8+B9	=+C8+C9	=+D8+D9	=+E8+E9	=SUM(B10:E10)
11	Selling and Administrative Expenses	=-SGA!B13	=-SGA!C13	=-SGA!D13	=-SGA!E13	=SUM(B11:E11)
12	Net Income	=+B10+B11	=+C10+C11	=+D10+D11	=+E10+E11	=+F10+F11

Figure B.10 Budgeted income statement.

The current assets section includes cash, which is derived from the ending cash balance in the cash budget. Accounts receivable is calculated using the net sales for the current period times and prior period times the associated collection rates and summing the result with prior accounts receivable. The inventory component is broken down into direct materials, work-in-process, and finished goods, all of which are linked to the cost of goods sold budget.

Long-term assets include property, plant, and equipment, which remains consistent in our example, and accumulated depreciation, which adjusts based on depreciation expenses recorded in the cash budget. The net value of long-term assets is summed with current assets to arrive at total assets, which represent the company's total resources. The current liabilities section primarily consists of accounts payable, which is calculated similarly to accounts receivable and based on current purchases, minus cash disbursements for material purchases and netted with the prior balance.

The owners' equity section incorporates retained earnings from prior periods and the projected net income, which is pulled from the budgeted income statement. The total liabilities and equity are calculated as the sum of liabilities and owners' equity, which must match the total assets to ensure the balance sheet remains balanced. Figure B.11 illustrates the budgeted balance sheet results followed by the formulas.

The use of spreadsheets in the budgeting process gives companies a flexible and cost-effective tool for integrating the various segments of their business. Spreadsheets allow for the various budgets to be interconnected, making it a dynamic tool that can be used for planning and forecasting.

	A	B	C	D	E	F
1		Bob Wills' Custom Wheel Company				
2		Budgeted Balance Sheet				
3		Year Ending December 20XX				
4						
5		Beginning Balance	1	2	3	4
6	Current Assets					
7	Cash	205,000	230,359	265,490	352,267	392,968
8	Accounts Receivable	200,000	200,000	205,200	215,600	200,000
9	Inventory					
10	Raw Material	9,672	11,904	13,764	9,672	9,672
11	Work in Process	2,922	3,895	2,435	2,922	2,922
12	Finished Goods	24,000	29,216	38,954	24,346	29,216
13	Total Current Assets	441,594	475,374	525,843	604,807	634,777
14	Long Term Assets					
15	PP&E	500,000	500,000	500,000	500,000	500,000
16	Accumulated Depreciation	(200,000)	(206,000)	(212,000)	(218,000)	(224,000)
17	Total Long Term Assets	300,000	294,000	288,000	282,000	276,000
18	Total Assets	741,594	769,374	813,843	886,807	910,777
19						
20	Current Liabilities					
21	Accounts Payable	200,000	200,171	201,622	202,267	199,948
22	Total Liabilities	200,000	200,171	201,622	202,267	199,948
23	Owners Equity	541,594	569,203	612,221	684,540	710,829
24	Total Liabilities and Equity	741,594	769,374	813,843	886,807	910,777

Figure B.11 Budgeted balance sheet.

Key Terms

sales budget An estimate of expected revenue for each period, detailing projected units sold and their selling prices.

production budget A plan that sets the number of units a company must manufacture to meet forecasted sales and desired ending inventory levels.

direct material budget A schedule that specifies the quantity and cost of direct materials or goods that must be bought to support the production budget and inventory policies.

labor budget A forecast of direct labor hours and costs required to produce the planned output.

overhead budget A projection of all indirect manufacturing costs (variable and fixed) needed for the forecasted production volume.

cost of goods sold budget A calculation that summarizes the expected manufacturing or purchase costs of the units planned to be sold during the period.

selling and administrative budget An estimate of all non-manufacturing operating expenses, both variable and fixed, needed to support sales and administrative functions.

budgeted income statement A pro-forma statement that combines all operating budgets to project expected revenues, expenses, and net income.
cash budget A detailed forecast of cash inflows and outflows, showing expected cash position and financing needs for each period.
budgeted balance sheet A forward-looking statement of financial position that estimates the company's assets, liabilities, and equity at the end of the budget period.

LEARNING ACTIVITY B.1

Refer to LA_B.1 Supplied with this appendix. Complete the tabs to develop an operating budget in Excel for Amor Artisan Hair Accessories.

INDEX

D

Printed and bound by CPI Group (UK) Ltd, Croydon, CR0 4YY
11/07/2025
14702107-0001